CONVENIENT
FOOD

Remove far from me vanity and lies:
GIVE ME NEITHER POVERTY NOR RICHES;
feed me with food convenient for me.

Proverbs 30:8

"Don't give me too much or too little. Just give me enough to live on." That's my commentary on this verse, and its message of balance and contentment fit my goal for this book perfectly. Sometimes eating healthy becomes an excuse to eat too much and obsess over food preparation, but God calls us to a higher standard. *Convenient Food* focuses on real, simple ingredients that are smart on calories, big on flavor, and easy on the wallet. In this book you'll find a vast array of savory main dishes and sides, but don't worry – I still enjoy desserts in moderation! My new commitment to a balanced diet doesn't mean that I cut out decadent ice cream entirely, but it does mean that I don't make such recipes every week…and my portions are smaller when I do choose to enjoy something rich. As you cook your way through *Convenient Food*, chew slowly and savor each bite!

COVER PHOTOS :: Briana Thomas Burkholder and Katelyn Thomas
LAYOUT + DESIGN :: Abigail Troyer Miller and Grace Troyer
All Bible verses are taken from the King James Version.

Carlisle Printing
OF WALNUT CREEK LTD

800.927.4196 • carlisleprinting.com
2673 Township Road 421 • Sugarcreek, Ohio 44681
To order more copies, please visit BRIANA-THOMAS.COM.

to Ryan

Thank you for encouraging my dreams and putting up with my long hours. Thank you for eating everything I set before you without complaint and enjoying it. Thank you for bringing discount salads home when I was busy typing up recipes. Thank you for listening when I was discouraged and stressed out with this project and showing me that things weren't as bad as they seemed in the moment. Above all, thank you for supporting my plan to slow down. All my love,

This cookbook is not affiliated with or endorsed by Trim Healthy Mama. I have done my best to make sure that all the recipes included are compatible with that healthy eating plan, but as always, read the book *Trim Healthy Mama Plan: Keep it Simple. Keep it Sane.* or the quick start guide at the beginning of *Trim Healthy Table* (both available from trimhealthymama.com) and use your own discernment based on the information therein. Trim Healthy Mama is a healthy eating lifestyle that includes all food groups. It focuses on a low-glycemic diet centered around protein and separates carbs and fats to allow the metabolism to function at its best.

I may be married to a doctor, but I'm not a doctor, nutritionist, or allergy expert. When determining if my recipes are right for your diet, please use your own best judgment as advised by your physician – and use common sense.

CAUTIONS

You may notice that some of the recipes in this book contain raw eggs. It's only fair to warn you that consuming raw or undercooked meats, poultry, seafood, shellfish, or eggs may increase your risk of foodborne illness. Eat raw eggs at your own risk, and if they make you nervous, use pasteurized whole eggs in their place. You can purchase these from some grocery stores or make your own (Google it).

Some of the recipes in this book require you to blend hot liquids. Guess what? This can be dangerous! Blending hot liquids can cause pressure to build up in your blender, which can in turn create an explosion of hot liquid that would be very detrimental to the health and wellbeing of you and your kitchen. When you blend hot liquids, don't fill the blender all the way up. Carefully vent the blender periodically to let pressure escape. An immersion blender can be a safer option for blending hot liquids. Just use common sense, please.

The subject of ingesting essential oils is a volatile one these days. Some of my recipes use essential oils for flavor, so before making these recipes, please do your own research regarding the safety of ingesting essential oils and the best brands to use. If you are not comfortable ingesting essential oils, bypass the recipes that use them or substitute a corresponding extract flavor, to taste.

TABLE OF contents

THIS ISN'T A *foreword* EITHER

Forewords are notorious for being boring, so in my first book, *Necessary Food*, I wrote a non-foreword. People read it, so I'm going to see if I can fool y'all once again.

» WHO AM I? «

» Bree-AH-nah. Not Bree-ANN-ah.

» I grew up as a Thomas in upstate South Carolina with a wonderful family and a bunch of horses. In February 2018, I married Ryan Burkholder, M.D. and moved to northern Louisiana where he is doing his Internal Medicine residency. God only knows where we'll settle down eventually, but we're enjoying Louisiana for now!

» Having been married a grand total of six months at the time of writing this, my life has changed a great deal lately. I used to be very passionate about horses and horse training, but after getting married this country gal got transplanted to the city – sans horse. I miss country life (and privacy, and trees, and mountains) a lot, but I hope that the future holds a nice spot down a back road for Ryan and me and maybe my cantankerous old horse, Traveler. And possibly some cantankerous children, should we ever have any of those.

» Other hobbies of mine include reading, music, and visiting museums with my husband. When it comes to books, I prefer true stories and well-written wit. Dating a doctor opened up a whole new world of very interesting literature to me; books written by doctors and nurses with senses of humor and the irony of life are always entertaining and often thought-provoking. As far as music goes,

singing with Laudate Mennonite Ensemble in 2016 and 2018, going to South Africa for three weeks in 2017 with Aspire Ensemble, and attending Shenandoah Christian Music Camp for a few years have been some of the best experiences of my life.

» Who am I? Most importantly I am a child of God. A relationship with God through the redemptive work of Jesus Christ is the most important part of my life, and I strive to live according to God's loving commands in His Word – the Bible. (Since many of you ask, I am conservative Mennonite by denomination. My husband is from that background as well.)

» NECESSARY FOOD «

I started blogging healthy recipes after graduating from high school in 2013, partly as a creative outlet and partly because I wanted to get into photography and horse training as a business and thought that posting recipes would give me a captive audience upon whom I could someday spring my "real" business ventures. People actually really liked the recipes I posted, I soon realized that I could make money blogging, self-employment and cooking appealed to me, and the rest is history. After a few years my readers asked for my recipes in book form, so *Necessary Food* was born in December 2016 after a long, arduous labor. "I'm never doing that again," said I. (More about that later.)

Necessary Food contains a lot of my basic recipes, so (shameless plug) you should really buy it to go along with *Convenient Food* if you don't already have it. (It's available on my website.) Both books include a lot of traditional Mennonite foods made healthy, many inspired by the old black-and-white church cookbooks my mom always used. Some recipes are just straight-up Briana with no prior inspiration, so watch out for those.

≫ HOW DR. RYAN SHOWED UP ≪

You're going to have to go to my website to read the full love story, parts one and two, because there's not room for it all here. I'll give you the basics.

I was 21 and single. I had escaped three terms of Bible school, two music camps, and countless music events unscathed...then the first Sunday morning in April 2017, some guy showed up at my church. I had no idea who he was, but he was pretty good-looking and wore nice shoes. I heard around the grapevine that he was in med school in Florida. We didn't really talk that morning, but he was around again that evening at a church event and struck up a conversation with me. We ended up eating together and really hit it off – to the point that people were already making smart remarks about something romantic brewing. Before the young man (whose name was Ryan) left that evening, he motioned me out onto the porch at church. I had no idea what he wanted, and I was sure I would never see him again so the thought that he could possibly be interested in me never crossed my mind. (I'm not typically this naïve, I promise.) I followed Ryan out onto the porch, saying as we went, "So, I never asked – what brought you to the area?" We stepped onto the porch, the door shut behind us, and he looked at me and said (in complete sincerity), "You did."

I like to think I remained calm and composed. I stared at him mutely with a raised eyebrow, waiting for him to explain himself. He went on to say that he had come across my blog and thought he would like to get to know me better...and could we go out for coffee the next day? He wasn't asking for a relationship – just a chat – but I wanted to get my dad's permission first. Unfortunately my dad was in Missouri preaching that weekend. I told Ryan that I would call my dad that evening and let him know our answer in the morning. To make a long story short, we invited Ryan to come over to our house for supper on Tuesday night where he was able to meet my dad and spend time with my family. The two of us talked for a few hours and I heard all about his family (who are wonderful people), his church background (also Mennonite), and his career (he graduated from medical school a month and a half after we met). I really, really liked him – and I liked that he wasn't the type to beat around the bush. By the end of the week he had called my dad to ask if he could start a relationship with me. Long-distance dating with someone in his intern year of residency is not the easiest thing to do, and being the rather intense individuals that we both are, we got engaged that November and married in February. Being married and living in the same house is much better than trying to do the whole long-distance thing.

I realize that at first brush our story probably sounds like a creepy stalking situation, but Anabaptist circles are fairly close-knit and Ryan had called a few people to get references on me before driving eight hours and showing up at my church. We found out as we got to know each other that we had some mutual connections and had even gone to the same music camp – just in different years. To be honest, I would've been a lot more skeptical about him if he would've contacted me before meeting me in person, but as it stood, I had already developed a liking for him before I even knew why he was at my church.

Ryan's intensity, decisiveness, and out-of-the-box thinking are some of the things that I really appreciate about him. He's one of the most sincere individuals I've ever met, and he puts on no pretense. Over and over I'm amazed at how well we complement and balance each other, and I like to tell people that marriage has been the most refining yet rewarding experience of my life.

Thankfully Ryan has always had an interest in fitness and healthy eating, so eating the way I'm used to cooking was no hardship for him – in fact, he loves it! If I say, "This has cottage cheese in it to cut down on calories and add protein" he says, "Great! I'll have seconds!" He's the least picky person I've ever known, and he's delighted to not have to cook for himself anymore.

>> MY FOOD STRATEGIES <<

I've eaten a low-glycemic diet since 2013 (following the Trim Healthy Mama plan), and it's become a way of life for me. I eat this way because I feel so much better doing so and I want to take care of the body God has given me. I never really had a lot of weight to lose, but I have lost some and managed to maintain a healthy weight despite doing a lot of traveling in the past few years. I'd like to lose a few more pounds, and these are some of the strategies that have been helping me trim down even more in the past year:

Contentment

This one is first for a reason. We people of the civilized world are spoiled people. We are picky people. We are entitled people. I speak of myself first and foremost! How much food do I actually need to eat to be healthy? Do I really need dessert with most meals? What are the eternal consequences of having to eat a food I don't particularly enjoy because it's what's available? If we could learn to live more simply and not over-satiate ourselves on a regular basis, we would be happier people, we would be skinnier people,

and most importantly, we would be more effective in the kingdom of God. Ryan has been a big conviction and encouragement to me in this area. He is one of the most grateful people I know. He doesn't expect much, but he genuinely enjoys the most simple pleasures of life and is thankful for the most trivial things. That's how I want to be in all of life, including my eating habits! Ryan has taught me that less can be so much more. You can enjoy a small piece of cheesecake even more than a big piece of cheesecake if you don't have it every day and you savor every bite.

Eat to live. Don't live to eat.

This one goes hand in hand with the previous point. Food is definitely a gift to be enjoyed and I don't see anything wrong with making an effort to cook yummy things, but food – and even a "healthy lifestyle" – can easily become an idol. If the preparation and consumption of food become an all-consuming passion to the exclusion of other, more important things in life, food has become an idol to me, and idols are sin. Even if you don't really enjoy cooking but are getting overwhelmed because it feels like you're always either creating dirty dishes or washing them, it's time to simplify! Being a slave to food any which way you look at it is no way to live. Keep things simple (there's nothing wrong with eating the same thing multiple times a week) and focus on savoring the creative process as well as the eating process. Chew slowly and enjoy what you're putting into your body. If you're scared to fellowship with friends because you don't want a shred of sugar to pass your purist lips…(don't take this wrong, but) get over it. There is balance on both sides of the equation! Learn to enjoy your food, but don't let it eat you instead of the other way around! Food is a gift God has given us to sustain us.

Chill out

You'd be amazed at the effect stress has on your ability to lose weight! Do your best to get plenty of sleep (obviously circumstances can affect this, but we choose how to use our free time…), rest in God and allow Him to give you a peaceful state of mind, and slow down and savor your food instead of gulping it. All these things will not only improve your ability to lose weight and your quality of life in general, but they're great spiritual exercises as well! Self-control is a Biblical principle; and for me, choosing to live a calmer, more relaxed life takes a lot of self control!

Now that I've gotten married and seen how much work goes into running a household (even a household of two, and I know the responsibility will multiply with the addition of a family in the future), I'm trying to simplify even more! I fix simpler, whole foods. Baked squash, roasted sweet potatoes, cubed melon, salads…these are my go-tos. Eating simply with only one side dish (or none) is OK, and serving things right out of cooking pots only makes sense, especially if you don't have a dishwasher! We don't need so much fuss in our lives!

Exercise

Living a more exercise-conscious lifestyle has really helped me lose weight! For me, exercise varies by seasons of life. Last year I got into running and it really helped me get into shape. When I got married and started working on this book, I was a desk potato for many months and hated the inactivity! Only now am I able to prioritize exercise again. Summertime in Louisiana isn't conducive to running outside, so for now I try to go walking or biking and hope to take up running again this fall. When I get into a more active frame of mind, I start looking for ways to get more exercise – such as

doing squats while waiting for my tea to heat in the microwave. Can you lose weight without exercise? Definitely! Some people lose more easily than others, though, and having an extra catalyst to boost my metabolism makes a huge difference in my personal ability to lose weight. And I like feeling stronger! If physical issues or time constraints limit your ability to exercise, just do what you can and keep the "exercise-conscious lifestyle" premise in mind. Just like little snacks all day long add up around your waist, taking the stairs instead of the elevator or doing 20 squats while waiting on the microwave will add up too!

Fill up on veggies!

Non-starchy veggies are low in calories and high in fiber and nutrients, making them the perfect thing to fill up on! Put your meals over a bed of salad to get your veggies in. Hamburgers, spaghetti meat, grilled chicken, leftover meatloaf, hard-boiled eggs, baked salmon, canned chickpeas… pretty much any protein source can become a salad! Putting frozen veggies in your shakes can be a great way to get a dose of veggies too.

Bring on the glucomannan!

Glucomannan is a natural thickener that helps balance the blood sugar and slows down the absorption of fats, aiding weight loss. It really fills you up so you don't need to eat as much, and I use it as much as I can! The texture can take some getting used to; try decreasing the amount used if your recipe turns out slimy. I use glucomannan in hot drinks like Cranberry Nog (page 286) or hot chocolate a lot, and if a recipe doesn't call for as much as I want to use (at least half a teaspoon), I just add more for a thicker, more filling drink! (Sometimes it turns into a hot pudding, but I'm good with that.) It works great to thicken shakes as well.

Cut needless calories

One of the things I love about the Trim Healthy Mama plan is that I don't have to count calories! However, being calorie conscious is a very good thing! Did you know that there are 4 calories per gram of protein and carbohydrates, but 9 calories per gram of fat? We totally need fats to remain healthy, but we do need to be aware of the fact that they're twice as calorie-dense as some other macronutrients. Switching up the types of meals you make (Healthy Fats, Healthy Carbs, Low Carb/Low Fat, etc.) switches up your calorie load. Sure, I can have coconut oil, butter, and even peanut butter and cream cheese, but eating cheesecake after every meal is just overkill! Recently I've tried to focus more on the cleaner-burning foundation fats like butter and coconut oil and keep the peanut butter and cream cheese to very moderate doses. I don't need two tablespoons of peanut butter on each stalk of celery! Learn to savor a thin layer! Coconut oil is a great fat to use, but if you don't need a full tablespoon to make a recipe taste good, why add the calories? If you can use salsa as a salad topping once in awhile instead of a fatty dressing like Ranch, why not – or go half and half? It's little things like that that will either add to or subtract from your overall calorie consumption.

Do I really need dessert with every meal?

Even though I often don't use as much sweetener as a lot of people do, I am a dessertaholic! They don't call me the Ice Cream Queen for no reason. After starting to eat healthy and hearing the "You can have cake for breakfast!" mantra, I grew accustomed to having dessert after every meal. Unfortunately many of them were heavy desserts tacked onto already-heavy meals, and that made for a lot of calories! I wasn't necessarily gaining weight, but I wasn't losing either. Over the past year, I've cut back on dessert a LOT. Not having large quantities of sweets on hand is helpful for me because if I have them, I'll eat them! (But if you need to have healthy sweets around to keep you from raiding your family's stash of cookies, go for it. Just try to moderate your intake.)

Don't get me wrong, I make sweets sometimes, but they're more of a special occasion now instead of a constant. When I eat a rich dessert, I view it as part of my overall meal and try to cut back on my overall portions to "make room for" the dessert. If I want something sweet to finish out my meal, I might have a small piece of 85% dark chocolate – and I mean small! Not even a whole section! Just enough to give me that sweet finish on my tongue. If you savor it, it's worth so much more. I actually had a hard time eating so many desserts while recipe testing for this cookbook (and my freezer is currently full of flops that I really don't feel like eating…haha). I've lost my taste for heavy stuff on a regular basis. Now I'd rather have fruit! Or baked oatmeal cakes (such as the ones found in the Breakfast section)! Or Strawberry Frozen Kefir (page 315)!

"Baked squash,
roasted sweet potatoes,
cubed melon, salads…
these are my go-tos."

➤➤ A GROWN-UP SEQUEL ◄◄

After publishing *Necessary Food*, I never wanted to go through such a stressful experience again... but I also knew that I wouldn't be able to rest until I published a sequel. I had so many more recipe ideas! "Publishing again in two years should be doable," I thought. "Two years will give me plenty of time to spread the process out." And maybe it would've, but then Ryan came along and I started a relationship, dated long-distance, planned a wedding, got married, and moved in those two years. And did a lot of traveling and singing outside of that as well. In hindsight, I probably should've pushed this project off for another year, but I didn't, and here it is. I'd like to tell you a little bit about what makes this book so special and sets it apart from *Necessary Food*.

A little while after I published *Necessary Food*, I made supper for my family one night and heard, "Your food is starting to all taste the same." They were right. I usually just used what my mom had on hand without doing any shopping myself, and she usually bought the same things. Inspired, I went to the grocery store myself and browsed – and was amazed by the array of ingredients that I didn't even know existed! I bought some fresh supplies, went home, and made Barbacoa Pork Tacos (page 84). They were a smashing success with my family!

After getting married, I've been having a lot of fun doing my own shopping. I usually buy fresh meats and vegetables on sale, and they're actually often cheaper than their frozen counterparts! Ah...fresh ingredients – there's nothing like some fresh ginger, fresh cilantro, or fresh jalapeños to add next-level flavor to a dish! These ingredients aren't expensive, but they make all the difference between boring and alive. A well-stocked spice cabinet is imperative as well, and I've been venturing into Indian and Asian spices. I try to be fairly authentic, but my aim with the recipes in this book is to create good flavors inspired by cuisines while doing them the Briana way with a twist, making them easy and attainable. Ryan has been an asset to my explorations into new cuisines; he loves scouting out new restaurants!

I want this book to be a grown-up sequel to *Necessary Food*, building on the basics but using a greater variety of fresh ingredients, better technique, and science and experimentation to push boundaries and develop recipes that are big on flavor but often lighter on calories. I've also tried to keep more of my allergy readers in mind, especially those with dairy allergies. I've even experimented with some egg-free baking, although I still have a long way to go in that department. I don't personally deal with any allergies so allergy-friendly recipes will probably never be my sole focus, but I do want to provide options for everyone. This book is heavier in the areas I now gravitate towards with more savory dishes, fewer desserts, more Healthy Carbs options, and lots of baked oatmeal and ice cream recipes. I've attempted to find a balance between budget-friendly ingredients and really good food, and I hope you're able to find recipes in this book that you want to make over and over again!

Convenient Food includes recipes published on my website between August 2016 and May 2018, but about half of the book is made up of cookbook-exclusive recipes! A neat note on the name: Carmen, one of my blog readers, recently messaged me and pointed out Proverbs 30:8 as possible inspiration for my second cookbook title. The verse sounded familiar, so I dug back in my archives – and sure enough! I had jotted down the same verse a year ago for a sequel! The title *Convenient Food* instantly felt right. I love how God uses other people as confirmation in our lives.

≫ MY IDENTITY CRISIS ≪

The process of this book was not easy. In fact, it caused the first five months of my marriage to be some of the hardest in my life because I faced a major collision of work and personal life. As a single girl living at home with my family, I could hole up in the basement and write cookbooks until midnight every night and no one was the wiser. After I got married I quickly realized that a house – even a small house – takes longer to keep up than I realized. And shopping! Who knew that grocery shopping could take the better part of an afternoon? My to-do lists have always been overly ambitious, but suddenly they were just plain impossible to accomplish. That was an overwhelming feeling.

I've always had a serious problem with over-committing myself. Part of it is a daily consequence of my obsessive compulsive disorder, which constantly tries to trick me into believing that I'm responsible for things I'm not and I have to do as much as I possibly can, and more, in order to be good enough. For months I tried desperately to be "super wife" and keep the house clean, pantry and fridge full, and laundry done while still working the full time+ hours that I had worked as a single woman. I had to finish this second cookbook so it could be published before the holidays this year! Anything less would be doing less than my best, and that would be sin. (This is how my personal experience with OCD works.) Meanwhile, I was an emotional mess and completely stressed out. I was stuck in a downward spiral that I didn't know how to get out of, and my brain was always running at 500 miles per hour. I couldn't relax enough to enjoy spending time with my husband without feeling guilty for the work we weren't getting accomplished, and I couldn't wind down enough to go to sleep so I'd lie awake for an hour or two every night.

In July 2018 I worked frantically and managed to get the cookbook recipes and pictures sent to my designers the day before Ryan and I left for a trip to Pennsylvania to attend his brother's wedding and for me to start rehearsal with Laudate Mennonite Ensemble. That trip was truly a God-send. Ryan was able to take a week of vacation, and we spent time with family and just did things together on a more relaxed time table. No work for either of us. On tour with Laudate, I had a decent amount of bus time in which to just sit in silence. I wasn't always actively thinking about things, but this was honestly, truly the first time since I got married that my brain had a chance to completely unwind. While I was watching scenery out the bus window and catching snippets of conversation, my brain was thrumming in the background, processing all the changes I had experienced in the past five months. I was able to observe some women who really inspired me with the intentional way they separated their full personal and work lives successfully, giving me hope that I could learn to do that too. Then I got this earth-shattering thought – "What if I set work hours for myself?"

That may sound laughably obvious to most of you, but for me it was a completely new idea. I've always felt the need to work as long as there is work to be done. Don't leave anything unfinished. Since I commit to so much, there is always work to be done, so I'm always working! The thought that maybe it's not lazy to have some free time even when I still have work to do was a new one. I also have always had a hard time viewing housework as "real work." I enjoy it so much that it must be lazy to take time to just focus on cleaning and organizing, right? After getting married I just loved being a wife and homemaker, but I felt guilty to spend too much time on that and not enough time on blogging and working on my cookbook.

Some things have changed in my life, and I think they'll keep changing as I mature and grow by the grace of God. I'm setting work hours for myself. I'm setting aside time every day to enjoy keeping my house in order – and I'm viewing that work with as much weight as bookkeeping, supervising cookbook design, and writing new blog posts. Blogging and publishing are officially becoming my hobby – not my career. I'm going to do this for fun, y'all! If I keep the right perspective on it, it is fun! I'm doing more spontaneous things. Being more sociable. Having more company. After I get this cookbook published, I'll probably keep revamping my schedule to work less and less. I will keep blogging, but I'm going to blog when I feel like it and have something to blog about. Since I love blogging, you might see me quite a bit – but I can take breaks, too. And if I ever have children, I can take off for months if I want to! I have a feeling I'll always come back, because I love having a creative outlet and a space to write. As far as future cookbooks go, we'll see. I will not be publishing another book with deadlines. Future works might be more or less compilations of blog recipes without so many cookbook exclusives. I'd like to do more in the ebook realm in the future, but only if I feel like it and it doesn't infringe on my personal life. Blogging is definitely where my heart is.

So…do I regret making myself this busy and jumping right into cookbook #2 after getting married? My mom asked me that question, and after ruminating on it, my answer was no. I'm so stubborn and thick-headed that it literally almost took an emotional breakdown for God to get my attention and for me to realize that I just can't live life like this. I had to be taken to the breaking point in order to change my path. Am I sorry that the first five months of my marriage had to go through this? Yes. But I'm glad it happened now rather than later.

Who is this Briana? This is Briana Burkholder. Briana Thomas really built a name for herself and held herself to very high expectations, but her identity has changed and she no longer needs to keep up with a certain performance level to be worth something. She has a God Who loves her and a husband who takes care of her and encourages her to do what she loves. She'll probably always struggle with the need to perform, but she knows that God will faithfully show her when she needs to reevaluate her priorities.

PS – I've kept my maiden name for my website and social media accounts because that's what people have always known me as and I don't want to confuse them, but I'm really and truly Briana Burkholder for all practical purposes.

≫ IN CONCLUSION ≪

Please stop by my website for more recipes, life stories, tips for starting and maintaining a healthy lifestyle, and whatever else I can come up with. I'm a human being, not an institution or corporation, and I value being real and transparent. Y'all are the reason I blog and write cookbooks. Thanks for being part of my life!

Visit BRIANA-THOMAS.COM for more recipes, life stories, and so much more!

ingredients + baking tips

» Overnight refrigeration immensely improves the taste and texture of most baked goods made with alternative flours and sweeteners.

» When storing spinach, lettuce, fresh herbs, berries, or other fresh ingredients that tend to spoil quickly, place paper towels in the container with the food to absorb moisture and keep the ingredients fresh longer.

» Store all baked goods in the fridge or freezer unless otherwise noted. These recipes don't have preservatives so they won't keep very long on the counter.

» Don't be afraid to think outside the box with recipes! I often use my baked oatmeal recipes as cake-like desserts in a Healthy Carbs setting. Some condiments, like Bri's Adobo Sauce (page 477), make great salad dressings!

» See a glaze or marinade that strikes your fancy in the Main Dishes section? Feel free to get creative and use it on other cuts or types of meat!

» Want to bake a recipe that calls for a microwave? Start with 350° and bake baked goods until a toothpick inserted into the center comes out cleanly or the center of the item springs back when lightly pressed (unless the recipe tells you to leave it on the slightly underdone side). Please note that some recipes that are formulated for a microwave will actually have a better texture in the microwave than in an oven, but in general you should be able to bake instead of microwave without much problem.

» Some protein powders clump if they get too hot. If using protein powder in a hot drink, add it to the hot liquid after adding all other ingredients, right before blending. If whisking protein powder into hot oatmeal, add the protein powder after cooking the oatmeal and give the oatmeal a minute to cool down before doing so. I use Swanson brand whey protein powder and don't usually have issues with clumping, so I'm guessing some brands are more prone to the problem than others.

» Don't boil soups or gravies after adding dairy products: they'll curdle.

» Cooking rice or baking chicken breasts? Make extra and freeze leftovers to use in future recipes like soups and quesadillas or enchiladas.

» See a great sale on meat? Buy up at the lower price, divide the meat into portions perfect for your family, and freeze! Sometimes I get fresh chicken breasts on sale and freeze them individually on a sheet pan, then transfer to a bag for easy portioning for recipes later.

» When you make dirty dishes, rinse them and let them soak with hot water and soap to minimize cleanup later.

» You don't need to wash measuring cups that have only touched dry ingredients!

» You can usually double a recipe created for an 8"x8" pan and put it in a 9"x13" pan. Likewise you can halve a recipe for a 9"x13" pan and make it in an 8"x8" pan instead.

» Glucomannan and xanthan gum can generally be interchanged in recipes in the same amount. I do have slight preferences of one over the other in certain cases, so I always call for the one I prefer.

» When a recipe calls for glucomannan or xanthan gum, add it while whisking so it doesn't clump. If either is blended in a blender with other ingredients, add it to the blender last, right before blending.

» Sour cream and Greek yogurt can usually be substituted for each other in recipes unless otherwise noted. (Watch the fat content in Healthy Carbs and Low Carb/Low Fat recipes.) Yogurt is tangier in flavor but has more protein.

≫ ALLERGY NOTES ≪

I don't have any allergies myself, but now that I've blogged for several years I've become a lot more aware of just how many people have to deal with allergies every day. You have my sympathy: substituting for common ingredients isn't always easy! Most of my recipes are naturally gluten free if you're mindful of using non-contaminated ingredients, and I've tried to become conscious of providing more dairy-free recipes. Egg-free baking is one thing that I haven't had much success with in my limited attempts, but many desserts outside of the cake and muffin realm are naturally egg free so you should be able to find plenty of options. (And check out Bri's Best Fudgy Brownies (page 391) and Chocolate Chip Cookie Pie (page 389)!) Briana's Baking Mix (page 345) is nut free (provided that you are able to use coconut products), so most of you with tree nut allergies should be able to make use of that.

I wish I would be able to make every recipe work for everyone, but since that is humanly impossible, I've done my best to provide at least some options for everyone. I'll list some common ingredient swaps here, but keep in mind that my recipes are tested as written and these swaps may or may not work in every recipe. Substitution is experimentation. If you're unfamiliar with substituting ingredients (and even if you're an old pro!), I recommend checking out online forums to get practical suggestions from other people with allergies regarding substitutions they've found to be helpful and foolproof. I am by no means an allergy expert!

In general, you can...

» Use unsweetened carton almond milk, cashew milk, and coconut milk interchangeably. (Please note that carton coconut milk is different nutritionally from canned coconut milk!)

» Switch between whey protein powder and collagen (which is dairy free). Collagen is not quite as creamy as whey protein powder, but I personally prefer the taste (or lack thereof) of collagen over whey protein powder in a lot of applications.

» Use coconut oil instead of butter for a dairy-free option. Use refined coconut oil if you don't want a coconut flavor. You can even purchase butter-flavored coconut oil that is completely non-dairy! Coconut oil may not produce the same richness of flavor as butter, but then I haven't personally tried the butter-flavored coconut oil so that may be the ticket!

» Leave cheese off of things that are otherwise dairy-free as long as the cheese is not an integral part of the structure (for example, part of a dough). You will obviously lose the cheese flavor, but if the other flavors are great, you may have just created a winner of a dairy-free dinner. Feel free to add other toppings – like salsa – to things like casseroles to bring out more flavor in place of a cheese topping.

These may require a little more experimentation, but you could also try…

» Substituting unsweetened applesauce for Greek yogurt or sour cream for a dairy-free swap in Healthy Carbs baked goods. The end result may be wetter and more gooey.

» Substituting full-fat canned coconut milk or coconut cream in place of half and half or heavy cream for a dairy-free substitute.

» Natural sunflower butter in place of peanut butter for a nut-free option. (I've never personally done this, which is why I'm putting it in the more experimental category…haha. I've heard from allergy peeps who do this, though.)

first date weekend

≫ FLOURS ≪

» **ALMOND FLOUR** (HF): I use very little of this because of the price and the fact that many of my readers have nut allergies. I hoard my almond flour for use in crusts because it does a great job there. I recommend blanched almond flour for the best look and texture in recipes; it doesn't include the almond skins, which make the end product heavier and a little bit gritty. (As you can see in a picture or two in this book, I didn't always use a blanched version.)

» **BRIANA'S BAKING MIX** (LC/LF in limited amounts, HF in larger quantities): This is a recipe for a blend of alternative flours that I have created and use in many of my recipes for a better texture than you'd get if just using a single flour. You can find the recipe and information on how my baking mix compares to THM Baking Blend on page 345.

» **CHICKPEA FLOUR** (HC): Also known as "besan," this flour is typically found in Indian cuisine and has a strong flavor. It can be purchased from ethnic grocery stores and some more mainstream retailers. I didn't use it a lot in this book because I'm still finding out how it acts in recipes, but I hope to implement it more in the future.

» **COCONUT FLOUR** (HF): This flour is tricky to bake with because it soaks up a tremendous amount of liquid, but it's fairly budget friendly and readily available online and in many local stores. Coconut flour soaks up a lot more liquid than almond flour and golden flaxmeal and requires lots of "conditioners" such as eggs, sour cream, Greek yogurt, and liquids. If you know how to use it, it works great! If you don't, your baked goods will be crumbly and gritty. Substitutions can be especially tricky with this flour because of these variables. On its own coconut flour can have a faint coconut flavor, but in a blend with other flours (in my baking mix, for example), I don't usually notice any coconut flavor.

» **COLLAGEN** (LC/LF): Collagen is a great way to add extra protein and structure to baked goods and can usually be used as a dairy-free substitute for whey protein powder in baking recipes. I typically use Great Lakes brand available from many online retailers, but there are lots of options on the market.

» **DEFATTED PEANUT FLOUR** (LC/LF in limited amounts, HF in larger quantities): This is a great way to add peanut butter flavor and protein to baked goods without all the calories of peanut butter! I use Protein Plus brand available from several online retailers. (Make sure that the brand you use doesn't contain added sugar in the ingredients.)

» **GOLDEN FLAXMEAL** (HF): Back in South Carolina I bought golden flax seeds from a bulk food store and ground them into flour in a coffee grinder, but here in Louisiana I don't have access to any bulk food stores so I buy golden flaxmeal already ground. Golden flax tastes way better than dark flax! Golden flaxmeal can be hard to find locally, but it's easily sourced from online health food stores. Flaxmeal is cheap and versatile, but use too much with no other prominent flavors to mask it and you'll definitely taste flax. For this reason I typically keep it to add cheap bulk to my baking mix. Too much flaxmeal can add an eggy texture to baked goods. Almond flour can usually work as a substitute for flaxmeal (unless the flaxmeal is being used as an egg substitute), but be careful substituting flaxmeal into recipes that call for almond flour since flaxmeal is much stronger in flavor.

» **MASA FLOUR** (HC): Corn products are high on the glycemic index and will spike your blood sugar, so I generally keep them to a Healthy Carbs setting and only use them occasionally in small amounts. However, masa flour goes through a nixtamalization process that breaks it down to a state that's kinder to your blood sugar (the same thing that sprouting does to wheat to produce sprouted wheat flour). I still don't use it often,

but it makes a great lower-glycemic cornbread for a treat! Walmart carries big bags of Maseca brand masa flour in the Hispanic foods section, and it's extremely cheap. The ingredients should read something like, "Corn treated with hydrated lime." (Lime is what breaks the corn down in the nixtamalization process.)

» **OAT BRAN** (HC): Oat bran is what a lot of people end up with when they're trying to find oat fiber. Just as the name suggests, it's made up of only the bran of the oat and is high in fiber. I use Bob's Red Mill brand, which you can find at many local grocery stores as well as in online health food stores.

» **OAT FLOUR** (HC): Not to be confused with oat fiber, oat flour is simply ground-up oats and thus a carb source. (You can make your own oat flour in a good blender or coffee grinder using old-fashioned or quick oats. If a recipe calls for oat flour, measure after grinding unless otherwise specified.) Oat flour is not interchangeable with oat fiber because of the differences in nutritional info as well as the extreme texture differences. Things made with oat flour tend to be slightly gummy, so I often combine it with oat fiber for a better texture. This combination makes great muffins!

» **OAT FIBER** (LC/LF): Oat fiber is not the same thing as oat flour! Oat fiber is made by grinding only the hull of the oat, has no carbs or fats, and is a very fine, dry flour that soaks up a lot of liquid. I like to use it to thicken gravies, soups, and puddings, and I also use it combined with other flours to add a fluffier texture to baked goods. Like coconut flour, oat fiber soaks up a lot of liquid and your end product can be gritty if too much oat fiber is used. Oat fiber can only be purchased online. Different brands vary drastically, and a bad brand can make your baked goods taste nasty! Look for a brand that has a very light color and flavor. I've always purchased LifeSource brand from Netrition.com and had very good success with it; I can't personally vouch for any other brands. Since oat fiber is such a unique flour, I don't know of any

5

foolproof substitutes for it. Some people substitute with psyllium husk flakes, which are easier to find locally, but I haven't personally tried that and have heard some anecdotal evidence that they don't work as a substitute in every recipe.

» **WHEY PROTEIN POWDER** (LC/LF): Whey protein powder can be a great way to add protein and structure to baked goods! Look for a whey protein powder without added fillers or sweeteners (1 gram of net carbs or less per serving). I use Swanson brand whey protein powder and have always had good success with it. (Available online.) Collagen can usually be substituted for whey protein powder, but I don't always recommend substituting the other way around. In certain recipes, like my pudding cakes, collagen works better.

Visit BRIANA-THOMAS.COM/ CONVENIENTFOODRESOURCES to find links to the products I use and recommend!

» FLOUR TIPS «

» Use a blend of alternative flours for best texture and taste. (You can find the recipe for my baking mix on page 345.)

» To properly measure flours, use one measuring scoop to scoop the flour into another measuring scoop, then level off the top with a knife. This ensures that the flour isn't packed into the measuring cup. (You should at least fluff the flour with your measuring scoop before measuring to prevent packing if you don't feel like using two measuring scoops.)

» Many alternative flours are thirstier than regular ol' white flour and require plenty of liquids and "conditioners" (water, eggs, sour cream, Greek yogurt, etc.) in order to turn out something semi-fluffy and moist.

» Most of the alternative flours I use in this book are naturally gluten free, so they lack the structure of gluten, which is a protein. Gluten is what gives breads their structure and cakes their fluff. Since alternative flours lack this structural element, adding other proteins, such as eggs or some protein powder or collagen, can help provide structure to gluten-free baked goods.

» The best advice I can give you when it comes to substituting flours is to not substitute unless you're pretty savvy with alternative baking or are open to producing some flops in the name of experience. Different flours soak up different amounts of liquid and have different properties that you have to work around, so flour substitution definitely comes with a learning curve.

» SWEETENERS «

» THM PURE STEVIA EXTRACT POWDER: This sweetener is super concentrated and is measured in "doonks." (A doonk is $1/32$ teaspoon.) Because it's so concentrated, it's the most economical sweetener in this list, and I use it where I can. Not everyone is a fan of the taste of stevia, especially when just coming off of sugar, but Trim Healthy Mama produces the best-tasting stevia I've found. It's more "forgiving" than other brands if you accidentally use too much. Less is definitely more in the stevia department, and one doonk is perfect for sweetening a mug of hot tea. You can find the THM sweeteners in the Trim Healthy Mama online store and from a few other retailers.

» THM SUPER SWEET BLEND: This is my favorite all-purpose sweetener! To me it's the perfect combination of economy and taste, and I use it for most of my baking.

» THM GENTLE SWEET: This sweetener is called "Gentle Sweet" for a reason; it has a lower concentration of stevia and is extra gentle on taste buds that are still coming off of sugar! This sweetener comes in powdered form and is still quite a bit more concentrated than sugar, though it's less concentrated than pure stevia and Super Sweet Blend.

» TRUVIA: Truvia measures similar to THM Gentle Sweet and is usually available locally.

» ERYTHRITOL: I personally don't care for the flavor and peculiar cooling sensation of erythritol, so I rarely use it. It measures similar to sugar and is often available locally as well as online.

» XYLITOL: Xylitol is great in that it tastes good, measures similar to sugar, and keeps ice cream from freezing hard, but it's poisonous to dogs and doesn't agree with everyone's digestive tracts. Xylitol can cause gas and bloating, so start with small amounts and work your way up to see how it affects you and let your body adjust. Available locally and online.

» SWEETENER TIPS «

» Don't use straight stevia to sweeten chocolate or coffee things; the bitter notes of both clash. A granulated sweetener such as THM Gentle Sweet, Truvia, or xylitol will work better in chocolate settings.

» I often use a combination of THM Pure Stevia Extract Powder and a granulated sweetener for cost efficiency and better flavor. "Layering" sweeteners is a great way to round out the sweetness profile of baked goods made with alternative sweeteners. Using various sweeteners in different layers makes for a more rounded sweetness that might be more palatable to you than just using one type of sweetener all the way through.

» Heat dissipates sweetness. Keep this in mind as you taste batters before baking. If you got too much sweetener in it, chances are after baking and refrigeration, it'll be edible. If you under-sweetened, better luck next time.

» As a general rule, less is more when it comes to alternative sweeteners, especially pure stevia. Start with less than you think you'll need, taste, and keep adding sweetener a little bit at a time, tasting as you go. Less concentrated sweeteners like xylitol and THM Gentle Sweet are more forgiving sweeteners for people who are getting used to alternative sweeteners.

» Feel free to try substituting your favorite low-glycemic sweeteners (to taste) for the sweeteners I have listed in recipes unless otherwise noted. Some recipes specifically call for a granulated sweetener for bulk or texture purposes. For help estimating how much sweetener you'll need in place of what I have listed, check out the Trim Healthy Mama Sweetener Conversion Chart. (Google will help you find it.) I always recommend starting with less sweetener than you think you'll need, then adding more to taste. There are even more sweetener options out there than what I've listed here (Swerve, Pyure, monk fruit extract), but I haven't personally tried any outside of this list.

» Some people complain that my recipes aren't as sweet as the typical American diet. I say it's all a matter of perspective! I've heard from plenty of people who say they love that my recipes aren't as sweet, so I know I'm not the only one! My mom always took sugar out of regular ol' unhealthy recipes, and fine dining and European cuisine take a different approach to sweetness than most of modern America. However, please feel free to add more sweetener to my recipes if that's what you're used to. Less concentrated sweeteners are often better for this than concentrated sweeteners like pure stevia and THM Super Sweet Blend. Tasting and adjusting is the best, most foolproof way to make sure you're happy with the sweetness of the end result.

» OTHER UNIQUE INGREDIENTS «

In general, product brands don't matter a whole lot to me, and I just try to find the best quality for the best price. Feel free to use whatever brands you prefer as long as they fit into the healthy eating lifestyle you follow. To save space, I'm using this section to cover a lot of info about the products I use instead of making notes about them in each recipe. Don't be frightened at the list – you don't need all of these ingredients! Some of them are only used in a few recipes and aren't things that I always keep on hand.

» **ANCHO CHILES:** These are dried poblano peppers commonly used in Mexican cuisine and can be found in the ethnic food section of your local grocery store.

» **BALSAMIC VINEGAR:** Look for a balsamic vinegar with no more than 2 grams of net carbs per serving.

» **BAOBAB POWDER:** A quick Google search will yield lots of reasons that baobab powder is the next greatest health supplement. I think it tastes cool – rather puckery, like tart raspberries or lemon. Readily available from online health stores.

» **BOUILLON:** I recommend a high-quality bouillon like Better Than Bouillon. (I consider this to fall under the "2 grams of sugar or less per serving" rule for storebought condiments.)

» **CANNED COCONUT MILK** (full fat or light): Thai Kitchen brand from Walmart and other local grocery stores is a good quality option. Shake coconut milk before measuring: it separates. To my taste buds, coconut milk doesn't really add a coconut flavor to things like soups, curries, and rice pudding; but I can taste it a little more in ice cream. I use it in certain recipes for authenticity as well as non-dairy creaminess.

» **CHANA DAL:** Chana dal are dried split chickpeas; I purchased mine from a local Indian grocery store. Do not substitute lentils for chana dal, or vice versa, as they have different cooking times (in my experience, at least!).

» **CHIA SEEDS:** These are a natural thickener that I like to use in puddings, porridges, and egg-free baking. Available locally.

» **COCONUT OIL:** I use refined coconut oil to eliminate any coconut flavor. This is a great non-dairy cooking oil. I prefer Nutiva brand, which I purchase off of Amazon in a big bucket, but you can find many options at your local grocery store – including a completely non-dairy butter-flavored coconut oil!

» **COLLAGEN:** Collagen is a great non-dairy protein powder for shakes, smoothies, hot drinks, oatmeal, baking…you name it! It has almost no flavor, but it's not quite as fluffy and creamy as whey protein powder. The two can generally be substituted for each other, but I do prefer each in different capacities and list the one I prefer in recipes.

» **CONDIMENTS:** When purchasing store-bought condiments, look for options with 2 grams of sugar or less per serving.

» **COOKING SPRAY:** I use an olive oil spray. Coconut oil would be better because it's more stable at high heat, but I've heard it doesn't keep things from sticking as well so I haven't tried it.

» **CRANBERRIES:** These are often only readily available over the holidays, so in the fall I buy a lot on sale and freeze them for the rest of the year.

» **CURRY POWDER:** I used the generic yellow curry powder available from most American grocery stores and Walmart in my recipes.

» **DREAMFIELDS PASTA:** Dreamfields pasta has a special coating on it that supposedly reduces its impact on blood sugar, but overcooking or reheating the pasta takes away the low-glycemic effect. There has been a ton of hype about whether or not Dreamfields is actually low-glycemic; the general consensus is that each individual needs to see how it affects his or her blood sugar and make a personal decision. If you find your weight loss stalling, Dreamfields pasta would be an item to cut back on. I hardly ever use it, but once in awhile it's nice to fill a pasta craving when veggies just won't cut it. You can usually find Dreamfields at your local grocery store (or Walmart) with the other pasta products.

» **ESPRESSO INSTANT COFFEE POWDER:** I use Medaglia D'Oro brand espresso instant coffee, which I found at my local grocery store. I prefer its flavor over that of regular instant coffee.

» **ESSENTIAL OILS:** I used essential oils in a few recipes for a better flavor than what I could achieve with extracts (specifically peppermint extract, which tends to taste like toothpaste). Please do your own research on ingesting essential oils and come to a personal decision. If you're not comfortable ingesting essential oils, use a corresponding extract to taste.

» **EXTRACTS/FLAVORINGS:** I usually use Watkins brand extracts and flavorings from Walmart. The new THM Natural Burst Extracts are much more potent than the extracts I used in these recipes, so keep that in mind if substituting.

» **FROZEN DICED (OR CUT) OKRA:** Okra is a great blood sugar balancer! I recommend using storebought frozen diced okra in recipes because it has been blanched before freezing. (Or blanch your own fresh okra before freezing.) Blanching helps cut some of the slime and makes the okra disintegrate into recipes better. I personally don't mind using fresh okra in recipes, but it's definitely slimier and produces a lovely snot-like texture in milkshakes. In recipes that call for blending, blend okra very well to reduce slime and produce a smooth texture. I've heard anecdotal evidence that okra contains an enzyme that can sometimes react with other ingredients and produce a vomit-like taste, so if that happens to you, don't blame me. Blame the okra.

» **GLUCOMANNAN:** Glucomannan is a natural thickener made from the konjac root. Different brands of glucomannan can vary in strength, so if you notice an odd texture in recipes made with it, try decreasing the amount used. I use Konjac Foods brand and have never had an issue with sliminess, but unfortunately this brand has been recently discontinued and I haven't tried any other brands yet. If you don't have glucomannan, try substituting xanthan gum in the same amount.

» **GRATED PARMESAN CHEESE:** When I refer to this in my recipes, I'm talking about the kind that comes in a shakable container with a green lid and doesn't have a very high fat content.

» **JOSEPH'S REDUCED CARB/FLAX, OAT BRAN & WHOLE WHEAT PITA OR LAVASH BREAD:** These are great bread options for low-carb sandwiches, pizzas, and quesadillas. You can find Joseph's products locally at some Walmarts and grocery stores, or you can purchase them online from Netrition.com.

» **KEFIR:** This is a fermented product that reminds me of drinkable yogurt. (I've only ever used dairy kefir.) Different types of kefir can be used in different fuel settings. Regular storebought kefir is single fermented; use low-fat single-fermented kefir in a Healthy Carbs setting. If you double ferment your kefir (Google it), some of the carbs are eaten up. Low-fat double-fermented kefir is Low Carb/Low Fat, and full-fat double-fermented kefir belongs in a Healthy Fats setting. Some kefir is actually lactose free, so keep that in mind if you have allergies.

» **LENTILS:** Lentils are a great source of plant-based protein and slow-burning carbs! Do not substitute lentils for chana dal, or vice versa, as they have different cooking times (in my experience, at least!). Available from local grocery stores alongside the dry beans.

» **LORANN FLAVOR OILS:** These are really concentrated flavorings that you measure in drops, not teaspoons. They can be found in cake decorating stores and Hobby Lobby as well as online from Netrition.com or Amazon.

» **LOW-CARB OR REDUCED-CARB TORTILLAS**: When purchasing low-carb tortillas, look for brands with 6 grams of net carbs or less per tortilla.

(Subtract dietary fiber from the total carb count to calculate net carbs.) I've tried nearly every brand out there and my favorite brand is whichever is the cheapest at the time.

» **MOLASSES:** I use Grandma's molasses because the nutritional info isn't that much different from blackstrap molasses, but it tastes much better. If using blackstrap molasses, you may want to use a little less than the amounts I call for. Molasses is not a low-glycemic ingredient, but I use it occasionally in small amounts for flavor, sticking to ¼ teaspoon or less per serving. If you don't want to use molasses, try a dash of maple extract in its place for a similar flavor (but not quite the same).

» **NATURAL PEANUT BUTTER:** I use Smucker's brand natural peanut butter (from Walmart) that contains just peanuts and salt and has a very intense peanut flavor. If your peanut butter contains a low-glycemic sweetener or no salt, adjust my recipes accordingly.

» **NO-SUGAR-ADDED KETCHUP:** It can be hard to find no-sugar-added ketchup in stores, but there are plenty of easy homemade low-carb ketchup recipes online. Or you can do like I do and just use regular storebought ketchup which is technically not allowed on the healthy eating plan I follow but probably won't do you too much harm in the grand scheme of things. My recipes assume you are using regular ketchup or a sweetened homemade version.

» **NO-SUGAR-ADDED PASTA SAUCE**: All pasta/pizza/spaghetti sauces will have sugar listed in the nutritional info because of natural sugars in tomatoes, but you want to look for a sauce that has no added sugar in the ingredients. Priano brand from Aldi is good.

» **RED CURRY PASTE:** This is available from a lot of local grocery stores in the ethnic foods aisle (near the Thai foods); you can also find it online. I use Mae Ploy brand. It's pretty spicy, so you don't need to use much!

» **SALT:** I just use regular store brand table salt in my recipes. If using salt with larger crystals (such as sea salt) you may need to add a bit more.

» **SPROUTED BREAD:** I like Aldi's Simply Nature Sprouted 7 Grain Bread for a storebought option. If you want to make your own bread, try my cold-fermented Homemade Bread recipe on page 160 of *Necessary Food*. (Regular wheat flour goes through a simple fermentation in the fridge – no sprouted flour or sourdough starter needed.)

» **SUGAR-FREE CHOCOLATE:** Lily's and Trim Healthy Mama brands are good sources for chocolate chips sweetened with decent low-glycemic sweeteners. For a more budget-friendly option, chop up 85% dark chocolate bars from your local grocery store. (I prefer Moser Roth brand from Aldi, but American-made brands are OK too. Europeans just make better chocolate.) If using 85% dark chocolate in place of sugar-free chocolate chips, you may need to add a little more sweetener to the batter of whatever you're making.

» **SUGAR-FREE CHOCOLATE SYRUP:** There are plenty of low-carb chocolate syrup recipes online, and Hershey's sugar-free chocolate syrup is sweetened mostly with erythritol!

» **SUGAR-FREE PANCAKE SYRUP:** Make your own Waffle & Pancake Syrup (page 491)! You can find some syrups sweetened with acceptable sweeteners online, but they're few and far between (and pricey). I personally just buy a store brand sugar-free syrup sweetened with Splenda and keep it for occasional use.

» **TAHINI:** This is an amazing ingredient made of 100% ground sesame seeds with the consistency of runny peanut butter. I use it to make hummus and baba ghanoush. Since I couldn't find any brands without sugar locally, even at ethnic grocery stores, I bought Baron's brand from Amazon. It contains only ground sesame seeds and is absolutely delicious and high quality.

» **TANDOORI PASTE:** I used Tiger Tiger brand tandoori paste (medium heat) in the recipes in this book. It contains a small amount of tamarind concentrate, which has a high glycemic index, but the sugars per serving are fairly low so I'm personally fine with using it in a Healthy Carbs setting. Look for this brand in your local grocery store or online.

» **TONY CHACHERE'S ORIGINAL CREOLE SEASONING:** I can find Tony's all day long at local grocery stores here in Louisiana, but if you can't locate it in your area you can purchase it from Amazon. This seasoning adds so much flavor to recipes – and you only have to get one spice shaker out of your pantry! Tony's has a high salt content so keep that in mind when using it and don't add large amounts of both salt and Tony's seasoning.

» **UNSWEETENED COCONUT FLAKES:** I usually buy these in the baking aisle at Walmart, but you can find them in most local grocery stores.

» **VEGETABLE GLYCERIN:** A clear liquid that helps give ice cream a creamy texture and stay scoopable instead of icy when frozen, then thawed. Vegetable glycerin also helps keep the ice cream from creating a thick frozen layer on your ice cream canister. I purchase Essential Depot brand from Amazon.

» **WHEY PROTEIN POWDER:** Whey protein is a good way to add protein and creaminess to shakes, smoothies, hot drinks, oatmeal, and baking. I personally don't care for the taste without cover-up flavors present, so in some applications I prefer to use collagen. The two can generally be substituted for each other, but I do prefer each in different capacities and list the one I prefer in recipes. Look for a whey protein powder without added fillers or sweeteners (1 gram of net carbs or less per serving). I use Swanson brand whey protein powder and have always had good success with it. (Available online.)

» XANTHAN GUM: This is a natural thickening agent that can be found in most local grocery and bulk food stores these days. It is generally interchangeable with glucomannan, but I do prefer each for different things and list the one I prefer in recipes. I like to use a combination of oat fiber and xanthan gum to thicken gravies and soups without slime.

A NOTE ON GELATIN:

I typically use Knox gelatin in my recipes because it dissolves the best and I can find it cheaper than I can find beef gelatin (such as Great Lakes or Trim Healthy Mama brand). Knox gelatin is a bit stronger than beef gelatin, so for every teaspoon of Knox gelatin called for in a recipe, use 1 + ¼ teaspoon of either THM Just Gelatin or Great Lakes gelatin.

» EQUIPMENT «

» BLENDER: A good blender is definitely one of my must-have appliances (although it was one I did without for a few months after I got married!). I've used a Ninja and while it's not a bad value for the price, I definitely prefer the results of a Vitamix. There's a big difference. I bought a used one off of Ebay, which is a slightly risky proposition but has worked for me so far.

» BOSCH MIXER: My mom had a nice Bosch mixer, so after I got married I got a used Ebay model. Someday when I'm rich and famous and have a bigger kitchen, I'll upgrade since the one I got is obviously old and makes quite a racket. I really don't use it that much – mostly for bread or large batches of things. Most of the time I try to make do with a hand mixer because my counter space in our little house is limited and I don't have a dishwasher.

» COFFEE/SPICE GRINDER: This is a must-have for grinding oats and flax seeds into flour and powdering sweetener and chia seeds.

» DUTCH OVEN: I've always wanted a Dutch oven – you know, a pretty enamel-coated cast iron version to grace my stovetop. Lo and behold, some of Ryan's coworkers gave us a 5.5-quart Dutch oven for a wedding gift! I use it all the time! It's so handy to be able to brown meats in it, then stick them right in the oven to bake.

» HAND MIXER: Yup, this is my go-to for everything from cheesecakes to frosting. With a small house and no dishwasher, if I can't make it with my hand mixer, I probably won't make it.

» ICE CREAM MAKER: I have used a Cuisinart ICE-21 1.5-quart automatic countertop ice cream churn for many years and love it. It's so easy to use!

» IMMERSION BLENDER: This is another go-to, especially in a small house. If I can use my immersion blender instead of a full-size blender to minimize cleanup, I most certainly will. It's helpful for blending hot liquids without the danger of a pressure buildup as well.

» SLOW COOKER: I use my Crock-Pot a lot for make-ahead suppers and fellowship meal dishes.

» WAFFLE IRON: I just use a regular nonstick waffle iron. Check out page 39 for a note on how to keep waffles from sticking.

» I've tried to list ingredients in the order that I would use them. In some recipes, all the dry ingredients are listed first because they're whisked together before the wet ingredients are added. In recipes where wet and dry ingredients are added at the same time, I list them in order of measurement but list the dry ingredient first so you can use the same measuring utensil for both dry and wet.

» If a specific ingredient is mentioned (i.e. "salted butter"), there's a reason for that. If the recipe does not specify, assume that it doesn't matter. (For example, in a recipe that just calls for "butter" instead of specifying "salted butter," assume that you can use either salted or unsalted butter.) The same rule applies to gelatin. If a recipe calls for "plain gelatin," assume that any brand will work in the same amount.

» According to some people, I undersweeten things. If I have a suspicion that some people will want more sweetener in a recipe, I make a note of that beside the sweetener that I suggest you increase (generally the less concentrated sweetener). Always taste and add more sweetener if necessary whether I suggest it in the recipe or not. I don't want you to be disappointed! I usually only use xylitol when I want it for anti-freezing or caramelization effects, so substitute for it at your own risk.

» If a recipe calls for "2 cups spinach (chopped)," measure the spinach, then chop it. If the recipe calls for "2 cups chopped spinach," chop the spinach first, then measure it.

» "1 tablespoon THM Super Sweet Blend (powdered)" means to measure a tablespoon of the sweetener, then powder it in a coffee grinder or spice grinder before using it in the recipe.

» I used half-tablespoon measurements when already working in tablespoons instead of parceling out the measurement into tablespoons + teaspoons. Tupperware sells measuring spoons with half-tablespoon measurements, and I'm sure other companies do too. If you don't have a half-tablespoon measurement, eyeball it. Or measure out 1½ teaspoons.

» When a recipe gives a range for an ingredient, start with the smaller amount, then taste and add more if desired.

» I tend to use reduced-fat cream cheese and sour cream in my recipes (unless otherwise noted) to cut down on needless calories. Feel free to use full-fat ingredients in a Healthy Fats setting if you prefer. Reduced-fat cream cheese usually doesn't have to be softened before use, but you'll probably need to soften full-fat cream cheese if substituting it into a recipe.

» All spices and herbs are in their dried forms unless otherwise noted.

» I always use part-skim mozzarella.

» I use large eggs from Walmart.

» Use thawed, drained meats unless otherwise indicated.

» Unless otherwise noted, thaw and drain frozen fruit before adding it to recipes.

» "Chicken breasts (chunked)" just means that you should cut the chicken into bite-sized pieces.

» "Coined" means "cut into coin-shaped pieces." I used this description with things like carrots and sausage links.

» If I say "rinse and drain," that's what I mean. If I say "drain," just drain.

» I use a conventional oven in my recipes. If you have a convection oven, you may need to decrease the baking times.

» Unless otherwise noted, store all recipes in the fridge or freezer. These recipes don't have sugar for preservation, so even baked goods will spoil quickly at room temperature.

» Serving sizes are an inexact science and really depend on your own personal metabolism and activity level. Eat until you're satisfied, but don't stuff yourself. Obviously hungry boys usually eat more than little girls, so in calculating serving sizes I just tried to eyeball average portions to give you an idea of how many people a recipe will serve.

» There are a medley of meal sizes in this book because of my personal journey when writing it. If you have a large family, multiply the recipes as many times as you need to! If you have a small family and find some of the recipes too big, enjoy having leftovers, freeze some for later, or halve the recipes.

» Recipe creation is a science. Substitution is an experiment. It's welcome, and I do it all the time, but for best results, use the ingredients given.

trip to Dallas

self-timer engagement picture

my kitchen

our living room

fuel types

HEALTHY FATS

recipes that focus on healthy fats and keep carbs to a minimum

FOUNDATION FATS

recipes that focus on basic fats that are easy for the body to digest, such as those from coconut oil, butter, eggs, and meat (This category omits ingredients such as cheese, heavy whipping cream, nuts, and cream cheese that are fine to use in a Healthy Fats setting but can sometimes be overdone.)

HEALTHY CARBS

recipes that focus on healthy carbs and keep fats to a minimum

LOW CARB/LOW FAT

recipes that don't contain significant sources of either carbs or fats

HEALTHY CARBS & HEALTHY FATS

recipes that use healthy carbs and healthy fats in the same recipe (Recipes in this category are great for people who don't need to lose weight, but if you'd like to lose a few pounds, keep these recipes for special occasions.)

Note: On occasion I've abbreviated fuel types to save space.

breakfast

apple pie baked oatmeal

2 cups old-fashioned oats

1¼ cups unsweetened almond milk

¾ cup egg whites

1 teaspoon cinnamon

1 teaspoon each maple, vanilla extract

½ teaspoon baking powder

½ teaspoon salt

¼ teaspoon THM Pure Stevia Extract Powder

⅛ teaspoon ground cloves

2 med. unpeeled apples (grated)

¼ cup xylitol

1 tablespoon lemon juice

¼ teaspoon cinnamon

These baked oatmeal recipes have a dense cake-like texture because the batter is refrigerated overnight before baking. I don't recommend skipping that step, but I know people who have and still liked them…. I love to make a batch or two of baked oatmeal, cut it into servings, and keep it in the fridge for a quick breakfast, snack, or dessert. These baked oatmeal recipes contain protein on their own so you don't need to add anything to complete your meal or snack, but if you want to add more protein in the form of low-fat cottage cheese or Greek yogurt to keep you full longer, be my guest!

Mix the oatmeal ingredients together and pour into a greased 8"x8" pan. Spread out evenly.

Mix the grated apple, xylitol, lemon juice, and cinnamon together. Spread on top of the oatmeal layer, using your fingers to gently distribute it if necessary so the apple doesn't become completely submerged in the excess oatmeal liquid. (This liquid will soak into the oats overnight, don't worry.)

Refrigerate the unbaked oatmeal overnight. In the morning, bake at 350° for 40-45 minutes, let cool for a few minutes to solidify before cutting, then enjoy! Store leftovers in refrigerator and enjoy cold or reheat.

"There, too," remarked Alleyne, as they rode on again, "that which seems to the eye to be dead is still FULL OF THE SAP OF LIFE, even as the vines were. Thus God hath written Himself and His laws very broadly on all that is around us, if our poor dull eyes and duller souls could but read what He hath set before us."

SIR ARTHUR CONAN COYLE
THE WHITE COMPANY

cherry pie baked oatmeal

HEALTHY CARBS | SERVES 8

4 cups old-fashioned oats

2 cups water

1 cup unsweetened applesauce

1 cup egg whites

2 teaspoons cinnamon

2 teaspoons vanilla extract

1 teaspoon baking powder

1 teaspoon salt

1 teaspoon molasses

⅜ teaspoon THM Pure Stevia Extract Powder

1 (26 oz.) can tart cherries canned
   in water (drained)

1½ teaspoons THM Super Sweet Blend

Mix the first section of ingredients together and refrigerate overnight. (If you want the oatmeal to be sweeter, add some THM Super Sweet Blend or other granulated sweetener in addition to the stevia used. I liked it as written.)

The next day, pour the oatmeal batter into a greased 9"x13" pan and spread it out evenly.

Toss the cherries with the Super Sweet Blend. Make a well in the center of each of 8 pieces in the oatmeal batter in the pan; divide the cherries among the holes. Push the cherries down into the oatmeal batter a bit. Bake the oatmeal at 350° for 45 minutes or until it is moist but not mushy in the center.

Enjoy the baked oatmeal warm or cold. I like to eat it with unsweetened almond milk and some extra Super Sweet Blend on top.

I love the taste of tart cherries and was delighted to find some at a discount grocery store in Ohio when I was working there one summer. If you can't find tart cherries in your area, I've given substitution suggestions below.

note

If you can't find canned tart cherries, you could try using frozen sweet cherries or flavorful berries such as blueberries, blackberries, or raspberries. The can of cherries I used yielded about 2½ cups of cherries. Thaw and drain frozen fruit before using in this recipe.

banana bread baked oatmeal

4 cups old-fashioned oats

2 cups unsweetened almond milk

1 cup unsweetened applesauce

1 cup egg whites

2 med. bananas (mashed)

2 teaspoons cinnamon

2 teaspoons banana extract

1 teaspoon baking powder

1 teaspoon salt

1 teaspoon vanilla extract

¼ teaspoon THM Pure Stevia Extract Powder

¼ teaspoon ground cloves

Chopped pecans

Sugar-free chocolate chips (for topping)

Mix the first section of ingredients together and refrigerate overnight. The next day, spread the batter into a greased 9"x13" pan, top with a sprinkling of chopped pecans and sugar-free chocolate chips (just a garnish amount so you don't overdo the fats), and bake at 350° for 40 minutes. This baked oatmeal is good warm or cold, but the banana bread flavors are strongest when warm.

note

If you want the baked oatmeal to be sweeter, add a few teaspoons of THM Super Sweet Blend. Neither Ryan nor I like our food to be too sweet, and the chocolate chips add a few pops of sweetness, so this amount of stevia was the perfect sweetness for us.

Nor let his eye see sin, but through my tears.
PHINEAS FLETCHER - "DROP, DROP, SLOW TEARS"

pineapple rightside-up baked oatmeal

HEALTHY CARBS | SERVES 4

2 cups old-fashioned oats

1¼ cups unsweetened almond milk

¾ cup egg whites

1 teaspoon cinnamon

1 teaspoon vanilla extract

½ teaspoon baking powder

½ teaspoon salt

¼ teaspoon THM Pure Stevia Extract Powder

1 cup pineapple chunks canned in juice (drained)

1 teaspoon THM Super Sweet Blend

1 teaspoon molasses

Mix the first section of ingredients together and pour into a greased 8"x8" pan or 9" pie plate.

Mash the pineapple chunks, Super Sweet Blend, and molasses together with a pastry cutter until the pineapple is in small pieces. Pour this mixture (including the juice that came out of the pineapple when mashing it) on top of the oatmeal layer and spread it out. Cover and refrigerate overnight.

In the morning, bake the oatmeal at 350° for 45 minutes. Let it cool for a few minutes to solidify before cutting and serving. Store leftovers in the refrigerator. It's good warm or cold!

ginger peach oatmeal cake

2 cups old-fashioned oats

1 cup unsweetened almond milk

½ cup unsweetened applesauce

½ cup egg whites

1 teaspoon molasses

1 teaspoon vanilla extract

½ teaspoon baking powder

½ teaspoon each cinnamon, ginger, salt

½ teaspoon maple extract

¼ teaspoon ground cloves

⅛ teaspoon + 2 doonks THM Pure Stevia
    Extract Powder

1½ cups peeled, chopped peaches

Beat all the ingredients except the peaches together. Fold in the peaches gently. Cover and refrigerate overnight.

In the morning, pour the mixture into a greased 9" pie plate and bake at 350° for 35 minutes. Serve warm with reduced-fat cream cheese (1½ tablespoons per serving to stay in HC mode) and sugar-free syrup, or refrigerate it and eat it cold.

note

If you don't plan to top this cake with sugar-free syrup, you may wish to add more sweetener.

maple & "brown sugar" baked oatmeal squares

HEALTHY CARBS | SERVES 8

4 cups old-fashioned oats

2 cups unsweetened almond milk

1 cup unsweetened applesauce

1 cup egg whites

1 tablespoon cinnamon

2 teaspoons molasses

2 teaspoons maple extract

2 teaspoons vanilla extract

1 teaspoon baking powder

1 teaspoon salt

¼ teaspoon THM Pure Stevia Extract Powder

These basic baked oatmeal squares are supremely easy and make a great grab-and-go breakfast for me and the hubby.

Mix the ingredients together and refrigerate overnight. The next day, spread the batter into a greased 9"x13" pan and bake at 350° for 40 minutes. This baked oatmeal is good warm or cold. You can top it with low-fat Greek or regular yogurt, low-fat cottage cheese, THM Super Sweet Blend, cinnamon, sugar-free syrup, etc.

note

If you want the baked oatmeal to be sweeter, add a few teaspoons of THM Super Sweet Blend. Neither Ryan nor I like our food to be too sweet, so this amount of stevia was the perfect sweetness for us.

mocha chip baked oatmeal

2 cups old-fashioned oats

1 cup brewed coffee

½ cup low-fat Greek yogurt or
    unsweetened applesauce

½ cup unsweetened almond milk

½ cup egg whites

1½ tablespoons cocoa powder

1 tablespoon THM Super Sweet Blend
    (or more, to taste)

2 teaspoons espresso instant coffee powder

1 teaspoon baking powder

1 teaspoon cinnamon

1 teaspoon vanilla extract

½ teaspoon salt

Sugar-free chocolate chips or chopped
    85% dark chocolate (for topping)

Stir all the ingredients together (except the chocolate chips), cover, and refrigerate overnight. In the morning, pour the mixture into a greased 9" pie plate, top with a sprinkling of sugar-free chocolate chips or chopped 85% dark chocolate, and bake at 350° for 35 minutes. Remove the baked oatmeal from the oven and let it cool 5-10 minutes before cutting into it. Leftovers are great cold out of the fridge!

OPTIONAL JAVA GREEK YOGURT TOPPING ▼

Whisk 2 cups low-fat Greek yogurt, ½ cup unsweetened almond milk, 1½ teaspoons espresso instant coffee powder, ¼ teaspoon vanilla extract, and 3-4 doonks THM Pure Stevia Extract Powder until smooth. Serve on top of Mocha Chip Baked Oatmeal.

note

• Feel free to add more espresso powder for a stronger coffee flavor!

• Since sugar-free chocolate chips and 85% dark chocolate are fat sources, keep them to a garnish amount in this recipe that focuses on healthy carbs.

pumpkin chip baked oatmeal

HEALTHY CARBS | SERVES 4

2 cups old-fashioned oats

1 cup unsweetened almond milk

¾ cup canned pumpkin

½ cup egg whites

2 teaspoons pumpkin pie spice

1 teaspoon each vanilla, maple extract

¾ teaspoon baking powder

½ teaspoon salt

¼ teaspoon THM Pure Stevia Extract Powder

Sugar-free chocolate chips or chopped
   85% dark chocolate (for topping)

Mix all the ingredients but the chocolate chips together, spread into a greased 9" pie plate, cover, and refrigerate overnight.

In the morning, add a sprinkling of chocolate chips to the top of the baked oatmeal and bake at 350° for 30-35 minutes until the center is not mushy and wet.

I prefer to eat this baked oatmeal warm with a drizzle of Hershey's sugar-free chocolate syrup (it's sweetened primarily with erythritol!). Leftovers keep well in the fridge or freezer, but I like to heat them up before eating because heating brings out more pumpkin spice flavor.

TIP ▼

Most of my baked oatmeal recipes made in an 8"x8" pan or 9" pie plate can easily be doubled for a 9"x13" pan. Bake a little longer if necessary.

note

• Feel free to add a few teaspoons of a granulated sweetener if you want the baked oatmeal to be sweeter.

• If you're a coffee lover, you might want to try using brewed coffee in place of some of the almond milk! I'm not a coffee drinker and the thought of pumpkin with coffee grosses me out, but I just thought I'd throw the idea out there because if I were a coffee drinker I would probably try it.

• Keep the chocolate chips to just a sprinkling because they are a fat source and we want to keep this recipe focused on healthy carbs.

cranberry orange baked oatmeal muffins

HEALTHY CARBS | YIELDS 12 MUFFINS

2 cups old-fashioned oats
1½ cups unsweetened almond milk
1 cup cranberries (whole or chopped)
¾ cup egg whites
1 lg. orange (peeled, chopped)
1 teaspoon cinnamon
1 teaspoon vanilla extract
½ teaspoon salt
¼ teaspoon THM Pure Stevia Extract Powder
¼ teaspoon each cardamom,
    ginger, ground cloves

1 tablespoon apple cider vinegar
1 teaspoon baking powder

Whisk the first set of ingredients together and refrigerate overnight. Feel free to add a dash of orange extract for extra orange flavor!

In the morning, whisk in the vinegar and baking powder. Divide the batter among 12 greased muffin tin holes and bake at 350° for 35 minutes. Enjoy warm or cold; I like to reheat cold muffins in the microwave for 15 seconds. I recommend 3 muffins per serving.

THINGS WHICH MATTER MOST
must never be at the mercy
of things which matter least.

JOHANN WOLFGANG VON GOETHE

SHOULD I ADD MORE PROTEIN? ▼

Oats contain protein on their own, so you're not required to add extra protein to your baked oatmeal or regular oatmeal breakfast. However, you might want to so you don't get hungry an hour after you eat! My baked oatmeal recipes contain egg whites for extra protein already, but you can serve them with a side of low-fat yogurt, Greek yogurt, or cottage cheese. You could also add a scoop of collagen to your hot tea or coffee to add extra protein. To add protein to regular hot oatmeal, stir in some egg whites, protein powder, or collagen after cooking the oatmeal and taking it off the heat. (Whisk in egg whites immediately after cooking so the oatmeal is hot enough to cook them, but wait a little bit before adding protein powder or collagen so they don't clump.)

easy chocolate oatmeal

1⅓ cups water
½ cup old-fashioned oats
Hearty dash salt

1 tablespoon cocoa powder
3-4 doonks THM Pure Stevia Extract Powder

Sliced banana
Unsweetened almond milk

Microwave the first three ingredients together in a large bowl for 3-4 minutes. (I use a large serving bowl so the oatmeal doesn't run over in the microwave.) You could also cook this mixture on the stovetop until the desired consistency is reached. Stir the cocoa powder and sweetener into the oatmeal. Top with a moderate amount of sliced banana and a splash of almond milk if desired. (Sometimes I stir a little almond milk into the oatmeal along with the cocoa powder and sweetener if I want it to be thinner or not so dark chocolatey.)

That's the base recipe, but I almost always dress it up a tad. I usually stir in 2 tablespoons of whey protein powder along with the cocoa powder to add protein. Sometimes I stir in a teaspoon of coconut oil or smear a teaspoon of peanut butter on top of the oatmeal after stirring the cocoa powder in. (Smearing it on top instead of stirring it in gives you more noticeable peanut butter flavor.) A sprinkling of sugar-free chocolate chips on top is good too, but remember to keep your added fat to 5 grams or less to avoid combining too many carbs and fats.

note

• You may be wondering about the banana and oatmeal together in one meal. Aren't they both carb sources? Yep, but according to my Google research, half a medium banana and a half cup serving of oats comes to about 35 grams net carbs.
• In my experience, cocoa powder gets more bitter when it's cooked, so stirring it into the oatmeal *after* cooking is important!

creamy pb&j oatmeal

1 cup water
½ cup old-fashioned oats

⅓ cup unsweetened almond milk
3 tablespoons defatted peanut flour
⅛ teaspoon salt
⅛ teaspoon THM Pure Stevia Extract Powder

Sliced strawberries

Microwave the water and oats for 3-4 minutes or until soft. (Alternatively you could cook them on the stovetop until the desired consistency is achieved.)

Whisk in the almond milk, peanut flour, salt, and stevia. Top with sliced strawberries and enjoy!

Defatted peanut flour adds protein to this oatmeal to keep you full longer!

And God said unto Moses,
I AM THAT I AM:
and he said, Thus shalt thou
say unto the children of Israel,
I AM hath sent me unto you.
EXODUS 3:14

Jesus said unto them,
Verily, verily, I say unto you,
Before Abraham was, I am.
JOHN 8:58

note

• To make the strawberries more of a jam-like consistency, mash them up and cook them with the oats and water in the first step.
• To make this an overnight oatmeal, try omitting the cooking step and adding a scant ½ teaspoon glucomannan. Shake all the ingredients together in a pint-sized jar with a lid and refrigerate overnight.
• For a twist, feel free to add some cocoa powder!

overnight oatmeal survival packets

HEALTHY CARBS | SERVES 1

DRY INGREDIENTS
½ cup old-fashioned oats
2 tablespoons whey protein powder or collagen
1 tablespoon cocoa powder
½ teaspoon glucomannan (slightly rounded)
⅛ teaspoon salt
⅛ teaspoon THM Pure Stevia Extract Powder

1½ cups water and/or unsweetened almond milk

Measure the dry ingredients into individual sealable plastic bags or containers. The ingredients listed make one packet, so simply add those ingredients to as many packets as you need.

The night before you want to eat your oatmeal, add one packet to a pint-sized glass jar, put a lid on it, and shake it to evenly distribute the dry ingredients. Add 1½ cups of liquid; I like to use a combination of water and almond milk, but just water works too if that's all you have. Put the lid on the jar again and shake it well to combine the dry and wet ingredients, then refrigerate overnight to thicken.

POSSIBLE ADDITIONS ▼
chili powder, defatted peanut flour, espresso instant coffee powder

These are my go-to make-ahead breakfasts while I'm traveling; they've gotten me through choir tours and music camps! Starting the day out right encourages healthy choices throughout the day and minimizes damage when you don't have an abundance of healthy options away from home.

minimalist version

Use all water and don't even refrigerate. Eat oatmeal at lukewarm temperature in the morning. I have done this.

my favorite version

Use whey protein powder instead of collagen for a creamier result and mix with 1 cup water and ½ cup unsweetened almond milk. Refrigerate properly.

baobab burst muesli

¾ cup unsweetened almond milk

½ cup old-fashioned oats

½ cup low-fat cottage cheese

2 tablespoons baobab powder

1 teaspoon THM Super Sweet Blend
   (or more, to taste)

3 doonks THM Pure Stevia Extract Powder

Dash salt

½ cup dark sweet cherries (or fruit of choice)

Whisk the first section of ingredients together, then stir in the cherries. Refrigerate overnight and enjoy cold in the morning! You can top with some extra Super Sweet Blend for additional sweetness and berries for additional volume if you like.

I love the fruity flavors of the baobab and cherry together! I used cottage cheese because that's what I had on hand and it's milder in flavor than Greek yogurt, but feel free to substitute with low-fat Greek yogurt if you prefer.

pb&j muesli

HEALTHY CARBS | SERVES 1

⅔ cup unsweetened almond milk

½ cup old-fashioned oats

½ cup low-fat cottage cheese

3 tablespoons defatted peanut flour

2 doonks THM Pure Stevia Extract Powder

Dash vanilla extract

Dash salt

½ cup frozen strawberries

THM Super Sweet Blend

Stir the first section of ingredients together and refrigerate overnight. In the morning, microwave the strawberry slices to thaw, then mash them with a fork. Top the muesli with the strawberry "jam" and Super Sweet Blend to taste. (Or just top the muesli with sliced fresh strawberries if you prefer.) Enjoy!

french toast for one

¼ cup unsweetened almond milk
¼ cup egg whites
¼ teaspoon cinnamon
1 doonk THM Pure Stevia Extract Powder
Dash salt
Dash vanilla extract

2 pieces sprouted or cold-fermented bread
    (such as the Homemade Bread on
    page 160 of *Necessary Food*)
Granulated sweetener
Sugar-free syrup

Whisk the first set of ingredients together. Soak the bread in the mixture for a few minutes, flipping it to make sure both sides get coated.

Meanwhile, heat a skillet over medium-high heat. When it is good and hot, spray it with cooking spray and fry the pieces of bread on both sides until toasted.

Sprinkle the French toast with some additional granulated sweetener of your choice and serve with sugar-free syrup. I like to top mine with some low-fat Greek yogurt or cottage cheese (for extra protein) and some sliced banana (only an inch or two, thinly sliced, so as not to overdo the carbs).

There are some egg whites in the dipping mixture for this French toast, but I recommend adding a bit more protein, either in the form of low-fat Greek yogurt or cottage cheese on top of your French toast or just by adding some collagen to your tea or coffee.

note

If you multiply this recipe for your family, you won't need to multiply the soaking mixture as many times as the bread. You'll have some liquid left over from this recipe (because you need enough volume to be able to soak the bread), but you can always fry it up and eat it like scrambled eggs.

peanut butter, banana & chocolate stuffed french toast

HEALTHY CARBS | SERVES 1

3 tablespoons defatted peanut flour
3 tablespoons water
½ - ¾ teaspoon THM Super Sweet Blend
Hearty dash salt

2 slices sprouted bread
3" banana (sliced)

2 tablespoons unsweetened almond milk
2 tablespoons egg whites

Cooking spray
Cocoa powder and additional
    THM Super Sweet Blend
Sugar-free syrup and/or
    sugar-free chocolate syrup

Whisk the peanut flour, water, Super Sweet Blend, and salt together and spread half on one piece of bread and half on the other. Top the peanut butter on both slices of bread with the sliced banana, then put the bread together as a sandwich.

Whisk the almond milk and egg whites in a bowl.

Heat a non-stick pan over medium heat. When it is hot, dip the sandwich in the egg mixture for a few seconds on each side. Spray the pan with a light coating of cooking spray and fry the French toast for a few minutes on each side until toasted. (I cover it with a lid while frying to make sure it heats all the way through.)

 Sprinkle a light dusting of cocoa powder and additional Super Sweet Blend onto each side of the French toast and serve with sugar-free syrup and/or sugar-free chocolate syrup.

note

• I used Aldi's Simply Nature Sprouted 7 Grain Bread, but you can use your favorite Healthy Carbs bread! I prefer thin slices for stuffed French toast.
• I don't feel the need to add extra protein to this breakfast because the sprouted bread, egg whites, and peanut flour all have some protein.

pumpkin stuffed french toast

HEALTHY CARBS | SERVES 1

2 slices sprouted bread
1 tablespoon reduced-fat cream cheese

2 tablespoons canned pumpkin
¾ teaspoon THM Super Sweet Blend
¼ teaspoon pumpkin pie spice
Dash salt

2 tablespoons unsweetened almond milk
2 tablespoons egg whites
Dash vanilla extract

Cooking spray
Additional pumpkin pie spice
Sugar-free syrup and/or sugar-free chocolate syrup

Spread the cream cheese on one slice of bread.

Mix the pumpkin, Super Sweet Blend, pumpkin pie spice, and salt together and spread over the cream cheese. Top with the other slice of bread to make a sandwich.

Whisk the almond milk, egg whites, and vanilla in a bowl.

Heat a non-stick pan over medium heat. When it is hot, dip the sandwich in the egg mixture for a few seconds on each side. Spray the pan with a light coating of cooking spray and fry the French toast for a few minutes on each side until toasted. (I cover it with a lid while frying to make sure it heats all the way through.) Sprinkle a little extra pumpkin pie spice on the stuffed French toast and serve with sugar-free syrup and/or sugar-free chocolate syrup.

Sprouted bread (such as Aldi's Simply Nature Sprouted 7 Grain Bread that I used in this recipe) does tend to be chewier than its traditional counterpart in French toast recipes, but I can put up with that knowing that my blood sugar isn't being yanked out of whack! The effect is still quite nice, on the whole.

note

I recommend adding a little protein with this stuffed French toast to hold you over until your next meal. 2 slices of the sprouted bread I was using contain 6 grams protein, but adding a side of low-fat Greek yogurt or a scoop of collagen to your coffee or tea would be ideal.

french toast casserole

4 cups cubed sprouted or cold-fermented
bread (such as the Homemade Bread
recipe on page 160 of *Necessary Food*)
1 cup blueberries

¾ cup unsweetened almond milk
¾ cup egg whites
1 teaspoon THM Super Sweet Blend
(or more, to taste)
1 teaspoon cinnamon
½ teaspoon baking powder
½ teaspoon vanilla extract
⅛ teaspoon salt
⅛ teaspoon THM Pure Stevia Extract Powder
¼ teaspoon xanthan gum

3 oz. reduced-fat cream cheese

Spread the cubed bread into a greased
8"x8" baking dish. Top with the blueberries.

Blend (or beat) the second set of ingredients
together and pour over the top of the
casserole.

Soften the cream cheese and whisk in a dash
of water to thin it down enough to dollop
and spread over the top of the dish. Cover
and refrigerate overnight.

In the morning, bake the casserole (uncovered)
at 375° for 45-50 minutes or until the top of
the casserole is as crunchy as you like it. Let
the casserole cool for 5-10 minutes before
serving, then serve with sugar-free syrup.

note

• If you don't plan to top this casserole with sugar-
free syrup, you may wish to add more THM Super
Sweet Blend. The fat from the cream cheese
comes to 4.5 grams per serving if the casserole is
cut into 4 large servings.
• Feel free to use any berries you like in this
recipe! You could add fruit (like peaches or pears)
instead if you prefer, but go easy on that because
you already have a carb source in the form of the
bread used in this casserole.

four vanilla waffles

LOW CARB/LOW FAT | SERVES 4

¾ cup Briana's Baking Mix

2 teaspoons baking powder

½ teaspoon xanthan gum

¼ teaspoon salt

¼ teaspoon THM Pure Stevia Extract Powder

¾ cup egg whites

½ cup low-fat Greek yogurt

½ cup water

1 teaspoon vanilla extract

Whisk the dry ingredients. Add the wet ingredients and mix well. Bake in a well-greased nonstick waffle iron until done. (This recipe will take a little longer to bake than "regular" waffles.) My waffle iron uses about half a cup of batter per waffle; it is not a Belgian-style waffle maker. Freeze leftover waffles and reheat in a toaster.

My baking mix is Low Carb/Low Fat in controlled amounts as used in this recipe, but keep additional fats to a minimum to stay in Low Carb/Low Fat mode. I like to top these waffles with low-fat cottage cheese and Blueberry Jam (page 487). Peanut butter made with defatted peanut flour and some sugar-free syrup would be a great topping option as well, or you can load up on your regular Healthy Fats toppings like natural peanut butter or cream cheese (and sugar-free chocolate chips!) to turn these into a Healthy Fats meal.

If you've made and loved the Strawberry Shortcake Waffle (page 41) as so many people have, you'll love being able to make a bigger batch of them using this recipe! Feed them to your family for breakfast or supper (because who doesn't love breakfast for dinner?), or freeze them and keep them on hand for your own grab-and-go breakfasts throughout the week. These waffles are light – not dense like a lot of low-carb waffles tend to be – and they have a yummy vanilla flavor that reminds me of Nilla Wafers.

note

I don't recommend using THM Baking Blend in this recipe since these waffles are on the fragile side and my baking mix is sturdier.

cheater "sourdough" waffles

HEALTHY CARBS I YIELDS 7 WAFFLES

2 cups whole wheat flour

1 tablespoon baking powder

1 teaspoon instant yeast

½ teaspoon THM Super Sweet Blend

½ teaspoon salt

1¼ cups unsweetened almond milk

1 cup hot tap water

½ cup egg whites

1 tablespoon butter or coconut oil (melted)

1 teaspoon honey

Whisk the dry ingredients in a large plastic mixing bowl. (Use one that has an airtight lid, like a Tupperware bowl.) Add the wet ingredients and mix again. Let the bowl sit out on the counter until you can see that the yeast is active and the mixture is rising. Cover the bowl with the lid, seal it, and refrigerate the batter for 3 days. (Keep an eye on the lid and reseal it if necessary.)

After 3 days of cold fermentation, give the batter a brisk stir to reincorporate the top layer, then bake the batter in a greased waffle iron. (Amount of batter will vary depending on the waffle iron. Mine uses a rounded third cup.) You may need to bake the waffles a little longer than normal waffles to get a crispy exterior. The waffle batter has a soured taste, but almost all of that disappears when you bake it.

I like to enjoy my waffles with peanut butter made from defatted peanut flour and sugar-free syrup. (Check out page 491 for a recipe.) Store leftover waffles in the fridge or freezer and reheat in a toaster.

I call these Cheater "Sourdough" Waffles because you get the souring taste and action of sourdough, but you don't need to mess with a starter! These waffles have a nice crispy finish thanks to the bit of gluten structure that remains after the wheat flour has been fermented. However, since the flour has been fermented and the gluten has been broken down, the waffles aren't as crispy crisp as a waffle made with regular white flour, and they do have a bit of "chew." You might need a knife to help cut them cleanly. Don't get me wrong – they are crispy. I was absolutely delighted when I picked up my first completed waffle and felt just how crispy it was. These are not limp and soggy waffles!

note

• I recommend using carton pasteurized egg whites to cut down on the chance of bacteria breeding in your waffle batter.

• I use honey in very small amounts like this for the purpose of activating yeast. Many of the sugars in the honey are eaten up during the fermentation period in this recipe.

• I have not tried keeping this batter for more than 3 days, but I don't recommend keeping it around much longer than that because the fermented flavor will get stronger and there are things in the batter (like egg whites) that I wouldn't want to risk spoiling.

• You can try making this batter as pancakes, but I prefer it as waffles because the texture just fits better. If you make this batter as pancakes, spread it out fairly thin so the pancakes aren't thick and gummy.

• The liquids and flours were specifically formulated for the cold fermentation technique. If you have sprouted wheat flour or sourdough starter that you would like to use, I recommend finding another recipe.

HOW TO KEEP WAFFLES FROM STICKING ▼

Use a nonstick waffle iron. (I've never used a fancy waffle iron; a Walmart model should work just fine.) Spray it well with cooking spray. I use olive oil spray because I've heard that coconut oil spray doesn't work as well for nonstick uses. If you're making multiple waffles, spray the waffle maker between each waffle.

When you're finished making waffles, wipe the waffle maker with a paper towel. Do not wash with soap and water. Wiping the greased waffle iron down with a paper towel "seasons" the coating similar to how you would care for cast iron ware. I don't know that this has been scientifically proven; this is just what I've picked up from personal experience.

chocolate waffles for two

¼ cup + 2 tablespoons Briana's Baking Mix

3 tablespoons cocoa powder

2 teaspoons THM Super Sweet Blend

¾ teaspoon baking powder

¼ teaspoon xanthan gum

⅛ teaspoon salt

3 doonks THM Pure Stevia Extract Powder

¾ cup hot tap water

1 tablespoon refined coconut oil

2 eggs

Whisk the dry ingredients.

Add the hot water and coconut oil and whisk (the hot water will melt the coconut oil without having to melt it separately - nifty, huh?), then add the eggs and whisk again. The batter will be fairly loose. Set it aside for 5 minutes.

After 5 minutes, make your waffles. (This recipe makes 2 standard-sized waffles.) Be sure to grease the waffle iron. You'll need to bake these waffles a bit longer than you would "normal" waffles.

I like to serve these waffles with natural peanut butter and the Blueberry Topping from page 493. Yum!

Leftover waffles keep well in the fridge. You can either heat them up in the toaster or just enjoy them cold! Sometimes I eat them cold with a little peanut butter and a squirt of Reddi-wip if I need a quick dessert.

note

These waffles aren't super sweet on their own, so if you're not topping them with a sweet syrup, you'll probably need to add some extra THM Super Sweet Blend.

strawberry shortcake waffle

LOW CARB/LOW FAT | SERVES I

3 tablespoons Briana's Baking Mix
½ teaspoon baking powder
⅛ teaspoon xanthan gum
2 doonks THM Pure Stevia Extract Powder
1⁄16 teaspoon salt

3 tablespoons egg whites
2 tablespoons low-fat Greek yogurt
2 tablespoons water
Hearty dash vanilla extract

Whisk the dry ingredients. Add the wet ingredients and mix again. Bake in a greased waffle iron until slightly crispy on the outside. Top with your choice of toppings and enjoy!

TOPPING SUGGESTIONS ▼
low carb/low fat sliced strawberries, low-fat cottage cheese, squirt of Reddi-wip
healthy fats homemade sweetened whipped cream

> BLEST IS THE MAN, FOREVER BLEST,
> Whose guilt is pardoned by his God, Whose sins with sorrow are confessed And covered with his Savior's blood. ISAAC WATTS

The original blog post for this recipe said, "This waffle was so good that I tried it out on a friend who was visiting for the weekend. There were no leftovers." That "friend" was Ryan, who was my boyfriend at the time and is now my husband. He really did like those waffles! Slightly crispy on the outside but soft on the inside, this waffle has the perfect texture. It reminds me of a Nilla Wafer thanks to a hearty dash of vanilla extract.

note

My baking mix is Low Carb/Low Fat in controlled amounts as used in this recipe, but keep any additional fats to a minimum to stay in Low Carb/Low Fat mode.

pb&j protein waffle

LOW CARB/LOW FAT | SERVES 1

¼ cup defatted peanut flour

½ teaspoon baking powder

⅛ teaspoon xanthan gum

2 doonks THM Pure Stevia Extract Powder

¹⁄₁₆ teaspoon salt

Dash cinnamon (optional)

3 tablespoons egg whites

2 tablespoons low-fat Greek yogurt

2 tablespoons water

Sliced strawberries and sugar-free syrup

Whisk the dry ingredients. Add the wet ingredients and mix well. Bake in a greased waffle iron. The outside will get a little crispy when it's done. Top with sliced strawberries and sugar-free syrup and enjoy!

Peanut flour has an incredible amount of protein at 16 grams in a quarter cup! Add some egg whites and Greek yogurt in this waffle and you're up over 20 grams of protein! That means that even though this waffle pulls back on the carb and fat sources, it's quite filling. Because defatted peanut flour has around 4 grams of fat in a serving, don't add any extra fats on top of the waffle if you want to stay in Low Carb/Low Fat mode. I like to eat it with sliced strawberries and sugar-free syrup.

crispy protein waffle

HEALTHY FATS | SERVES I

1 egg

3 tablespoons Briana's Baking Mix

3 tablespoons water

2 tablespoons collagen

½ teaspoon baking powder

2 doonks THM Pure Stevia Extract Powder

Dash vanilla extract

Dash each cinnamon, salt

Whisk the egg. Add the rest of the ingredients and mix well. Bake in a well-greased waffle iron, then top with your favorite fixin's and enjoy! Hey, omitting the sweetener, vanilla, and cinnamon and making it into a savory waffle sandwich would be great too!

This is the best, most normal-tasting healthy waffle I've had to date. The added protein helps it crisp up like a regular waffle and I am in love. My favorite toppings: natural peanut butter, blueberries, and sugar-free syrup. If you want a family-sized waffle recipe similar to this, try the 5 Ingredient Waffles on page 13 of *Necessary Food*.

> To those who have sought
> Thee Thou never saidst, No;
> Now wash me, and I shall be
> WHITER THAN SNOW.
>
> JAMES NICHOLSON - "LORD JESUS,
> I LONG TO BE PERFECTLY WHOLE"

apple cinnamon waffle

HEALTHY CARBS | SERVES I

⅓ cup oat flour
½ teaspoon baking powder
½ teaspoon cinnamon
3 doonks THM Pure Stevia Extract Powder
Dash salt

¼ cup egg whites
2 tablespoons Greek yogurt
2 tablespoons water
½ cup chopped apple

Whisk the dry ingredients.

Add the egg whites, Greek yogurt, and water and mix until smooth. Fold in the chopped apple.

Bake the batter in a greased waffle iron. When the waffle is done, top with low-fat cottage cheese and some sugar-free syrup and enjoy!

cornbread waffle

¼ cup + 2 tablespoons water

¼ cup egg whites

3 tablespoons masa flour

2 tablespoons oat fiber

2 tablespoons Greek yogurt

½ teaspoon baking powder

¼ teaspoon cinnamon

⅛ teaspoon turmeric (for color)

3 doonks THM Pure Stevia Extract Powder

Dash salt (don't skimp on this)

Whisk the ingredients together until smooth. Bake in a greased waffle iron. Top with low-fat cottage cheese and sugar-free syrup (page 491) or Cranberry Syrup (page 492).

If you're one of those odd people that eats chicken with waffles, this would be a good waffle contender! Personally I like this waffle with some Cranberry Syrup (page 492). For a more traditional palate, top this waffle with sugar-free syrup. Want a combination of carbs and fats for something special? Add a nice pat of butter on top!

mocha waffle

LOW CARB / LOW FAT I SERVES I

2½ tablespoons Briana's Baking Mix

2½ teaspoons espresso instant coffee powder

2 teaspoons cocoa powder

½ teaspoon baking powder

⅛ teaspoon xanthan gum

2 doonks THM Pure Stevia Extract Powder
   (or more, to taste)

1/16 teaspoon salt

3 tablespoons egg whites

2 tablespoons low-fat Greek yogurt

2 tablespoons water

Whisk the dry ingredients, then add the wet ingredients and whisk again. Taste and add more coffee and sweetener if desired. Bake in a well-greased waffle iron (it will take a little longer than a normal waffle), top with your choice of toppings, and enjoy!

TOPPING SUGGESTIONS ▼

low carb/low fat low-fat cottage cheese, 1 tablespoon reduced-fat cream cheese, sugar-free syrup, sugar-free chocolate syrup

healthy fats cream cheese, sugar-free chocolate chips, 85% dark chocolate

healthy carbs sliced banana (and any of the LC/LF options)

peanut butter granola

¼ cup salted butter

2 tablespoons natural peanut butter

1½ teaspoons cinnamon

1 teaspoon each vanilla, maple extract

¼ teaspoon salt

⅛ teaspoon + 2 doonks THM Pure
Stevia Extract Powder

4 cups unsweetened coconut flakes

1 cup golden flaxmeal

1 cup salted cocktail peanuts (finely chopped)

2 teaspoons THM Super Sweet Blend
(or more, to taste)

Heat the first set of ingredients together in a saucepan and whisk until smooth. Add the second section of ingredients and stir well. Spread the granola onto a baking sheet and bake at 375° for 8-10 minutes until the granola is toasty brown on top. Stir the granola and return it to the oven for about 3 more minutes or until the top is brown. Remove the granola from the oven, stir it again, and let it cool completely before putting it in a sealable container for storage. It will keep in a cool, dry place (like your cupboard) for several weeks.

You can enjoy this yummy granola with some unsweetened almond milk for breakfast (add a source of protein, like some cottage cheese), on ice cream, or as part of a yogurt parfait! I'm not good at calculating serving sizes for stuff like this, but it's pretty calorie dense so I wouldn't fill up on it.

note

You can also add some sugar-free chocolate chips to the granola after it has cooled!

oat bran blueberry pancakes

HEALTHY CARBS I YIELDS 6 PANCAKES

1½ cups oat bran
¾ cup unsweetened almond milk
¾ cup egg whites
2½ teaspoons THM Super Sweet Blend
2 teaspoons baking powder
1 teaspoon vanilla extract
½ teaspoon each cinnamon, salt

Blueberries (no need to thaw if frozen)

Whisk the ingredients (except the blueberries) until smooth. Fry in a lightly-greased nonstick pan, using ⅓ cup batter for each pancake. Sprinkle some blueberries evenly onto each circle of uncooked pancake batter. Fry the pancakes until golden brown on both sides and not mushy in the center. (Frying on medium-low heat lets the pancakes cook through without burning.)

TOPPING SUGGESTIONS ▼

Waffle & Pancake Syrup from page 491, peanut butter made with defatted peanut flour, low-fat cottage cheese or Greek yogurt, fruit

At last – a pancake recipe that doesn't require fermentation or expensive sprouted flour but has a more traditional texture than pancakes made with oat flour! These pancakes are super easy to mix up and remind me of whole wheat pancakes, thick and hearty like the ones my grandma makes.

Oat bran is what a lot of people end up with when they're trying to find oat fiber. Just as the name suggests, it's made up of only the bran of the oat and is high in fiber. I use Bob's Red Mill brand, which you can find at many local grocery stores as well as in online health food stores.

note

Oat bran is not that carby, so you can really have as many pancakes as you want. (Each contains about 5 grams net carbs from the oat bran.) However, they're quite filling, so you probably won't need more than 2 or 3.

Obedience is the fruit of faith. CHRISTINA ROSSETTI

easy make-ahead breakfast quiche

HEALTHY FATS I SERVES 8

1 tablespoon salted butter
3 med. garlic cloves (minced)
1 med. onion (chopped)
1 lb. ground turkey sausage

12 eggs
2 cups chopped fresh greens of choice
Dime-sized bunch fresh cilantro (chopped)
¾ teaspoon Tony Chachere's
   Creole Seasoning

1½ cups shredded cheese
   of choice (for topping)

Melt the butter in a skillet and add the garlic and onion. Add the sausage and cook everything together until the sausage is fully cooked. Chop the sausage fine. (I used turkey sausage so I wouldn't have to drain the grease.)

Mix the second set of ingredients together, then add the sausage mixture (juice and all). Spread into a greased 9"x13" pan and top with the cheese. Bake at 350° for 30 minutes or until set. You can eat this quiche cold or hot. I like to top with sour cream and salsa.

note

Try turnip greens, mustard greens, collard greens, or spinach as the greens in this recipe. I recommend not using tough stems in this recipe since they won't have time to cook down.

> When one man dies, one chapter is not torn out of the book, but translated into a better language. JOHN DONNE

biscuity sour cream & chive egg muffins

HEALTHY FATS I YIELDS 12 MUFFINS

2 cups loosely-packed chopped fresh spinach

½ med. onion (chopped)

6 eggs

1 cup shredded cheese of choice

½ cup Briana's Baking Mix

½ cup sour cream

1½ teaspoons baking powder

1½ teaspoons chives

½ teaspoon salt

¼ teaspoon each garlic powder, black pepper

Dash cayenne pepper

Beat the ingredients together well. Grease a muffin tin and fill each hole with ¼ cup batter. Bake at 350° for 25-30 minutes (until set). Store in the fridge for a grab-and-go breakfast.

These breakfast muffins are good warm or cold! I like to dip them in ketchup or mustard, but they're good on their own too. You could easily double the batch to have plenty of muffins on hand to put in your family's lunches throughout the week.

okra & fried egg skillet

Refined coconut oil
1 cup diced okra (fresh or frozen)
2-3 eggs
Garlic salt, nutritional yeast,
    black pepper (to taste)

Sauté the okra in the coconut oil in a small skillet over medium-high heat until tender. Crack the eggs on top of the okra and reduce the heat to medium-low. Season with garlic salt, nutritional yeast, and black pepper and cover the pan with a lid. Let the eggs cook until the tops are set but the yolks are still runny. Enjoy!

"God He knows that I am not worthy to be her humble servant. It is easy, lady, for a man to ride forth in the light of day, and do his devoir when all men have eyes for him. But in a woman's heart there is a strength and truth which asks no praise, and can but be known to him whose treasure it is."
SIR ARTHUR CONAN COYLE
THE WHITE COMPANY

sausage & okra breakfast

2 teaspoons refined coconut oil
⅔ cup chopped sausage links
  of choice (pre-cooked)
1 cup diced okra (fresh or frozen)
Garlic salt, curry powder (to taste)

Heat the coconut oil in a frying pan over medium-high heat. Add the sausage and sear it, then add the okra and sauté until soft. Season with garlic salt and curry powder to taste.

I used a beef sausage in this and it was delicious!

Thy words were found,
and I did eat them;
  and thy word was unto me
the joy and rejoicing of
  mine heart: for I am called
by thy name,
O LORD GOD OF HOSTS.

JEREMIAH 15:16

note

You could definitely top this breakfast with a fried egg or two, but I wanted to demonstrate an egg-free breakfast option for those of you who are tired of eggs every morning (or have an egg allergy).

hot chia porridge

HEALTHY FATS   I   SERVES I

3 tablespoons chia seeds

1 tablespoon beef gelatin

½ teaspoon glucomannan

⅛ teaspoon salt (slightly rounded)

⅛ teaspoon THM Pure Stevia Extract Powder

1 cup unsweetened almond milk

½ cup water

Hearty dash vanilla extract

1-2 teaspoons salted butter

THM Super Sweet Blend

Cinnamon

Grind the chia seeds to powder in a coffee grinder. Whisk the dry ingredients (including the powdered chia) in a small saucepan. Add the almond milk, water, and vanilla and whisk again until smooth. Bring to a boil, then reduce the heat and simmer (uncovered) for 5 minutes to thicken, whisking occasionally. Top with salted butter and Super Sweet Blend and cinnamon to taste. Berries or sugar-free syrup are good toppings too. Enjoy!

chocolate cranberry almond porridge

HEALTHY FATS | SERVES I

3 tablespoons chia seeds
1 tablespoon beef gelatin
1 tablespoon cocoa powder
½ teaspoon glucomannan
⅛ teaspoon THM Pure Stevia Extract Powder
⅛ teaspoon salt

1 cup unsweetened almond milk
¾ cup water
½ cup cranberries (fresh or frozen)
2 teaspoons coconut oil
½ teaspoon almond extract

Grind the chia seeds to powder in a coffee grinder. Whisk the dry ingredients (including the chia powder) in a small saucepan. Add the wet ingredients and whisk again until smooth. Bring to a boil to thicken, then simmer for 5-10 minutes or until the cranberries are softened to your liking. (Whisk occasionally.) Serve with your choice of toppings!

TOPPING SUGGESTIONS ▼
half and half or cream, sugar-free chocolate syrup, additional cranberries, almonds, THM Super Sweet Blend

chunky monkey chia pudding

HEALTHY FATS | SERVES I

1 cup unsweetened almond milk
½ cup water
3 tablespoons chia seeds
1 teaspoon banana flavoring
½ teaspoon vanilla extract
3 doonks THM Pure Stevia Extract Powder
¹⁄₁₆ teaspoon salt

½ cup cottage cheese
1½ tablespoons natural peanut butter
Sprinkling of sugar-free chocolate chips

Whisk the first set of ingredients together in a saucepan and bring to a boil. Remove from the heat. Whisk in the cottage cheese and peanut butter. Sprinkle with some sugar-free chocolate chips. Enjoy warm for a thinner consistency, or cover and refrigerate overnight for a very thick pudding.

Don't like chocolate, peanut butter, and banana all together? Leave something out and make it either chocolate peanut butter or peanut butter banana!

note

• Banana flavoring/extract can vary in strength, so I suggest starting with ½ teaspoon, then adding more as desired. Personal taste buds vary a lot when it comes to banana flavoring. Feel free to leave it out entirely if banana isn't your thing.
• You can mash the cottage cheese with a fork before stirring it into the pudding to remove most of the lumps.

breakfast corn pudding

HEALTHY CARBS | SERVES |

¼ cup + 2 tablespoons masa flour
3 tablespoons collagen
½ teaspoon glucomannan
¼ teaspoon salt (scant)
2 doonks THM Pure Stevia Extract Powder

1 cup unsweetened almond milk
½ cup water
½ teaspoon vanilla extract

1 teaspoon salted butter
THM Super Sweet Blend
Cinnamon
Sugar-free syrup

Whisk the first section of ingredients in a small saucepan. Add the almond milk, water, and vanilla and whisk again. Bring to a boil and cook on the stovetop until thickened. I like to let the corn pudding cool just a bit before eating because the corn flavor shows up more when it's not piping hot. Top with your favorite toppings (I've listed mine above) and enjoy! This pudding is very thick and filling because of the glucomannan, but if you're still hungry, have some low-fat Greek yogurt on the side.

This corn pudding is like other cornmeal mush I've had – on the bland side and suited to be a canvas for your favorite toppings, but a warming comfort food nonetheless. Even when broken down by nixtamalization (the process used to make masa flour), corn is not the most weight loss friendly food, so I would keep this corn pudding to an occasional treat.

note

• I don't recommend substituting whey protein powder for the collagen in this recipe.
• Maple extract or blueberries would be good additions to this pudding!

ADOBO PORK TACOS
PG 86

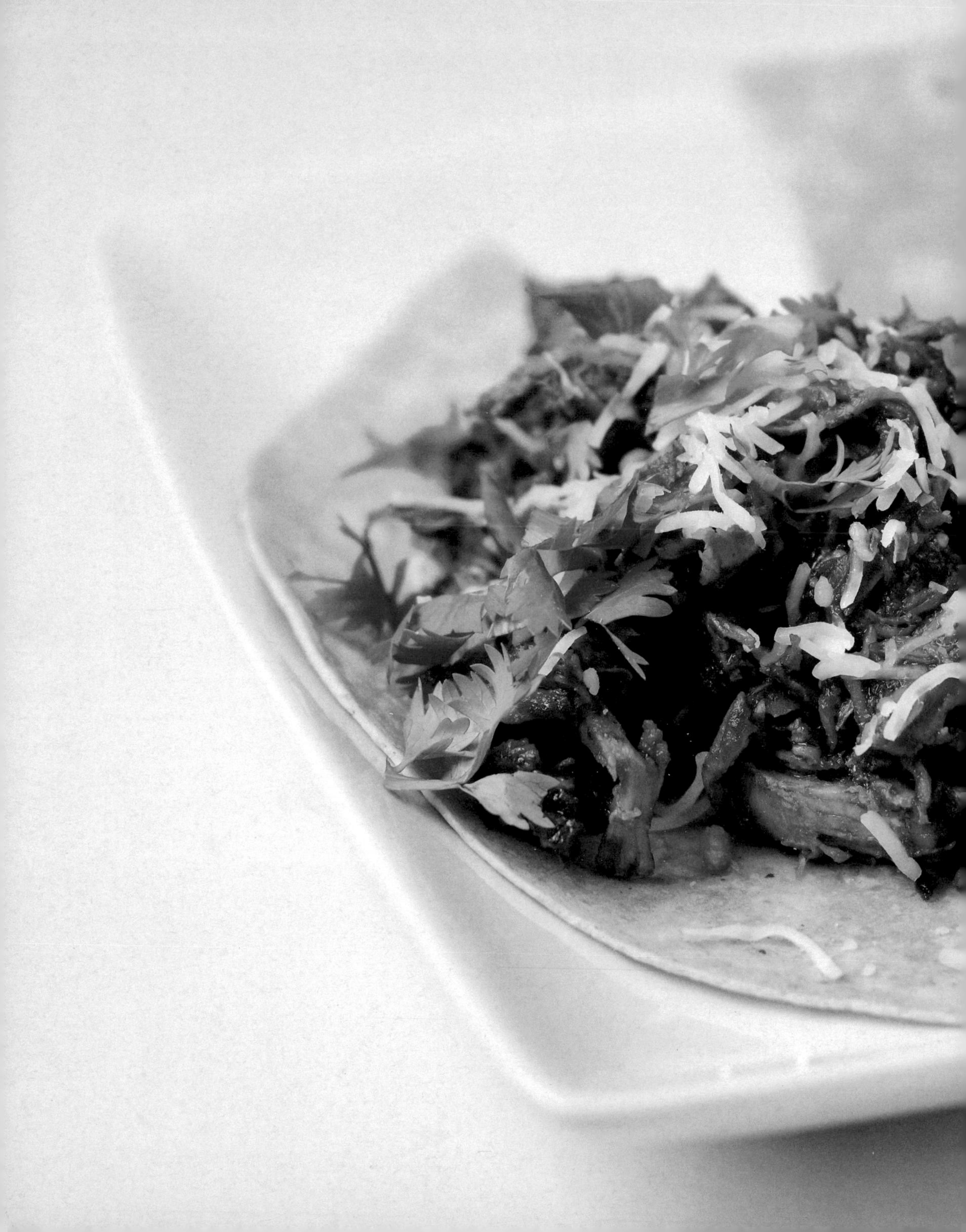

main dishes

main dishes

SINGLE SERVE
cornbread in a bowl + beans **177**
creamy sweet potato bisque **150**
kate's weird pasta veggie bowl **176**
leftover turkey fried wrap **179**
quinoa lunch bowl **175**
strawberry, ham & swiss quesadilla **178**
strawberry, ham & swiss salad **174**

SLOW COOKER
basic-ally delicious slow cooker curry **153**
black bean stew **143**
black beans (over cilantro lime rice) **157**
black eyed pea soup **148**
brown gravy beef stew **151**
bulgogi-flavored beef & broccoli **158**
easy cheesy fiesta chowder **144**
hunter's venison stew over rice **152**
nutty slow cooker curry **156**
philly cheesesteak beef roast **159**
slow cooker salsa verde chicken **160**
sweet potato chana dal curry **154**

SOUPS + STEWS
black bean stew **143**
black eyed pea soup **148**
brown gravy beef stew **151**
colorful chicken chili **145**
creamy broccoli bacon chowder **138**
creamy sweet potato bisque **150**
easy cheesy fiesta chowder **144**
easy southwest soup **142**
gumbo **126**

ham & "potato" chowder **139**
happy harvest soup **147**
hearty barbecue soup **146**
hunter's venison stew over rice **152**
lasagna soup **149**
lentil, carrot & roasted red pepper soup **136**
mom's chicken soup **137**
springy cabbage & sausage soup **141**
turkey pot pie chowder **140**

STOVETOP + SKILLET DINNERS
cajun sausage, red beans & rice skillet **120**
chicken in creamy dill sauce **108**
colorful sweet & sour chicken stir-fry **110**
creamy chicken gravy **107**
creamy eggs & spinach **122**
easy mixed rice & beans **121**
ground beef stroganoff **113**
jambalaya **130**
kale, mushroom & ham skillet **119**
korean barbecue pan-fried chickpeas **123**
lemon butter fried tilapia **100**
one pot pineapple chicken & rice **131**
pan-fried chicken strips **105**
pan-fried mushroom chicken **104**
philly cheesesteak skillet **111**
shrimp & cheddar "grits" **103**
skillet sausage & cornbread supper **116**
skillet yumzetti **117**
spaghetti three ways **115**
sweet onion teriyaki stir-fry **109**
western burgers **112**
zucchini fritter pizzas **118**

proteins

BEEF

CHICKEN

MEATLESS

black bean stew **143**
black beans (over cilantro lime rice) **157**
black eyed pea soup **148**
chana dal & greens **134**
chickpea curry over caulitoes **124**
cornbread in a bowl + beans **177**
creamy eggs & spinach **122**
creamy sweet potato bisque **150**
easy mixed rice & beans **121**
easy southwest soup **142**
korean barbecue pan-fried chickpeas **123**
lentil, carrot & roasted red pepper soup **136**
sweet potato chana dal curry **154**

PORK

adobo pork tacos **86**
barbacoa pork tacos **84**
breakfast burritos **70**
bri's baked barbecue ribs **90**
"brown sugar" glazed ham **89**
creamy broccoli bacon chowder **138**
glazed pork steaks **92**
gumbo **126**
ham & "potato" chowder **139**
happy harvest soup **147**
hawaiian pizza bake **74**
kale, mushroom & ham skillet **119**
kate's weird pasta veggie bowl **176**
lasagna soup **149**
lasagna stuffed spaghetti squash **75**
pizza boats **78**
sausage packets **93**
sausage patty quiche **71**

skillet sausage & cornbread supper **116**
skillet yumzetti **117**
springy cabbage & sausage soup **141**
strawberry balsamic glazed pork **87**
strawberry, ham & swiss quesadilla **178**
strawberry, ham & swiss salad **174**
zucchini fritter pizzas **118**
zucchini lasagna **77**

SEAFOOD

italian salmon bake **81**
jambalaya **130**
lemon butter fried tilapia **100**
shrimp & cheddar "grits" **103**
simple "brown sugar" grilled salmon **161**
simple soy salmon **162**
spiced baked tilapia **99**
sweet pepper shrimp curry **101**

TURKEY

cajun sausage, red beans & rice skillet **120**
easy thai turkey meatballs **67**
jambalaya **130**
leftover turkey fried wrap **179**
loaded cornbread casserole **73**
sausage packets **93**
spaghetti three ways **115**
springy cabbage & sausage soup **141**
turkey pot pie chowder **140**
zucchini fritter pizzas **118**

VENISON

hunter's venison stew over rice **152**
loaded cornbread casserole **73**
spaghetti three ways **115**

italian meatball casserole

HEALTHY FATS | SERVES 14-16

MEATBALLS

2½ - 3 lb. ground beef

1 cup unsweetened almond milk

½ cup old-fashioned oats

½ cup grated Parmesan cheese
   (the green can kind)

2 eggs

1 tablespoon each dried minced onion,
   Italian seasoning

2 teaspoons salt

1 teaspoon each oregano, sage, black pepper

1 (24 oz.) jar no-sugar-added pasta sauce

Shredded mozzarella cheese

Knead the meatball ingredients together (I use my hands) until thoroughly mixed. Form into golf-ball-sized meatballs and place into 2 greased 9"x13" pans.

Pour the pasta sauce over the meatballs and top with as much cheese as you like. Bake (uncovered) at 350° for 30 minutes or until done.

note

• This amount of oats adds less than 1 gram of net carbs per meatball.

• All pasta/pizza/spaghetti sauce will have sugar listed in the nutritional info because tomatoes contain natural sugars, but you need to look for a sauce that has no added sugar in the ingredients. We buy Priano brand from Aldi.

This casserole doesn't take many ingredients and can be thrown together in a hurry! Yes, it is very possible to make meatballs in a hurry. Simply use your hands to pinch off the meatball mixture in golf-ball-sized blobs and plop them in a dish. You can take the time to roll them nice and pretty if you so desire, but I usually omit that step. They get covered with sauce and cheese anyway! Since this recipe makes two 9"x13" pans of meatballs, you'll probably have leftovers for another meal. Score! This would also be a good recipe to use if you're taking supper over to someone else and want to make enough for your family and their family combined without making two separate dinners.

When I served this to my family, I paired it with cabbage sautéed in butter and garlic salt, salad, and some corn for the children.

southwestern meatloaf

HEALTHY FATS | SERVES 8-10

MEATLOAF

1 cup salsa of choice

½ cup grated Parmesan cheese
   (the green can kind)

2 eggs

2 tablespoons sriracha

2½ teaspoons Tony Chachere's
   Creole Seasoning

Dime-sized bunch fresh cilantro (chopped)

2½ lb. ground beef

TOPPING

1 lg. onion (sliced)

1 tablespoon salted butter

1 cup shredded cheddar cheese

Whisk all the meatloaf ingredients (except the ground beef) together. Add the ground beef and mix well. (I use my hands for this.) Press the meatloaf mixture into a greased 9"x13" baking pan, then use your hand to make a slight trough around the outside of the meatloaf for the grease to drain off. (Basically just make sure the meatloaf doesn't go all the way to the sides of the pan.)

Sauté the sliced onion in the butter until nice and brown, then stir in the cheese and spread the onion/cheese mixture over the top of the meatloaf.

Bake the meatloaf (uncovered) at 350° for 50-60 minutes or until done all the way through. (We bake it for a full hour because we like it more on the crispy side.) I like to slice and serve the meatloaf on a separate plate to get it out of the grease.

This meatloaf is so good. The family liked it, I liked it, and I'm pretty sure you're going to like it too. It's worth making for the topping alone. That fried onion + cheese concept is definitely getting used in future recipes....

easy saucy meatballs

HEALTHY FATS I SERVES 4-5

1 lb. ground beef

¼ cup Briana's Baking Mix

¼ cup grated Parmesan cheese
   (the green can kind)

¼ cup unsweetened almond milk

1 egg

½ teaspoon each garlic powder,
   onion powder, salt

¼ teaspoon black pepper

TOPPING

½ cup no-sugar-added ketchup

2 teaspoons yellow mustard

¾ teaspoon THM Super Sweet Blend

½ teaspoon molasses

⅛ teaspoon liquid smoke

Mix the first section of ingredients together. (I whisk all the non-meat ingredients together, then add the meat and use my hands to knead the mixture.) Use a 1½-tablespoon cookie scoop to scoop the mixture into a greased 9"x13" baking dish; the recipe will make 18-20 meatballs. Use your hands to roll the meatballs smooth.

Whisk the topping ingredients together. Dollop some sauce onto each meatball. Bake the meatballs at 400° for 25 minutes or until cooked through.

These meatballs are easy to make and so delicious! The sauce comes from my mom's meatloaf recipe, which you can find on page 42 of *Necessary Food*.

easy thai turkey meatballs

HEALTHY FATS I SERVES 4-6

1 lb. ground turkey

½ cup grated Parmesan cheese
(the green can kind)

⅓ cup Briana's Baking Mix

¼ cup light canned coconut milk

1 egg

2 tablespoons reduced-sodium soy sauce

1 tablespoon natural peanut butter

1 tablespoon sriracha

1 teaspoon each chili powder, onion powder

½ teaspoon each ginger, salt, black pepper

Mix the ingredients together. (I whisk all the non-meat ingredients together, then add the meat and use my hands to knead the mixture.) Use a 1½-tablespoon cookie scoop to scoop the mixture onto a greased cookie sheet; the recipe will make about 23 meatballs. I didn't roll the balls smooth with my hands because this is a wetter "dough." Bake at 350° for 20 minutes or until cooked through.

These flavorful meatballs have such a light texture! I served them with sautéed cabbage that I seasoned with onion powder and salt and dressed with some of the Asian Vinaigrette from page 482.

beef enchiladas with homemade enchilada sauce

HEALTHY FATS I SERVES 11+

ENCHILADA SAUCE

1 (28 oz.) can diced tomatoes (no salt added)

1 med. onion (chopped)

1 lg. jalapeño (seeded, chopped)

4 lg. garlic cloves (peeled)

1 tablespoon chili powder

2 teaspoons each cumin, smoked paprika

1½ teaspoons salt

1 teaspoon black pepper

ENCHILADAS

2 lb. ground beef (cooked, crumbled, drained)

2 cups shredded cheddar cheese

1 cup sour cream

1 cup Homemade Enchilada Sauce

½ cup fresh cilantro (chopped)

1 (6 oz.) can black olives (drained, sliced)

11 low-carb tortillas

3 cups Homemade Enchilada Sauce

Additional shredded cheddar cheese (for topping)

Chopped fresh cilantro (for garnish)

Blend the enchilada sauce ingredients until smooth. Use liquid and all from the canned tomatoes, and leave the jalapeño seeds in if you want heat. Set aside. (Makes 4 cups.)

Stir the first section of enchilada ingredients together, reserving some of the sliced black olives for garnish. Feel free to add some well-drained canned green chilies or chopped jalapeño for heat. Fill each low-carb tortilla with a level half cup of filling, then roll up and place seam side down in a greased baking dish. (I used a very large casserole pan and an 8"x8" pan.)

Bake (uncovered) at 350° for 15 minutes. Remove from the oven and top with the rest of the Homemade Enchilada Sauce (about 3 cups), a few handfuls of shredded cheddar cheese, and the reserved sliced black olives. Bake for another 15 minutes until the enchiladas are hot and bubby and the cheese is melted. Garnish with fresh chopped cilantro after baking if desired. Serve with sour cream, salsa, chopped lettuce, and guacamole (page 454).

This recipe makes 11 enchiladas, but I often only eat a half. Enchiladas made with low-carb tortillas tend to be best fresh, but you can reheat leftovers in the oven.

enchiladas verdes

4 cups shredded cooked chicken

1 (16 oz.) jar salsa verde (divided)

2 cups packed fresh spinach (chopped)

1 sm. onion (diced)

¼ cup fresh cilantro (chopped)

1 cup shredded mozzarella cheese

1 cup sour cream

½ teaspoon each garlic powder, black pepper

8 low-carb tortillas

Additional shredded mozzarella (for topping)

Mix the chicken, ½ cup salsa verde, spinach, onion, cilantro, cheese, sour cream, and seasonings to combine.

Divide the filling among the tortillas. Fold the tortillas up enchilada-style and place in a greased baking dish. (I use a 9"x13" pan and an 8"x8" pan.)

Bake (uncovered) at 350° for 15 minutes. Remove the pans from the oven, top the enchiladas with the rest of the jar of salsa verde and additional shredded mozzarella and return to the oven. Bake at 350° for another 15 minutes or until heated through. Broil the enchiladas for a few minutes at the end of baking if desired to brown the cheese.

Serve with sour cream and additional salsa verde.

This recipe makes 8 enchiladas, but I personally often just eat a half so depending on how hungry your family is, this recipe may provide more than 8 servings.

For there are three that bear
record in heaven,
the FATHER, the WORD,
and the HOLY GHOST:
and these three are ONE.
1 JOHN 5:7

breakfast burritos

8 eggs

½ teaspoon each dill weed, garlic powder,
    parsley flakes

¼ teaspoon each salt, black pepper

3 cups loosely-packed fresh spinach (chopped)

1 tablespoon salted butter

1 cup diced leftover ham

½ cup shredded cheddar cheese

1 tablespoon Dijon mustard

4 low-carb tortillas

Dijon mustard, shredded cheese of choice,
    and parsley flakes (for topping)

Beat the eggs and seasonings together, then add the spinach and stir. Cook the eggs and spinach in the butter in a skillet until soft set, stirring often. (The eggs will continue cooking in the burritos.)

Stir the ham, cheddar cheese, and Dijon into the hot eggs. Mix until everything is evenly distributed. Divide the filling among 4 low-carb tortillas. Roll them up and place seam side down in a small greased casserole dish. Brush the burritos with a little additional Dijon, then top with a few handfuls of shredded cheese and garnish with some parsley. Bake (uncovered) at 350° for 25 minutes. The recipe makes 4 burritos, but I often just eat a half because they're very filling.

These breakfast burritos make a great dinner, but they're dry enough that leftovers make a good grab-and-go breakfast when wrapped individually! You can serve them with salsa (which adds moisture since they aren't baked with a sauce), but the flavors are great on their own too.

Read as you taste fruit
    or savor wine, or enjoy
    friendship, love or life.
GEORGE HERBERT

sausage patty quiche

HEALTHY FATS | SERVES 10-12

12 uncooked sausage patties (I used pork)

3 cups finely-chopped fresh broccoli
1 med. onion (chopped)
6 eggs
1 cup shredded cheddar cheese
⅓ cup unsweetened almond milk
½ teaspoon each dill weed, garlic powder,
    paprika, salt

1 cup shredded mozzarella cheese
3 small colorful peppers, sliced horizontally
    (for garnish)

Place the sausage patties in the bottom of a greased 9"x13" pan. (They should cover the bottom of the pan.) Mix the second set of ingredients together with a hand mixer and pour the mixture over the sausage. Top the casserole with the mozzarella cheese and sliced peppers and bake (uncovered) at 350° for 45 minutes or until solid in the middle.

note

•The broccoli should be very finely chopped. I shave/chop the florets with a knife, then grate the stems on a cheese grater and use those too so I don't waste any. You could try using frozen broccoli, but you probably won't be able to cut it into such fine pieces. You can use other vegetables to replace the broccoli, but the casserole might be more watery.

•If you don't want to use sausage patties, just use a layer of cooked crumbled sausage. You could even just mix this right in with the egg mixture.

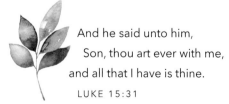

And he said unto him,
    Son, thou art ever with me,
and all that I have is thine.
LUKE 15:31

fiesta casserole

3 lb. ground beef

1 med. onion (chopped)

2 teaspoons each chili powder, cumin, garlic powder, paprika

1½ teaspoons salt

2 cups cottage cheese

1 cup shredded cheddar cheese

½ cup half and half

2 teaspoons each cilantro, dill weed, nutritional yeast

1 (10 oz.) can diced tomatoes with green chilies (drained)

1 (6 oz.) can black olives (drained)

Additional shredded cheddar cheese (for topping)

Cook the ground beef in a large skillet. Drain it well and chop it fine, then return it to the skillet. Add the chopped onion and seasonings and stir to combine. Divide the meat into the bottom of a greased 9"x13" pan and a greased 8"x8" pan.

Mix the cottage cheese, shredded cheddar, half and half, and seasonings together with a hand mixer. Spread the mixture over the meat in both pans. Drain the tomatoes and olives very well, slice the olives, and divide these veggies over the cottage cheese mixture in both pans.

Bake at 350° for 30-35 minutes or until the casseroles are hot and bubbly. During the last ten minutes of baking, sprinkle the top of both pans with shredded cheddar cheese to melt. I like to add a moderate amount of cheese that doesn't quite cover the tomatoes and olives. Once the casseroles are hot and the cheese is melted, let them cool on the counter for 10 minutes before serving to solidify. Eat 'em plain or top with sour cream and salsa.

Before I was married, this recipe made enough for 2 meals for our family of 6. Don't want to eat it twice? I bet you could freeze any leftovers and reheat at a later date when you need supper in a jiffy! This casserole isn't spicy, so feel free to add some jalapeños for heat.

loaded cornbread casserole

1 lb. lean ground beef, venison, or turkey

1 lg. colorful bell pepper (chopped)
1 med. onion (chopped)
2 lg. jalapeños (chopped)
3 lg. garlic cloves (minced)
½ cup fresh cilantro (chopped)

1 (15 oz.) can dark red kidney beans (drained)
1 teaspoon each chili powder, cumin, salt
½ teaspoon ground sage

CORNBREAD LAYER
1 cup masa flour
1 cup water
¾ cup egg whites
⅔ cup oat flour
2 teaspoons THM Super Sweet Blend
1½ teaspoons baking powder
1 teaspoon salt
½ teaspoon each cumin, onion powder
½ teaspoon turmeric (for color)

Brown the meat until fully cooked. Crumble. Rinse in hot water after cooking if not 96% lean or leaner. Drain and set aside.

Sauté the bell pepper, onion, jalapeños, garlic, and cilantro in a non-stick skillet until mostly tender. Drain any juices, then add the meat, kidney beans, and seasonings.

Mix the cornbread ingredients together and spread the batter into a greased 9"x13" pan. Top evenly with the meat and veggie mixture.

Use a spatula to mix them together a bit. Don't stir everything up, especially not on the bottom, but stir enough that you see cornbread batter distributed through the veggies.

Bake at 350° for 30-40 minutes. 30 minutes is done, but still on the gooier casserole side. Bake longer to dry it out a little if you prefer. Serve with low-fat sour cream, salsa, and chopped lettuce.

note

2 jalapeños are pretty spicy for my tastes, but Ryan loves spice so I try to accommodate once in awhile. Feel free to use only 1 jalapeño or remove the seeds and membranes for less spice.

hawaiian pizza bake

8 oz. fresh mushrooms (sliced)

1 med. onion (chopped)

1 lg. colorful bell pepper (chopped)

1 cup no-sugar-added pasta sauce

1 cup low-fat cottage cheese

1 teaspoon each garlic powder, oregano

1 (20 oz.) can pineapple chunks in juice
   (drained very well)

6 oz. Canadian bacon (chopped)

¾ cup shredded part-skim mozzarella cheese

Spread the mushrooms, onion, and bell pepper evenly in a greased 9"x13" baking pan. Spread the pasta sauce and cottage cheese evenly over that, and sprinkle the garlic powder and oregano over the top. Drain the pineapple very well in a colander and use a potato masher to break it down a bit and remove more juice. Spread evenly over the other layers in the pan. Distribute the Canadian bacon and cheese evenly over the top.

Bake (uncovered) for 30 minutes at 400°. Remove the pan from the oven, tilt one edge of the pan up and use a spoon to remove excess liquid accumulated from the veggies and pineapple. (I removed about ¾ cup.) Return the pan to the oven for 10 minutes. Remove it from the oven again and remove any extra runny juice. There shouldn't be a lot; thicker juice is OK. Let the pizza bake cool for 5-10 minutes before serving. Feel free to season with salt and pepper at the table.

I didn't add any salt to the pizza bake because of the salty ingredients used but thought it benefitted from some additional seasoning.

I love Hawaiian pizza, and this pizza bake gives you all the good stuff: the toppings! Salty Canadian bacon (which is very low in fat) and sweet pineapple are a winning combination.

note

You have room for another moderate carb source in your meal, but don't add any more fat. The cottage cheese, Canadian bacon, and mozzarella add about 4.4 grams of fat to each of 6 servings.

lasagna stuffed spaghetti squash

HEALTHY FATS I SERVES 4

1 (3 lb.) spaghetti squash

1 lb. ground sausage
¾ cup no-sugar-added pasta sauce

½ cup cottage cheese or ricotta cheese
½ cup shredded mozzarella cheese
1 teaspoon Italian seasoning
½ teaspoon each garlic powder,
   black pepper

Shredded mozzarella cheese and
   Italian seasoning (for topping)

Cut the spaghetti squash in half lengthwise and place cut side down in a baking pan. Add a quarter inch of water to the pan, cover the pan with foil, and bake at 350° until the squash is mostly soft (about 40 minutes).

Meanwhile, fry the sausage. Drain the grease and chop the sausage fine. Stir in the pasta sauce.

Mix the cottage or ricotta cheese, mozzarella cheese, Italian seasoning, garlic powder, and pepper together.

When the squash is done, scoop the seeds out of each half. Dump the water out of the baking pan and place the squash in the pan cut side up. Divide the sausage mixture between the 2 halves. Divide the cheese mixture between the 2 halves; spread it on top of the sausage mixture. Top each half with additional shredded mozzarella and some Italian seasoning for garnish. Bake (uncovered) at 350° until the cheese is melted and everything is hot (about 30 minutes). Cut each squash half in half again and serve.

lasagna cabbage rolls or enchiladas

HEALTHY FATS I SERVES 15-20

18-20 lg. cabbage leaves
(the outer leaves of 2 lg. cabbages) or
9-10 low-carb tortillas, or a combination of both

2½ lb. ground beef
1 med. onion (chopped)

¾ cup no-sugar-added pasta sauce
1½ teaspoons each Italian seasoning, oregano
1 teaspoon each sage, salt

15 oz. ricotta cheese
1½ cups shredded mozzarella cheese
¾ teaspoon garlic powder
½ teaspoon black pepper

Additional pasta sauce and shredded
mozzarella cheese for topping (a 24-oz. jar
of pasta sauce and a quart bag of shredded
mozzarella work well for the entire recipe,
including the amounts used in the
previous sections)

If using cabbage leaves, prepare them by blanching them in boiling water for 2 minutes. Remove from the water and set aside.

Fry the ground beef and onion together until the ground beef is cooked through. Drain the grease and chop the meat fine, then return the ground beef and onion to the skillet and add the pasta sauce and seasonings. Mix well.

Mix the ricotta, mozzarella, garlic powder, and pepper together. Grease two 9"x13" pans, then prepare the rolls. The cabbage leaves take half the amount of filling that low-carb tortillas do. Divide the ground beef mixture and the ricotta mixture among the cabbage leaves and/or wraps, using a spoon of each on each cabbage leaf or tortilla. (You'll use more ground beef mixture than ricotta mixture in each.) Wrap the cabbage rolls up like you would wrap presents and place them seam down in the pans. For the tortillas, just roll them up lengthwise like you would enchiladas. Place them in the pans seam side down. Top the cabbage rolls and/ or tortillas with additional pasta sauce and mozzarella cheese, then bake (uncovered) at 375° for 30 minutes.

zucchini lasagna

HEALTHY FATS I SERVES 10-12

2 sm.-med. zucchini
Salt

2½ lb. ground beef (or ground sausage,
   or a combination)
½ med. onion (chopped)

1½ cups no-sugar-added pasta sauce
2 teaspoons oregano
1½ teaspoons salt
1 teaspoon sage
½ teaspoon black pepper

15 oz. ricotta cheese
2 cups shredded mozzarella cheese
1 teaspoon each garlic powder,
   Italian seasoning

Additional shredded mozzarella cheese
   and Italian seasoning for topping

Slice the zucchini lengthwise in ⅛"-¼" slices (basically as thin as you can slice it by hand with a knife). Lay the slices on a baking sheet and sprinkle lightly with salt, then bake at 400° for 10 minutes to remove excess moisture. Remove the zucchini from the oven and set aside, then turn the oven down to 350°. (You can start cooking the meat while the zucchini is in the oven.)

Brown the ground beef (and/or sausage) and onion together until the meat is cooked through. Drain well, then stir in the pasta sauce, oregano, salt, sage, and pepper.

Mix the ricotta, mozzarella, garlic powder, and Italian seasoning together with a spatula or hand mixer. To assemble the casserole, layer half the zucchini slices, half the meat mixture, all the cheese mixture, the rest of the zucchini, and the rest of the meat mixture in a 9"x13" pan in that order. Top with additional shredded mozzarella and sprinkle with more Italian seasoning. Bake (uncovered) at 350° for 30 minutes or until heated through. Let the casserole cool for 5 minutes to solidify a bit before serving.

Much to my surprise, my whole family liked this lasagna with its nontraditional noodle substitute. My dad even called it "good," and that's saying something! The simple step of roasting the zucchini before putting it in the casserole cuts down on the soupiness that often accompanies veggie lasagnas.

note

• I prefer ricotta to cottage cheese in this lasagna because ricotta is much less wet and adding vegetables to lasagna always presents a moisture problem.
• I went light on the pasta sauce – again, to cut down on moisture. Take a look at the meat and pasta sauce mixture and add more pasta sauce if you prefer.

pizza boats

4 sm.-med. zucchini

1 lb. (3 cups) cooked ground beef
  and/or ground sausage
1½ cups no-sugar-added pasta sauce
½ sm. onion (chopped)
½ cup chopped green bell pepper
1 teaspoon Italian seasoning
¼ teaspoon black pepper

Shredded mozzarella cheese
Pepperoni slices (cut into quarters)

Bake the whole zucchini in a covered roaster at 350° for 30 minutes. (Do not add water to roaster.)

Meanwhile, add the meat, pizza sauce, vegetables, and seasonings to a skillet on the stove and heat (uncovered to let moisture evaporate).

When the zucchini are done, remove them from the oven, trim the ends off, cut them in half down the middle, use a knife to make two cuts in a V-shape down the center of each half, and use a spoon to scrape out the seeds. Place the zucchini boats on a baking pan, fill them with the meat mixture, top each with mozzarella and some pepperoni pieces, and bake (uncovered) at 350° for 20 minutes or until the cheese is melted and browning.

note

Feel free to leave the onions and peppers out – or add more veggies like sliced black olives and fresh mushrooms!

Lord, send me anywhere,
ONLY GO WITH ME.
Lay any burden on me, only sustain me; and sever every tie, but the tie that binds me to Thy service and Thy heart.
DAVID LIVINGSTONE

italian chicken bake

3½ - 4 lb. boneless skinless
   chicken thighs (fat trimmed)
1 med. onion (sliced)
8 oz. fresh mushrooms (halved)
1 cup black olives (halved)
1 (24 oz.) jar no-sugar-added pasta sauce
1 tablespoon Italian seasoning
½ teaspoon each garlic powder, salt,
   black pepper
Shredded mozzarella cheese and
   Italian seasoning (for topping)

Place the chicken thighs in a large greased casserole dish or roaster. (I used a 10"x12" pan for plenty of room.) Top with the onion, mushrooms, and olives. Pour the sauce over everything and sprinkle the seasonings over the top. Top with a few handfuls of cheese and some Italian seasoning, then bake uncovered at 375° for 1 hour or until the chicken is cooked through.

note

You could try using chicken breasts in this instead of chicken thighs, but it may not take as long to bake (depending on the thickness of the meat you use).

greek chicken bake

HEALTHY CARBS | SERVES 8-10

2 lb. chicken breasts (chunked)

2 cups fresh spinach (chopped)

8 oz. fresh mushrooms (sliced)

1 sm. onion (chopped)

2 cups low-fat chicken broth

1½ cups uncooked quinoa (rinsed, drained)

1 (14 oz.) can quartered artichoke hearts
    (drained, chopped)

1 (10 oz.) can mild diced tomatoes with
    green chilies (drained)

⅔ cup light canned coconut milk

1½ teaspoons each basil, oregano

1½ teaspoons salt (my chicken broth
    was salted as well)

1 teaspoon each garlic powder, mint

½ teaspoon black pepper

Feta or other cheese of choice (for topping)

1 lg. lemon (sliced)

Mix the first column of ingredients together and spread in a 9"x13" pan. Top with a light sprinkling of feta or your cheese of choice (keep fats minimal) and arrange the lemon slices on top. Cover with foil and bake at 400° for 45 minutes, then remove the foil and bake an additional 15 minutes, or until the chicken is cooked through and the quinoa is tender.

note

The light coconut milk adds about 1 gram of fat per serving.

italian salmon bake

2 lb. fresh broccoli and/or cauliflower
   (chopped into florets)
8 oz. fresh mushrooms (halved)
1 med. onion (sliced)
1 med. tomato (chopped)
Cooking spray of choice *or* melted butter
   or coconut oil
Garlic powder, salt, and black pepper

3 tablespoons salted butter
2 tablespoons red wine vinegar
2-3 lg. garlic cloves (minced)
1 teaspoon each basil, dill weed, oregano,
   parsley flakes, salt
½ teaspoon black pepper
2 lb. salmon filets

Shredded mozzarella cheese

Place the vegetables on a sheet pan and spray generously with cooking spray (olive oil or coconut oil spray) or drizzle with a little melted butter or coconut oil. Season generously with garlic powder, salt, and pepper and toss to coat. Bake at 400° for 30 minutes or until the vegetables are mostly tender.

Meanwhile, combine the butter, vinegar, minced garlic, and seasonings and heat them together in the microwave or on the stovetop to melt the butter. Pour the mixture over the salmon filets and massage them with your hands to coat. Set aside until the vegetables are done baking.

When the vegetables are mostly tender, remove the pan from the oven and place the salmon filets over the vegetables on the pan. Sprinkle lightly with shredded mozzarella cheese and return the pan to the oven for 15-20 minutes or until the salmon is done. (It will flake with a fork.)

My whole family loved this flavorful meal-on-a-pan! Start with fresh vegetables for best results.

note

• For a Foundation Fats meal, omit the onion, tomato, and cheese.
• If using frozen salmon, thaw it completely before trying to coat it with the butter mixture!

roast beef dinner

1 tablespoon salted butter

2 tablespoons Worcestershire sauce

2½ - 3 lb. beef chuck roast

Celery salt, garlic powder, black pepper (to taste)

1 sm. onion (halved)

1 (16 oz.) pkg. radishes (trimmed)

1 sm. head fresh broccoli (chopped into florets)

6 carrots (peeled)

Heat the butter and Worcestershire sauce in a large Dutch oven on the stovetop. Add the roast and sear on all sides. Season with celery salt, garlic powder, and pepper. After searing, leave the roast in the Dutch oven and top with vegetables. (Slice large carrots and radishes in half.) Season the veggies with more celery salt, garlic powder, and pepper. Cover and bake at 250° for 4 hours or until the meat can be pulled apart easily and the vegetables are tender. Pull the roast apart and discard excess fat, then pour the meat juices over the top and serve.

Radishes are one of my favorite low-carb potato substitutes. When cooked or baked, they lose a lot of their pungent flavor. I wouldn't try to pass these off as potatoes to your family, but I really enjoy them for what they are: baked radishes.

note

• Feel free to add more vegetables depending on the size of your family. I was making this roast dinner for just Ryan and me. If you're in weight loss mode, keep your carrot consumption to a minimum in a Healthy Fats meal. (These were mostly for my husband, and they're usually a favorite with children as well.) Fresh mushrooms would be a great addition to this dinner! Sweet potato and butternut squash chunks would be great to include for children and skinny husbands as well.

• If you want to make a real spread, serve this with Sour Cream & Chive Smashed Caulitoes (page 196) and make gravy with the beef broth by thickening it with 1 tablespoon of oat fiber and ¼ teaspoon of xanthan gum per cup of broth.

roast beef melts

HEALTHY FATS | SERVES 2-3

2 low-carb tortillas
2 cups leftover shredded beef roast
½ cup shredded cheese of choice
Salt and black pepper (to taste)

I like to heat the leftover roast in the microwave to melt any fat off and make it easier to shred. Drain well. Divide the shredded roast beef over the tortillas. Top each tortilla with half of the cheese and season to taste. (I used a finely-shredded white queso cheese that melts really well.)

Bake at 425° for 15-20 minutes or until toasty and as crispy as you like. I actually like to turn the heat down after 20 minutes and leave them in the oven for an additional 10-15 minutes to dry out even further, but they're good both ways. Cut each "pizza" into quarters with a pizza cutter. Eat plain or top with your favorite condiments...barbecue sauce (page 475), ketchup, guacamole (page 454), sour cream....

Serving sizes depend on how hungry you are. A whole pizza is pretty calorie dense, but a hardworking man (or woman!) could pull it off. 2-3 quarters are enough for me. Serve with a salad or crudités and French Onion Veggie Dip (page 458).

barbacoa pork tacos

BARBACOA SAUCE

2 ancho chiles (seeds and stems removed)

2 cups chicken broth (hot)

1 med. onion (peeled)

½ cup fresh cilantro

3 chipotle peppers packed in adobo sauce

6 lg. garlic cloves (peeled)

½ cup fresh lime juice (approx. 4 limes)

¼ cup apple cider vinegar

1 tablespoon each cumin, oregano

1 tablespoon adobo sauce (from can of peppers)

2 teaspoons molasses

¼ teaspoon ground cloves

¼ teaspoon THM Pure Stevia Extract Powder

8 lb. pork loin or beef or pork roast of choice
Salt (to taste)

First, make the sauce. Add the dried ancho chiles and hot broth to a blender first so the chiles can soak while you add the rest of the ingredients. When all the ingredients have been added, blend 'em up until everything is smooth.

Place the pork loin or roast(s) of your choice in a large greased roaster with lid. You can trim the fat off if you like, or don't bother if you don't like. Poke lots of holes in the top of the meat so the sauce can get down inside, then pour all the sauce over the meat, cover, and bake at 350° for an hour. You will be baking for a total of 8 hours.

After an hour, turn the oven down to 200°. You will bake for a total of 5 hours at this temperature. After 2 hours at 200° (or when the pork loin or roast is done all the way through), cut it up into smaller chunks so it can submerge in its own juice. Put it back in the oven for 3 more hours.

After a total of 5 hours at 200°, shred the meat (I used a meat fork and a table fork) and return it to the juice. Taste and add salt as necessary. (Salt really helps balance the flavors.) Turn the oven up to 275° and bake for another 2 hours, then serve with the rest of the taco fixin's. Leftover meat is even better after it has been refrigerated in its juice overnight. The flavors intensify and it gets more tender.

FOR THE TACOS ▼

low-carb tortillas, guacamole (page 454), diced onions, chopped fresh cilantro, shredded cheese, sour cream, lime wedges

When my family told me that all my food was starting to taste the same, I went shopping for new ingredients. Ancho chiles, chipotle peppers packed in adobo sauce, fresh cilantro, and fresh limes were all easy to find at my local grocery store and were just what I needed to get out of my cooking rut. A delicious barbacoa sauce was the result (so delicious that I drank it plain out of the blender). I was a little skeptical that my family would like something as out-of-the-box as pork tacos with all the authentic fixin's – but to my surprise, they all loved them! My siblings informed me that they much prefer when I let them create their own food instead of mixing everything up into a casserole. My dad's comment was my favorite: "That was worth eating!"

note

• This recipe is not sweet or spicy because I wanted to keep it family friendly. Feel free to add more hot peppers or sweetener!

• You could try baking chicken breasts in this sauce to use in a Low Carb/Low Fat or Healthy Carbs setting! (Chicken probably won't need to bake as long. Pork benefits from a longer baking time to break down the fibers.) You could serve shredded barbacoa chicken over the Cilantro Lime Rice on page 205 for a Healthy Carbs meal! (Omit the guacamole and use only a sprinkling of part-skim mozzarella and some low-fat sour cream on top.)

• I used one big pork loin to make a huge roaster full of shredded pork. We can get pork loin very inexpensively from Sam's Club so I use it wherever I can, but using a fattier meat like beef roast or pork shoulder would give you a more tender result.

• Don't want a taco? Eat this meat over salad with all the taco toppings!

adobo pork tacos

HEALTHY FATS I SERVES 5-6

1 tablespoon salted butter
2 lb. Boston butt pork roast
2 cups Bri's Adobo Sauce (page 477) (divided)

Sear the roast in the butter on all sides in a Dutch oven on the stovetop. Top with 1½ cups of Bri's Adobo Sauce, then cover and bake at 350° for 1 hour and 40 minutes or until tender and able to be pulled apart. Shred the roast and submerge in the juices, then cover and bake 1 hour longer. The meat will soak up most of the sauce and even get a little charred around the edges. Add another half cup of adobo sauce and stir well before serving to shred the meat even more.

Serve the pulled pork in tacos made with low-carb tortillas, fresh cilantro, chopped onion, some white queso cheese, and a squeeze of fresh lime juice. Or enjoy it over salad!

If you have some of my adobo sauce in your fridge, this recipe couldn't be easier! The pulled pork soaks up some powerful flavors from the adobo sauce and gets a little crispy, then it's rehydrated with even more sauce. The result is a tender pulled pork with a deep, rich flavor - perfect for tacos!

note

Boston butt really cooks down because of the high fat content, so servings may vary. If pork isn't your thing, feel free to try a different meat (keeping in mind that some meats won't need baked as long). I got a bunch of Boston butt on sale cheap, and this South Carolina gal likes her pulled pork. I bet this recipe would be good with beef or chicken, though!

strawberry balsamic glazed pork

HEALTHY FATS | SERVES 5-6

1 cup mashed strawberries

3 tablespoons balsamic vinegar

2 tablespoons Dijon mustard

1 teaspoon each garlic powder, salt

½ teaspoon THM Super Sweet Blend

½ teaspoon black pepper

2 lb. Boston butt pork roast

1 tablespoon refined coconut oil

Blend the first section of ingredients together until smooth. Sear the roast in the coconut oil on all sides in a Dutch oven on the stovetop. Pour the strawberry glaze over the seared roast, cover, and bake at 350° for 1 hour and 40 minutes or until tender and able to be pulled apart. Shred the roast and submerge in the juices, then cover and bake 30 minutes longer. Serve the pulled pork on its own, in tacos, or on salad (my favorite!). Leftovers are great crisped up in a skillet.

Optional: Bake (uncovered) a little longer for a crispier texture. Ryan likes his meat dry, so I often do this.

This pulled pork has a neat, slightly fruity flavor from the strawberries! Try it over spinach with shredded mozzarella, chopped pecans, sliced fresh strawberries, and the Balsamic & Lime Vinaigrette from page 481.

note

Boston butt really cooks down because of the high fat content, so servings may vary. If pork isn't your thing, feel free to try a different meat (keeping in mind that some meats won't need baked as long). I got a bunch of Boston butt on sale cheap, and this South Carolina gal likes her pulled pork. I bet this recipe would be good with beef or chicken, though!

> PRAYER
> should be the key of the day and the lock of the night.
> GEORGE HERBERT

"brown sugar" glazed ham

HEALTHY FATS | SERVINGS WILL VARY

Smoked butt portion fully-cooked
  bone-in ham (mine was around 9 lb.)

GLAZE
8 tablespoons butter
2 tablespoons Dijon mustard
3-4 teaspoons THM Super Sweet Blend
  (to taste)
1 teaspoon garlic powder
1 teaspoon maple extract
¼ teaspoon ground cloves
8 drops orange essential oil
  (or orange extract to taste)

Unwrap the ham and bake in a baking dish or roaster (with sides to catch the juices) according to package directions. I cover mine with foil until I'm ready to glaze it.

Once you get the ham in the oven, make the glaze. Melt the ingredients together in a saucepan and whisk until emulsified and thick. Take the pan off the heat and let it cool.

Thirty minutes before the ham is done baking (according to the baking time on your ham package), remove it from the oven. Remove the foil. Score the outer fat layer in a crosshatch pattern before glazing to let the glaze get down into the meat better. (Not gonna lie, this is also for aesthetics.) Brush the exterior of the ham with half of the glaze, then return the ham to the oven (uncovered). I like to turn the oven up to 400° for the last half hour to help caramelize the exterior of the glazed ham. After another 15 minutes, remove the ham from the oven again and brush with the remaining glaze. Return the ham to the oven and bake for another 15 minutes. Remove the ham from the oven and let it rest about 15 minutes before slicing and serving.

The combination of flavors in this glaze reminds me of a honey- or brown sugar-glazed ham! I love the Dijon mustard paired with the other flavors and don't recommend omitting or substituting for it. (It doesn't make the glaze taste overtly mustardy.) Don't forget to save the ham juice and leftover ham bits for another recipe! Try some Ham & "Potato" Chowder (page 139), Breakfast Burritos (page 70), or Slow-Cooked Ham & Collards (page 199)!

note

• Look for a ham with as few carbs as possible. Avoid those marketed as honey- or brown sugar-glazed. The weight can vary by a few pounds and be fine with this glaze recipe.

• I used salted butter since that's what I had on hand and it tasted fine, but ham is usually fairly salty on its own so I would use unsalted butter if I had it.

• Do your own research before ingesting essential oils and make your own informed decision regarding brands and use. If you don't want to use orange essential oil, feel free to just add some orange extract (to taste) to the glaze instead.

bri's baked barbecue ribs

HEALTHY FATS | SERVES 6 (HALF RACK APIECE)

3 racks pork loin back ribs (8-9 lb.)

SPICE RUB
1 tablespoon each chili powder, paprika
½ tablespoon each onion powder, salt
1 teaspoon each dry mustard, THM Super
    Sweet Blend, black pepper
½ tsp cumin

BRI'S RIB SAUCE
1½ cups no-sugar-added ketchup
¼ cup yellow mustard
2 tablespoons salted butter
2 tablespoons sriracha
1 tablespoon THM Super Sweet Blend
    (or more, to taste)
1 tablespoon apple cider vinegar
1½ teaspoons molasses
1 teaspoon each chili powder, onion powder,
    paprika
1 teaspoon liquid smoke
½ teaspoon cumin

Whisk the spice rub ingredients together. Place the ribs on two baking sheets (two racks on one, one rack on the other), flesh side up, and rub the spice rub evenly over the top of each. Cover the baking pans with foil and bake at 250° for 5½ hours.

Turn the oven up to 350°, remove the foil from the pans, and bake the ribs for an additional 30 minutes, basting the top of the rib racks with barbecue sauce twice within

that time. (I remove the ribs from the oven, baste them, return them to the oven for 15 minutes, remove and baste again, and bake for the last 15 minutes.) You can use my rib sauce or about 2 cups of your favorite sugar-free barbecue sauce. Don't skimp on the sauce, and enjoy those ribs!

BRI'S RIB SAUCE
Whisk the ingredients together in a saucepan and simmer, uncovered, for 10 minutes. Taste and adjust sweetness and spices as desired. I used the whole batch on these ribs.

Looking for a special occasion meal to make at home? These finger-lickin' good, fall-off-the-bone-tender pork ribs are actually very simple to make and pack succulent flavor at a fraction of the price of a steakhouse. I purchased a package of 3 large pork loin back racks of ribs at Sam's Club for about $25; that's a half rack apiece for our family of 6 (when I was living at home before I was married), but we were full on 2 racks for supper and some of us enjoyed the other rack the next day for lunch! That comes to about $2.78 per serving…which really isn't that bad when you're talking about a special rib meal.

The rib sauce here is a thickish basting sauce but would also make a great dipping sauce! It's a little sweet, a little spicy (hello, sriracha!), and has more mustard than some of my other barbecue sauces (but not overpoweringly so).

glazed pork steaks

2 tablespoons Worcestershire sauce

1 tablespoon butter

2 lg. pork shoulder blade steaks or pork chops

Onion powder, salt, black pepper (to taste)

GLAZE

¼ cup tomato paste

2 tablespoons lime juice

2 tablespoons reduced-sodium soy sauce

1 tablespoon yellow mustard

1½ teaspoons THM Super Sweet Blend

½ teaspoon molasses

Heat the Worcestershire sauce and butter in a Dutch oven on the stovetop. Brown the steaks on both sides, seasoning with onion powder, salt, and pepper while frying. (My steaks were pretty large so I had to brown them one at a time.)

Whisk the glaze ingredients together. Brush half the glaze over each steak and layer the steaks in the Dutch oven (leave the drippings in there). Bake (covered) at 350° until the steaks are cooked through. Mine were ¾" shoulder blade steaks and took about 30 minutes, but check earlier than that for thinner cuts of meat.

I found some pork shoulder blade steaks on clearance at our local grocery store and discovered that they're really tender due to their high fat content. If you're not into all that marbling, use leaner pork chops to make this recipe (less grease but not quite as tender). Browning the meat gives the steaks amazing flavor, and finishing them off in the oven helps them cook evenly. And don't forget about that glaze! It's based off of my mom's meatloaf glaze and the combination of sweet and sour is spot on.

note

• Feel free to multiply the recipe, fry the steaks or pork chops all at once in a large electric skillet, then layer in a Dutch oven or covered casserole dish with the glaze and bake as directed.

• The glaze itself is Low Carb/Low Fat, so feel free to use it on other meats in other meal types as well!

sausage packets

13 oz. fully-cooked smoked sausage of choice
2 lg. colorful bell peppers (sliced)
8 oz. fresh mushrooms
Tony Chachere's Creole Seasoning and
    garlic powder (to taste)

Slice the sausage into 8 pieces, then cut the pieces in half lengthwise. Place 4 pieces in each of 4 squares of tinfoil.

Cut the mushrooms in half if they're large. Divide them and the sliced peppers among the pieces of foil. Season each packet generously with Tony's and garlic powder, or use your own favorite (salty) seasoning blend.

Fold and pinch the foil to create a sealed packet with a seam on the top only. Place the packets in the oven seam side up and bake at 400° for 30 minutes or until the veggies are tender.

People can top their individual packets with their favorite sauces, such as Ranch dressing, ketchup, Perfect Barbecue Sauce (page 475), Bri's Adobo Sauce (page 477), or Cow Sauce (page 478).

note

• I used Aldi Fit & Active Lean Turkey Polska Kielbasa to cut down on grease.
• You can substitute your favorite veggies for the mushrooms and peppers if you prefer. I used these because they're my favorites and they cook quickly.

I had camping in mind when creating these easy sausage and veggie packets; I bet they would work great in a campfire! They're basically a meal in one, and you can customize them with your favorite non-starchy veggies, seasonings, and sauces. I personally don't have a problem with baking things in foil once in awhile, but if you stay away from that, there are tutorials online that will show you how to make parchment paper packets.

sheet pan chicken fajitas

HEALTHY FATS | SERVES 10

2½ lb. chicken breasts (chunked)

1 lg. onion (sliced)

1 lg. green bell pepper (sliced)

8 oz. fresh mushrooms (sliced)

¼ cup fresh cilantro (chopped)

3 lg. garlic cloves (minced)

1½ teaspoons salt

1 teaspoon each chili powder, cumin, paprika

½ teaspoon black pepper

2 tablespoons salted butter (melted)

Low-carb tortillas

TOPPING OPTIONS ▼

sour cream, shredded cheese, salsa, guacamole (page 454), sliced jalapeños, natural peanut butter (if you're like my dad)

Spread the chicken, onion, bell pepper, and mushrooms on a cookie sheet (with sides to hold the juices). Sprinkle with the cilantro, minced garlic, and seasonings and pour the butter on top. Stir to coat. Bake at 350° for 25 minutes or until the chicken is cooked through.

Serve with low-carb tortillas and your choice of toppings.

A loaded fajita is quite filling, so I don't even serve any sides with this meal. Everyone is stuffed! If you have voracious eaters, a nice salad or steamed veggie would be a good side item.

mango chutney chicken

HEALTHY CARBS | SERVES 3

1½ cups chopped mango

½ sm. onion (chopped)

2 tablespoons apple cider vinegar

¾ teaspoon salt

½ teaspoon THM Super Sweet Blend

½ teaspoon maple extract

¼ teaspoon each curry powder, ginger, black pepper

Cayenne pepper (to taste)

2 med. chicken breasts (approx. 1 lb.)

Mash the first section of ingredients together with a potato masher to get the juices flowing but still leave some mango pieces intact. Place the chicken breasts in a small greased casserole dish and top with the mango mixture. Cover and bake at 350° for 30 minutes, then uncover and bake until the chicken is cooked through. (Mine took 30 more minutes.) If you like, you could serve this chicken over a moderate serving of cooked brown rice to soak up the juices, but it's good on its own as well.

note

I used fresh mango, but frozen would probably work too.

teriyaki baked chicken over rice

HEALTHY CARBS | SERVES 8-10

¾ cup reduced-sodium soy sauce

½ cup water

2 lg. garlic cloves (minced)

¾ teaspoon paprika

2 doonks THM Pure Stevia Extract Powder

¼ teaspoon xanthan gum

1 (20 oz.) can pineapple chunks in juice (drained)

2½ lb. chicken breasts (chunked)

Brown rice seasoned with garlic salt and
    pepper (for serving)

Whisk the first set of ingredients together. Add the xanthan gum while whisking so it doesn't clump. Stir in the pineapple.

Place the chicken in a greased 9"x13" pan. Pour the sauce over the top and bake (uncovered) at 350° for 30 minutes or until the chicken is cooked through. Serve over brown rice.

note

You can have ¾ cup of cooked brown rice with this as well as a moderate side of steamed carrots and come in right at about 45 grams of net carbs.

crispy chicken thighs

FOUNDATION FATS | SERVES 6-8

4 lb. bone-in chicken thighs (about 8 thighs)
2 tablespoons butter or refined coconut oil
2 tablespoons Worcestershire sauce
Dill weed, onion powder, oregano, parsley,
   salt, black pepper (to taste)

Heat the butter and Worcestershire sauce in a skillet. Brown the chicken thighs on all sides in the butter, then transfer them to a baking pan (I use a large pizza pan with sides) and sprinkle generously with the seasonings listed. Bake (uncovered) at 400° for 40-50 minutes or until the chicken is cooked all the way through.

I love me some crispy chicken skin! Frying the chicken before finishing it off in the oven gives you terrific flavor, tender meat, and a crispy exterior.

garlic herb broasted drumsticks

FOUNDATION FATS I SERVES 4

2 tablespoons salted butter (melted)

2 tablespoons Worcestershire sauce

½ teaspoon each basil, garlic powder,
parsley flakes, black pepper

¼ teaspoon each dill weed,
smoked paprika, thyme, salt

2½ lb. chicken drumsticks (about 8 drumsticks)

Whisk the first section of ingredients together.

Place an oven-safe rack on top of a cookie sheet. (I use an uncoated cooling rack safe for high temperatures.) Place the drumsticks on the rack (this keeps them up out of the juices, allowing them to stay dry and not get soggy), then baste them with the butter mixture.

Roast the drumsticks in the middle of the oven at 400° until cooked through (50-60 minutes).

I use bone-in, skin-on drumsticks for the most tender result. You could follow the same instructions but baste the drumsticks with my Perfect Barbecue Sauce (page 475) or Bri's Adobo Sauce (page 477) instead of the garlic herb mixture. (These would be Healthy Fats meals.)

spiced baked tilapia

2 tilapia filets
Chili powder, cumin, dill weed, garlic powder,
   salt, black pepper (to taste)

Place the filets in a greased baking dish and
season generously with the seasonings above.
Bake at 350° for about 20 minutes or just until
the fish flakes with a fork. (Check at 15 minutes
to make sure you don't overbake it.)

Serve over salad with fresh cilantro, chopped
onion, a squeeze of lime juice, and salsa to create
a Low Carb/Low Fat meal, or enjoy with a carb
source like lentils to create a Healthy Carbs meal.

lemon butter fried tilapia

FOUNDATION FATS | SERVES 4

4 tilapia filets

2 tablespoons butter

2 tablespoons lemon juice

Dill weed, garlic powder, salt,
    black pepper (to taste)

Fry the fish in a large frying pan or electric skillet on both sides in the butter and lemon juice until the fish flakes with a fork. (Or fry in two batches in a smaller pan, using half the butter and lemon juice each time.) Season liberally with the dill weed, garlic powder, salt, and pepper.

sweet pepper shrimp curry

LOW CARB/LOW FAT | SERVES 3-4

1 cup light canned coconut milk

1 lg. red bell pepper (julienned)

1 med. jalapeño (seeds removed, chopped)

1 tablespoon fresh minced ginger

2 teaspoons tarragon

2 teaspoons minced garlic

2 teaspoons lemon juice

1 teaspoon onion powder

½ teaspoon each turmeric, salt

¼ teaspoon THM Super Sweet Blend

12 oz. small peeled and deveined raw shrimp

Low-glycemic noodles of choice (for serving)

Bring the first section of ingredients to a boil in a skillet on the stovetop. Simmer (uncovered) until the peppers are tender (but not mushy). Add the shrimp and cook until the shrimp are opaque and firm. Serve over the noodles of your choice.

This easy skillet curry has some amazing flavors going on, so make sure you savor the delicious sauce coating your noodles. The jalapeño gives it some significant heat, at least to my wimpy palate. If you don't eat shrimp, you could try substituting chicken or fish.

TIP ▼

Shake canned coconut milk before measuring. It separates.

note

Using light canned coconut milk, this recipe just sneaks in as Low Carb/Low Fat. Using full-fat coconut milk (which would be amazing!) or adding more fat to the meal would turn this into a Healthy Fats meal. You can serve it over non-starchy veggies (like baked spaghetti squash) to stay in LC/LF mode. Dreamfields pasta is too high in calories to be technically LC/LF, so if you serve this over Dreamfields like I did, I'm not quite sure what it is... other than *yummy!* I'd just call it a light HF meal. You could also serve it over the Garlic Butter Zoodles on page 183 for a true HF meal. (The combination of fats from both recipes will put you in HF mode even though both could be LC/LF on their own.)

shrimp & cheddar "grits"

HEALTHY FATS | SERVES 4

"GRITS"
2 lb. fresh cauliflower florets

1½ cups shredded cheddar cheese
¼ cup masa flour
2 tablespoons salted butter
2 teaspoons dried minced onion
1 teaspoon each salt, black pepper

SHRIMP
4 slices high-quality pork bacon (chopped)
12 oz. small peeled and deveined
   raw shrimp (drained)
1 tablespoon lemon juice
2 teaspoons parsley flakes
2 teaspoons minced garlic
Salt & pepper

Steam the cauliflower in an inch or two of water in a covered saucepan until soft. You want it to be cooked *al dente*, not mushy. Drain the cauliflower very well in a colander, pressing excess moisture out of it. Return it to the saucepan. Use an immersion blender to mash the cauliflower, but don't puree it to a super smooth consistency. (The immersion blender will give you better control over the texture than a regular blender will.) Add the rest of the grits ingredients, stir to combine, cover, and leave the grits on the stove over low heat to let the cheese melt, stirring occasionally. Leave the pan on the heat for at least 10 minutes to let the flavors meld. Meanwhile, make the shrimp.

Fry the bacon in a pan until crispy. Remove the bacon and set it aside, leaving the grease in the pan. Add the shrimp to the bacon grease. Add the other ingredients as well and cook (uncovered) till the shrimp become opaque and firm. Add the bacon back in, season with salt and pepper to taste, and serve over grits.

So they're not your traditional cheddar grits, but they have the same flavors and some of the same texture! Masa flour gives these cauliflower "grits" a bit of corn flavor in a way that won't spike your blood sugar. I tweaked a Food Network recipe to make my own low-carb version of a classic, and Ryan declared it, "Phenomenal!" These may not be grits, but they're close enough for me, especially with the addition of plenty of cheese and butter to make a creamy texture and bind it all together.

note

• See page 5 for a note on masa flour. The masa flour in this recipe adds about 5 grams net carbs per serving.
• Serve these "grits" with fried eggs for a yummy country breakfast!

pan-fried mushroom chicken

HEALTHY FATS | SERVES 4

2 med. chicken breasts (approx 1¼ lb.)

2 tablespoons salted butter

1 tablespoon Worcestershire sauce

2 teaspoons minced garlic

8 oz. fresh mushrooms (sliced)

1 sm. onion (sliced)

½ teaspoon each basil, salt

¼ teaspoon black pepper

Baked spaghetti squash or your favorite low-carb noodle substitute (for serving)

Slice each chicken breast through the center like you're butterflying it, but cut it all the way through so you have 2 thin filets from each breast. Pound filets to uniform thickness.

Heat a skillet on the stovetop. Add the butter to melt, then add the Worcestershire sauce and garlic. Sauté the garlic a bit, then add the chicken. Add the mushrooms and onions on top of the chicken, then cover the skillet.

When the chicken has a good sear on one side, season the skillet with the basil, salt, and pepper. Flip the ingredients in the skillet so the mushrooms and onions are on the bottom and the chicken is on top - with the seared side up so the other side can get some heat now. Cover the skillet again and fry until the chicken is cooked through. (When the chicken is nearly done, remove the lid so the juices can reduce.)

Serve the chicken, mushrooms, and onions over baked spaghetti squash or your favorite low-carb "noodle" to soak up the yummy pan juices. Add additional salt at the table if you like.

note

I like to bake a spaghetti squash (cut in half) until tender, remove the seeds, remove the flesh from the rind, and keep it in the fridge to warm up as a quick side dish. A large squash lasts Ryan and me for a few meals!

pan-fried chicken strips

BREADING

1 (3.5 oz.) pkg. plain pork rinds

½ cup oat fiber

1 teaspoon each onion powder, paprika

½ teaspoon each salt, black pepper

EGG WASH

2 eggs

2 tablespoons sriracha

2½ lb. chicken tenders

Salted butter

Worcestershire sauce

Blend the breading ingredients together (I used our Vitamix blender with a tamper, but a food processor would probably work as well or better) until it is powdery and there are no chunks of pork rinds left. Set aside.

Whisk the eggs and sriracha together well. Heat a skillet (I used an electric skillet) and add 2 tablespoons salted butter and 1 tablespoon Worcestershire sauce. Dip the chicken into the egg wash, then the breading. Fry on both sides until done. I do this in two batches and replenish the butter and Worcestershire sauce for the second batch. Keep the first batch of chicken in the oven on Warm while you fry the second batch.

Leftover chicken is great warmed up in a frying pan, then topped with Swiss cheese, lettuce, Ranch, and sriracha in a low-carb tortilla!

note

• You could use this breading on other things too! (This recipe makes about 2 cups.) If you make extra, keep it in a separate container and only pour out as much as you need so you don't contaminate all of it with raw meat. Keep unused breading in the freezer indefinitely.

• For an easy dipping sauce, mix Ranch dressing with a little sriracha! This is a great way to get some heat in without setting the whole family on fire. (The chicken itself isn't that spicy.) The Cow Sauce on page 478 would be another great dipping option.

japanese chicken

¾ cup oat fiber

¾ cup golden flaxmeal

4 tablespoons salted butter

2½ lb. chicken tenders or
    chicken breasts cut into strips

2 eggs (beaten)

SAUCE

¾ cup reduced-sodium soy sauce

¾ cup water

½ cup + 2 tablespoons white vinegar

1 tablespoon THM Super Sweet Blend

2 teaspoons garlic powder

1 teaspoon salt

1½ teaspoons xanthan gum

Whisk the oat fiber and flaxmeal together to make a breading.

Heat the butter in a skillet.

Roll the chicken strips in the beaten egg, then in the breading, and fry the strips in the butter on both sides just until golden brown.

Transfer the chicken strips to baking dishes. I used a 9"x13" and a 7½"x11" baking dish.

Whisk the sauce ingredients together, adding the xanthan gum last slowly while whisking so it doesn't clump. Pour the sauce over the chicken, then bake (uncovered) at 350° for 30 minutes or until the chicken is done.

In case you're not familiar with it, Japanese chicken is breaded, fried, then baked with a delicious sweet-and-sour sauce for a super-duper-tender result!

note

Feel free to add more sweetener to the sauce, if desired. My family liked this amount of vinegar, but feel free to decrease it if it's too much for you.

creamy chicken gravy

LOW CARB/LOW FAT | SERVES 8-10

2 lb. chicken breasts

1 lg. onion (chopped)

Dime-sized bunch fresh cilantro (chopped)

1 teaspoon each basil, curry powder, dill weed,
    garlic powder, parsley flakes

½ teaspoon each salt, black pepper

1½ cups fat-free Greek yogurt

¾ cup unsweetened almond milk

⅓ cup grated Parmesan cheese
    (the green can kind)

Heat a large skillet or kettle, then add the first set of ingredients. Reduce the heat to medium or medium-low and cover. (The lower the heat, the longer the cook time, but the more tender the chicken.)

Stir occasionally. You can chop the chicken up a bit to speed up the cooking time.

When the chicken is done, reduce the heat to low. Chop the chicken up fine with a pastry cutter, then add the Greek yogurt, almond milk, and cheese. Stir, then simmer uncovered for 15 minutes. Taste and add more salt if necessary.

Serve over steamed broccoli or baked spaghetti squash for a Low Carb/Low Fat meal or Seasoned Quinoa (page 203) for a Healthy Carbs meal.

note

The grated Parmesan adds 1.5 grams fat per serving when divided over 8 servings.

chicken in creamy dill sauce

1 tablespoon salted butter

3 lg. garlic cloves (minced)

3 lb. chicken breasts (chunked)

½ cup fresh dill (chopped)

½ teaspoon black pepper

1½ cups fat-free Greek yogurt

⅓ cup grated Parmesan cheese
  (the green can kind)

Salt (if needed)

Brown the butter in an electric skillet, then add the garlic and sauté for a minute or two. Add the chicken, dill, and pepper and cook (uncovered) until done, stirring occasionally.

When the chicken is done and the juices run clear, turn the skillet down to Simmer and add the Greek yogurt and Parmesan cheese. Stir to combine everything and let the sauce heat to your desired temperature. (Do not boil after adding the yogurt or the sauce will break.)

Serve the chicken over sautéed cabbage or steamed broccoli for a Low Carb/Low Fat meal, or over brown rice seasoned with garlic salt and pepper for a Healthy Carbs meal. I make 2 cups of dry rice for our family of 6, but if you have big eaters you can do a little more. Serve the chicken and rice with green peas for a complete meal; I actually like to stir the peas into my chicken and rice because the sweetness of the peas helps balance the slight tanginess of the Greek yogurt in the sauce.

note

• The butter and Parmesan cheese add a small amount of fat to each serving, but it stays well beneath 5 grams per serving.

• Feel free to substitute another fresh herb of your choice for the dill. You could also try using dried dill (in a much smaller amount), but the flavor just isn't the same.

sweet onion teriyaki stir-fry

STIR-FRY (SERVES 8)

1 lg. onion (chopped)

1 med. orange (peeled, chopped)

⅔ cup water

⅓ cup reduced-sodium soy sauce

1 teaspoon minced garlic

½ teaspoon THM Super Sweet Blend

½ teaspoon ginger

½ teaspoon xanthan gum

3 lb. chicken breasts (chunked)

Salt (to taste, if needed)

SEASONED BROWN RICE (SERVES 6)

4 cups cooked brown rice (unseasoned)

2 tablespoons hot water

1 teaspoon chicken bouillon

2 tablespoons reduced-sodium soy sauce

½ teaspoon each dill weed, onion powder

¼ teaspoon black pepper

Salt (to taste, if needed)

Add the first section of ingredients to an electric skillet, sprinkling in the xanthan gum while whisking to avoid clumping. Bring the sauce ingredients to a boil, then add the chicken. Cover and cook until the chicken is done. Taste and add salt if desired. Serve over seasoned brown rice.

Make the rice while the chicken cooks. Dissolve the chicken bouillon in the hot water and add it and the rest of the ingredients to the rice. Stir and heat. Serve.

I designed this stir-fry recipe to go over the rice, but the rice makes a great side dish on its own! Serve this chicken and rice with a side of green peas and you have dinner.

note

Feel free to add some veggies to the stir-fry if you like. You can also add a dash of orange extract for extra orange flavor and/or increase the sweetener.

colorful sweet & sour chicken stir-fry

HEALTHY CARBS | SERVES 5-6

SAUCE

1 (20 oz.) can pineapple tidbits
    in juice (drained)

1" cube fresh ginger (peeled, chopped)

4 lg. garlic cloves (peeled)

½ cup rice vinegar

½ cup no-sugar-added ketchup

2 tablespoons reduced-sodium soy sauce

1 teaspoon THM Super Sweet Blend

½ teaspoon each salt, black pepper

2 teaspoons refined coconut oil

2 lg. chicken breasts (approx. 1 lb.)
    (chunked)

2 lg. colorful bell peppers (sliced)

1 med. onion (chopped)

1 (15 oz.) can cut baby corn (drained)

1 (8 oz.) can water chestnuts (drained)

½ teaspoon salt (or more, to taste)

Cooked brown rice (for serving)

Blend the sauce ingredients together until smooth. Set aside.

Heat the coconut oil in a Dutch oven or electric skillet. Add the chicken. Add the sauce, sliced peppers, onion, baby corn, and water chestnuts. Stir, then cover and cook until the chicken is done and the veggies are soft. Add salt to taste. Feel free to add some heat with cayenne pepper or chili flakes. Cook 10-15 minutes longer to let the flavors develop, then serve over moderate portions of brown rice.

Yummy sweet and sour sauce soaks down into the rice, which helps balance out what would otherwise be fairly strong flavors. Ryan and I both loved this fresh-tasting, colorful stir-fry.

philly cheesesteak skillet

HEALTHY FATS I SERVES 8

3 tablespoons butter
1 med. onion (sliced)

2½ lb. flank steak (thinly sliced)
¼ cup no-sugar-added ketchup
2 tablespoons Worcestershire sauce
2 teaspoons apple cider vinegar
½ teaspoon THM Super Sweet Blend
¼ teaspoon black pepper
Garlic salt (to taste)

Mozzarella and/or Swiss cheese

Sauté the sliced onion in the butter in a skillet (electric or on the stovetop) until it starts to brown.

Pound the sliced steak to an even thickness with a meat mallet, then add it and the rest of the ingredients (except the cheese) to the onions. Cover and cook until the beef is done to your liking, stirring occasionally.

Turn the heat off and top the dinner with the cheese of your choice. Cover the skillet until the cheese melts. Serve.

note

• Feel free to add sliced mushrooms and green bell peppers with the onions. I didn't have any fresh mushrooms on hand and I don't care for green bell peppers.
• I'm sure this would be good made with chicken as well!

western burgers

VEGGIES

8 oz. fresh mushrooms (sliced)

1 med. onion (sliced)

1 tablespoon salted butter

½ teaspoon salt

¼ teaspoon each garlic powder,
   black pepper

BURGERS

1 lb. ground beef

1 tablespoon Worcestershire sauce

½ teaspoon each chili powder,
   garlic powder,
   smoked paprika, salt

¼ teaspoon black pepper

Bri's Adobo Sauce (page 477) or
   Perfect Barbecue Sauce (page 475)

Cheese of choice

Chopped lettuce or low-carb
   wraps (for serving)

Sauté the mushrooms and onions in the butter until tender. Season with salt, garlic powder, and pepper. Keep warm while making the burgers.

Mash the burger ingredients together and form 4 patties. Fry in a skillet on the stovetop, or grill them. After cooking on one side and flipping, top each with a generous blop of adobo or barbecue sauce. Top with a slice of cheese (or some shredded cheese) and put the lid on the skillet (or grill) to melt the cheese. If pan-frying, I like to turn the heat down low after putting the lid on to let the burgers finish cooking slowly so the cheese has plenty of time to melt without letting the burgers get overcooked.

Serve the burgers with the sautéed mushrooms and onions on a salad or in low-carb wraps (or use your favorite low-carb bun option).

Ryan and I both loved these flavorful burgers! There are too many veggies to fit onto 4 sandwiches, but if you're making a salad – load 'er up!

ground beef stroganoff

HEALTHY FATS I SERVES 4

1 lb. lean ground beef
8 oz. fresh mushrooms (chopped)

1 cup sour cream
¼ cup half and half
1½ tablespoons Worcestershire sauce
2 teaspoons parsley flakes
1½ teaspoons onion powder
¾ - 1 teaspoon salt (to taste)
¾ teaspoon smoked paprika
½ teaspoon black pepper

Garlic Butter Zoodles (page 183) or your
    favorite low-carb noodle substitute
    (for serving)

Sauté the ground beef and mushrooms together in a skillet. Cook until the meat is done; chop it up fine while it browns. (Use a lean ground beef, or even ground turkey or venison, so you don't have to drain the grease and lose the yummy broth. A little grease is good for flavor.)

Reduce the heat and add the rest of the ingredients to the skillet with the meat, mushrooms, and pan juices. Stir to combine. Cover and simmer gently for 15-20 minutes to let the flavors develop. Do not boil or the dairy will get grainy. Taste and adjust salt and seasonings if needed. If the stroganoff is too thick, add half and half a little bit at a time until your desired consistency is reached. If it's too thin, cook it uncovered for awhile to reduce the liquid. If grease pools on top, just skim it off with a spoon.

Serve the stroganoff over zoodles or your low-carb "noodle" of choice.

note

If your family doesn't like mushrooms, chop them up fine so you still have the flavor but the mushrooms will be indistinguishable from the beef in the gravy. Whatever you do, don't announce that supper has mushrooms in it!

spaghetti three ways

1 lb. ground meat of choice
3 cups no-sugar-added pasta sauce
Garlic powder, Italian seasoning, black pepper
Salt (if needed)

Noodles of choice (for serving)
Grated Parmesan cheese (the green can kind)

Brown the meat in a skillet. Crumble, drain the grease off (and rinse in hot water if needed – see options below), then add the pasta sauce, using more or less to bring the spaghetti sauce to your desired consistency. Add your desired seasonings to taste; this may depend on the pasta sauce you use. Add salt if necessary. (Most pasta sauces are quite salty already.) Cook a bit to let the flavors meld.

Serve the spaghetti sauce over your low-glycemic noodles of choice and top with grated Parmesan cheese if desired.

HEALTHY FATS

Use ground beef. Serve over Dreamfields pasta; Garlic, Butter & Herb Roasted Spaghetti Squash (page 183); Garlic Butter Zoodles (page 183); or any of the LC/LF noodle options below. Top with as much Parmesan cheese as you like.

HEALTHY CARBS

Use 96% or leaner ground beef, venison, or turkey (or rinse the leanest you can find in hot water after cooking). Serve over black bean pasta or a starchy veggie like roasted or boiled sweet potato. (You must include a carb source to be in Healthy Carbs mode!) Keep Parmesan cheese to a sprinkling.

LOW CARB/LOW FAT

Use 96% or leaner ground beef, venison, or turkey (or rinse the leanest you can find in hot water after cooking). Serve over steamed broccoli, steamed cauliflower, sautéed cabbage, or Trim Healthy Noodles. (Keep added fats to a minimum!) Keep Parmesan cheese to a sprinkling.

Spaghetti was always my mom's go-to Wednesday night pre-church supper since it was so quick to make. The options are endless!

note

• Make this meal even easier by keeping cooked and crumbled ground beef, turkey, or venison in your freezer.
• Jarred pasta sauces taste way better than canned sauces.
• In a Healthy Fats setting, you could even include some pre-baked meatballs in the sauce, such as the meatballs from the Italian Meatball Casserole on page 64.

skillet sausage & cornbread supper

1 lb. ground pork sausage

1 med. onion (chopped)

CORNBREAD BATTER

¾ cup oat fiber

⅓ cup Briana's Baking Mix

⅓ cup masa flour

2 teaspoons nutritional yeast flakes

1½ teaspoons baking powder

1 teaspoon THM Super Sweet Blend

½ teaspoon garlic powder

½ teaspoon salt (scant)

¼ teaspoon each sage, turmeric (for color),
   black pepper

¾ cup water

⅔ cup sour cream

½ cup unsweetened almond milk

3 eggs

Shredded cheese of choice (for topping)

Heat a 12" cast iron skillet on the stovetop. When the skillet is hot, fry the sausage. When it's nearly done, add the chopped onion and let both sauté (uncovered) until the onion is tender.

While the sausage and onion are frying, make the cornbread batter. Whisk the dry ingredients, then add the wet ingredients and whisk until smooth.

Pour the cornbread batter over the top of the cooked sausage and onion. (There shouldn't be much liquid at the bottom of the pan by now; if there is, let it cook uncovered longer so the moisture evaporates. Do not drain the sausage grease.) Cover the pan and cook undisturbed over medium heat for 10 minutes. At that point scramble everything together, cover again, and cook for 5 more minutes. Scramble again, top with shredded cheese, and cook (uncovered this time) for another 5-10 minutes until the cornbread is done, the cheese is melted, and the "casserole" isn't soggy. Serve. You might enjoy topping it with ketchup or some of my Perfect Barbecue Sauce (page 475).

note

• See my note on masa flour on page 5. There are 3.5 grams net carbs per serving from the masa flour when divided among 8 servings.

• If you don't have a cast iron skillet, you should probably try another method of preparation, like layering the recipe in a baking dish and baking until the cornbread is done all the way through. Anecdotal evidence from my readers indicates that making this recipe in a regular skillet doesn't distribute the heat as well, so the cornbread is apt to burn if left to cook on the stovetop in the times I have listed in the recipe. (Alternatively you could just stir the recipe more often to avoid burning and end up with a more scrambled result.)

skillet yumzetti

HEALTHY FATS | SERVES 6-7

1 lb. ground pork sausage

1½ cups shredded cheddar cheese
1 cup frozen green peas
1 cup unsweetened almond milk
½ cup no-sugar-added ketchup
⅓ cup mayonnaise
2 teaspoons Worcestershire sauce
½ teaspoon garlic powder
¼ teaspoon black pepper
¼ teaspoon THM Super Sweet Blend (optional)

2 cups dry Dreamfields pasta of choice

Fry the sausage (uncovered) in a large skillet. Chop it fine. When the sausage is cooked, drain the grease if there's a lot there. If there's not too much, I just leave it in the pan for flavor. Reduce the heat to medium-low and add the second section of ingredients. Stir, then cover the skillet until the cheese melts.

Meanwhile, cook the pasta according to package directions.

When the cheese has melted, stir the skillet mixture again. When the pasta is cooked *al dente* (don't overcook!), drain it and add it to the skillet and stir to coat. Serve immediately.

This easy skillet dinner is based off of a casserole that my mom used to make. My version is modified quite a bit from the original, but the creamy casserole-y goodness is the same.

Since you can't cook Dreamfields twice without losing its special coating, I made this a skillet dinner instead of a casserole and just stirred the cooked noodles into the sauce right before serving.

note

• Keep in mind that Dreamfields pasta has a special coating on it that supposedly reduces its impact on blood sugar, but overcooking or reheating the pasta takes away the low-glycemic effect. Eat the casserole leftovers cold (it's quite good like this!) or reheat and serve them to your children. Don't want to use Dreamfields? Just omit some of the almond milk and serve the sausage mixture over zoodles, spaghetti squash, or broccoli!

• Feel free to replace some of the ketchup with sour cream for less tomato flavor.

zucchini fritter pizzas

2 cups freshly-grated zucchini

3 eggs

½ cup oat fiber

½ teaspoon baking powder

½ teaspoon each garlic powder,
    salt, black pepper

½ tablespoon butter

No-sugar-added pasta sauce
Shredded mozzarella cheese
Pepperoni

Mix the first section of ingredients well. (I use a fork.) Divide the mixture to make two large fritters in pancake shapes. Fry them in the butter in a skillet till nice and brown on the bottom, then flip and top them with the pasta sauce, cheese, and pepperoni so the toppings can get hot while the bottom of the fritter is frying. (Top the fritters just like you would top a pizza!) You don't want to burn the fritters, but neither do you want them to be soggy. Frying for a good little while on a lower heat, especially toward the end, is a good idea so the toppings can heat up but the bottom of the fritter won't burn. When the bottom of the fritter is brown and the cheese is melted, enjoy!

I'm not a big zucchini fan, but the pizza toppings make me feel like I'm eating something unhealthy when I'm really not. Please note: the fritter is NOT meant to taste like a pizza crust. Rather, the toppings are meant to cover up the zucchini. Happily, they succeed, and the whole effect is scrumptious.

note

I use part-skim mozzarella and turkey pepperoni to cut down on unnecessary calories.

kale, mushroom & ham skillet

FOUNDATION FATS | SERVES 2-3 (4-5 AS A SIDE DISH)

1 cup chopped cooked ham

8 oz. fresh mushrooms (sliced)

2 lg. garlic cloves (minced)

2 tablespoons refined coconut oil

6 oz. chopped fresh kale

Salt & pepper

Dash apple cider vinegar

Sauté the ham, mushrooms, and garlic in the coconut oil to get a nice crisp on them, then add the kale, cover the pan, and let the kale wilt a bit. Season with salt and pepper and a dash of apple cider vinegar, stir, and let the kale continue to cook as soft as you like it.

cajun sausage, red beans & rice skillet

1 med. onion (chopped)

2 tablespoons water

3 cups cooked brown rice (unseasoned)

1 (15 oz.) can dark red kidney beans (drained)

6.5 oz. smoked lean turkey sausage
   of choice (coined)

Dime-sized bunch fresh cilantro (chopped)

¼ cup water

1½ teaspoons smoked paprika

1 teaspoon oregano

½ teaspoon each garlic powder,
   salt, black pepper

Cayenne pepper (to taste)

1½ teaspoons apple cider vinegar (optional)

⅛ teaspoon THM Super Sweet Blend (optional)

Sauté the onion in 2 tablespoons of water in a skillet to start softening. Add the second section of ingredients, stir, cover, and simmer for 15 minutes to heat it all the way through and let the flavors develop. Taste and add the apple cider vinegar and sweetener to round out the flavors if desired. Add more salt if needed. Cover and simmer 5 more minutes after any additions. I like to serve this skillet meal with fat-free Greek yogurt, salsa, and chopped lettuce on top for a cross-cultural meal.

I don't recommend adding any more fats or carbs to your meal, so serve with a non-starchy vegetable side. You could even add non-starchy veggies to the skillet meal itself to stretch it further and allow larger servings.

This isn't meant to be traditional Cajun red beans and rice, but rather a quick skillet dinner with some of the same flavors!

note

• I used half of a 13-oz. pkg. Aldi Fit & Active Lean Turkey Polska Kielbasa.

• Leave the sausage out to make a great side dish!

easy mixed rice & beans

6 cups cooked brown rice (unseasoned)

2 (15.5 oz.) cans mild chili beans

1 (15.5 oz.) can black beans

5 stems fresh cilantro (chopped)

1 tablespoon dried minced onion

2 teaspoons apple cider vinegar

1 teaspoon each chili powder, garlic powder, paprika, salt

½ teaspoon liquid smoke

¼ - ½ teaspoon THM Super Sweet Blend

Mix all the ingredients together in a large bowl. (Add the entire contents of the bean cans, juice and all.) I like to refrigerate the rice and beans overnight for best flavor, but if you want to use it for dinner, heating it up and simmering for 15 minutes will suffice. Heat leftovers or serve cold; it's good both ways! Feel free to top with low-fat sour cream and salsa.

I didn't even cook this recipe when I made it – just dumped everything together, stirred it up, and put it in the fridge. Some days I ate the rice and beans cold, some days I warmed it up, some days I ate it by itself, some days in a wrap. Over a salad would be a great option, too! It keeps in the fridge for a few days, but I don't recommend keeping it for longer than a week because beans spoil pretty quickly in my experience (and smell horrific!). If you don't think you'll be able to eat this much right away, freeze some for later.

creamy eggs & spinach

1 tablespoon butter

2 cups fresh spinach (or more)

6 eggs

⅓ cup sour cream

Chives, garlic powder, salt,
   black pepper (to taste)

Shredded cheese of choice (for topping)

Sauté the spinach in the butter in a skillet. Once the spinach is wilted, add the eggs and sour cream and stir to scramble. Fry over medium-low heat, stirring continually. Season to taste. Turn the burner off before the eggs are completely set so they don't get overcooked. Add some cheese on top, cover the skillet with a lid, and leave it on the burner to let the eggs steam to finish cooking and the cheese melt from the residual heat.

I call these "Honeymoon Eggs" because the first time I made eggs like this was on our honeymoon in a little cabin in the mountains. Someone visiting before us left some sour cream in the refrigerator, so I made creamy scrambled eggs and spinach with it. This is now one of my favorite ways to eat eggs! You can enjoy them on their own or serve with salsa or ketchup.

korean barbecue pan-fried chickpeas

1 (15.5 oz.) can chickpeas
  (rinsed and drained)
2 tablespoons reduced-sodium soy sauce
1 teaspoon toasted sesame oil
1 teaspoon sriracha
½ teaspoon THM Super Sweet Blend
½ teaspoon garlic powder
¼ teaspoon each ginger, black pepper
Salt (to taste, if needed)

Combine the ingredients in a skillet and fry over medium to medium-high heat, stirring occasionally. You can take the pan off the heat once the chickpeas are hot if you want more sauce, or you can let the liquid evaporate and caramelize by cooking longer. The latter option will yield a drier chickpea with stronger flavor. Serve the chickpeas over lettuce or with broccoli, cauli rice, or cabbage "noodles." Or serve in a low-carb wrap with lettuce, sriracha, and homemade yogurt like I did.

These fried chickpeas are based off of a crunchy Korean barbecue-flavored chickpea snack I love (which has some questionable ingredients). To stay in Healthy Carbs mode I couldn't use much oil on these chickpeas, so don't expect them to be crispy. However, the flavor is amazing!

The just shall live by his faith. HABAKKUK 2:4B

chickpea curry over caulitoes

1 lg. onion (chopped)

3 lg. garlic cloves (minced)

1 tablespoon refined coconut oil

4 (15.5 oz.) cans chickpeas (drained)

3 cups water

½ cup no-sugar-added ketchup

10 stalks fresh cilantro (chopped)

2 tablespoons curry powder

2 teaspoons chili powder

2 teaspoons chicken bouillon

1½ cups frozen green peas

Salt (to taste)

Sauté the onion and garlic in the coconut oil in a large skillet until browned. Add the second section of ingredients and stir, then cover and simmer for 30 minutes, stirring occasionally. Halfway through, use a potato masher to mash some of the chickpeas to help thicken the sauce to your liking. Towards the end of cooking, add the green peas and salt to taste. Serve over mashed caulitoes. Leftovers are even better the next day!

note

• Feel free to add more veggies to this curry!

• As written, this recipe is pretty mild. Feel free to up the spice if you're into heat. I needed to keep it kid-friendly for my family, and to be honest, I don't handle heat well myself!

Disclaimer: this curry is probably not authentic.... I like to serve it over the mashed caulitoes because they form a mild base to balance out the spice. You'll notice that the mashed caulitoes recipe makes about half the servings of the curry recipe. That's because only half of our family likes mashed cauliflower.

CLASSIC MASHED CAULITOES
LOW CARB/LOW FAT | SERVES 4-5

2 lb. fresh cauliflower

¼ cup + 2 tablespoons fat-free Greek yogurt

½ teaspoon each onion powder,
    salt (slightly rounded)

¼ teaspoon black pepper

Steam the cauliflower in a covered saucepan in a small amount of water. Drain the steamed cauliflower in a colander. Use a potato masher to break down the cauliflower in the colander and press it down to get as much liquid out as possible. Return the cauliflower to the kettle you cooked it in, add the Greek yogurt and seasonings, and blend with an immersion blender until smooth.

"And 'twill be when you understand that your idol has feet of clay that you'll learn the real lesson of love," said Blakeney earnestly. "Is it love to worship a saint in heaven, whom you dare not touch, who hovers above you like a cloud, which floats away from you even as you gaze? TO LOVE IS TO FEEL ONE BEING IN THE WORLD AT ONE WITH US, our equal in sin as well as in virtue. To love, for us men, is to clasp one woman with our arms, feeling that SHE LIVES AND BREATHES JUST AS WE DO, suffers as we do, thinks with us, loves with us, and, above all, sins with us. Your mock saint who stands in a niche is not a woman if she have not suffered, still less a woman if she have not sinned. Fall at the feet of your idol an you wish, but drag her down to your level after that—the only level she should ever reach, that of your heart." BARONESS EMMUSKA ORCZY - *I WILL REPAY*

gumbo

HEALTHY FATS | SERVES 8-10

10 tablespoons salted butter

¾ cup oat fiber

3 cups chopped onion

3 cups chopped green bell pepper

2 cups chopped celery

6 med. garlic cloves (minced)

3 bay leaves (remove before eating)

1 tablespoon parsley flakes

2 teaspoons Tony Chachere's Creole Seasoning
   (or more, to taste)

2 teaspoons each oregano, smoked paprika

1 teaspoon each thyme, black pepper

8 cups unsalted chicken stock

6 bone-in chicken thighs (approx. 3 lb.)
   (skin and excess fat removed)

14 oz. fully-cooked smoked andouille
   sausage (coined)

4 cups frozen diced okra

Additional Tony's (to taste)

Cayenne pepper (to taste)

2 teaspoons gumbo filé powder

In a large (5.5 quarts or larger) Dutch oven on the stovetop, melt the butter. Add the oat fiber and cook over medium heat until the mixture is a rich brown, stirring often so it doesn't burn. (Stir constantly toward the end.) The roux may seem a little dry at the beginning, but it'll loosen up as it cooks. I like to start it out on medium heat, then reduce the heat a bit as it cooks so it doesn't burn. Baby it, and get it as dark as you can without burning it for best flavor. If the roux starts to smoke or boil, it's too hot. Reduce the heat, stir like mad, and pull the pan off the heat a bit to cool down. If it burns, start over. The roux should be the color of melted semi-sweet chocolate when finished.

Add the chopped onion, bell pepper, and celery and stir to combine. Sauté for 5 minutes. While sautéing, add the garlic, bay leaves, and seasonings.

After sautéing, add the chicken stock, whole chicken thighs, sausage, and okra. Bring to a boil, then reduce the heat and simmer uncovered for 2 hours, stirring occasionally. After 2 hours, remove the chicken thighs from the pot and take the meat off the bones. Shred the meat and return it to the pot, giving it a good stir to break the ingredients apart. Taste and add additional Tony's and cayenne as desired. I usually add another 2 ½ teaspoons of Tony's to bring the salt level up to where it needs to be. Adjust the salt and spice levels to your own taste! Remove the pot from the heat and stir in the filé powder.

Serve the gumbo on its own, over cauliflower rice to stay in the Healthy Fats category, or over brown rice if you don't mind combining carbs and fats.

I feel a little self conscious publishing a gumbo recipe when I've only recently become a Louisiana resident, but I did do my research before embarking on my gumbo journey! One of Ryan's coworkers, a true son of Louisiana named Caleb, gave me the run-down on several Louisiana specialties like gumbo and jambalaya. He's the one who told me to use chicken thighs to make good gumbo – and he was right! I love them in this recipe; they stay tender and just fall apart into shreds. (And using bone-in chicken adds flavor and nutrients.) Ryan said my gumbo was amazing and couldn't stop gushing over it, so even if I've made some major *faux pas* in this recipe, I'm owning this gumbo.

I know that people say to use either okra or filé powder and not both for a traditional gumbo, but I like it with both for best flavor and texture and have seen quite a few recipes that agree with me. If I learned anything in my gumbo research, it's that gumbo is a highly personalized art form, so I'd be delighted if you use my recipe as a springboard to make your own individualized gumbo.

When cooked this long, the flavors really develop and the ingredients (especially the okra) break down and help thicken the broth. The okra is not slimy! I like my gumbo thick and filling because I usually eat it on its own, not with rice, but if you want a thinner, more traditional consistency, add more broth and/or decrease the okra and chicken. You could leave the filé out as well, since it helps thicken the gumbo.

note

• Chop the veggies before making the roux so they're ready to go when the roux is done.
• Do not substitute for the oat fiber.
• Normally it's acceptable to use either salted or unsalted broth in recipes and adjust the added salt accordingly, but I use Tony Chachere's Creole Seasoning (which is salty) in this recipe for seasoning, so using a high quality unsalted chicken stock gave me the best flavor and control over the salt levels.
• My husband hates grease. If yours does too, you can use a spoon to skim the grease off the top of the gumbo before adding the additional seasonings at the end. However, the grease is where some of the dark, nutty flavor notes are! It's up to you. My local Louisiana friends say that this is why you serve gumbo with cornbread…to soak up the yummy grease. You can find a cornbread recipe on page 167 of *Necessary Food*.
• If you can't find gumbo filé powder you can leave it out, but I recommend it for the best taste and texture. (It helps thicken the gumbo.)
• Gumbo is even better the next day!

JAMBALAYA

jambalaya

HEALTHY CARBS | SERVES 6

1 tablespoon refined coconut oil

1 tablespoon minced garlic

1 lg. onion (chopped)

1 lg. red bell pepper (chopped)

2 cups chopped celery

6.5 oz. smoked lean turkey sausage of
choice (coined)

4 cups fat-free chicken broth

1 tablespoon Tony Chachere's Creole
Seasoning (or more, to taste)

2 bay leaves (discard before serving)

1½ teaspoons each oregano, smoked paprika

½ teaspoon black pepper

1½ cups uncooked brown rice

12 oz. small peeled and deveined raw shrimp

Sauté the first section of ingredients in a big soup kettle for 5 minutes.

Add the second section of ingredients and bring to a boil. Cover and simmer for 15 minutes.

Add the rice, stir, and bring to a boil again. Cover and simmer undisturbed for 50-60 minutes or until the rice is soft.

Taste and adjust the salt and spice levels to your taste. 1 tablespoon of Tony's seasoning was the perfect salt and heat level for me since I used salted chicken broth, but if you used unsalted chicken broth, you may need more Tony's and/or regular salt. Also feel free to add cayenne pepper if you want the jambalaya to be spicier. Add the shrimp, stir, and simmer (covered) for 5 minutes or until the shrimp are firm and pink. Serve.

Here's another Cajun classic...Mrs. Burkholder's version. It's definitely one of my favorite recipes in this book! This jambalaya is saucier than some. I've seen it done saucy and I've seen it done dry, but I like mine on the wetter side, so that's how I made it. Feel free to use less chicken broth for a drier result. Jambalaya often contains chicken as well as sausage and shrimp, but I thought two proteins were enough so I picked my favorites. If you like tomatoes in your jambalaya, feel free to add some, but I went the Cajun direction instead of Creole (well, except for the Tony Chachere's Creole Seasoning shortcut, but Tony's is pretty much a staple of all Louisiana cuisine).

note

• To stay in Healthy Carbs territory, don't add any additional fat to your meal. The coconut oil and turkey sausage add almost 5 grams of fat per serving.

• I used half of a 13-oz. pkg. Aldi Fit & Active Lean Turkey Polska Kielbasa.

one pot pineapple chicken & rice

HEALTHY CARBS I SERVES 4-5

1 lb. chicken breasts (chunked)

3 cups chopped cabbage

½ med. onion (chopped)

2 cups water

1 cup uncooked brown rice

¼ cup reduced-sodium soy sauce

2 teaspoons rice vinegar

¾ teaspoon salt

½ teaspoon each Chinese five spice,
　　garlic powder, sesame seeds

¼ teaspoon black pepper

1 cup crushed pineapple canned
　　in juice (drained)

½ teaspoon THM Super Sweet Blend (optional)

Stir the first section of ingredients together in a Dutch oven on the stovetop. Cover and bring to a boil, then turn the heat down and simmer (covered and undisturbed) for 50 minutes. Add the pineapple. Add the sweetener to round out the flavors if desired, stir, cover, and cook for 10 more minutes (or longer if necessary to soften the rice). Serve with additional sesame seeds and sriracha if desired.

bri's easy kettle curry

HEALTHY CARBS I SERVES 12-14

4½ cups water

2 cups uncooked brown basmati rice

3 med. carrots (coined)

1 med. onion (chopped)

3 lg. garlic cloves (minced)

4 cups shredded cooked chicken breast

1 lb. frozen broccoli florets

1 lb. frozen green peas

8 oz. fresh mushrooms (sliced)

2 cups unsweetened almond milk

¾ cup reduced-sodium soy sauce

2 tablespoons curry powder

2 tablespoons sriracha

1 teaspoon THM Super Sweet Blend

Salt (if necessary)

Bring the water to a boil in a large soup kettle. (I used a 6-quart kettle.) Rinse and drain the rice to remove excess starch and add it and the carrots, onion, and garlic to the water. Return to a boil, cover, reduce the heat, and cook for 30 minutes or until the rice is tender.

Add the rest of the ingredients, stir, taste, and add more curry powder or sriracha if desired. Add salt as necessary. Simmer for 20-30 minutes or until the vegetables are soft and the flavors are good.

India meets the Orient in this one pot supper stop. It uses healthy convenience foods (like pre-cooked chicken) and packs a bold flavor punch! If you want to make this even easier, use 3-4 pounds of frozen stir-fry vegetables to replace the onion, carrots, broccoli, peas, and mushrooms. (Add these after cooking the rice.)

note

If you're a flavor/spice wimp, start with only 1 tablespoon each of curry powder and sriracha, then taste and add more until the flavors meet your approval.

thai curry

1 tablespoon refined coconut oil
1 med. onion (diced)
1 tablespoon finely-grated fresh ginger
2 lg. garlic cloves (minced)
2½ lb. chicken breasts (chunked)
½ cup reduced-sodium soy sauce
2 tablespoons red curry paste
2½ teaspoons THM Super Sweet Blend

2 (13.66 oz.) cans light coconut milk
2 cups chicken broth
2 lb. frozen stir-fry vegetables
¼ teaspoon xanthan gum (optional)
Salt (if needed)

Melt the coconut oil in a large soup kettle. Add the onion, ginger, and garlic and sauté until they start to soften. Add the chicken, soy sauce, curry paste, and Super Sweet Blend and cook until the chicken is cooked through.

Add the coconut milk, chicken broth, and vegetables and simmer (uncovered) until the vegetables are tender. Sprinkle the xanthan gum over the top of the soup in a fine layer for a slightly thicker broth if desired, then stir it in. Let the soup simmer for 20-30 minutes if you can to let the flavors develop. Taste and add salt and additional sweetener if desired. (The salt needed will vary depending on the saltiness of the chicken broth used.)

Warning – this can get spicy! When I first created the recipe, I added a teaspoon of crushed red pepper flakes and my whole family was sweating and steaming! If you're a spice lover, feel free to repeat my mistake. If you're not, you may want to start with only one tablespoon of curry paste, then add more as desired. This curry is based off of an amazing curry I had at the first Thai restaurant I ever visited (with my then-boyfriend, Ryan). The foundation of fresh onion, ginger, and garlic paired with red curry paste and the creamy, subtly sweet coconut milk is a-maz-ing.

note

Please don't omit the fresh ginger! It adds such a good flavor that dried ginger just can't match in this kind of recipe!

chana dal & greens

3 cups low-fat chicken broth

1½ cups dry chana dal (soaked in water
    overnight, drained)

6 cups loosely-packed chopped fresh
    mustard greens

2 med. Roma tomatoes (chopped)

1 med. onion (chopped)

½ cup fresh cilantro (chopped)

1 med. jalapeño (diced)

1" cube fresh ginger (peeled, minced)

1 cup light canned coconut milk

¾ cup unsweetened applesauce

¼ cup tandoori paste

¼ cup tomato paste

1 tablespoon curry powder

1 tablespoon minced garlic

1 teaspoon THM Super Sweet Blend

1 teaspoon each cumin, ground coriander,
    turmeric

Salt (to taste)

Lime juice (optional, to taste)

Cooked brown rice (for serving)

Bring the first section of ingredients to a boil in a Dutch oven on the stovetop, then cover and simmer for an hour, stirring occasionally.

After cooking for an hour, add salt to taste. If you want a little more acidity, add a dash of lime juice. Cook for an additional 30-60 minutes to let the chana dal continue softening and round out the flavors. I like to leave the pot uncovered for at least part of that time to let the curry thicken. When the curry is done, serve over cooked brown rice. (I recommend sticking to half a cup of brown rice per serving to not overdo the carbs. You could add some non-starchy veggies to round out your meal.) I really enjoy leftovers on their own (cold!) as a soup/stew the next day after they've thickened in the fridge overnight.

This curry is sort of a grownup version of the Chickpea Curry over Caulitoes on page 124. That one is good and definitely has fewer ingredients than this recipe, but this curry has more depth of flavor (and is hopefully a little more authentic, even though it has a bit of a southern fusion flair).

note

• Can't find mustard greens in your grocery store? Try using other greens, such as turnip greens, kale, or spinach. Hardier greens like mustard and turnip may hold up better.

• As written, this curry has a medium spice level. Feel free to add more or less spice with a hotter or more mild tandoori paste or more or less jalapeño, as desired.

• The light coconut milk adds 2.25 grams of fat to each of 6 servings.

lentil, carrot & roasted red pepper soup

HEALTHY CARBS | SERVES 5-6

5 cups water

1½ cups dry lentils (rinsed, drained)

8 med. carrots (peeled, chopped
 into large pieces)

1 lg. onion (chopped)

1 (12 oz.) jar roasted red peppers (undrained)

3 lg. garlic cloves (smashed)

½ cup unsweetened applesauce

¼ cup nutritional yeast

2 tablespoons fresh peeled and
 chopped ginger

2 teaspoons each chili powder,
 oregano, tarragon

1 teaspoon each ground coriander,
 ground fennel, black pepper

3 tablespoons apple cider vinegar

2½ teaspoons salt (or more, to taste)

½ teaspoon liquid smoke

Add the first set of ingredients to a large soup kettle, cover, and bring to a boil, then reduce the heat and simmer until the lentils and vegetables are soft - about 40 minutes. Blend everything with an immersion blender until smooth, then add the vinegar, salt, and liquid smoke. Add more liquid if it's too thick. Taste and adjust as desired. Simmer for 15 minutes more (or longer). Serve with reduced-fat sour cream or a swirl of light canned coconut milk for creaminess (keep fats minimal). Garnish with carrot ribbons (made with a vegetable peeler) and tarragon if you want to be fancy.

This reminds me of a vegetarian Indian "chili soup" because it's so hearty and comforting with warm, rich flavors. Those flavors are even better the next day; I love to eat leftovers cold for lunch.

note

You could probably use low-fat chicken broth in place of the water and omit the nutritional yeast. Adjust salt if needed depending on the saltiness of your chicken broth. Feel free to add some cayenne pepper, chili flakes, or hot peppers to the soup for spice.

mom's chicken soup

HEALTHY CARBS | SERVES 12-14

9 cups low-fat chicken broth
2 cups chopped carrots
2 cups chopped celery
1 large onion (finely chopped)

4-6 cups diced cooked chicken breast
4 cups cooked barley (unseasoned)
1 tablespoon each cilantro, parsley flakes
½ teaspoon each basil, dill weed
2 lg. garlic cloves (minced)
Chicken bouillon (to taste)
Salt (to taste)

Add the broth and vegetables to a large soup kettle and cook until tender.

Add the rest of the ingredients and simmer over low heat until everything is heated through. If possible, simmer for an hour or two to let the flavors meld. Taste and add some chicken bouillon for a stronger flavor if desired, then taste and add as much salt as needed (don't skimp on this).

note

• You can use chicken broth left from cooking chicken or just make your own with chicken bouillon and water.
• If using the lesser amount of chicken, you may wish to increase the amount of vegetables.
• 1 cup uncooked barley yields about 4 cups cooked.

My mom makes the best soup - especially the best chicken barley soup. It used to be chicken noodle soup, but when we started eating healthier, we switched out barley for the noodles and love it just as much. Even my younger siblings (who can be picky on certain things) really like the barley in this soup! I've tried to recreate my mom's chicken soup before, but as is my habit when making soup, I added everything from the fridge that needed to be used up and the end result was nothing close to my mom's. My mom's chicken soup is very simple. It's a classic. Instead of trying again on my own, I asked my mom to make the soup like she usually does and write down the recipe for me. She lovingly obliged.

creamy broccoli bacon chowder

HEALTHY FATS | SERVES 10-12

2-3 lb. pork bacon

2 tablespoons salted butter
1 med. onion (chopped)
2 teaspoons minced garlic

2 lb. cauliflower florets (fresh or frozen)
2 lb. broccoli florets (fresh or frozen)
3 cups chicken broth
3 cups water
Salt (to taste)
1 teaspoon black pepper

2 cups shredded mozzarella cheese
1½ cups cottage cheese
1 (8 oz.) pkg. reduced-fat cream cheese

I like to fry the bacon while I make the soup. However you decide to do it, fry, drain, and crumble the bacon before serving the soup. The bacon will be added as a garnish on top.

To make the soup, sauté the onion and garlic in the butter in a large soup kettle until nice and brown. Add the cauliflower, broccoli, chicken broth, water, salt, and pepper and bring to a boil, then reduce the heat until the soup is lightly bubbling and cook until the vegetables are tender.

When the vegetables are tender, turn the heat to low, wait until the soup stops bubbling, and add the cheese, cottage cheese, and cream cheese. Let them melt for a bit, then use an immersion blender to puree everything to a smooth consistency. Let the soup simmer for 10 minutes (do not boil), taste and add more salt if necessary, then serve with bacon bits and additional shredded cheese as a garnish.

I happen to love pureed soups. After serving this to my family, I realized that not everyone does. To me, pureed soups mean dignified special-occasion lunches at Panera Bread, but apparently some little children relive baby food memories when confronted with such sophisticated yumminess. They loved the flavor – weren't fans of the texture. In this case, I decided to pull rank and publish it anyway.

note

• If you don't want to mess with frying bacon, you could just stir some real bacon bits into the soup at the very end. (Whatever amount will please your family.) I thought the freshly-fried crunchy bacon on top added good texture, but we've tried it both ways and both are good.
• If your family wants a little texture in the soup, you could remove some (not all) of the broccoli and cauliflower from the pot right before melting the cheeses in the broth and pureeing everything smooth, then add them back in at the end.

ham & "potato" chowder

HEALTHY FATS I SERVES 8-10

1 (16 oz.) pkg. radishes (trimmed, chopped)
1 med. onion (chopped)
1 tablespoon butter (or congealed fat from
   the top of refrigerated ham juice)

3 lb. cauliflower florets (fresh or frozen)
4 cups water
1 cup strong ham juice

4 cups diced cooked ham
1 (8 oz.) pkg. reduced-fat cream cheese
3 tablespoons Dijon mustard
2 tablespoons nutritional yeast
2 teaspoons parsley flakes
1 teaspoon each garlic powder,
   smoked paprika, black pepper
Salt (to taste, if needed)

Sauté the chopped radishes and onion in the butter in a large soup kettle for a few minutes. Add the cauliflower, water, and ham juice. Cover and cook until the cauliflower is soft.

When the cauliflower is soft, use an immersion blender to blend some of the cauliflower, leaving as many radish chunks as possible intact. Add the third set of ingredients. Use a potato masher to mash the unblended vegetables to uniform chunks and thicken the soup further.

Let the chowder simmer uncovered (don't boil) for 15 minutes to let the chowder thicken and the flavors meld.

I used the juice and leftover ham from the glazed ham recipe on page 89, and it really took this chowder up a notch! You don't really taste the Dijon mustard in this soup; it adds a nice backdrop and depth of flavor without being overtly mustardy. If your soup turns out a little bit pink, don't panic! That would be the radishes making their presence known. (Maybe it's their last protest against being called "potatoes.") The brilliant red color of the radish skin majorly fades when cooking, but a little bit remains.

note

The ham juice I'm talking about is the liquid left from baking a ham. It's very strong in flavor - stronger than broth. Refrigerate overnight and remove the fat from the top before using.

turkey pot pie chowder

2 tablespoons turkey fat or butter

1 lg. onion (chopped)

3 med. carrots (peeled and coined)

1-2 cups frozen green peas

1 lb. frozen green beans

2 cups strong turkey juice

4 cups water

1 cup cottage cheese

1 cup grated Parmesan cheese
   (the green can kind)

1 cup heavy whipping cream

¼ cup oat fiber

2 teaspoons parsley flakes

2 teaspoons turkey or chicken bouillon

½ teaspoon xanthan gum

½ teaspoon each garlic powder, black pepper

2 cups water

8 cups leftover chopped turkey
   (white and/or dark meat)

Salt (if needed)

In a large soup kettle, cook the first section of ingredients together until the vegetables are tender.

Blend the second section of ingredients together until smooth. Add the blended mixture to the cooked vegetables in the soup kettle. Use the additional 2 cups of water to clean out the blender; add this water to the soup kettle as well.

Add the turkey to the soup and simmer for 10-15 minutes. Taste and add salt and additional seasonings if desired.

note

The turkey juice I used was the liquid left from baking a whole deviled turkey. The spices my mom used on the deviled turkey added great flavor to this soup, so if you aren't using broth and meat from a deviled turkey, consider adding some extra spices that are traditionally used in deviled turkey. (You can look up recipes online.) Feel free to adjust the turkey juice, water, and turkey bouillon according to what you have on hand. In other words, if you have more than 2 cups of turkey juice, feel free to use it in place of some of the water and bouillon.

springy cabbage & sausage soup

HEALTHY FATS | SERVES 4

1 tablespoon salted butter

2 lg. garlic cloves (minced)

1 med. onion (chopped)

½ med. head fresh cabbage (chopped)

1 sm. carrot (grated or shaved into ribbons
    with a vegetable peeler)

6.5 oz. smoked sausage of choice (coined)

3 cups chicken broth

1 cup frozen green peas

¾ cup half and half

½ teaspoon dill weed

¼ teaspoon each thyme, black pepper

Dash cayenne pepper

Zest and juice from 1 small lemon

Salt (to taste)

Heat the butter in a soup kettle and add the garlic and onion. Sauté for a few minutes, then add the cabbage, carrot, and sausage. Sauté until the vegetables start to soften.

Add the second section of ingredients and simmer until the vegetables are soft. (Don't boil or the half and half may get a little weird.)

I love the unique flavors in this fresh, springy soup! Fresh mushrooms would be a great addition.

note

• I used half of a 13-oz. pkg. Aldi Fit & Active Lean Turkey Polska Kielbasa.

• Start with the juice from half a lemon. I liked a whole lemon's worth of juice, but it might be too lemony for some people.

They go from strength to strength. PSALM 84:7A

easy southwest soup

HEALTHY CARBS | SERVES 8-10

5 cups low-fat chicken broth

3 cups cooked brown rice

2 (16 oz.) cans fat-free refried beans

1 (16 oz.) can chili beans (undrained)

1 (15 oz.) can black beans (rinsed, drained)

1 (10 oz.) can diced tomatoes
   with green chilies

1 cup whole kernel corn

1 lg. onion (chopped)

2 teaspoons each cumin, smoked paprika

½ teaspoon black pepper

½ teaspoon liquid smoke

Salt (to taste)

Cayenne pepper (to taste)

Nickel-sized bunch fresh cilantro (chopped)

Combine everything but the cilantro in a large soup kettle. Cover and bring to a boil, then reduce the heat and simmer until the vegetables are tender. Add the chopped cilantro right before serving. Serve with reduced-fat sour cream or Greek yogurt and a squirt of lime juice or dollop of salsa (like the Goldmine Salsa on page 453) for some bright acidity.

note

• Use mild or spicy diced tomatoes with green chilies and chili beans depending on your desired heat level.

• I found this soup to be very filling meatless as written, but feel free to add some chopped cooked chicken breast to appease meat eaters.

• You may wish to add water or more chicken broth when reheating leftovers to thin them out a bit.

black bean stew

HEALTHY CARBS | SERVES 8-10

2 lb. dry black beans
1 lg. onion (chopped)
5 lg. garlic cloves (minced)

½ cup fresh cilantro (chopped)
1 tablespoon each chili powder, paprika
1 tablespoon chicken bouillon
2 teaspoons cumin
2 teaspoons lime juice
1½ teaspoons salt (may vary according to
   the saltiness of your chicken bouillon)
½ teaspoon THM Super Sweet Blend
½ teaspoon liquid smoke
Additional water as needed

Rinse and drain the beans and put them in a large slow cooker. (I used a 6-quart slow cooker.) Cover the beans with water to about 1½" above the surface of the beans. Add the onion and garlic and cook on High for 3½ hours or until the beans are soft enough to mash. Do not add more water during this time, but do stir the beans occasionally.

Mash the beans with a potato masher until they are your desired consistency. I like to leave some texture. Add additional water as desired; I added an extra 2 cups. Add the second set of ingredients and stir, then cook on Low for 2 hours. Serve.

You can top this stew with low-fat sour cream and a small sprinkling of cheese, but keep fats to a minimum as this meal focuses on healthy carbs.

note

Leftover beans refrigerated overnight will probably need extra liquid added before reheating because they will absorb water in the fridge. Or leave them thick and serve them in low-carb or sprouted tortillas! I like to have these beans on hand for lunches throughout the week, but if they last for more than a few days I would freeze them since beans tend to spoil quickly in my experience.

easy cheesy fiesta chowder

3 lb. chicken breasts

2 teaspoons each cilantro, dill weed

1½ teaspoons each chili powder, cumin,
   garlic powder, paprika

4 cups chicken broth

3 cups shredded cheddar cheese

1 cup heavy whipping cream

1 (14.5 oz.) can diced tomatoes

1 (6 oz.) can black olives (drained, sliced)

1 cup frozen green peas

Salt (to taste)

Cook the chicken breasts and spices in a large slow cooker (at least 6 quarts) on High for 2 hours or until the chicken is cooked through. (This will take longer if the chicken is frozen.) Shred the chicken in the slow cooker using two forks. Don't drain the broth.

Add the rest of the ingredients, stir, and cook on High for an hour or until the soup is hot and the cheese is melted. Stir and serve.

This soup goes great with the Sour Cream Cornbread recipe on page 167 of *Necessary Food*!

colorful chicken chili

HEALTHY CARBS I SERVES 10-12

1 cup chopped colorful bell pepper

1 lg. onion (chopped)

1 med. jalapeño (chopped)

5 lg. garlic cloves (minced)

4 cups low-fat chicken broth

4 cups shredded cooked chicken breast

2 (10 oz.) cans mild diced tomatoes
   with green chilies

1 (15.5 oz.) can great northern
   beans (drained)

1 (15 oz.) can black beans (drained)

1 (15 oz.) can corn (drained)

1 (13.66 oz.) can light coconut milk

1 cup fresh cilantro (chopped)

¼ cup + 2 tablespoons nutritional yeast

1 tablespoon lime juice

2 teaspoons cumin

1 teaspoon each chili powder,
   smoked paprika

½ teaspoon black pepper

Salt (to taste)

Dry sauté the bell pepper, onion, jalapeño, and garlic in a large soup kettle or Dutch oven on the stovetop until the vegetables start to soften. Add the rest of the ingredients, cover, and bring to a boil, then reduce the heat and simmer for 20-30 minutes until the vegetables are soft. (I like them on the *al dente* side, not cooked to mush.)

note

• Corn needs to be kept to very moderate amounts if you're in weight loss mode, but this amount spread over so many servings (this is a serious pot of soup) isn't very much.

• The coconut milk adds 2.25 grams of fat to each of 10 servings.

• As written, this soup is not very spicy. Feel free to add more jalapeños and/or use spicy diced tomatoes with green chilies.

hearty barbecue soup

HEALTHY CARBS | SERVES 15-18

1 lg. onion (chopped)

3 lg. garlic cloves (minced)

1 (29 oz.) can tomato sauce

3 cups water

1 (15.5 oz.) can mild chili beans (undrained)

6-8 cups shredded cooked chicken breast

2 (15.5 oz.) cans mild chili beans (undrained)

4 cups cooked brown rice

2 cups low-fat chicken broth

1 cup whole kernel corn

1 tablespoon parsley flakes

1 tablespoon THM Super Sweet Blend

1 tablespoon yellow mustard

2 teaspoons cumin

1 teaspoon molasses

1 teaspoon liquid smoke

½ teaspoon black pepper

Salt (to taste)

WATCH IT! This makes a lot of soup! I could barely fit it into a 6-quart kettle, so if you have a bigger pot, you might want to use it so you don't have to stir as tentatively as I did.

Dry sauté the onion and garlic in the kettle for just a bit to make them aromatic before adding the tomato sauce, water, and one can of chili beans. Puree the mixture with an immersion blender until smooth (or transfer to a regular blender to blend, then back to the kettle). Add the rest of the ingredients and simmer (uncovered) for 30 minutes to let the flavors settle out. Taste and add salt and/or more seasonings to taste. This makes a fairly thick, hearty soup, so feel free to thin it down a little with more chicken broth or water, especially when reheating. (The soup will thicken up after it sits in the fridge for awhile because of the beans and rice.)

I absolutely love to make soup, in fact I've joked before that soup is one of my love languages. Got leftovers? Make soup. Need leftovers? Make soup. Don't know what to make for supper? Make soup. It's so versatile, so yummy, so warm and comforting. In this case I was on a barbecue kick and wanted to see if I could make a Healthy Carbs soup that had the flavors of barbecue sauce. It worked!

note

• Chili beans do contain a bit of sugar, but the ones we buy (from Aldi) have only 2 grams of sugar per serving, and you're not going to be eating nearly a serving in this soup. The juice from the canned chili beans adds a lot of good flavor to this soup without having to get out half the spices in your cupboard, so keep that in mind if you omit them and use a different type of bean instead. I was going for quick and easy.

• While corn is not super weight loss friendly, it's OK in small amounts in a Healthy Carbs setting for flavor. 1 cup is stretched over a huge pot of soup here, so you're only getting 1 tablespoon or less per serving. I do like the little bit of sweetness it adds.

happy harvest soup

1 lb. ground beef
1 lb. ground sausage (I used pork)

½ med. head cabbage (thinly sliced)
1 lg. onion (chopped)
2 cups water

2 cups tomato juice
2 cups water
2 cups frozen green peas
1 (14.5 oz.) can diced tomatoes
4-8 oz. fresh mushrooms (sliced)
¼ cup reduced-sodium soy sauce
2 teaspoons each chili powder, garlic powder,
    nutritional yeast
1 teaspoon ginger
¾ teaspoon THM Super Sweet Blend
¾ teaspoon cinnamon
Salt (to taste)

1½ cups heavy whipping cream

Brown the ground beef and sausage in a skillet until cooked through. Drain the grease off and chop the meat finely.

Meanwhile, in a large covered soup kettle, cook the cabbage and onion in 2 cups of water. When they are mostly soft, add the meat and the third section of ingredients. Simmer until all the vegetables are soft.

When the vegetables are soft, add the cream (do not boil the soup after this point).

Taste and adjust the flavors as desired. Simmer for 10-15 minutes, then serve.

This soup combines lots of vegetables, flavorful sausage, rich tomato juice and cream, and some unexpected spices to create a delicious taste of fall in every bite. The crowning touches are a little THM Super Sweet Blend and cinnamon – just enough to add a hint of fall flavor reminiscent of pumpkin and spice, but not enough to take over. It's different, yes, but it's a good different. Leave the sweetener and cinnamon out if you feel you must, but trust me on this one. You might be pleasantly surprised.

black eyed pea soup

1 lb. dry black eyed peas (soak overnight)
2 tablespoons apple cider vinegar

6 cups water
2 cups strong beef juice (fat scraped off)
3 lg. carrots (coined)
1 med. onion (chopped)
2 teaspoons minced garlic

8 oz. fresh mushrooms (halved)
2 teaspoons salt (or more, to taste)
2 teaspoons each basil, oregano, paprika
1 teaspoon garlic powder
½ teaspoon black pepper
½ teaspoon liquid smoke
⅛ teaspoon red pepper (or more, for spice)
3 doonks THM Pure Stevia Extract Powder

2 cups diced okra (fresh or frozen)

The night before, cover the dry black eyed peas with plenty of water and the apple cider vinegar in a glass bowl (with several inches of water covering the beans to allow for expansion). Refrigerate overnight.

In the morning, rinse and drain the peas and add them to a 6-quart slow cooker. Add the water, beef juice, carrots, onion, and garlic and cook on High for 2 hours. After 2 hours, turn the heat down to Low.

Cook for 5 hours on Low, then add the mushrooms and seasonings. Blend the okra with some of the broth until completely

smooth, then stir it into the soup. Several hours of cooking will let the flavors meld and obliterate the okra completely. Cook for 3 more hours on Low, or until the beans are soft, the okra is indistinguishable, and the flavors have melded.

note

This "beef juice" was broth left from baking a roast for Sunday dinner, so it was pretty strong and had great flavor. We refrigerated it overnight and removed the fat that rose to the surface to make it acceptable for use in a Healthy Carbs setting. If you're using regular fat-free beef broth that isn't as strong as this "beef juice," use more of it and replace some of the water for better flavor. I bet fat-free ham juice/broth would be great in this soup as well!

lasagna soup

1-2 lb. ground pork sausage
1 med. onion (chopped)
3 lg. garlic cloves (minced)

½ cup oat fiber
1 teaspoon xanthan gum

6 cups water
1 (29 oz.) can tomato sauce
½ med. head cabbage (finely chopped)
2 cups fresh spinach (packed)

2 cups shredded mozzarella cheese
2 cups cottage cheese
1 cup heavy whipping cream
1 tablespoon Italian seasoning
2 teaspoons each oregano, parsley
½ teaspoon black pepper
Salt (if necessary)

Sauté the sausage, onion, and garlic together in a big soup kettle until the sausage is cooked through. Sprinkle the oat fiber and xanthan gum over the sausage in a fine layer and stir to distribute evenly. Add the water, tomato sauce, cabbage, and spinach and cook until the cabbage is tender. Add the rest of the ingredients and simmer for 15-20 minutes (do not boil once the dairy is added) to give the flavors a chance to develop and let the cheese melt, stirring occasionally. Serve with additional shredded mozzarella and parsley if desired.

This soup reminds me of the sauce mixture that gravitates to the bottom of the casserole dish after a crowd of people have been served from a pan of lasagna. You know, the goop immediately scooped up by nerds like me who don't want to eat the lasagna noodles but also don't want to be seen with a pile of discarded noodles pushed to the sides of their plates, discreetly covered with napkins.

note

• I only used 1 pound of sausage and thought it was enough with all the other stuff in the soup, but if you're serving major meat eaters, use 2 pounds.
• I didn't blend the cottage cheese because I wanted a little texture reminiscent of the ricotta layer in a lasagna. Most of the cottage cheese breaks down anyway while cooking. If you don't want to risk it, blend the cottage cheese with a bit of soup broth to eliminate any chunks.

creamy sweet potato bisque

HEALTHY CARBS | SERVES I

1 cup baked sweet potato

1 cup water

⅓ cup low-fat cottage cheese

2 teaspoons apple cider vinegar

1 teaspoon chicken bouillon

¼ teaspoon each cinnamon, garlic powder

1 doonk THM Pure Stevia Extract Powder

Dash each ginger, black pepper

Blend all the ingredients together in a high-powered blender for 1-2 minutes or until completely smooth. If your blender has a soup setting, you can use that; or you can blend everything smooth, then heat in the microwave or on the stove. Feel free to multiply this easy soup for your family!

It's important to get protein into every meal, and the protein source in this soup is the cottage cheese. The ⅓ cup of cottage cheese in this soup adds 8 grams of protein, so if you're not eating any other protein source with the soup, you may wish to add a scoop of collagen or gelatin to hold you over longer.

brown gravy beef stew

HEALTHY FATS I SERVES 8-10

2½ lb. beef chuck roast (chunked)

¼ cup oat fiber

2 teaspoons parsley flakes

½ teaspoon black pepper

1 tablespoon Worcestershire sauce

2 teaspoons minced garlic

1 bay leaf (remove before serving)

1 med. onion (chopped)

1 med. carrot (coined)

1 cup chopped celery

1 (16 oz.) pkg. radishes (trimmed, halved)

2 cups beef broth

8 oz. fresh mushrooms (halved)

¼ cup oat fiber

1 teaspoon xanthan gum

Salt (to taste)

If using a fatty cut of meat, trim excess fat off as much as possible. Place beef cubes in a slow cooker (4-quart slow cooker or larger). Sprinkle the oat fiber, parsley, and pepper over meat and stir to coat. Add the Worcestershire sauce, garlic, bay leaf, onion, carrot, celery, radishes, and beef broth. Leave the veggies on top and don't stir. Cook on High for 3½ hours or until the beef is cooked through.

Stir everything together and add the mushrooms. Remove two cups of broth from the stew and whisk in the additional oat fiber and xanthan gum, adding the xanthan gum while whisking so it doesn't clump. Stir the thickened broth back into the stew. Taste and add salt as desired (will vary according to the saltiness of the broth you used). Continue cooking the stew on High for about 3 more hours until the meat is falling apart, the stew is thickened, and the veggies are tender.

Oat fiber and xanthan gum is my favorite thickening combo for a non-slimy stew or gravy. Ryan declared this thick brown gravy stew the perfect consistency and called it, "My style." He loves anything beef and reminds me of that fact when I feed him too much chicken.

note

Don't use glucomannan in place of the xanthan gum; it tends to be slimier.

hunter's venison stew over rice

HEALTHY CARBS I SERVES 10-12

2 lg. sweet potatoes

8 med. carrots

1 med. onion

2 cups water

½ cup reduced-sodium soy sauce

½ cup water

3 tablespoons oat fiber

3 tablespoons tomato paste

1 teaspoon each garlic powder, paprika, salt

½ teaspoon ground mustard, sage,
    black pepper

½ teaspoon liquid smoke

½ teaspoon xanthan gum

3 lb. venison roast

1 teaspoon xanthan gum

Wash the sweet potatoes and carrots and cut them up into 3" chunks. (This isn't rocket science, and I don't peel them.) If the carrots are really big around, cut them in half so they'll cook through. Place the sweet potato and carrot chunks in the bottom of a slow cooker that holds 6 quarts or more. Cut the onion into thick slices and put it on top. Pour two cups of water over the vegetables.

In a mixing bowl, whisk the second section of ingredients. (Add the xanthan gum while whisking so it doesn't clump.)

Cut the venison roast into 1½" chunks and fold them into the sauce. Pour the venison and sauce over the top of the vegetables in the slow cooker. Do not stir.

Cover and cook on High for 3 hours, then stir. Remove one cup of broth and whisk 1 teaspoon xanthan gum into it. Pour this mixture into the slow cooker and stir again. Cook on High for another hour or until the vegetables are soft and the meat cooked through, then turn the slow cooker to Low until serving.

Serve over brown rice. Since you already have some carbs in the form of the sweet potatoes and to a lesser extent, the carrots, go easy on the rice.

basic-ally delicious slow cooker curry

HEALTHY FATS | SERVES 3-4

1 lb. chicken breasts (chunked)

1 sm. onion (chopped)

1" cube fresh ginger (peeled, diced)

3 lg. garlic cloves (minced)

1 (13.66 oz.) can light coconut milk

3 tablespoons tomato paste

1 tablespoon salted butter

¾ teaspoon salt (or more, to taste)

½ teaspoon black pepper

Cayenne pepper (to taste)

Cauli rice, baked spaghetti squash, or other
non-starchy veggies (for serving)

Stir all the ingredients together in a slow cooker. (I used a 4-quart slow cooker.) Cook on High for about 2 hours or until the chicken is cooked through. Leave it on High, open the lid a crack with a wooden spoon, and cook for another 2 hours until the sauce is thickened to your liking. Cook on the Keep Warm setting with the lid closed until serving; another 1-2 hours to continue developing flavors is great. Serve over cauli rice or your favorite non-starchy veggie.

TO MAKE EASY CAULI RICE: Cook fresh cauliflower florets with a bit of water in a covered kettle until crisp-tender (not mushy). Drain in a colander. In the colander, mash into rice-sized pieces with a potato masher. Transfer back to kettle to reheat/keep warm or serve immediately. Feel free to fry the cauli rice in a little butter and season it with garlic powder, salt, and pepper for additional flavor.

This easy slow cooker curry has all the basic but delicious flavors of a standard curry you'd get at an Indian restaurant!

note

• You could also serve this curry over brown rice for a delicious combination of carbs and fats.
• Curries are often even better the next day, and I love to eat them cold for lunch!

sweet potato chana dal curry

3 cups sweet potato cubes (I left the skin on)

2 cups low-fat chicken broth

1½ cups dry chana dal (soaked in water overnight, drained)

1 med. onion (chopped)

⅔ cup light canned coconut milk

1" cube fresh ginger (peeled, diced)

1 tablespoon + 1 teaspoon curry powder

1 teaspoon THM Super Sweet Blend

1 teaspoon garlic powder

½ teaspoon each turmeric, black pepper

30 raisins (optional)

Salt (to taste)

Cayenne pepper (to taste)

Combine all the ingredients (except the salt and cayenne) in a slow cooker. (I used a 4-quart slow cooker.) Cook on High for 5 hours or until the chana dal is soft and starting to break down into a thick stew.

Taste and add salt and cayenne pepper to taste. I added 1¼ teaspoons salt (my chicken broth was salted) and ⅛ teaspoon cayenne. Add these right before serving; do not add salt before the chana dal is soft.

On its own, this curry is very thick and filling, like a stew. You have a few options: 1) eat it plain like that, 2) serve it over a non-starchy veggie like cauli rice, broccoli, or spaghetti squash to help fill you up, or 3) add more chicken broth or water to thin it down to a soupier consistency. If you thin it down, do so half an hour or so before serving. (The curry will thicken even more as it cools, and leftovers will really thicken up in the fridge.) Stir and serve. I like to let it cool a few minutes before serving; the flavors are better when it's not piping hot.

This recipe was inspired by a sweet potato lentil curry that Ryan remembers fondly from his college days. I don't know how close I got to the original, but we both loved this version!

note

• Raisins are not generally part of a low-glycemic diet because they're full of concentrated natural sugars, but 6 raisins per person as an occasional treat won't do much damage. Ryan's favorite sweet potato curry included raisins, so I threw them in as an homage to him.

• I don't recommend exceeding one-fifth of the batch or adding other carb sources to your meal since the chana dal and sweet potato make this curry rather carb heavy. I tried various amounts of chana dal and sweet potato to try to reduce the carb count and allow for bigger servings, but this combination worked best for thickness and flavor. You can round out your meal with non-starchy veggies and a Low Carb/Low Fat glucomannan shake to help fill you up.

nutty slow cooker curry

1 cup light canned coconut milk

2 tablespoons natural peanut butter

2 tablespoons reduced-sodium soy sauce

1" cube fresh ginger (peeled, thinly sliced)

1-3 teaspoons red curry paste (to taste)

2 teaspoons minced garlic

1 teaspoon onion powder

¾ teaspoon THM Super Sweet Blend
  (or more, to taste)

½ teaspoon black pepper

1 lb. chicken breasts (chunked)

1 lg. red bell pepper (sliced)

12 oz. frozen broccoli florets

Salt (to taste, if needed)

⅓ cup cashew halves and pieces

Baked spaghetti squash (for serving)

Stir the first section of ingredients together in the slow cooker. (I used a 4-quart slow cooker.) Start with 1 teaspoon curry paste, then taste and add more to match your desired spice level. (The heat intensifies with cooking, and 3 teaspoons make it pretty spicy to my tastes, but I'm a spice wimp.) Add the chicken, red pepper strips, and frozen broccoli, in that order. Do not stir. Cook on High for 2 hours or until the chicken is cooked through. Stir everything together, then taste and add salt if needed. You can also add more sweetener for a sweeter curry. Cook on the Keep Warm setting for another hour to let the flavors develop, then sprinkle the cashews on top and serve over baked spaghetti squash.

This curry is so easy to make! It's on the thicker side, meant to be served over something (like spaghetti squash) instead of on its own as a soup or stew.

note

• I use kitchen shears to easily snip chicken into small pieces.

• A lot of curries taste best (and thicken up a bit) when they're not piping hot.

black beans (over cilantro lime rice)

6 cups water

14 oz. dry black beans (rinsed, drained)

1 lg. onion (chopped)

⅓ cup fresh cilantro (chopped)

1 med. jalapeño (chopped)

4 lg. garlic cloves (minced)

2 tablespoons chicken bouillon

1 tablespoon cumin

1 teaspoon black pepper

2 tablespoons apple cider vinegar

Salt (to taste, if needed)

Cilantro Lime Rice (page 205) (for serving)

Combine the first section of ingredients in a slow cooker (I used a 4-quart slow cooker) and cook on High until the beans are tender, stirring occasionally. Mine always take a very long time (8+ hours), so start in the morning to give them plenty of time. Half an hour before serving, add the vinegar and taste and add salt if needed. Smash some of the beans with a potato masher to thicken the broth if you like. Serve over Cilantro Lime Rice with chopped lettuce, salsa, and fat-free Greek yogurt. (Stick to ½ - ¾ cup rice to not overdo the carbs.)

note

• You could use low-fat chicken broth in place of the water and chicken bouillon.

• This recipe isn't that spicy, so feel free to add more jalapeños if you want more heat.

And into whatsoever city ye enter, and they receive you, eat such things as are set before you. LUKE 10:8

bulgogi-flavored beef & broccoli

HEALTHY FATS I SERVES 6-8

2½ lb. beef chuck roast
1 med. onion (chopped)

SAUCE
⅔ cup low-sodium soy sauce
2 tablespoons minced fresh ginger
2 tablespoons apple cider vinegar
2 tablespoons toasted sesame oil
1 tablespoon + 1 teaspoon
    THM Super Sweet Blend
1 tablespoon minced garlic
1 teaspoon crushed red pepper
1 teaspoon molasses
½ teaspoon black pepper

Salt (to taste)
2 lb. frozen broccoli florets

Place the roast in a 4-quart slow cooker. Top with the onion. Whisk the sauce ingredients together and pour over top. Cook on High for about 4 hours or until the meat is tender and can be pulled apart easily. Pull the meat apart, then taste and add salt as desired. Add the frozen broccoli, stir everything together, and continue cooking on High for 1 - 1½ hours or until the broccoli is tender and everything is hot. Garnish with sesame seeds if desired, then serve.

Traditional bulgogi uses a different cut of meat and a different cooking method, but this recipe has some of the same amazing flavors combined with tender beef. Broccoli turns this slow cooker dish into a meal on its own.

note

• Never substitute dried ground ginger in a recipe that calls for fresh ginger. They taste so different and you won't get the same effect.
• Using a larger slow cooker than a recipe calls for may make recipes cook faster. It's always great to check things early to prevent overcooking.

philly cheesesteak beef roast

HEALTHY FATS | SERVES 6-8

1 tablespoon salted butter

2 tablespoons Worcestershire sauce

2½ - 3 lb. beef chuck roast

1 teaspoon each garlic powder, oregano,
   parsley flakes, salt, black pepper

1 tablespoon salted butter

1 med. onion (sliced)

1 lg. green bell pepper (sliced)

1 lg. colorful bell pepper (sliced)

8 oz. fresh mushrooms (sliced)

½ teaspoon each garlic powder, salt,
   black pepper

Shredded white cheese of choice

Heat the butter and Worcestershire sauce in a large skillet or Dutch oven on the stovetop. Add the roast and sear on all sides. Place the roast in a slow cooker (I used a 4-quart slow cooker) and sprinkle with the garlic powder, oregano, parsley, salt, and pepper.

Heat the second tablespoon of butter in the same skillet or Dutch oven and add the sliced onion, peppers, and mushrooms. Season with garlic powder, salt, and pepper and sauté until the vegetables soften a bit – just enough to take the crunch off and coat them in the meat juices. Pour the sautéed veggies over the roast in the slow cooker and cook on High for 4-5 hours or until the meat is tender and can be pulled apart.

Pull the meat apart in the slow cooker, top with the shredded white cheese of your choice (queso cheese melts well), close the slow cooker lid, and let the cheese melt before serving. (Or transfer the meat and veggies to a serving plate, top with cheese, and pop it in the oven to melt it quickly, like I did.)

This roast dinner is perfect to put in the slow cooker before church Sunday morning! Mine usually ends up cooking for a full 5 hours until we get home from church, which is a little too long in a perfect world, but it's still very tasty. If you're craving a sandwich, serve it up in a low-carb tortilla or between 2 slices of low-carb bread.

slow cooker salsa verde chicken

LOW CARB / LOW FAT | SERVES 4

2 med. chicken breasts (approx. 1¼ lb.)
1 cup salsa verde
⅓ cup fresh cilantro (chopped)
½ teaspoon each cumin, garlic powder

Stir the ingredients together in a slow cooker. (I used a 4-quart slow cooker.) Cook on High for 2 hours or until the chicken is cooked through. Shred the chicken with 2 forks, then taste and add salt if needed. (My salsa was salty enough that I didn't add any.) Leave the chicken on the Keep Warm setting until serving; I like to let it soak in the juices for awhile.

SERVING SUGGESTIONS ▼

low carb/low fat Serve over salad or in a low-carb tortilla with chopped onion, chopped tomato, fresh cilantro, a squeeze of lime juice, and low-fat sour cream.
healthy fats Same as above, but add cheese, guacamole, sliced olives, and/or full-fat sour cream.
healthy carbs Serve with seasoned brown rice, quinoa, or lentils and roasted or steamed carrots. (Recipes like these can be found in the Side Dishes section of this book.)

Ryan says, "Phenomenal!" This recipe couldn't really get any easier, but it has such good flavor. The serving options are endless!

note

• I used a medium strength salsa verde (La Preferida brand, from Walmart), which had some kick. Use your favorite kind!
• You could try using a chunk of pork butt instead of chicken in this recipe for some Healthy Fats pork tacos. Adjust cooking time if necessary.

simple "brown sugar" grilled salmon

LOW CARB/LOW FAT I SERVES 8

8 wild-caught salmon filets (2 lb.)

1 tablespoon refined coconut oil
1 teaspoon garlic salt
1 teaspoon molasses
1 teaspoon maple extract
½ teaspoon THM Super Sweet Blend
½ teaspoon black pepper

Melt the coconut oil. Let it get fairly warm so it won't immediately congeal on the salmon filets. Whisk the garlic salt, molasses, maple extract, Super Sweet Blend, and black pepper into the hot coconut oil. Pour the mixture over the salmon and use your hands to coat the filets. Do this quickly before the coconut oil solidifies. (Make sure the filets are completely thawed for best results.)

Grill the salmon for 2-4 minutes on each side (I grill the skin side first) or just until the fish flakes to the touch of a fork. Grill time will vary according to the thickness of the filets.

note

• If you omit the molasses, this recipe can be used as part of a Foundation Fats meal! To make it truly FF, add some more healthy foundational fats to round out the meal (since such a small amount of coconut oil per serving is used here). A nice pat of butter on top of the grilled salmon would work just fine!

• The coconut oil used in this recipe falls well within Low Carb/Low Fat guidelines.

SIDE DISH IDEAS ▼

low carb/low fat steamed cauliflower, ½ cup serving of green peas
healthy fats steamed cauliflower with cheese or butter, salad with cheese and Ranch dressing
foundation fats cabbage sautéed with butter and garlic salt, salad with olive oil and vinegar dressing (no cheese)
healthy carbs steamed carrots with garlic salt and dill weed, Seasoned Quinoa (page 203)

simple soy salmon

LOW CARB/LOW FAT | SERVES 8

8 wild-caught salmon filets (2 lb.)
3 tablespoons reduced-sodium soy sauce
Sriracha
1 tablespoon refined coconut oil (melted)

1 teaspoon each garlic powder, paprika
½ teaspoon THM Super Sweet Blend
⅜ teaspoon ginger
Salt (to taste)

Place the salmon filets on a cookie sheet and pour the soy sauce over them. Add a hearty squirt of sriracha as well. Heat the coconut oil until it is fairly warm so it won't instantly congeal on the salmon. Pour it over the salmon filets and use your hands to coat the filets with the soy sauce, sriracha, and coconut oil on both sides. (Make sure the filets are completely thawed for best results.)

Whisk the spices and sweetener and sprinkle evenly over one side of the salmon filets. (If your filets have skin, spice the non-skin side.) Let the filets marinate for 30 minutes. Sprinkle with salt right before grilling.

Grill the filets for 2-4 minutes on each side or until the fish flakes with a fork. (Grill time will vary according to the thickness of the filets.)

I often pull the filets off the grill just a teensy bit before I think they're done and let them rest in a covered pan for a few minutes to finish them off with residual heat so I don't over-cook them.

Sometimes I completely omit the coconut oil so I don't have to bother melting it. The salmon is a tad drier without it but still tastes really good.

note

You can have up to 1 teaspoon added fat in a Low Carb/Low Fat setting, so you're good to go here!

pineapple marinated chicken

HEALTHY CARBS | SERVES 8-10

MARINADE

1 (20 oz.) can pineapple chunks
   in juice (drained)

¾ cup reduced-sodium soy sauce

½ cup water

¼ cup apple cider vinegar

3 lg. garlic cloves (peeled)

1 teaspoon paprika

2 doonks THM Pure Stevia Extract Powder

2½ lb. chicken tenders or chicken breasts
   cut into strips

Blend the marinade ingredients together in a blender until smooth. Pour over the chicken (it's OK if the chicken is still frozen) and refrigerate in a sealed container for 24 hours.

Grill on both sides until done, basting the chicken generously with extra marinade once before flipping.

MARINATING MEATS ▼

You'll notice that some of these marinated chicken recipes call for grilling, while others have baking instructions. You can do either! I prefer the flavor of grilled meats, but after I got married and moved I didn't have a grill, so I improvised. Marinating still gives you great flavor and tenderness even if the meat isn't destined for the grill.

My whole family loved this chicken, and I was happy to have found another easy Healthy Carbs meal! As you can see, I paired the chicken with fresh veggies and some cantaloupe cubes for a colorful plate. Got leftovers? Not a problem. This chicken would be great on a low-carb wrap or over a salad for lunch.

note

To clarify, you are using the pineapple *chunks* in the marinade, not the juice.

asian grilled chicken

LOW CARB / LOW FAT | SERVES 10

MARINADE
1 cup reduced-sodium soy sauce
½ cup water
2 tablespoons rice vinegar
2 tablespoons sriracha
1 lg. garlic clove (peeled)
1" cube fresh ginger
⅛ teaspoon THM Pure Stevia Extract Powder

3 lb. chicken tenders or chicken breasts
   cut into strips

Blend the marinade ingredients together until smooth. Pour over chicken and marinate for 6-8 hours. Grill on both sides until cooked through.

note

• The fresh ginger is imperative! It has a totally different flavor than dried ginger does. You can find a whole ginger root in the produce section of your grocery store and it will keep for a long time in the fridge.

• Feel free to use this marinade on any meat! Since it has no significant carb or fat sources, it can be used in any meal type. The type of meat you use will determine the fuel type of your meal. If you use a fatty meat (like chicken thighs or drumsticks), you have a Healthy Fats meal, but if you use a lean meat such as pork tenderloin or white meat poultry, you have a Low Carb/Low Fat meal that can be turned into a Healthy Carbs meal by adding a carb source.

• For a Healthy Carbs meal, grill some pineapple rings alongside the chicken! (I don't like to add the pineapple rings to the marinade because they get too soft and lose their bright flavor. Just pop them on the grill plain.)

• Pictured with Pineapple Sweet & Sour Sauce (page 479), Sweet & Sour Rice (page 207), and Steamed Dilly Carrots (page 188)

easy yogurt marinated chicken

HEALTHY CARBS | SERVES 6-8

1½ cups plain low-fat yogurt

3 tablespoons chickpea flour

2 tablespoons lemon juice

1 tablespoon + 1 teaspoon curry powder

1½ teaspoons each garlic powder, salt

1 teaspoon black pepper

2 lb. chicken tenders or chicken breasts
   cut into strips

Whisk the first section of ingredients together. Pour over the chicken in a sealable container and marinate in the fridge for 6+ hours or overnight.

Grill the chicken on both sides until done or bake on a greased pan at 350° for about 25 minutes or until cooked through.

This easy marinated chicken copies some of the flavors of tandoori chicken but keeps the process very simple. It has great flavor, and the chickpea flour helps more of the marinade stick to the chicken. (For a note on chickpea flour, check out page 4.)

note

• This chicken leans in the HC direction because of the plain yogurt and chickpea flour used, but you'll need an additional carb source to create a true Healthy Carbs meal. Serve it with Sunshine Rice (page 206) and some steamed broccoli! You could also serve it with Faux Tabbouleh (page 230) like I did for a multicultural, delicious meal.
• The marinade (sans raw chicken and minus some salt) would make a great dipping sauce!

ranch marinated chicken

HEALTHY FATS | SERVES 6-8

¾ cup mayonnaise

¾ cup water

2 tablespoons red wine vinegar

1½ teaspoons salt

1 teaspoon each dill weed, garlic powder, oregano, parsley flakes, black pepper

2 lb. chicken tenders or chicken breasts cut into strips

Whisk the first section of ingredients together until smooth. Pour over the chicken in a sealable container and marinate in the fridge for 6+ hours or overnight.

Grill the chicken on both sides until done or bake on a greased pan at 350° for about 25 minutes or until cooked through.

Ryan said this was "White House quality." The marinade really permeates the chicken with great flavor and makes it tender.

note

I actually used 1 tablespoon fresh dill weed because I grow it and love the flavor, but dried will work too.

saucy marinated chicken

LOW CARB/LOW FAT | SERVES 6-8

1 cup no-sugar-added ketchup

3 tablespoons apple cider vinegar

1½ tablespoons yellow mustard

1½ teaspoons THM Super Sweet Blend

1 teaspoon each garlic powder,
    smoked paprika, salt

1 teaspoon molasses

½ teaspoon black pepper

¼ teaspoon liquid smoke

2 lb. chicken tenders or chicken breasts
    cut into strips

Whisk the first section of ingredients together until smooth. Pour over the chicken in a sealable container and marinate in the fridge for 6+ hours or overnight.

Grill the chicken on both sides until done or bake on a greased pan at 350° for about 25 minutes or until cooked through.

note

• My husband does not enjoy salty food, so I often err on the conservative side with sodium levels. I thought this chicken needed a little more salt, but he thought it was good as-is. Verdict: add an extra ¼ - ½ teaspoon salt to the marinade or add additional salt at the table.

• Smoked paprika is worth a trip to the store! I don't recommend substituting regular paprika unless you absolutely have to because you'll

The marinade on this chicken is based off my mom's meatloaf topping, which I love. (You can find my mom's meatloaf recipe on page 42 of *Necessary Food*.) The simple flavors make a great kid-friendly dinner.

miss out on some amazing smoky flavor. You can find smoked paprika at Walmart or your local grocery store.

• Marinating chicken to bake or grill is one of my favorite strategies for a simple supper. Much of the prep work is done in advance, and most marinades are easy to throw together. Pair the grilled or baked chicken with a spinach salad or simple roasted veggies and dinner is served!

cilantro & lime marinated chicken

LOW CARB/LOW FAT | SERVES 8-10

1 cup water

1 cup fresh cilantro

1 med. ancho chile (stem and seeds removed)

¼ cup + 2 tablespoons apple cider vinegar

¼ cup + 2 tablespoons lime juice

1 tablespoon minced garlic

1½ teaspoons salt

1 teaspoon each onion powder, black pepper

½ teaspoon THM Super Sweet Blend

½ teaspoon liquid smoke

3 lb. chicken tenders or chicken breasts
   cut into strips

Blend the first section of ingredients together until smooth. Pour over the chicken in a sealable container and marinate in the fridge for 6+ hours or overnight.

Grill the chicken on both sides until done or bake on a greased pan at 350° for about 25 minutes or until cooked through.

note

I kept the salt on the low side since I often eat this chicken as part of a burrito bowl with salty ingredients. Feel free to add more salt (½ – ¾ teaspoon) if eating the chicken on its own.

burrito bowls

HEALTHY FATS, HEALTHY CARBS, OR LOW CARB/LOW FAT

NUETRAL (LOW CARB/LOW FAT)
lettuce, Cilantro & Lime Marinated Chicken (above), chopped tomato, chopped onion, chopped fresh cilantro, chopped jalapeño, salsa, low-fat sour cream or Greek yogurt, small sprinkling of part-skim shredded cheese

HEALTHY CARBS
brown rice, Slow Cooker Pinto Beans (page 210), rinsed and drained canned black beans, small amount of corn, Goldmine Salsa (page 453)

HEALTHY FATS
full-fat sour cream, shredded cheese, chopped avocado, guacamole (page 454)

Create your own customized burrito bowls! The neutral ingredients can be used with either carbs or fats.

chicken caesar salad

1) Place several chicken breasts on a greased cookie sheet and season generously with Italian seasoning, dill weed, garlic powder, salt, and pepper. Bake (uncovered) at 375° until the chicken is cooked through. (Slice a piece open and make sure the juices inside run clear instead of pink.) Baking time will vary according to the thickness of your chicken. Store in the refrigerator for future Caesar salads.

2) Chop a bunch of lettuce. Toss the lettuce and some shredded white cheese of your choice (Parmesan is the classic, but mozzarella or white queso cheese works too) with enough Caesar dressing to coat it lightly. Top with black olives and sliced baked chicken. (You can warm the chicken or leave it cold.) Make as much salad as you need, but don't mix dressing into more than you'll eat in a sitting because the salad will get soggy if left over.

When using storebought dressings, look for brands with 2 grams of carbs or less per serving. Caesar usually falls into that because it's not typically sweetened! There are lots of easy recipes online for making your own Caesar salad dressing if you want to go that route. They don't usually include sugar, but make sure you use a healthy oil like olive oil to make them instead of vegetable oil.

OK, folks - this is one of the easiest meals you can make, and I'm not going to take the fun out of it by measuring. Here's what you do!

greek salads with quick tzatziki dressing

HEALTHY CARBS | SERVES 2

4-6 cups chopped romaine lettuce
2 cups shredded rotisserie chicken breast
1 cup cooked quinoa (seasoned as desired)
½ lg. English cucumber (chopped)
1 med. Roma tomato (chopped)
Sliced red onion (as desired)

QUICK TZATZIKI DRESSING
⅔ cup fat-free Greek yogurt
1 tablespoon lemon juice
¼ teaspoon each dill weed, mint
⅛ teaspoon each garlic powder, salt,
    black pepper

Assemble salads by dividing the ingredients into 2 bowls in the order given, with lettuce on the bottom. You can heat the chicken and quinoa if you like, but it's good cold too. I like to season the quinoa with garlic powder, salt, and pepper.

Whisk the dressing ingredients together and drizzle over the salads. Season the salads with additional salt and pepper if desired and enjoy!

note

• If you use homemade cooked chicken, season it before using it in these salads.
• You could have up to ¾ cup of cooked quinoa on each salad, but they're huge salads as it is so I didn't use that much. You can, though! Just use really big bowls.
• This tzatziki dressing would make a yummy dipping sauce!

The Lord thy God in the midst of thee is mighty;
   he will save, he will rejoice over thee with joy;
   he will rest in his love, he will joy over thee with singing.
ZEPHANIAH 3:17

fajita salads

2 teaspoons salted butter
1 med. green bell pepper (sliced)
½ med. onion (sliced)

1 lg. chicken breast (cut into strips
   or small pieces)
½ teaspoon each cilantro, salt
¼ teaspoon each chili powder, cumin,
   garlic powder, black pepper
Shredded white queso cheese (for topping)

4-6 cups chopped romaine lettuce
Salsa, guacamole (page 454), sour cream
   (for topping)

Heat the butter in a skillet, then sauté the bell pepper and onion to soften a bit. Add the chicken and seasonings and sauté until the chicken is cooked through. Top with some queso cheese and put the lid on the skillet so it will melt.

Divide the lettuce between 2 bowls and top with the chicken and veggies. Serve with your toppings of choice.

note

• If you want to be fancy, you could also add fresh mushrooms, chopped jalapeño, chopped tomato, sliced black olives, fresh cilantro, and fresh lime juice – either to the skillet or fresh on top of the salads. Instead of making salads, you could serve the chicken and veggies in low-carb tortillas with toppings. You could also add more non-starchy veggies to the skillet (like fresh mushrooms!) and enjoy it on its own as a stir-fry.

• For a Low Carb/Low Fat version, use only 1 teaspoon of butter for frying, keep the cheese to a garnish sprinkling, top with fat-free Greek yogurt instead of sour cream, and don't use any guacamole or olives.

asian chicken salad

HEALTHY FATS | SERVES 2

1½ cups shredded rotisserie chicken
   (white and/or dark meat)
Asian Vinaigrette (page 482)
4-6 cups chopped Romaine lettuce and spinach
Shredded cheese of choice
Pecans (or nuts of choice)

Warm the chicken in a skillet with a few tablespoons of the Asian Vinaigrette (enough to coat the chicken well). Pour the warm chicken over the shredded greens and toss to coat. Divide the salad between 2 bowls and top each with some shredded cheese and nuts of your choice. Serve with additional Asian Vinaigrette if needed.

SALAD SUGGESTIONS ▼
When it comes to salad, the sky's the limit! I love a good, creative salad for lunch or dinner. Top salads with leftover meats (such as grilled chicken or shredded pork), cooked beans or lentils, or hardboiled eggs for a protein source, then finish them off with whatever happens to be in the fridge. There are some great salad dressing recipes in this book, but you can think outside the box too. Salsa, vinegars of all kinds, soy sauce, barbecue sauce, and Bri's Adobo Sauce (page 477) all make great Low Carb/ Low Fat salad dressings for LC/LF or Healthy Carbs salads! Fruit, some soup broths, and Pineapple Sweet & Sour Sauce (page 479) all make great HC moisture options.

These salads taste gourmet, but they're super easy to make if you have some of my Asian Vinaigrette in your fridge. The vinaigrette caramelizes beautifully on the chicken! Hint: these salads are a great way to use rotisserie chicken on a night that you need a no-fuss dinner.

note
• If you use homemade cooked chicken, season it before using it in these salads.
• If you want to get fancy, toast the nuts in butter with some salt, cayenne pepper, and a little THM Super Sweet Blend. Feel free to add some chopped colorful peppers or other non-starchy veggies to the salad as well. I'm all for simple.

strawberry, ham & swiss salad

HEALTHY FATS | SERVES 1

DRESSING

1 tablespoon mayonnaise

1 tablespoon red wine vinegar

1 teaspoon horseradish spread
(or less if yours is really strong)

Dash each garlic salt, THM Super Sweet Blend

2 cups chopped romaine lettuce

1 cup chopped spinach

Chopped ham (unlimited!)

Chopped cucumber (unlimited!)

Up to 1 cup sliced strawberries

1-2 slices Swiss or Muenster cheese (chopped)

¼ cup pecans (chopped, if desired)

Whisk the dressing ingredients together and pour over the lettuce and spinach. Stir to coat. Top with the rest of the ingredients. Enjoy!

The directions and amounts for this single-serve salad can be tweaked according to your preferences. I've included some guidance for the topping ingredients so you know which ones to load up on and which ones to be careful with so you don't dump a boatload of unnecessary calories onto your salad.

quinoa lunch bowl

¼ cup uncooked quinoa

½ cup water

½ cup shredded cooked chicken breast

¼ teaspoon each onion powder, salt,
  black pepper

½ cup chopped tomato

½ cup chopped cucumber

1 tablespoon vinegar of choice or lemon juice

1 teaspoon tahini

Rinse and drain the quinoa and add it and the water to a saucepan. Cover, bring to a boil, then reduce the heat and cook until tender – about 15 minutes.

Add the chicken, onion powder, salt, and pepper to the quinoa and stir. Heat it if desired, then transfer it to a bowl. Top with the tomato, cucumber, and vinegar or lemon juice, then drizzle the tahini over the top. Enjoy!

This easy lunch bowl packs some cool textures and flavors! I used balsamic vinegar, but I'm sure red wine vinegar or lemon juice would also taste great! The tahini serves as your teaspoon of added fat in a Healthy Carbs meal.

kate's weird pasta veggie bowl

HEALTHY FATS | SERVES I

2 cups water
1½ cups fresh broccoli florets
¼ cup Dreamfields elbow pasta

¼ cup shredded cheddar cheese
Dash of half and half

Protein of choice (leftover cooked chicken,
    bacon, some diced lunch meat, etc.)
Garlic powder, salt, cracked pepper (to taste)
⅓ cup diced fresh tomato
Feta cheese

Bring the water to a boil in a saucepan. Add the broccoli and pasta, return to a boil, cover, and simmer for 8 minutes. Drain and return the broccoli and pasta to the pan.

Add the cheese and half and half, stir, and cover until the cheese melts. Stir again.

Add your protein, season with garlic powder/salt/pepper, and stir in the tomato. Top with a sprinkling of feta and enjoy!

note

• I used fresh broccoli so it would stay crisper. You could probably use frozen as well but it won't be as fresh and crisp and pretty.
• Don't trust Dreamfields? Use another low-glycemic pasta of your choice or just add more broccoli! Adjust cooking time for a different pasta if needed.

The credit for this one goes to my little sister Katelyn, as you may have gathered by the title of the recipe. She's always coming up with neat flavor combinations, and on occasion she'll let me try them. She never writes anything down, so after I tasted a bite of a noodle/veggie concoction she made that I really liked, I worked backwards to recreate it with my own spin. The result is this yummy pasta veggie bowl. It's awesome because it gives you a pasta fix without actually using much pasta, plus it incorporates plenty of veggies! There's a mixture of flavors, temperatures, and textures going on here that has to be nothing short of gourmet. (That's a code word for "weird.") Kate's a genius.

cornbread in a bowl + beans

HEALTHY CARBS I SERVES I

CORNBREAD

2 tablespoons masa flour

2 tablespoons oat fiber

¼ teaspoon baking powder (rounded)

¼ teaspoon THM Super Sweet Blend

Hearty dash salt (don't skimp on this!)

Dash turmeric (optional, for color)

3 tablespoons egg whites

2 tablespoons low-fat Greek yogurt

2 tablespoons water

BEANS

½ cup cooked black beans

2 tablespoons no-sugar-added ketchup

2 tablespoons water

1 teaspoon horseradish spread (decrease this amount if your horseradish is really strong)

Dash THM Super Sweet Blend

Cumin, garlic salt (to taste)

Whisk the cornbread dry ingredients. Add the wet ingredients and whisk again. Microwave for 1 minute and 45 seconds (or until a toothpick comes out cleanly) in a greased 2-cup glass Pyrex bowl.

Combine the bean ingredients and heat in the microwave or on the stovetop. Serve over the warm cornbread.

I've tested this cornbread recipe in the microwave as well as the oven, and much to my surprise, it actually tastes better when microwaved. It's fluffier and the flavor is better. Usually I find that baked goods taste better than microwaved ones, but for some reason that just doesn't hold true in this case. Feel free to use the cornbread in other applications as well – not just with the bean recipe listed here!

note

Because of the amount of masa flour, I recommend using this cornbread in a Healthy Carbs setting, but it actually doesn't contain enough carbs to be the carb source in your HC meal. Paired with the beans, it's perfect, but if you don't eat the cornbread with beans, add another moderate carb source to create a true HC meal.

strawberry, ham & swiss quesadilla

HEALTHY FATS | SERVES 1

1 low-carb tortilla

Mayonnaise

Horseradish spread

Sliced ham

Sliced Swiss cheese

Spinach

Sliced strawberries

Refined coconut oil (for frying)

Spread some mayo and horseradish spread onto a low-carb tortilla. On one half of the tortilla, layer some sliced ham, sliced Swiss cheese, fresh spinach, and a few strawberry slices. Fold the tortilla over onto itself to create a quesadilla and fry on both sides in hot coconut oil until crispy.

leftover turkey fried wrap

HEALTHY FATS I SERVES I

1 low-carb tortilla

Mayonnaise

Horseradish spread

Yellow mustard

Garlic herb seasoning

Leftover turkey

Cheese of choice

Fresh spinach

Refined coconut oil (for frying)

GRAVY

Turkey broth

Xanthan gum

Salt & pepper

Spread mayo, horseradish, and mustard onto half of the tortilla. Sprinkle with the garlic herb seasoning. Top with turkey pieces, cheese, and fresh spinach. Fold the tortilla over onto itself. Fry it on both sides in hot coconut oil until golden brown. You can enjoy right away or make some gravy to go on top.

For the gravy, heat some turkey broth in a pan. (I just use the same pan that I used to fry the wrap.) Sprinkle in a very small amount of xanthan gum while whisking (so the xanthan gum doesn't clump). Add enough xanthan gum to thicken the gravy to your liking, season with salt and pepper, then pour the gravy over the fried wrap and enjoy!

MASHED SWEET
POTATOES • PG 187

side dishes

garlic butter zoodles

LOW CARB/LOW FAT | SERVES 4

1 tablespoon butter
2 med. zucchini (spiralized)
Garlic powder, salt, black pepper (to taste)

Sauté the spiralized zucchini in the butter in a skillet just until *al dente*. Do not overcook or the zoodles will be mushy! Season with garlic powder, salt, and pepper, then serve. (Go easy on the salt if serving the zoodles with a salty gravy, but don't skimp on the garlic powder!)

Pictured with Ground Beef Stroganoff on page 113

note

I've marked this as a Low Carb/Low Fat recipe because the amount of butter used comes to less than a teaspoon per serving, but if you intend to eat more than one-fourth of the recipe (which is totally fine!) or add other fats to your meal, decrease the butter or keep the zoodles to a Healthy Fats setting.

garlic, butter & herb roasted spaghetti squash

FOUNDATION FATS | SERVES 4-6

1 (3 lb.) spaghetti squash

2 tablespoons butter (melted)
Dill weed, garlic powder, Italian seasoning,
   salt, black pepper (to taste)

Cut the squash in half and place cut side down in a covered baking dish. Bake at 350° until mostly tender (60-70 minutes). Remove the squash from the oven and scoop out the seeds. Place in the baking pan cut side up.

Brush the top of the squash with the melted butter and season generously with dill weed, garlic powder, Italian seasoning, salt, and pepper. (Don't skimp on the garlic!) Bake the squash (uncovered) at 350° until fork tender (about 30 minutes).

This recipe produces an *al dente* squash that "noodles" well with a fork. Enjoy as a side dish or serve spaghetti sauce over it!

roasted butternut squash

DIRECTIONS: Slice a butternut squash lengthwise and place on a cookie sheet with the cut sides up. Roast uncovered at 450° for 1 hour and 30 minutes or until tender and caramelized. Scoop out the seeds after baking. Add sweet or savory toppings of your choice!

Ryan and I went to a cabin in the mountains for a brief honeymoon, and we did our own cooking while we were there. While poking around Walmart looking for some easy meal ingredients, we grabbed a butternut squash which I roasted in the oven back at the cabin. Not having any of my usual baking pans or tinfoil, I just roasted it uncovered on a baking sheet. It took awhile to get soft, but I loved the caramelized result of a squash exposed to high

heat. It's so rich and nutty and flavorful; I eat it like candy! Even the skin and crispy roasted seeds are good. Eat this butternut squash on its own as a side dish, or use it as a vehicle for some of the Healthy Carbs curries in this book.

Butternut squash is one of the starchier squashes, so keep it to a half cup serving in a Healthy Fats or Low Carb/Low Fat setting. You can have all you want (with a teaspoon of butter) in a Healthy Carbs meal! On our honeymoon, I pan-fried leftover roasted squash with butter, cinnamon, and salt and it was delicious. Here at home, I'd add some THM Super Sweet Blend. With the amounts of squash and butter I used, I probably created a glorious combination of carbs and fats, but was I worried about that on my honeymoon? Nope.

maple butter roasted squash

1 (2 lb.) acorn or spaghetti squash

2 tablespoons salted butter (melted)
1 teaspoon THM Super Sweet Blend
1 teaspoon maple extract
½ teaspoon cinnamon
¼ teaspoon each salt, black pepper

Cut the squash in half and place cut side down in a covered baking dish. Bake at 350° until mostly tender; I baked my acorn squash for 70 minutes, but check at 40 minutes in case yours gets done quicker. Remove the squash from the oven and scoop out the seeds. Place in the baking pan cut side up.

Whisk the second set of ingredients together. Brush over the top of the squash, then bake the squash (uncovered) at 350° until fork tender (about 30 minutes).

If you're feeling fancy, you can serve this squash with some chopped pecans and a drizzle of sugar-free syrup. Feel free to add more salt or Super Sweet Blend to your portion at the table.

note

If using acorn squash, keep your serving to half a cup unless you're not concerned about weight loss or just want a special treat. You don't have to be as careful with spaghetti squash, since it's considered a non-starchy.

"One thousand aves and as many credos, said standing with arms outstretched before the shrine of the Virgin, may help thee to remember that the Creator hath given us two ears and but one mouth, as a token that there is twice the work for the one as for the other." SIR ARTHUR CONAN COYLE - *THE WHITE COMPANY*

roasted sweet potatoes three ways

....

HEALTHY CARBS

....

SEASONING OPTIONS ▼
- Garlic powder, salt, black pepper
- Tony Chachere's Creole Seasoning
- THM Super Sweet Blend, cinnamon, salt

Wash as many sweet potatoes as you need, then dry them. (I don't peel them.) Slice the sweet potatoes into rounds, fries, or long slabs (approximately ⅜" thick). Spread the sweet potatoes onto cookie sheets in a single layer. Lightly spray with cooking spray, then season with one of the above seasoning combinations.

Roast the sweet potatoes at 400° until tender, checking at 25 minutes and baking longer in 5 minute increments as needed (depending on thickness). I like to bake them a little longer, about 45 minutes, to caramelize.

This makes a super easy side dish – and the roasted sweet potatoes taste like candy, especially when you use a sweet topping! If you cut them thin (¼") and bake them awhile (45 minutes), then let them cool, they get kind of chewy (which I *love!*).

mashed sweet potatoes

2 lb. sweet potatoes

2 teaspoons salted butter

¾ teaspoon salt

¼ teaspoon each cinnamon, garlic powder,
  black pepper

Peel the sweet potatoes. Chop them into chunks, cover with water, and bring to a boil in a saucepan. Reduce heat and simmer until soft.

Drain the sweet potatoes well and add the second section of ingredients. Beat well with a hand mixer, then taste and add more seasonings if desired. Serve.

note

For a Healthy Carbs & Healthy Fats meal, feel free to add more butter. Since this recipe already has a few grams of added fat per serving from the small amount of butter used, keep the fat in the rest of your meal minimal if you want to stay in Healthy Carbs mode.

steamed dilly carrots

HEALTHY CARBS | SERVES 4-6

3 cups peeled and coined carrots

¼ cup water

2 teaspoons salted butter

1 teaspoon dill weed

¾ teaspoon garlic salt

Combine all the ingredients in a saucepan and cook (covered) over medium heat until tender, stirring occasionally. The liquid cooks off and the butter kind of caramelizes onto the carrots. Delicious!

note

The butter used here stays well within Healthy Carbs limits, but it does add good flavor!

roasted carrots

1 tablespoon refined coconut oil (melted)

1 tablespoon red wine vinegar

1 teaspoon honey

½ teaspoon maple extract

2 lb. fresh carrots (about 10
large carrots) (peeled)

Garlic salt, black pepper (to taste)

Whisk the coconut oil, vinegar, honey, and maple extract.

Slice the carrots in half unless they're pretty thin. Toss them with the dressing mixture and use your hands to make sure all the pieces get coated. Spread the carrots into a 9"x13" pan and season generously with garlic salt and black pepper.

Cover the pan with tinfoil and bake at 400° for 30 minutes. Remove the foil and increase the oven temperature to 450°. Bake for an additional 30 minutes or until the carrots are tender.

note

• Just want plain carrots? Omit the vinegar, honey, and maple extract.

• The coconut oil used here adds a miniscule amount of fat to each serving. The honey stays under ¼ teaspoon per serving, so it's within what I consider to be low-glycemic limits.

> After all, I thought, it is better and finer to love than to be loved, if it makes something
> in life so worthwhile that one is not loath to die for it.
> I forget my own life in the love of another life; and yet, such is the paradox,
> I never wanted so much to live as right now when I place the least value upon my own life.
> JACK LONDON - *THE SEA WOLF*

buttery garlic brussels sprouts

HEALTHY FATS | **SERVES 5**

2 tablespoons butter
1 garlic clove (minced)

1 lb. fresh Brussels sprouts (halved)
Salt & pepper

Sauté the garlic in the butter in a skillet until golden brown. Add the Brussels sprouts and sauté until tender. Season with salt and pepper.

note

• Please do not use frozen Brussels sprouts. Just don't. Fresh are infinitely better. Frozen become a soggy mess.
• Since Brussels sprouts are a little carbier than non-starchy veggies like green beans, keep them to ½ cup per serving in a Healthy Fats setting. If you are in maintenance mode and want to combine carbs and fats, Brussels sprouts cooked up in plenty of coconut oil or butter are a great way to do that!

roasted brussels sprouts

HEALTHY FATS | **SERVES 5**

1 lb. fresh Brussels sprouts
2 tablespoons refined coconut oil (melted)
Garlic salt

Toss the sprouts in the coconut oil, spread onto a cookie sheet, season with garlic salt, and bake at 400° for 25 minutes or until the desired tenderness is achieved, stirring halfway through.

note

• Please do not use frozen Brussels sprouts. Just don't. Fresh are infinitely better. Frozen become a soggy mess.
• Since Brussels sprouts are a little carbier than non-starchy veggies like green beans, keep them to ½ cup per serving in a Healthy Fats setting. If you are in maintenance mode and want to combine carbs and fats, Brussels sprouts cooked up in plenty of coconut oil or butter are a great way to do that!

special roasted brussels sprouts

HEALTHY FATS I SERVES 4-5

2 tablespoons refined coconut oil (melted)
2 tablespoons red wine vinegar
½ teaspoon THM Super Sweet Blend
½ teaspoon maple extract
¼ teaspoon black pepper

1 lb. fresh Brussels sprouts
Garlic salt

Whisk the first 5 ingredients together in a large bowl. Add the Brussels sprouts and toss to coat. Spread the sprouts on a cookie sheet, pour any excess liquid over the top, and sprinkle with garlic salt. Roast at 400° for 15 minutes. Stir. Return the sprouts to the oven to roast for another 10-15 minutes or until the desired tenderness is achieved.

note

• Please do not use frozen Brussels sprouts. Just don't. Fresh are infinitely better. Frozen become a soggy mess.
• Since Brussels sprouts are a little carbier than non-starchy veggies like green beans, keep them to ½ cup per serving in a Healthy Fats setting. If you are in maintenance mode and want to combine carbs and fats, Brussels sprouts cooked up in plenty of coconut oil or butter are a great way to do that!

There seems to be no middle ground for this poor vegetable. I'm personally in the "love it" camp, but I haven't always been. Brussels sprouts were never really on my radar until a year or two ago when my mom decided to buy some after hearing lots of great things about these mini cabbages. They were frozen. We added them to a roast that we baked during church for Sunday lunch, and the combination of the frozenness + long baking time made for mush. They didn't taste that bad, but the texture was just a little scary. Fast forward to the time when we found out that fresh Brussels sprouts are the only Brussels sprouts worth eating. We now love them sautéed in a pan or roasted in the oven just until they're tender. Delicious! I love this subtly sweet and sour take!

sautéed cabbage

LOW CARB/LOW FAT I SERVES 6-8

1 med. head cabbage (thinly sliced)
1 tablespoon butter
Garlic salt

Sauté the cabbage in the butter in a skillet over medium-high heat, stirring occasionally. I keep the cabbage covered when I'm not stirring it so it cooks faster. Season with garlic salt partway through cooking.

special sautéed cabbage

LOW CARB/LOW FAT I SERVES 3-4

2 teaspoons refined coconut oil
½ med. head cabbage (thinly sliced)
¾ teaspoon salt
½ teaspoon THM Super Sweet Blend
½ teaspoon garlic powder
¼ teaspoon black pepper
1-2 tablespoons red wine vinegar

Heat the coconut oil in a skillet over medium-high heat. Add the cabbage, salt, Super Sweet Blend, garlic powder, and pepper and stir. When the pan is nice and hot and the cabbage is cooking, add the vinegar (deglazing the pan), stir again, cover, and cook over medium-low heat until the cabbage is soft.

In case you haven't noticed, the sweet and sour combination of some sweetener and red wine vinegar with the balancing notes of garlic and black pepper is one of my favorite flavor combinations. It turns regular sautéed cabbage into something special!

note

Feel free to use more oil for a Healthy Fats meal.

cabbage, carrot & onion stir-fry

LOW CARB/LOW FAT | SERVES 3

1 teaspoon refined coconut oil

4-5 cups sliced cabbage

½ med. onion (sliced)

1 sm. carrot (shaved into ribbons with
   a vegetable peeler)

1 tablespoon rice vinegar

⅜ teaspoon salt (or more, to taste)

¼ teaspoon each dill weed, garlic powder,
   black pepper

Heat the oil in a skillet, then add the rest of the ingredients and stir. Cover and cook until the cabbage is tender, stirring occasionally.

garlic butter mushrooms

FOUNDATION FATS | SERVES 2

8 oz. fresh mushrooms

2 lg. garlic cloves (minced)

1 tablespoon butter

Dill weed, parsley flakes, salt, black pepper
(to taste)

Leave the mushrooms whole if small; halve
or quarter if large. Sauté the mushrooms and
garlic in the butter until the mushrooms are
tender. Season with dill weed, parsley flakes,
salt, and pepper while sautéing. Enjoy!

These delicious fresh mushrooms make the
perfect special romantic side dish! Well, garlic
aside.

sour cream & chive smashed caulitoes

HEALTHY FATS | SERVES 4-5

2 lb. fresh cauliflower florets

¼ cup sour cream
1 tablespoon salted butter
2 teaspoons chives
½ teaspoon each garlic powder, salt
¼ teaspoon black pepper

Steam the cauliflower in an inch of water in a covered saucepan until tender. Drain very well in a colander and press the liquid out.

Return the cauliflower to the saucepan and add the second set of ingredients. Mash with an immersion blender or hand mixer. Reheat if desired before serving.

"You would eat that at a restaurant!" – Dr. Ryan

note

To make the best mashed cauliflower, use fresh cauliflower, steam it instead of boiling it, drain it extremely well, and use an immersion blender or hand mixer to mash it. These let you take more control of the texture than a regular blender does so you can stop mixing before you end up with baby food.

southwest cauliflower

FOUNDATION FATS | SERVES 4-5

1 med. head cauliflower
   (chopped into bite-sized pieces)
2 tablespoons butter or bacon grease
Chili powder, cumin, dill weed,
   garlic salt (to taste)

Sauté the cauliflower in the butter in an uncovered skillet until the cauliflower starts to soften. Season, then cover and continue to cook until tender. (You could add some shredded cheese on top to melt for a regular Healthy Fats recipe.)

fancy sautéed greens

HEALTHY FATS I SERVES 2-3

1 tablespoon salted butter

6 cups chopped fresh greens of choice

1 tablespoon balsamic vinegar

½ teaspoon salt (or more, to taste)

¼ teaspoon THM Super Sweet Blend

¼ teaspoon each garlic powder, black pepper

Melt the butter in a skillet on the stovetop, then add the greens and other ingredients. Cover and cook until tender, stirring occasionally. Cook time will depend on the type of greens you use.

note

I used collard greens, but mustard or turnip greens would probably work better because they don't seem to take quite as long to soften. If none of the above are options where you live, try kale. I recommend not using tough stems in this recipe since they aren't being stewed and won't break down as much.

slow-cooked ham & collards

HEALTHY FATS | SERVES 4

Ham bone (with some scraps still
   attached) from butt portion ham
2 cups water
10 cups chopped fresh collard greens
1 med. onion (chopped)
4 lg. garlic cloves (minced)
2 tablespoons apple cider vinegar
½ teaspoon black pepper

1 teaspoon Tony Chachere's Creole Seasoning
½ teaspoon THM Super Sweet Blend

Add the first section of ingredients to a slow cooker (4 quarts or larger). Cook on High for 5 hours. Remove the ham bone from the slow cooker and pick the meat off. Discard the bone, add the meat to the slow cooker, and season with Tony's and Super Sweet Blend. Taste and add more Tony's if you want it saltier. Cook another 10 minutes to let the sweetener mellow out a bit, then serve.

I used this as a side dish, but you could add some chunks of leftover ham to make a main dish out of it. Serve with the Sour Cream Cornbread on page 167 of *Necessary Food* to soak up the juice!

note

• You could add more greens and seasonings per ham bone, but this was all that would fit in my 4-quart slow cooker.
• I like to use collards in this recipe because they hold up better to long cook times than some other greens, but you could try turnip greens, mustard greens, or kale. I use the stems and all.

As newborn babes, desire the sincere milk of the word, that ye may grow thereby. 1 PETER 2:2

creamy roasted eggplant

10 cups chopped eggplant
(approx. 2 med. eggplants)
⅓ cup mayonnaise
Dill weed, garlic powder, parsley flakes,
smoked paprika, salt, black pepper (to taste)

Toss the chopped eggplant with the mayo to coat. Spread it out onto a cookie sheet, season generously with the seasonings listed, and roast at 425° for 40 minutes.

Busting myths about underappreciated veggies one at a time – first Brussels sprouts, now eggplant! Roasting is a game changer.

note

• I didn't peel my eggplants, but you can if you like. The skins on large eggplants can be tough and a little bitter, so you may wish to peel them with a vegetable peeler. Honestly, I think it's easier to just bite the flesh out of the skins after roasting than peeling them beforehand. Smaller eggplants tend to be more tender with a better flavor.

• Not a fan of eggplant? You have to try it at least once, but if you want to substitute other non-starchy veggies (mushrooms, yellow squash, zucchini, okra, green beans) into this recipe, be my guest! Adjust the roasting time if necessary.

roasted okra

Fresh okra (washed, stems removed,
 sliced in half lengthwise)
Cooking spray of choice
 (coconut oil spray is ideal)
Garlic salt

Spread the sliced okra on a baking sheet and spray lightly with cooking spray. Season with garlic salt and bake at 450° until tender and browning, about 25-30 minutes. Flip once during baking.

CURRY ROASTED OKRA
Season generously with curry powder, garlic salt, and red pepper.

CREOLE ROASTED OKRA
Season generously with Tony Chachere's Creole Seasoning.

We eat this like candy! Roasting really helps cut the slime. I've only ever tried this with fresh okra, but frozen would probably work if thawed and drained well. (Patting it dry would be a good idea too.) You may not need to bake frozen okra as long since most frozen okra has been blanched before freezing.

note

• Instead of the cooking spray, you can melt some refined coconut oil or butter, then toss the okra in it to coat. Keep the added fat to a teaspoon or less per serving to stay in Low Carb/Low Fat mode. (Any more than this puts you into a Healthy Fats setting, which is just fine.)

• I vary baking times and temperatures according to what else I have in the oven. If I'm baking a casserole at 350°, I may bake the okra at that temperature as well for 20-30 minutes, then finish it off at a higher heat for 10 minutes or so until I get the crispiness I want. It ain't rocket science, folks.

roasted teriyaki broccoli

2 lb. frozen broccoli florets

¼ cup reduced-sodium soy sauce
2 tablespoons refined coconut oil
1 teaspoon THM Super Sweet Blend
1 teaspoon molasses

Garlic salt

Spread the frozen broccoli on a sheet pan. Heat the second section of ingredients together until the coconut oil is melted, then pour the mixture over the broccoli and stir quickly to coat before the coconut oil completely solidifies. Sprinkle with garlic salt and bake at 450° for about 25 minutes or until tender (do not stir).

This tastes like a high-quality version of a mall food court's Oriental restaurant. My mom loved it.

note

Thawing the frozen broccoli, then patting it dry before coating with the sauce would probably yield a drier roasted result, but I don't like to take the extra step. If you do this, you may not need to bake as long.

seasoned quinoa

3 cups water

1½ cups uncooked quinoa

2 springs fresh cilantro (chopped)

2 teaspoons dried minced onion

2 teaspoons chicken bouillon

Salt & pepper (if needed)

Rinse and drain the quinoa to remove any bitter coating.

Bring all the ingredients to a boil, then simmer (covered) for 15 minutes. Turn the heat off and leave the pan on the burner for 5 more minutes. Fluff the quinoa with a fork and serve.

I like to serve this quinoa with the Creamy Chicken Gravy on page 107.

note

Instead of the chicken bouillon and water, you could use 3 cups of low-fat chicken broth. If you use unseasoned chicken broth, be sure to add salt and pepper to the quinoa. If you use chicken bouillon this additional step may not be needed. You could try using different kinds of low-fat broth to change things up, if you like!

barbecue rice

4 cups cooked brown rice (unseasoned)

¾ cup no-sugar-added ketchup

1½ teaspoons chili powder

1 teaspoon each garlic powder, paprika

1 teaspoon THM Super Sweet Blend
   (or more, to taste)

¾ teaspoon salt

¾ teaspoon liquid smoke

Stir all the ingredients together until mixed well and heat in a covered saucepan. Taste and add more seasoning if desired.

cilantro lime rice

HEALTHY CARBS | SERVES 8

4 cups water
2 cups uncooked brown rice

⅓ cup fresh cilantro (chopped)
Juice of 1 med. fresh lime
1½ teaspoons salt (or more, to taste)
1 teaspoon onion powder
½ teaspoon THM Super Sweet Blend
½ teaspoon black pepper (scant)

Bring the water to a boil in a saucepan on the stove. Add the rice, cover, return to a boil, then reduce the heat and simmer 30 minutes or until the rice is soft. (Don't remove the lid or stir during that time. If the rice hasn't fluffed up and absorbed the water yet, cook a little longer.)

If there's a lot of water left in the kettle after the rice is soft, drain it off. I like to leave a little water in the bottom, and this water to rice ratio usually comes out about right for me. Add the second section of ingredients and fluff the rice with a fork to stir. (Stir as little as possible.) Taste and adjust as desired, then cover and leave the pan on a low burner for 10 minutes before serving. Use as a side dish or serve with the black bean recipe on page 157.

Pictured with Black Beans on page 157

note

Add some zest from the lime for a stronger lime flavor, if desired.

BROWN RICE SECRETS ▼

I love brown rice! It's so hearty and wholesome, and mine is always so soft. I do not recommend using instant brown rice; it never softens up for me. I just use regular ol' brown rice from Walmart. I put it in a saucepan with twice as much water as rice, cover it, bring it to a boil, then reduce the heat and simmer for anywhere between 30 and 50 minutes without removing the lid.

Using a glass lid is helpful so you can see the rice. Once it has obviously puffed up and absorbed the liquid, it's ready! Sometimes I take it off the heat and leave the lid on to steam it for another 5 minutes. Stir brown rice as little as possible after cooking to keep it nice and fluffy, not sticky. (Obviously adding all the yummy stuff to the brown rice recipes in this section and stirring them kind of defeats that purpose, but just stir as little as possible.)

sunshine rice

HEALTHY CARBS | SERVES 4

3 cups cooked brown rice (unseasoned)

1 sm. carrot (peeled and grated or shaved
   into ribbons with a vegetable peeler)

⅓ cup cranberries (chopped)

¼ cup water

2 tablespoons lemon juice

1 teaspoon each garlic powder, parsley flakes,
   turmeric, salt

½ teaspoon ground coriander, ginger

¼ teaspoon THM Super Sweet Blend

¼ teaspoon black pepper

Combine the ingredients in a skillet and bring it up to medium-high heat. Cover, reduce heat to low, and cook for 20 minutes to soften the vegetables and let the flavors develop.

"You make foods that are just bursting with flavor!"
– Dr. Ryan

sweet & sour rice

3 cups water

1½ cups uncooked brown rice

1 cup Pineapple Sweet & Sour Sauce (page 479)

½ teaspoon salt (slightly rounded)

Bring the water and rice to a boil, cover, turn the heat down, and simmer for 30-40 minutes or until the water has been absorbed. (Or just start with 3 cups cooked brown rice.) Add the sauce and salt, stir, and leave the rice on Low for 5-10 minutes to let the flavors meld into the rice. Serve.

This subtly sweet and sour rice uses my Pineapple Sweet & Sour Sauce for a side dish that is as easy as cook-some-rice, dump-sauce-in, stir, eat.

crunchy rice

3 cups leftover brown rice
Curry powder, garlic powder, salt, black pepper
Shredded cheese of choice (for topping)

Spread the rice out in a thin layer on a cookie sheet and season with the spices and herbs of your choice. Roast at 450° for about 25 minutes or until the rice is heated through and getting a little crunchy on both top and bottom. (We're not looking for break-your-teeth crunchy.) Top with a light sprinkling of your favorite cheese (you don't want to add too much fat); finely-shredded white queso cheese melts well. Return the pan to the oven to melt the cheese, then serve.

This is a great way to repurpose leftover rice! Enjoy it on its own or smother with some curry or your favorite sauce.

note

• Use unseasoned leftover brown rice, not fresh rice, for the most crunchy texture.
• Feel free to mix up the seasonings. Go a Mexican route with chili powder, cumin, onion powder, and smoked paprika; or do a garlic herb version.

mexican fried rice

2½ cups leftover brown rice (unseasoned)

1 tablespoon masa flour

¾ teaspoon each cumin, onion powder

½ teaspoon each chili powder, salt

¼ teaspoon each smoked paprika, black pepper

Shredded white queso cheese (for topping)

Spray a nonstick skillet with cooking spray. Add the rice and seasonings and stir, then fry undisturbed for awhile to heat and crisp up the bottom of the rice a bit. When everything is hot and the rice is slightly crunchy on the bottom, top with a sprinkling of queso cheese (just a little, since you're in Healthy Carbs mode) to melt. Serve when the cheese has melted.

Something about this combination of flavors reminds me of the rice that is usually served as a side at Mexican restaurants. The masa flour adds to the effect, so I definitely recommend adding it if you have it.

note

I like to use leftover cold brown rice instead of freshly cooked brown rice for a crunchier texture.

slow cooker pinto beans

3½ cups low-fat chicken broth

2 cups dry pinto beans (soaked in water overnight, drained)

1 med. onion (chopped)

½ cup fresh cilantro (chopped)

6 lg. garlic cloves (minced)

1½ teaspoons each cumin, smoked paprika

1 teaspoon black pepper

1 tablespoon apple cider vinegar

Salt (to taste)

Stir the first section of ingredients together in a slow cooker. (I used a 4-quart slow cooker.) Cook on High for 4 hours or until the beans are mostly soft. Add the vinegar and salt to taste and cook for 2 more hours on Low until the beans are completely tender and falling apart.

You can eat these beans on their own as a protein source, as a side dish, or as part of a burrito bowl!

REFRIED BEANS ▼

Turn this recipe into refried beans by blending them to the desired consistency with an immersion blender! If the refried beans are too runny for your taste, leave the slow cooker lid open a crack and cook the beans on High to reduce the liquid until the desired consistency is reached.

Without prompting, Ryan said these pinto beans remind him of Chipotle. I'll take that as a compliment! These beans make a delicious side dish, but I also love to use them in the Burrito Bowls on page 169. Don't forget to soak the dry pinto beans overnight before making this recipe.

note

• When cooking beans or lentils, don't add salt or acid until the beans or lentils are soft.

• Want beans and cornbread? Serve these beans over either of the cornbread recipes on pages 167-168 of *Necessary Food*!

barbecue baked bean medley

HEALTHY CARBS | YIELDS 4 QUARTS

1 (24 oz.) bag frozen baby lima beans

1 (12 oz.) bag frozen cut green beans

1 (15.5 oz.) can cannellini beans
   (rinsed and drained)

1 (15 oz.) can dark red kidney beans
   (rinsed and drained)

1 (6 oz.) can tomato paste

3 cups low-fat chicken broth

1 lg. onion (chopped)

2 tablespoons yellow mustard

2 tablespoons Worcestershire sauce

1 tablespoon THM Super Sweet Blend
   (or more, to taste)

2 teaspoons each chili powder, garlic powder

2 teaspoons molasses

1 teaspoon black pepper

3 tablespoons apple cider vinegar
Salt (to taste)

Stir the fist section of ingredients together in a slow cooker (4 quarts or larger). Cook on High for 3 hours or until hot and starting to bubble. Add the apple cider vinegar and salt to taste, then cook on Low for 3-4 hours or until tender but not mushy, stirring occasionally.

Leftovers make great lunches! You may need to add more water when reheating if you want the beans to be saucier.

This baked bean medley with its barbecue-ish sauce will be a hit at potlucks and picnics! If you have some spice lovers in the group, feel free to add some chopped jalapeños.

note

Leftover beans and lentils tend to thicken when refrigerated, so feel free to add more liquid when reheating to make them the consistency you like.

adobo baked beans

2 cups dry pinto beans (soaked in
   water overnight, drained)
1½ cups Bri's Adobo Sauce (page 477)
1½ cups low-fat chicken broth

½ cup fresh cilantro (chopped)
1 lg. jalapeño (seeds removed, chopped)
1 tablespoon lime juice
Salt (to taste)

Drain the pinto beans after soaking them overnight and add them to a slow cooker with the adobo sauce and chicken broth. (I used a 4-quart slow cooker.) Cook on High for 5½ hours or until the beans are soft.

Add the cilantro, jalapeño, lime juice, and salt. If the beans are thicker than you like, feel free to add more chicken broth or water. Cook on High for 30 more minutes to let the new additions soften (but not lose their freshness), then serve.

Having a batch of my adobo sauce on hand makes this recipe come together in a jiffy! I'm in love with that deep, rich sauce, and the fresh components added to this recipe not long before serving really make these baked beans pop. Don't forget to soak the dry pinto beans overnight before making this recipe.

note

• Feel free to leave the seeds in the jalapeño for more spice.
• Leftovers will thicken up after refrigeration, so feel free to add more liquid when reheating.
• Beans or lentils are a terrific make-ahead meal or lunch. If you have a busy schedule, make a big batch in the slow cooker and keep them in the fridge. I like to put them in a bowl and add all kinds of cool low-fat toppings.

comforting slow cooker lentils

HEALTHY CARBS | SERVES 6-8 (OR 4 AS A MAIN DISH)

1 lb. dry lentils (rinsed, drained)

3 cups low-fat chicken broth

2 cups water

1 med. onion (chopped)

2 teaspoons minced garlic

1 teaspoon each cumin, turmeric

½ teaspoon black pepper

½ cup fresh cilantro (chopped)

Salt (to taste)

Stir the first set of ingredients together in a slow cooker. (I used a 4-quart slow cooker.) Cook on High for 3 hours or until the lentils are mostly soft. Add the cilantro and salt to taste, stir, and cook on Keep Warm for another hour to let the flavors meld and allow the lentils to break down a bit. Serve.

This easy lentil recipe is very filling and can be used as a main dish or a side! (The same goes for the bean recipes in this section.) Lentils are high in both fiber and protein, and leftovers will make a great lunch (hot or cold!).

note

I don't specify the salt quantities in recipes like this because the amount of salt needed will vary according to how salty your chicken broth is. You'll need more salt if using an unsalted homemade broth versus making broth using chicken bouillon.

baked skillet dressing

CORNBREAD BASE

1¼ cups Briana's Baking Mix

⅓ cup masa flour

1 teaspoon THM Super Sweet Blend

1 teaspoon baking powder

½ teaspoon salt

¼ teaspoon turmeric (for color)

4 eggs

½ cup unsweetened almond milk

½ cup water

FOR THE DRESSING

4 tablespoons salted butter

1 med. onion (diced)

1 cup chopped celery

⅔ cup chopped cranberries

1 teaspoon THM Super Sweet Blend

1 teaspoon ground sage

½ teaspoon each oregano, thyme, black pepper

¼ teaspoon salt

⅔ cup chopped pecans

½ cup chicken broth (mine was salted)

1 egg

First, make the cornbread. Whisk the dry ingredients, then add the wet ingredients and mix well. Spread into a greased 9"x13" pan and bake at 350° for 22-24 minutes or until a toothpick inserted into the center comes out cleanly. Refrigerate to cool and set up completely, preferably overnight, before making the dressing.

When you're ready to make the dressing, cut the bread into small cubes. Melt the butter in a 12" cast iron skillet. Sauté the onion, celery, and cranberries *al dente*, adding the seasonings while they are cooking.

Add the cubed bread and pecans and stir gently to combine everything.

Whisk the chicken broth and egg together and pour over the dressing. Stir gently to coat. Transfer the cast iron skillet to the oven and bake (uncovered) at 350° until the dressing is crusty on top and the excess moisture has evaporated - about 25 minutes.

Although the fig tree shall not blossom, neither shall fruit be in the vines; the labour of the olive shall fail, and the fields shall yield no meat; the flock shall be cut off from the fold, and there shall be no herd in the stalls: Yet I will rejoice in the Lord, I WILL JOY IN THE GOD OF MY SALVATION.

HABAKKUK 3:17-18

There seem to be about as many variations of stuffing and dressing as there are people in this world! I've taken my favorite elements and made my own version. Feel free to tweak it to make it your own.

note

• Masa flour is a carb source, but in this amount it stays within Healthy Fats guidelines.

• I doubt this dressing would hold up well in a turkey.

• Pre-cooked ground sausage would be a great addition and could even turn this into a main dish!

• Don't have cast iron? Fry the dressing in a regular skillet on the stove (or an electric skillet), then transfer to a baking dish for the oven. You may need to bake longer.

• Feel free to try substituting your own favorite low-carb bread recipe (5-6 cups of cubed bread). For a combination of carbs and fats, sprouted bread cubes could be used instead, but you may need more broth because the bread will be drier.

• This cornbread recipe is meant to be used in the dressing, not baked and eaten on its own. It's kind of bland on its own, but it holds up well in this dressing. I made it dense on purpose.

cheesy party "potatoes"

HEALTHY FATS I SERVES 9

4 cups peeled, grated turnip (gently packed)
1 lb. frozen cauliflower florets (thawed)
Salt

1½ cups grated cheddar cheese
1 cup cottage cheese
1 tablespoon salted butter (softened)
1 lg. garlic clove (peeled)
2 teaspoons chicken bouillon
1 teaspoon each onion powder, parsley flakes
½ teaspoon black pepper
¼ teaspoon THM Super Sweet Blend
⅛ teaspoon turmeric (for color)

3 tablespoons oat fiber

½ cup grated cheddar cheese
Parsley flakes (for garnish)

Spread the grated turnip and cauliflower out on a baking sheet. Sprinkle lightly with salt and roast at 450° for 20 minutes. Turn the oven temperature down to 350° to prepare for baking the casserole.

While the veggies are baking, make the cheese mixture. Add the second section of ingredients to a blender and blend to a thick paste. (The chicken bouillon adds enough salt that I didn't need to add extra.)

Put the turnips and cauliflower in a mixing bowl and add the oat fiber. Use a pastry cutter to chop up the cauliflower and distribute the oat fiber at the same time. Add the cheese mixture and mix everything up with a spatula. Spread the mixture into a greased 8"x8" baking dish and top with the additional cheese and parsley flakes. Bake (uncovered) at 350° for 30-40 minutes until hot and bubbly and the veggies are tender.

While testing for this recipe, I made (and ate) many valiant attempts that ranged from super disgusting to almost palatable. The final recipe is yummy and garlicky with a surprising combination of non-starchy veggies that provide a taste and texture closer to hashbrown potatoes than anything I've tried before! They are NOT potatoes and therefore will not taste exactly like potatoes, but they do make a delicious and nutritious cheesy side dish that would be the perfect addition to your Thanksgiving or Christmas dinner!

I chose a combination of cauliflower and turnip for my favorite taste and texture, but you could try substituting grated jicama or radish for the turnip if you're up to a little experimenting, or even just use all cauliflower. Various vegetables may need longer baking times to soften up (especially jicama!). The texture may vary.

note

I used about 3 small turnips. Use SMALL turnips! Large turnips have a very strong flavor! And do not omit the peeling step!

salads

festive broccoli salad

HEALTHY FATS | SERVES 6-8

6 cups chopped fresh broccoli florets

1 cup chopped cranberries

⅔ cup chopped pecans

1 sm. onion (chopped)

⅔ cup mayonnaise

⅔ cup sour cream

2 tablespoons balsamic vinegar

2 teaspoons THM Super Sweet Blend

1 teaspoon salt

½ teaspoon each garlic powder, black pepper

Mix the ingredients together and serve! The textures are best the day of making it, but it keeps for a few days in the fridge. (It just gets softer.)

The cranberries give this salad a pinkish hue, hence the name. I love the unique combination of flavors – and the crunch of the pecans!

For wherein shall it be known here
that I and thy people have found grace in thy sight?
is it not in that thou goest with us? So shall we be
separated, I and thy people, from all the people that
are upon the face of the earth. And the Lord said unto
Moses, I will do this thing also that thou hast spoken:
FOR THOU HAST FOUND GRACE IN MY
SIGHT, AND I KNOW THEE BY NAME.
EXODUS 33:16-17

ranch cucumber salad

HEALTHY FATS | SERVES 2-3

3 cups sliced cucumber

¼ cup mayonnaise

½ teaspoon parsley flakes

¼ teaspoon each dill weed, onion powder, salt, black pepper

Mix the ingredients together. Taste and add more salt if needed. If you want to get fancy, add some sliced onion and chopped tomatoes. This salad is best fresh.

This is my new favorite cucumber salad. The end.

note

You could try using reduced-fat sour cream in place of the mayonnaise for a LC/LF version, but I'm partial to mayo.

three bean salad

1 (15.5 oz.) can cannellini beans

1 (15 oz.) can dark red kidney beans

1 (14.5 oz.) can cut green beans

1 med. onion (sliced)

1 cup water

¾ cup apple cider vinegar

¼ cup lime juice

1 tablespoon THM Super Sweet Blend

1¼ teaspoons salt

1 teaspoon each garlic powder, black pepper

Rinse and drain the beans. Set aside.

In a saucepan, bring the second set of ingredients to a boil. (I used a 2-quart saucepan so the liquid nearly covered the beans.) Cook until the onion starts to get translucent (but retains its crunch). Add the beans and stir once. Bring to a boil again, then cover, remove from the heat, and steep 10 minutes. Transfer to a new container to stop the cooking process. You don't want to overcook or stir too much so the beans stay firm. Chill for several hours or overnight before serving to let the sweetness mellow out. Serve with a slotted spoon so people don't end up with a plateful of pickling liquid. This bean salad keeps well in the fridge for a few days.

This bean salad is the perfect picnic food! It reminds me of a chow-chow relish and tastes like a sweet and sour pickle.

picnic radishto salad

2 (16 oz.) pkgs. radishes (washed, trimmed)

4 hardboiled eggs (chopped)
½ cup + 2 tablespoons mayonnaise
½ cup chopped celery
2 tablespoons yellow mustard
1 tablespoon apple cider vinegar
¾ teaspoon salt (or more, to taste)
½ teaspoon onion powder
¼ teaspoon THM Super Sweet Blend
    (or more, to taste)
¼ teaspoon each dill weed, black pepper

Smoked paprika (for garnish)

Boil the radishes until tender and easily pierced with a fork with no resistance. (Submerging the radishes in water to boil instead of just steaming them helps remove more red color faster, at least that's my hypothesis.) Drain the radishes very well in a colander. Mash the radishes in the colander with a potato masher to break them open and release more liquid. Use a paper towel to press/blot as much liquid out as possible. Transfer the radishes to a mixing bowl.

Add the rest of the ingredients to the radishes and stir to combine. Smash with a potato masher again to make the salad your desired consistency. (The radishes lend themselves more to a smashed "potato" salad than a chunky one. When smashed, they're less noticeable as radishes.) Taste and add a little more salt and/or sweetener if desired to round out the flavors. Refrigerate the salad overnight before serving for best flavor. Garnish with smoked paprika before serving.

I'm not one to call things what they're not, so I wouldn't call this a potato salad, but it definitely has the flavors of potato salad and it tastes amazing! Cooking the radishes makes them lose their bite, and refrigerating the salad overnight before serving lets them take on the other flavors in the salad.

pasta salad

1 (13.25 oz.) box dry Dreamfields
Penne Rigate pasta

2 cups chopped English cucumber
1 cup chopped Roma tomato or
halved cherry tomatoes
1 lg. colorful bell pepper (chopped)
1 sm. onion (chopped)
1 (8 oz.) block mozzarella cheese (cubed)
1 (6 oz.) can black olives (drained,
sliced in half if desired)
½ cup chopped turkey pepperoni

DRESSING
¾ cup olive oil
⅓ cup red wine vinegar
2 teaspoons Italian seasoning
1½ teaspoons salt (or more, to taste)
1½ teaspoons garlic powder
½ teaspoon THM Super Sweet Blend
½ teaspoon black pepper

This recipe makes a big bowl of pasta salad for a social gathering. It got great reviews at our church fellowship meal!

Cook the pasta *al dente* according to package directions. Rinse in cold water to stop the cooking process and drain well.

In a large bowl, combine the pasta with the second set of ingredients.

Whisk the dressing ingredients and toss the dressing with the pasta salad. Taste and add more salt if needed. Refrigerate until serving. The pasta salad keeps well, so you can make it a day ahead if you like.

note

See page 9 for a note on Dreamfields pasta. All the veggies in this pasta salad stretch the noodles so you're not eating so many, but if you don't want to use Dreamfields at all you could probably just add a lot more chopped veggies for a fresh vegetable salad with all the flavors of a pasta salad.

sophisticated coleslaw

6 cups shredded cabbage

⅓ cup + 1 tablespoons mayonnaise

⅓ cup sour cream

2-3 tablespoons red wine vinegar

1 teaspoon THM Super Sweet Blend
  (or more, to taste)

½ teaspoon each salt, black pepper

½ teaspoon maple extract

¼ teaspoon garlic powder

Mix the ingredients together, then taste and adjust as desired. Feel free to add more mayo or sour cream if it seems too dry, and add more Super Sweet Blend if you like a sweeter coleslaw. Refrigerate the coleslaw for 15 minutes before serving to let the flavors mellow out.

This coleslaw is unique, but not overwhelmingly so. I love the combination of red wine vinegar, some sweetener, garlic, black pepper, and a touch of maple.

mexican coleslaw

10 cups shredded cabbage

½ cup diced Roma tomato

DRESSING

2 cups low-fat sour cream or Greek yogurt

⅓ cup fresh cilantro (chopped)

3-4 tablespoons lime juice

1½ teaspoons each cumin, onion powder,
  black pepper

1 teaspoon salt (or more, to taste)

1 teaspoon chili powder

½ teaspoon THM Super Sweet Blend

Whisk the dressing ingredients together. Stir the cabbage, chopped tomato, dressing, and any additions together to combine. Taste and add more salt and/or sweetener if desired. Refrigerate for 15 minutes before serving (or longer) to let the flavors develop. The coleslaw is best the day you mix it together, but you could make the dressing a few days in advance and assemble it the day of, if you like.

LOW CARB/LOW FAT OPTIONS

Add chopped onion, a few sliced black olives, and/or diced jalapeño.

HEALTHY FATS OPTION

Use mayonnaise for part of the sour cream for a richer coleslaw. (The LC/LF options are fair game too.)

HEALTHY CARBS OPTIONS

Add a small amount of corn and/or rinsed and drained canned black beans. (The LC/LF options are fair game too.)

As written, this easy coleslaw is low in both carbs and fats. You can keep it simple, or you can make use of the optional add-ins.

cucumber raita

HEALTHY CARBS | SERVES 5

3 cups chopped English cucumber
½ cup chopped Roma tomato
½ teaspoon salt

2 cups plain low-fat yogurt
½ teaspoon mint
¼ teaspoon THM Super Sweet Blend
⅛ teaspoon ground coriander
Dash each cayenne pepper, onion powder, salt

Toss the cucumber, tomato, and salt together in a bowl and refrigerate for 30 minutes.

Drain any accumulated liquid and add the second set of ingredients to the bowl. Stir, then taste and adjust as desired. Refrigerate for 15 minutes before serving to let the flavors mellow out. The raita is best the day it's made.

Raita is a traditional Indian refresher and palate cleanser that helps cool down the heat of a spicy curry.

note

• Greek yogurt would be too thick for this recipe.
• Don't omit the mint! It adds a lot to this raita.

cantaloupe raita

6 cups chopped cantaloupe

2½ cups plain low-fat yogurt

2 teaspoons THM Super Sweet Blend

1 teaspoon each mint, poppy seeds

1 teaspoon vanilla extract

¼ teaspoon cinnamon

⅛ teaspoon ground cardamom

⅛ teaspoon salt (scant)

Mix the ingredients together, then taste and adjust if desired. Refrigerate for 15 minutes before serving to let the flavors mellow out. The raita keeps for a few days; stir before eating.

This one is a bit unique – is cantaloupe raita even a thing? I dunno, but I just thought it sounded good. Call it cantaloupe salad if you will. Since I was going more for raita than a fruit salad, this recipe isn't very sweet, but you can change that if you want.

note

Greek yogurt would be too thick for this recipe.

faux tabbouleh

5 cups finely-chopped fresh turnip greens

3½ cups cooked quinoa (cold)

1 cup chopped Roma tomato

⅓ cup lemon juice

1½ tablespoons olive oil

1 tablespoon fresh chopped dill weed

2 teaspoons each onion powder,
   parsley flakes

1½ teaspoons each mint, salt, black pepper

Mix the ingredients together, then taste and adjust as desired. Add a little more lemon juice if it's too dry or you want a stronger citrus flavor. The textures are best fresh, but the salad keeps well for a few days. (It just gets softer.)

note

• You can find large bunches of turnip greens in the produce section of your local grocery store, at least I've been able to in South Carolina and Louisiana. If you live up north, you may need to get creative. Maybe try kale?

• I cooked 1 cup of uncooked quinoa according to package directions for this amount of cooked quinoa.

• The olive oil adds 3.5 grams fat per serving (6 servings).

• If you don't have fresh dill, use 1 teaspoon dried dill in its place.

This salad, created with ingredients I had on hand, is so fresh and delicious! Even if it's lacking fresh parsley and couscous, it has similar textures and flavors to tabbouleh. If you think it's too far removed from the original to even be called a faux version, call it "Greens & Quinoa Salad" and enjoy it for what it is.

strawberry & balsamic chicken salad

HEALTHY FATS I SERVES 2-3

2 cups shredded cooked chicken breast

½ cup chopped fresh strawberries

⅓ cup chopped celery

⅓ cup chopped pecans

¼ cup + 2 tablespoons reduced-fat sour cream

¼ c mayonnaise

1½ tablespoons balsamic vinegar

½ teaspoon onion powder

¼ teaspoon each salt, black pepper

Mix the ingredients together and serve. I enjoy it in half a low-carb pita, on salad, or with sliced cucumbers or Ryvita or Wasa crackers (watch the carbs on those, of course). The chicken salad is freshest and crunchiest the day you make it, but it's definitely still edible for a day or two. (The strawberries get softer.)

The mixture of savory ingredients with the crunch of celery and pecans and the natural sweetness of fresh strawberries is a winning combination! I put some of this in Ryan's lunch with (unhealthy) crackers one day and he enjoyed it so much that he texted me about it!

note

You may need to reduce or omit the salt if using salty canned chicken breast.

mexican chicken salad

2 cups chopped cooked chicken breast
1 (16 oz.) can fat-free refried beans
½ cup chopped celery
½ cup fresh cilantro (chopped)
½ cup salsa of choice

Mix the ingredients together, then taste and add more seasonings if desired. Canned refried beans are usually already seasoned so you don't *have* to add anything else, but I think it's fun to add a dash of all my favorite spices to amp up the flavor. I added a squirt of sriracha, a dash of lime juice, some cumin, smoked paprika, and garlic powder. Add salt and pepper if you think the chicken salad needs it, and feel free to add cayenne or hot sauce for heat. You could also add a small amount of corn or some chopped jalapeño. Ryan tasted it and said it needed 2 teaspoons of chili powder. While 2 teaspoons would likely be overkill, I did sprinkle some chili powder in per his suggestion – and he was right. It was a good addition.

I ate this chicken salad in a low-carb wrap with some Mexican Fried Rice (page 209), reduced-fat sour cream, and lettuce. You could also serve it with Wasa or Ryvita crackers, over a salad, rolled up in big lettuce leaves, or with colorful peppers.

We're reinventing the chicken salad! I wanted to provide a dairy-free chicken salad recipe in this book, and thankfully refried beans make the perfect binder for a Mexican-themed chicken salad. You can keep it simple or make it as complicated as you want.

asian slaw & lettuce wraps

1 lb. fresh Brussels sprouts

2 cups shredded cooked chicken breast

1 (8 oz.) can water chestnuts (drained)

1 (15 oz.) can mandarin oranges
   (rinsed well and drained)

¼ cup reduced-sodium soy sauce

3 tablespoons rice vinegar

1½ teaspoons THM Super Sweet Blend

1 teaspoon salt

¾ teaspoon garlic powder

½ teaspoon ginger

Cayenne pepper (to taste)

Lettuce leaves (for serving)

Process the Brussels sprouts in a food processor to your desired texture. A fine slaw works well in lettuce wraps, but a coarser slaw may work better on its own. Add the chicken and water chestnuts and process again. Transfer the mixture to a mixing bowl. After rinsing and draining the mandarin oranges, mash them into small pieces with your fingers and add to the slaw. Add the rest of the ingredients, stir, taste, and adjust as needed. Let the slaw rest in the fridge for 15 minutes before serving to let the flavors develop. Serve in lettuce leaves as lettuce wraps, or enjoy on its own. The slaw is best the day you make it, but it's still good in the next day or two. (It just gets softer, like coleslaw.)

This slaw has a high veggie to chicken ratio, but feel free to adjust that if you're intending to use this for lunches and want more protein to keep you full. This recipe does include some Healthy Carbs ingredients, but you'll need to add more of a carb source to create a true HC meal.

note

• I haven't been able to find mandarin oranges canned in juice or water, so the next best option is the kind canned in Splenda. I get these and rinse very well before using them in this recipe.

• The slaw in these lettuce wraps is moist enough that they don't really need a sauce, but feel free to drizzle with additional soy sauce, sriracha, or the Pineapple Sweet & Sour Sauce from page 479.

classic egg salad

HEALTHY FATS | SERVES 6

12 hardboiled eggs

1 cup chopped celery

½ med. onion (chopped)

1 cup mayonnaise

½ cup reduced-fat sour cream or Greek yogurt

2 tablespoons yellow mustard

2-3 teaspoons lemon juice

¼ teaspoon each dill weed, smoked paprika,
  salt, black pepper

Crumble the eggs with a potato masher. Add the rest of the ingredients and mix together well. Everything will mash together – just how I like it. The egg salad keeps for a few days in the refrigerator. Serve it on low-carb tortillas or pitas, on sliced tomatoes, or in lettuce leaves.

Serve this egg salad on sliced tomatoes for a cute appetizer!

dilly ham salad

½ cup cubed cooked ham

½ cup chopped cucumber

½ cup Greek yogurt

2 tablespoons mayonnaise

1 tablespoon chopped fresh dill weed

Onion powder and THM Super
  Sweet Blend (to taste)

Salt (if needed)

1 Joseph's pita (halved)

Leaf lettuce

Stir the ham, cucumber, Greek yogurt, mayo, and dill together, then add onion powder and Super Sweet Blend to taste. (Don't skimp!) Add a sprinkle of salt as well if needed. Serve the ham salad in Joseph's pita halves with leaf lettuce.

I like to serve this ham salad in Joseph's pita halves with leaf lettuce. The recipe makes two sandwiches, but if you're really hungry, just go ahead and eat the whole recipe. It's legal. In that case, I recommend eating part of the salad in half a pita, then finishing off the salad with a spoon so you don't overdo the carbs (since both the pita and the Greek yogurt contribute a few carbs). Not feeling in a sandwich mood? Enjoy the salad on its own or over some shredded lettuce. The fresh dill in this recipe really makes the flavor, but if you don't have a good source for it, feel free to substitute another fresh herb of your choice or use ½ to 1 teaspoon of dried dill weed.

yummy salmon dip salad

LOW CARB/LOW FAT I YIELDS I QUART

1 (14.75 oz.) can wild-caught Alaskan
  salmon (drained well)
1 (8 oz.) pkg. reduced-fat cream cheese
1 cup low-fat cottage cheese
¼ cup + 2 tablespoons dill pickle
  relish (drained well)
¼ cup fresh dill weed (chopped)
½ teaspoon onion powder
Hearty dash each ground red pepper, lemon
  juice, THM Super Sweet Blend

Beat the salmon in a mixing bowl with a
hand mixer until the bones, skin, and meat
are broken down into a uniform consistency.
(Trust me on this one! You won't even know
they're there!)

Add the rest of the ingredients and beat
until smooth. There will be a little bit of
texture from the cottage cheese and pickle
relish, but that's fine. Taste and add more red
pepper, lemon juice, and Super Sweet Blend
as needed to balance the flavors; I usually
add about 3 dashes of each.

Garnish with paprika or fresh dill if desired.
Serve with vegetables and low-carb pitas
baked into chips or eat it in a low-carb pita or
over a salad. The dip keeps well in the fridge
for a few days, so you can make it ahead for
a party if you need to.

A ⅓ cup serving of this dip/salad is Low
Carb/Low Fat, but more than that is Healthy
Fats (albeit pretty light). There are about

10 grams of protein in ⅓ cup. A serving of
this salad on 2 Light Rye Wasa crackers would
make a good Low Carb/Low Fat snack.

Is it a veggie dip? Is it a salad – like a chicken salad,
but with salmon? You tell me!

note

If you don't have fresh dill you can try substituting
another fresh herb of your choice or substitute
dried dill (but it's not the same!). As a general rule
of thumb, use ⅓ as many dried herbs as the fresh
amount called for in a recipe. You may wish to start
with about 2 teaspoons of dried dill in this recipe,
then work your way up, tasting as you go.

yogurt fruit salad

2 apples of choice (cored, chopped)

1 lg. orange (peeled, chopped)

1 med. banana (sliced)

1 cup pineapple tidbits canned
in juice (drained)

1½ cups plain low-fat yogurt

2 teaspoons THM Super Sweet Blend

½ teaspoon vanilla extract

Dash salt

Toss the fruit together (the orange and pineapple juice will help keep the apple and banana from turning brown). Add the second set of ingredients and stir. Serve. The textures are best the day of, but leftovers are still good for a few days (just softer).

note

• Greek yogurt would be too thick for this recipe.

• I like to use a firm banana so it holds up well in this fruit salad.

apple salad

2½ cups chopped apples of choice
2 teaspoons lemon juice

1 cup Greek yogurt
3 tablespoons defatted peanut flour
2 tablespoons half and half
¼ teaspoon cinnamon
¼ teaspoon vanilla extract
3 doonks THM Pure Stevia Extract Powder
(or more, to taste)

Toss the chopped apple with the lemon juice.

Whisk the second section of ingredients in a separate bowl until smooth. Fold in the chopped apples and mix well to coat. Taste and add more sweetener if desired (amount may vary according to the sweetness of the apples you used). Serve immediately. This apple salad will keep for a few hours, but it's best served immediately, especially if you use apples that turn brown quickly. (The sweeter the apple, the quicker this will happen because of the high sugar content.)

note

For more texture and a little less tang, you can substitute half of the Greek yogurt with low-fat cottage cheese.

raspberry & grated apple gello salad

6 cups water

1½ cups red raspberries

2 tablespoons THM Super Sweet Blend
   (or more, to taste)

⅜ teaspoon salt

⅛ teaspoon THM Pure Stevia Extract Powder

2 tablespoons Knox gelatin

1 teaspoon raspberry extract

3 cups grated apple

3 tablespoons lemon juice

Bring the first section of ingredients to a boil in a saucepan on the stovetop. Remove from the heat and use an immersion blender to blend in the gelatin and raspberry extract. Blend until smooth, then run the mixture through a sieve to remove the seeds before pouring it into a serving bowl. Cool to room temperature. (You can put the bowl in the fridge or freezer to speed this process up, but don't let the salad gel.)

Wait to grate the apple until the gello has cooled. Toss the grated apple with the lemon juice and stir into the cooled gello. Cover and refrigerate overnight to firm up.

This refreshing gello salad is perfect for summertime! It's kid friendly, but Ryan loved it too....

note

If using beef gelatin, add 1½ teaspoons.

sparkling cherry berry gello salad

HEALTHY CARBS **|** SERVES 8-10

1 cup blueberries

1 cup cranberries

1 cup dark sweet cherries

1 cup water

¼ cup lime juice

2 tablespoons Knox gelatin

1 tablespoon + 1 teaspoon THM Super
  Sweet Blend (or more, to taste)

¼ teaspoon THM Pure Stevia Extract Powder

¼ teaspoon salt

3 cups orange-flavored sparkling water
  (not sweetened)

Bring the first set of ingredients to a boil in a saucepan. Remove from the heat and blend with an immersion blender until smooth. Add the sparkling water and stir to mix. Pour the mixture through a sieve to remove any large particles and seeds as well as the foam that will accumulate.

Pour the strained mixture into a mold or bowl and refrigerate for several hours or overnight until firm. Unmold and serve.

I love to eat this gello salad with low-fat cottage cheese for a light, refreshing snack! It's not heavy or overly carby at all (in fact, per serving it's probably more Low Carb/Low Fat than Healthy Carbs), so you can have as much as you want. As written, the recipe isn't overly sweet, so if you want a store-bought Jello sweetness, add more Super Sweet Blend or some THM Gentle Sweet. I prefer to concentrate on the fruity flavors.

note

If using beef gelatin, add 1½ teaspoons.

fancy cherry gello goblets

½ cup dark sweet cherries
½ cup water
1½ teaspoons Knox gelatin

1½ cups plain low-fat yogurt
2½ teaspoons THM Super Sweet Blend
(or more, to taste)
1 teaspoon vanilla extract

Bring the cherries and water to a boil in the microwave or on the stovetop. Remove from heat and whisk in the gelatin. Steep 2 minutes to dissolve.

Add the yogurt, Super Sweet Blend, and vanilla and blend with an immersion blender until smooth. Taste and add more sweetener if desired. Pour the mixture through a sieve to remove any large pieces of cherry skin, then pour into 2 goblets and refrigerate for several hours to set before serving.

This refreshing dessert is perfect for a date night! The gello has a silky-smooth panna cotta-esque texture.

note

• If using beef gelatin, add ⅜ teaspoon.
• I used regular yogurt, but Greek yogurt would probably work as well. It may be more tangy and make the gello thicker.
• You're welcome to try other fruits or berries in place of the cherries, but steer clear of fruits that can keep gelatin from setting, such as mango. If using berries and Greek yogurt, these gello cups would be Low Carb/Low Fat instead of Healthy Carbs.

CHOCOLATE
DREAMY • PG 261

shakes + drinks

some tips
FOR SUCCESS

These drinks and shakes are meant to be enjoyed with a meal or snack or on their own as a meal or snack – not sipped on throughout the day.

Some of these recipes call for crushed ice, which I like to use because it's easier on a blender and can be measured accurately. After I got married and moved, I didn't have an ice maker anymore, so I used ice cubes frozen in trays. If you don't have a way to make crushed ice, just eyeball the measurement with your ice cubes and adjust the amount to make the consistency you like.

I often use glucomannan to add a thick creaminess to my shakes. It promotes stable blood sugar and keeps me full longer. Brands vary in strength, so if you notice a funny texture from the glucomannan, decrease the amount and see if that helps. Glucomannan will clump upon contact with liquid, so I always add it right before blending so it doesn't have time to clump.

I like to blend shakes until they expand and get lighter in color. Protein powder, collagen, and glucomannan get creamier as they're blended, so blending longer gives you a creamier result (which is especially helpful in dairy-free recipes and recipes with okra or cauliflower). A high-powered blender like a Vitamix will do the best job with these recipes and will really upgrade your shake game!

classic strawberry milkshake

HEALTHY FATS I SERVES I

1 cup frozen strawberries

1 cup crushed ice

1 cup unsweetened almond milk

⅓ cup cottage cheese

3 tablespoons heavy whipping cream

2 tablespoons collagen

⅛ teaspoon THM Pure Stevia Extract Powder

Dash vanilla extract

¼ teaspoon glucomannan

Blend all the ingredients together until completely smooth. Enjoy!

You can top this with a squirt of Reddi-wip or a dab of homemade sweetened whipped cream if you like.

The cream in this recipe makes it more like a traditional milkshake, and since that's the only significant source of fats, the shake is still decently light, especially if this is your meal. The recipe makes quite a large milkshake (close to a quart), so if you're having it as dessert after a meal you may need to share with someone or cut the recipe in half.

note

Using low-fat cottage cheese and omitting the cream, this would be a Low Carb/Low Fat shake. (Stick with fat-free Reddi-wip for the top.)

Drink waters out of thine own cistern, and running waters out of thine own well. Let them be only thine own, and not strangers' with thee. Let thy fountain be blessed: and rejoice with the wife of thy youth. PROVERBS 5:15, 17-18

melty blueberry ice cream shake

1 cup crushed ice
1 cup unsweetened almond milk
½ cup frozen blueberries
½ med. banana
⅓ cup low-fat cottage cheese
2 tablespoons whey protein powder
¼ teaspoon glucomannan
2-3 doonks THM Pure Stevia Extract Powder

Blend the ingredients together until smooth.

The texture of this milkshake is like melty ice cream, hence the name. I used whey protein instead of collagen in this one for a creamier texture.

Let me never fall into the vulgar mistake
of dreaming that I am persecuted
whenever I am contradicted.

RALPH WALDO EMERSON

cookie dough shake

12 ice cubes

½ cup low-fat cottage cheese

½ cup unsweetened almond milk

¼ cup defatted peanut flour

¼ cup water

2-3 teaspoons THM Super Sweet Blend
(or more, to taste)

¼ teaspoon baking powder

1/16 teaspoon salt

Dash each vanilla, butter extracts

½ teaspoon glucomannan

Blend the ingredients together until smooth. Enjoy!

If you don't like funky veggies in your shakes and just want something "normal," this is for you! I didn't add any protein powder because the cottage cheese and peanut flour already offer a whopping 30 grams of protein between them. A sprinkling of sugar-free chocolate chips would be great in this shake. (They would make it a very light Healthy Fats treat.)

And Moses said unto the people, Fear ye not, stand still, and see the salvation of the Lord, which he will shew to you to day: for the Egyptians whom ye have seen to day, ye shall see them again no more for ever. The Lord shall fight for you, and ye shall hold your peace.
EXODUS 14:13-14

banana & peanut butter shake

1 sm. or ½ lg. banana (peeled, frozen)
½ cup low-fat cottage cheese
½ cup unsweetened almond milk
½ cup water
¼ cup defatted peanut flour
4 ice cubes (or more for a thicker shake)
2 doonks THM Pure Stevia Extract Powder
Dash maple extract

Blend ingredients together until smooth. Enjoy!

Between the peanut flour and cottage cheese, you have a good amount of protein going on here!

Room for pleasure, room for business –
BUT FOR CHRIST THE CRUCIFIED,
Not a place that He can enter
In the heart for which he died.
D. W. WHITTLE
"HAVE YOU ANY ROOM FOR JESUS?"

ryan's spinach smoothie

4 cups fresh spinach (loosely packed)

2 cups sliced strawberries (use frozen for a thicker shake)

1 cup unsweetened vanilla almond milk

1 banana

¼ cup collagen

1 teaspoon vanilla extract

⅛ teaspoon THM Pure Stevia Extract Powder (or more, to taste)

12 ice cubes

Add all the ingredients to a blender (I like to put the ice cubes on top) and blend until smooth. If you can't fit all the ice cubes in at the beginning, add some, blend, then add the rest and blend again. And more ice for a thicker shake if desired. Enjoy!

This smoothie is so refreshing and healthy! Ryan will gladly scarf this for a meal and is more than delighted if there are smoothie leftovers in the fridge for breakfast (he's so not picky). If you're not planning on sharing with someone, just cut the recipe in half.

five ingredient yogurt smoothie

HEALTHY CARBS | SERVES 1

1½ cups plain low-fat yogurt

1 cup sliced strawberries

½ med. banana

5 ice cubes

2-3 doonks THM Pure Stevia Extract Powder
(to taste)

Blend the ingredients until smooth. Taste and adjust the sweetener if needed; blend again. Enjoy!

This easy smoothie doesn't take any special ingredients! It's a great budget-friendly use for homemade yogurt.

note

• This smoothie has quite a few carbs, so I don't recommend adding any more to your meal or snack.

• If you want to substitute low-fat Greek yogurt for the plain yogurt, I would try using a cup of Greek yogurt and half a cup of unsweetened almond milk. Low-fat kefir (regular, or double-fermented to reduce carbs) would probably work as a substitute as well.

orange smoothie

1 cup chopped raw carrot

1 cup frozen peach slices

1 cup water

½ cup frozen strawberries

3" slice banana

6 ice cubes

3 tablespoons collagen

½ teaspoon vanilla extract

⅛ teaspoon THM Pure Stevia Extract Powder (or more, to taste)

⅛ teaspoon salt (scant)

½ teaspoon glucomannan

Blend the first set of ingredients until completely smooth. (I used a Vitamix blender.) Add the second section of ingredients and blend again until smooth. Enjoy! This smoothie contains quite a few carbs, so keep the rest of the carbs in your meal minimal.

Smoothies with goo-gobs of fruits and veggies in them are all the rage these days and can be purchased at nearly every grocery store, but most of them have very little fiber and protein – two important ingredients to reduce the effect of carbohydrates on your blood sugar. This smoothie keeps all the fiber of the fruits and veggies intact and adds protein and glucomannan, which slow down the absorption of sugars to your blood stream, helping prevent a blood sugar spike.

note

• Peeling the carrot is ideal for best taste, but I don't always bother.

• This amount of glucomannan produces a pretty thick smoothie that thickens as it sits. I absolutely love the "full" factor and health benefits it adds! I have a big appetite, but this smoothie keeps me full for quite awhile! Glucomannan can cover up flavor in large amounts, so feel free to reduce the amount by half if you prefer.

• If you don't mind a "green" taste and strange color, add a few handfuls of spinach for extra nutrition! I really like it this way.

peach smoothie

1 large peach (chunked)
1 cup crushed ice
1 cup unsweetened almond milk
½ cup low-fat cottage cheese
2 doonks THM Pure Stevia Extract Powder
Dash vanilla extract
¼ teaspoon glucomannan

Blend the ingredients together until smooth
and enjoy! Feel free to top the smoothie with
a squirt of fat-free Reddi-wip if you like.

note

• You can add more ice for a thicker shake; I
wanted more of a smoothie consistency.
• Feel free to add some whey protein or collagen
for additional protein. The cottage cheese adds
about 10 grams of protein on its own.

In truth, I have observed, down town,
that the fact of your ancestors doing
nothing is not considered good proof
that you can do anything.
GEORGE WILLIAM CURTIS
"TITBOTTOM'S SPECTACLES"

simple mixed berry smoothie

1 cup unsweetened almond milk
⅓ cup frozen blueberries
⅓ cup frozen strawberries
⅓ cup frozen cranberries
2 tablespoons collagen
1½ teaspoons THM Super Sweet Blend
  (or more, to taste)
Dash vanilla extract
½ teaspoon glucomannan

Blend the ingredients together until smooth and creamy. (Blend long enough that the mixture increases in volume and gets lighter in color.)

note

• Feel free to substitute other frozen berries of your choice for the ones I have listed here, but keep the blueberries to ⅓ cup or less if you want to stay in Low Carb/Low Fat mode since they're higher in natural sugars and there are other berries in the recipe as well. If you don't mind being in Healthy Carbs mode, use as many blueberries as you like.

• As always, feel free to increase the sweetener and/or decrease the glucomannan to match your personal preferences.

This is a more moderately-sized smoothie than many of my recipes, but it still delivers a hearty dose of glucomannan to balance your blood sugar and fill you up! I like this dairy-free version, but feel free to add a dollop of low-fat cottage cheese to make it creamier.

mango strawberry kefir smoothie

HEALTHY CARBS | SERVES 2

2 cups low-fat kefir

1 cup frozen mango chunks

1 cup frozen strawberries

½ teaspoon vanilla extract

2 doonks THM Pure Stevia Extract Powder

Blend the ingredients together until smooth. Feel free to add more sweetener if desired.

This smoothie is so refreshing! Mango and strawberry is definitely one of my favorite flavor combinations.

note

The kefir can be regular or double fermented.

pb&j kefir smoothie

1 cup double-fermented kefir

1 cup frozen sliced strawberries

½ cup unsweetened almond milk

2 tablespoons defatted peanut flour

1 tablespoon natural peanut butter

2 doonks THM Pure Stevia Extract Powder
  (or more, to taste)

Blend the ingredients together until smooth. Taste and add more sweetener if you like. Blend again after any additions and enjoy.

note

• The defatted peanut flour adds more peanut butter flavor and protein without adding a lot of fat. If you don't have it, you could try substituting with 1 tablespoon natural peanut butter (which is more calorie dense). You could also omit the peanut butter flavor entirely for a plain strawberry smoothie.

• For a LC/LF version, use low-fat double-fermented kefir and 3-4 tablespoons of defatted peanut flour (no peanut butter).

• The kefir provides protein, but you could add some collagen for extra protein to keep you full longer. You could also add a dash of vanilla to round out the flavors. I kept it simple.

> "God He knows that I am not worthy to be her humble servant. It is easy, lady, for a man to ride forth in the light of day, and do his devoir when all men have eyes for him. But in a woman's heart there is a strength and truth which asks no praise, and can but be known to him whose treasure it is."
> SIR ARTHUR CONAN COYLE
> *THE WHITE COMPANY*

grapefruit slushie

1 grapefruit (peeled, seeds removed)
1 cup crushed ice
½ cup water
2 tablespoons collagen
2 doonks THM Pure Stevia Extract Powder
Dash vanilla extract

Blend the ingredients together until smooth.
Enjoy!

note

• Collagen works better than whey protein in
this recipe.
• Slushies make a great low-calorie afternoon or
evening snack!

For if people occupy their time with pipes, and psalteries, and choirs, and dances, and Egyptian
clapping of hands, and such disorderly frivolities, they become quite immodest and difficult
to handle. They beat on cymbals and drums and make a noise on instruments of delusion. For
plainly such a party, as it seems to me, is a theatre of drunkenness.

For temperate harmonies are to be admitted [in the church]; but we are to banish as far
as possible from our healthy mind those liquid harmonies, which through pernicious
manipulations in the changes of tones, train a person to effeminacy and vulgarity. But sober
and modest tunes say "Farewell!" to the turbulence of drunkenness. Colorful harmonies are
therefore to be abandoned to immodest parties, and to complicated and vulgarly attractive
music. CLEMENT OF ALEXANDRIA - *THE INSTRUCTOR*, BK. II, CH. 4

peach slushie

HEALTHY CARBS | SERVES I

1 med.-lg. peach (peeled, stone removed,
   thawed if frozen)
1 cup crushed ice
½ cup water
2 tablespoons collagen
2 doonks THM Pure Stevia Extract Powder
Dash vanilla extract

Blend all the ingredients together until smooth and creamy. Enjoy!

note

• Collagen works better than whey protein in this recipe.

• A few raspberries would be a yummy addition!

HE SEEMED TO LOVE THEM:
to know how to separate
THE LITTLE GOOD that was in them,
from that hard crust of evil,
which misery had put around their hearts.
BARONESS EMMUSKA ORCZY - *I WILL REPAY*

banana milk

1 cup unsweetened almond milk
½ med. banana
4 ice cubes
2 tablespoons collagen
2 tablespoons low-fat cottage cheese
1-2 doonks THM Pure Stevia Extract Powder
Dash vanilla extract

Blend the ingredients together until smooth.
Enjoy!

note

• Feel free to add some banana extract for extra
flavor. You could also try adding strawberries or
defatted peanut flour.

• You can leave the cottage cheese out of the
Banana and Strawberry Milks to make them
dairy free, but they won't be as creamy. I don't
recommend using whey protein powder in
these recipes because you'll taste it. As long as
you're using the cottage cheese for creaminess,
you could omit the collagen if you don't have it
and just make sure you get another source of
protein with your meal or snack.

This Banana Milk makes a great pre-workout
snack! It includes protein as well as some healthy
energetic carbs in the form of half a banana. I
personally try to get several half bananas into my
diet every week because if I don't, my feet start
cramping up.

BY FAITH, for my cleansing I see Thy blood flow;
    Now wash me, and I shall be whiter than snow.
JAMES NICHOLSON - "LORD JESUS, I LONG TO BE PERFECTLY WHOLE"

strawberry milk

1 cup unsweetened almond milk

4 ice cubes

3 large strawberries (approx.
  ¼ cup fresh or frozen slices)

2 tablespoons collagen

2 tablespoons low-fat cottage cheese

2 doonks THM Pure Stevia Extract Powder
  (or more, to taste)

Dash vanilla extract

Blend the ingredients together until creamy and smooth. Taste and add more sweetener or strawberries if desired. Pour into a chilled glass and enjoy!

I admit, I enjoyed Nestlé's strawberry milk as a child. Now I've made my own healthy version with real ingredients and the same pink color – no red dye needed! I've been trying to incorporate lighter snacks into my life, and this strawberry milk fits the bill perfectly. It's a light Low Carb/Low Fat recipe, but it's still filling and creamy and packed with protein. It can be a snack on its own, a protein source for your breakfast, or a satisfying dessert after a Healthy Carbs meal! It's also perfect for an evening snack – something to fill your tummy without giving your body lots of excess fuel to burn right before bedtime. This strawberry milk is best when it's super cold, so I like to stick a glass in the freezer while I'm making the milk so I have a chilled glass waiting for my creamy pink deliciousness.

chocolate dreamy

LOW CARB / LOW FAT | SERVES 1

1½ cups crushed ice

1 cup frozen diced okra

1 cup unsweetened almond milk

⅓ cup low-fat cottage cheese

2 tablespoons whey protein powder

2 tablespoons half and half

1 tablespoon cocoa powder

¼ teaspoon baking powder

⅛ teaspoon THM Pure Stevia Extract Powder
   (or more, to taste)

Dash salt

¼ teaspoon glucomannan

Blend all the ingredients together until completely smooth and creamy. Enjoy!

note

Don't thaw the okra or the shake won't be as nice and thick! Use storebought frozen okra, or if you freeze your own, blanch it before freezing to help break it down, cut some of the slime, and get rid of some of the earthy taste.

This delicious chocolate shake has turned many an okra hater into an okra lover - or at least an okra tolerator! It's one of the most popular recipes on my website, and it reminds me of a Wendy's Frosty! I was originally intending for it to have a brownie batter flavor (hence the baking powder in the recipe), but when I tasted it I immediately thought, "Frosty!" I'm cool with that. It's not a killer dark chocolate like some healthy recipes tend to be; this shake is more along the lines of milk chocolate.

A good blender is definitely helpful when blending okra and other vegetables into creamy milkshakes. I never understood the okra hype until my mom bought a Vitamix. With a good blender, the okra is indistinguishable and adds a great smooth texture! And drinking my veggies in a milkshake? That's pretty cool.

And there's another country, I've heard of long ago,
Most dear to them that love her, most great to them that know;
   We may not count her armies, we may not see her King;
Her fortress is a faithful heart, her pride is suffering;
And soul by soul and silently her shining bounds increase,
   And her ways are ways of gentleness, and all her paths are peace.
CECIL SPRING RICE - "I VOW TO THEE, MY COUNTRY"

strawberry dreamy

LOW CARB / LOW FAT | SERVES I

1 cup frozen diced okra

1 cup frozen strawberries

1 cup unsweetened almond milk

¾ cup crushed ice

⅓ cup low-fat cottage cheese

2 tablespoons whey protein powder

2 tablespoons half and half

¼ teaspoon baking powder

3 doonks THM Pure Stevia Extract Powder

Dash vanilla extract

¼ teaspoon glucomannan

Blend all the ingredients in a high-powered blender until a smooth soft-serve consistency is reached. If in doubt, blend a little longer; the shake will taste better. (I used a Vitamix with a tamper and found that high speeds help this blend. If you find that your blender won't blend the mixture, thin it down into a shake with some more almond milk.) Enjoy!

This recipe makes a huge serving of soft-serve ice cream or a quart jar of strawberry shake. I enjoy the whole thing for lunch, but you can try cutting the recipe in half if you don't want so much.

This recipe makes a huge bowl of soft serve (or a huge jar of strawberry shake). My little sister saw my big bowl of ice cream – which was literally my lunch one day – and asked, "You're eating ALL of that?" It may make a big bowl of ice cream, but my other sister – the runner – was very impressed with the macros. I didn't run numbers, but there's nothing calorie-dense in this recipe. It includes protein and okra for a great health boost, though, and it kept me full all afternoon!

note

• Don't thaw the okra or the shake won't be as nice and thick! Use storebought frozen okra, or if you freeze your own, blanch it before freezing to help break it down, cut some of the slime, and get rid of some of the earthy taste.

• Feel free to add some defatted peanut flour to this shake for a PB&J option! You can add natural peanut butter, but that will turn this into a Healthy Fats recipe.

> But we never can prove the
> DELIGHTS OF HIS LOVE,
> until all on the altar we lay.
> JOHN HENRY SAMMIS
> "TRUST AND OBEY"

chocolate-covered cranberry superfood shake

LOW CARB/LOW FAT I SERVES I

1 cup frozen diced okra

1 cup unsweetened almond milk

1 cup water

⅔ cup frozen cranberries

⅓ cup low-fat cottage cheese

4 ice cubes

2 tablespoons collagen

1-2 tablespoons cocoa powder

⅛ teaspoon THM Pure Stevia Extract Powder
(or more, to taste)

½ teaspoon glucomannan

Blend the ingredients together until completely smooth and lighter in color. (My Vitamix does a great job.) Taste and add more cocoa powder and/or sweetener if desired. Do not under-blend! Blending well helps cut possible slime factor from the okra.

Hershey's sugar-free chocolate syrup makes a great topping! (It's sweetened mostly with erythritol and is available at many local grocery stores.)

The hearty dose of okra, cranberries, and glucomannan in this shake is full-on HEALTH in a jar and I will not apologize for the taste! It's probably not for everyone, but I love it! The recipe makes about a quart of very filling shake.

note

• The okra and cranberries need to be frozen so the shake has the right texture. I recommend using okra that has been blanched before freezing (like storebought okra) to cut down on slime.

• If the shake is too slimy for you, try decreasing the okra and/or glucomannan, or just chug it and embrace the health!

• Some frozen banana would be a good addition! (That would make this a Healthy Carbs shake.) You could also add some orange sections or orange extract.

• If you don't want a whole quart to drink, cut the recipe in half. I don't recommend making it with the intention of storing leftovers because the texture and flavor will be weird if it sits in the fridge.

cranberry orange superfood shake

1 cup unsweetened almond milk

¾ cup frozen diced okra

½ cup frozen cranberries

½ cup low-fat cottage cheese

1 orange (peeled, chunked)

4 ice cubes

3 doonks THM Pure Stevia Extract Powder

¼ teaspoon glucomannan

Blend the ingredients very well until completely smooth.

superfood breakfast smoothie

1 cup frozen diced okra

1 cup frozen blueberries

1 cup unsweetened almond milk

½ med. banana, 1 orange (peeled), or 1 peach

⅓ cup low-fat cottage cheese

2 tablespoons whey protein powder

¼ teaspoon cinnamon

3 doonks THM Pure Stevia Extract Powder

¼ teaspoon glucomannan

Blend all the ingredients together until completely smooth and enjoy!

I've noticed that a lot of okra recipes involve chocolate. I mean, who doesn't love a chocolate-covered vegetable, right? Chocolate is great, but sometimes I like other flavors too – and that's where this shake comes in. When paired with blueberries and other fruit (bananas, oranges, or peaches are great), okra flavor gets kind of lost…and to the picky palate, that's probably a good thing. If you've tried the Chocolate Dreamy and decided it's not for you, give this shake a try instead. You might find that you can handle okra better in this flavor combo. This recipe makes a large amount, so feel free to cut the recipe in half (but use the full amount of protein powder).

note

• I recommend using okra that has been blanched before freezing (like storebought okra) to cut down on slime.

• Be sure to use frozen okra and frozen blueberries since this recipe does not call for any ice. If you feel like a cup of okra is too much for you either in taste or texture, try subbing half of it with ice.

dreamy dairy-free chocolate shake

LOW CARB / LOW FAT | SERVES 1

1½ cups frozen cauliflower florets

1¼ cups unsweetened almond milk

2 tablespoons collagen

2 tablespoons cocoa powder

2 teaspoons THM Super Sweet Blend
(or more, to taste)

½ teaspoon vanilla extract

⅛ teaspoon salt

3 doonks THM Pure Stevia Extract Powder

½ teaspoon glucomannan

4 ice cubes (or more, to desired consistency)

Add all the ingredients except the ice to a high-powered blender. Add the glucomannan right before blending to avoid clumping. Blend until completely smooth (don't skimp on the blending; it should be a thick smoothie consistency), then add the ice and blend again until smooth. Taste and adjust. Does it need more sweetener? Do you want to add more ice for a thicker shake? Feel free to do so, then blend until smooth and enjoy!

Let me get this straight: this recipe is not just for the dairy-free peeps. It's for anyone who wants 1) a creamy chocolate milkshake experience, 2) a dose of non-starchy veggies, or 3) a very low-calorie, protein-rich snack. The cauliflower makes it so creamy!

You kind of need a pretty good blender to pulverize vegetables into unnoticeable smithereens if you plan to turn them into milkshakes. I was blenderless for a long time after I got married, but I finally bought myself a used Vitamix off of Ebay! The tamper was busted when I got it so I made this shake thinner than I normally would with my mom's Vitamix with tamper back home. If you have a working tamper, you may want to decrease the almond milk just a tad and/or add a little more ice. I made the shake thin enough that it would blend on its own in the blender without my having to take the lid off and keep scraping down the sides to get things to blend smoothly.

note

• I recommend using storebought frozen cauliflower florets because they have been blanched and will break down better in your shake. They also seem to be milder in flavor than fresh cauliflower. (The cauliflower needs to be frozen because it acts as part of the ice in the recipe.) I've heard from some blog readers that storebought riced cauliflower works well in this shake in the same amount if you don't have cauliflower florets.

• While this recipe doesn't have a fat source itself, it's Foundation Fats compliant! Add a fat source on the side and you have a Foundation Fats meal.

surprise birthday cake shake

LOW CARB / LOW FAT | SERVES 1

1 cup frozen cauliflower florets

1 cup unsweetened almond milk

4 ice cubes

2 tablespoons collagen

2½ teaspoons THM Super Sweet Blend
(or more, to taste)

¼ teaspoon baking powder

¼ teaspoon each almond extract,
butter extract, vanilla extract

Dash salt

2 drops yellow food coloring (optional)

½ teaspoon glucomannan

Blend the ingredients together until smooth and creamy. Blend long enough that the shake fluffs up and increases in volume. Enjoy!

Yep, there's a surprise in here all right! Don't let the cauliflower scare you; it makes this dairy-free shake super creamy! You'll never know it's there, AND you're getting some veggies in. This is one of my new favorite shakes! (I'm a sucker for cake batter anything.)

note

• I recommend using storebought frozen cauliflower because it has been blanched and will have a more mild flavor than unblanched cauliflower. The cauliflower needs to be frozen because it acts as part of the ice in the recipe.

• If you're dairy free, you may need to omit the butter extract.

pumpkin pie milkshake

1 cup frozen cauliflower florets

1 cup ice

1 cup unsweetened almond milk

½ cup canned pumpkin

½ cup cottage cheese

⅓ cup half and half

2 tablespoons whey protein powder

2 teaspoons THM Super Sweet Blend
   (or more, to taste)

½ teaspoon cinnamon

⅛ teaspoon ground cloves

2 doonks THM Pure Stevia Extract Powder

Dash vanilla extract

½ teaspoon glucomannan

Blend the ingredients together until completely smooth. Make sure you blend for a good long while so the shake gets nice and creamy.

The shake makes one very large serving or two more moderate servings. Half of the batch actually just sneaks into Low Carb/Low Fat range if you use low-fat cottage cheese. If sharing with someone and using this on its own as a snack, you should probably add a little extra protein powder.

Feel free to top with some Reddi-wip or homemade whipped cream (definitely Healthy Fats!).

I shared this shake with my mom who was ravenous after getting home from getting groceries, and she loved it! (Surprisingly, she still loved it after I informed her of the secret ingredient halfway through the glass.)

note

• I recommend using storebought frozen cauliflower because it has been blanched and will have a more mild flavor than unblanched cauliflower. The cauliflower needs to be frozen because it acts as part of the ice in the recipe.

• I chose to use whey protein powder in this instead of collagen for extra creaminess.

ice creamed coffee

HEALTHY FATS | SERVES 1-2

1½ cups cold coffee

1 cup frozen cauliflower florets

1 cup crushed ice

⅓ cup cottage cheese

⅓ cup half and half

2 tablespoons whey protein powder

2 teaspoons THM Super Sweet Blend
    (or more, to taste)

2 doonks THM Pure Stevia Extract Powder

Dash vanilla extract

½ teaspoon glucomannan

Blend the ingredients together until completely smooth. Make sure you blend for a good long while so the shake gets nice and creamy.

The shake makes one very large serving or two more moderate servings. Half of the batch actually just sneaks into Low Carb/Low Fat range if you use low-fat cottage cheese. If sharing with someone and using this on its own as a snack, you should probably add a little extra protein powder.

This is a DELICIOUS healthy version of a popular fast food drink from the ultimate chicken store. Don't be afraid of the cauliflower – it turns the shake into an incredible texture and you don't even taste it!

note

• I recommend using storebought frozen cauliflower because it has been blanched and will have a more mild flavor than unblanched cauliflower. The cauliflower needs to be frozen because it acts as part of the ice in the recipe.

• I chose to use whey protein powder in this instead of collagen for extra creaminess.

grab & go iced coffee

6 cups cold coffee

1 cup unsweetened almond milk

½ cup heavy whipping cream

¼ cup + 2 tablespoons collagen

2 tablespoons cocoa powder

2 teaspoons vanilla extract

¼ teaspoon salt

⅛ teaspoon glucomannan

Sweetener of choice (to taste)

Blend all the ingredients together, adding the glucomannan right before blending so it doesn't clump. Taste and adjust the sweetener to what you like. I used ⅛ teaspoon THM Pure Stevia Extract Powder and 2 tablespoons THM Super Sweet Blend, which Ryan thought was too sweet on the day I made it but was fine after overnight refrigeration. If you're used to the storebought sugary iced coffees, I recommend using a less concentrated sweetener like THM Gentle Sweet instead of the concentrated sweeteners I used. (A less concentrated sweetener isn't as budget friendly but will balance better with coffee and chocolate, two bitter flavors.) According to the online sweetener conversion chart you'd need a little over half a cup of THM Gentle Sweet to replace the sweeteners I used, but I would start with a third cup, taste, and work up from there. Blend after any additions and store in the refrigerator. Shake before serving.

This iced coffee is meant to be used as a snack or as part of a meal, not sipped on all day. Each serving has 11 grams of protein! For the record, Ryan really likes it.

note

• Feel free to add a dash of your favorite coffee shop flavor, such as hazelnut, maple, or caramel extract.

• I don't recommend substituting whey protein powder for the collagen. It may not dissolve as well and you'll probably taste it unpleasantly.

vanilla frappé

7 coffee ice cubes (coffee frozen in
standard ice cube trays)

1 cup unsweetened almond milk

2 tablespoons collagen

1 teaspoon THM Super Sweet Blend
(or more, to taste)

1 teaspoon vanilla extract

3 doonks THM Pure Stevia Extract Powder

½ teaspoon glucomannan

Blend all the ingredients together in a high-powered blender until smooth. If you want a thicker frappé, add another ice cube or two and blend some more. Top with a squirt of fat-free Reddi-wip and some sugar-free chocolate syrup and enjoy!

note

• I love this frappé as written and wanted to keep it dairy free, but if you want a richer result, feel free to add a few tablespoons of half and half or heavy whipping cream. Three tablespoons of half and half will keep you in Low Carb/Low Fat territory, but using over one tablespoon of heavy whipping cream will give you a Healthy Fats drink.

• As written (without toppings), this frappé can actually be used in a Foundation Fats setting! It doesn't have any fats of its own but can help fill you up along with an FF meal. Do not add half and half or heavy cream if using this in an FF setting.

Ye also, as lively stones,
are built up a spiritual house,
AN HOLY PRIESTHOOD,
to offer up spiritual sacrifices,
acceptable to God by Jesus
Christ. 1 PETER 2:5

mocha frappé

7 coffee ice cubes (coffee frozen in
   standard ice cube trays)
1 cup unsweetened almond milk
2 tablespoons collagen
1 tablespoon cocoa powder (scant)
1½ teaspoons THM Super Sweet Blend
1 teaspoon vanilla extract
3 doonks THM Pure Stevia Extract Powder
½ teaspoon glucomannan

Blend all the ingredients together in a high-powered blender until smooth.

note

• As written, this frappé is Low Carb/Low Fat and dairy free (not to mention delicious). For a slightly creamier LC/LF frappé that isn't dairy free, replace 3 tablespoons of the almond milk with half and half. Add a dash of cream for a Healthy Fats drink.

• For an HF mocha chip frappé, feel free to add a handful of sugar-free chocolate chips or a square of 85% dark chocolate with the other ingredients in the blender, then garnish with homemade whipped cream or a squirt of Reddi-wip and a sprinkling of additional chocolate chips.

• As written (without toppings), this frappé can actually be used in a Foundation Fats setting! It doesn't have any fats of its own but can help fill you up along with an FF meal. Do not add half and half or heavy cream if using this in an FF setting.

I am two fools, I know, for loving, and for saying so in whining poetry.
JOHN DONNE

s'mores frappé

7 coffee ice cubes (coffee frozen in
   standard ice cube trays)
1 cup unsweetened almond milk
2 tablespoons collagen
2 tablespoons defatted peanut flour
2 teaspoons cocoa powder
2 teaspoons THM Super Sweet Blend
   (or more, to taste)
1 teaspoon vanilla extract
2 doonks THM Pure Stevia Extract Powder
Dash cinnamon
½ teaspoon glucomannan

Blend all the ingredients together in a high-powered blender until smooth. If you want a thicker frappé, add a couple extra coffee ice cubes, and feel free to add more THM Super Sweet Blend if you so desire. Enjoy!

Let me explain the flavors here. You have coffee, because -> coffee frappé. You have defatted peanut flour because -> s'mores should always have peanut butter. You have cocoa because -> you don't need that one explained. And the cinnamon? Because -> cinnamon graham crackers.

note

For a creamier Healthy Fats frappé, you could use a tablespoon or two of natural peanut butter in place of the defatted peanut flour. You could also replace a few tablespoons of the almond milk with half and half or heavy whipping cream. I like it as-is for a very light snack, but feel free to tweak!

pb&j frappé

1½ cups crushed ice

1 cup unsweetened almond milk

¼ cup + 2 tablespoons half and half

½ cup frozen blueberries

¼ cup defatted peanut flour

2 tablespoons collagen

1 teaspoon THM Super Sweet Blend
   (or more, to taste)

1 teaspoon vanilla extract

3 doonks THM Pure Stevia Extract Powder

½ teaspoon glucomannan

Blend the ingredients together in a high-powered blender until smooth.

note

• To make this frappé Low Carb/Low Fat, try using more almond milk in place of the half and half. (The defatted peanut flour already adds 4 grams of fat.)

• For a richer, creamier (and more calorie dense) frappé you can use 2 tablespoons of natural peanut butter in place of the defatted peanut flour.

• Feel free to substitute other frozen berries for the blueberries. Raspberries would be better than strawberries since they are stronger in flavor. Hey, even cranberries would be cool! (You may need to add more sweetener.)

If you're not a coffee lover, this unique frappé flavor was made with you in mind! Since a frappé is a blended drink with ice and doesn't necessarily include coffee as some may think, I feel fully justified in calling this concoction a frappé.

peppermint chip frappé

HEALTHY FATS | SERVES 1

1½ cups crushed ice

1 cup unsweetened almond milk

3 tablespoons heavy whipping cream

2 tablespoons collagen

2 tablespoons cottage cheese

1 teaspoon THM Super Sweet Blend
(or more, to taste)

¼ teaspoon peppermint extract

¼ teaspoon vanilla extract

2 doonks THM Pure Stevia Extract Powder

2 drops red food coloring (optional)

Small chunk of 85% dark chocolate

3 sugar-free peppermints (whole)

¼ teaspoon glucomannan (rounded)

Blend the ingredients together in a high-powered blender until smooth. (See note about chocolate and peppermints.) Enjoy!

note

• I just put the chocolate and peppermints in the blender whole and let them blend with everything else so they blended pretty fine, but if you want bigger, get-stuck-in-the-straw chunks, blend the frappé, then add the chocolate and peppermints and pulse to get the size chunks you want.

• Feel free to add more peppermint extract if you like (especially if you don't have any sugar-free peppermints to add to the frappé). I try not to add too much peppermint extract because it leaves a sharp taste.

TAKE THEREFORE
NO THOUGHT
for the morrow:
for the morrow shall
take thought for the things of itself.
Sufficient unto the day
is the evil thereof.

MATTHEW 6:34

velvety earl grey

1 cup unsweetened almond milk

1 cup water

1 Earl Grey tea bag

2 tablespoons whey protein powder

2 teaspoons refined coconut oil

1 teaspoon salted butter

½ teaspoon vanilla extract

3 doonks THM Pure Stevia Extract Powder

Dash salt

Heat the almond milk, water, and tea bag together until the desired temperature is reached. (I do this in a big mug in the microwave.) Let it steep for a few minutes.

Remove the tea bag, add the rest of the ingredients, and blend with an immersion blender until smooth and creamy. Enjoy!

VELVETY DRINKS ▼

In case you're wondering, "Velvety" is my description for my recipes that incorporate coconut oil, butter, and protein powder into a super-creamy blended drink that will rev your metabolism with its foundational fats. I like to use them as afternoon snacks or a dessert after a Healthy Fats or Low Carb/Low Fat meal. You can use protein-filled drinks like this as a meal on occasion, but a) I highly recommend that you get plenty of "real," whole foods into your body as well, and b) it

might not be enough to fill you up when your body is expecting larger quantities. I like to heat the liquid for these drinks in a really big mug in the microwave, then use an immersion blender to blend in the rest of the ingredients so I don't have to wash a big blender or worry about pressure buildup when blending hot liquids in a closed container. You can blend the heated liquid along with the rest of the ingredients in a regular blender instead of using an immersion blender, but vent the blender as needed to relieve pressure. Always be very careful when blending hot liquids, and use common sense. (Both methods are mentioned in these recipes because I didn't discover the mug/immersion blender trick at the beginning of my Velvety career.)

velvety cappuccino

1 cup unsweetened almond milk

1 cup brewed coffee

2 tablespoons whey protein powder

1 tablespoon refined coconut oil

2 teaspoons cocoa powder

1 teaspoon THM Super Sweet Blend
   (or more, to taste)

1 teaspoon butter

2 doonks THM Pure Stevia Extract Powder

Dash salt

Dash vanilla extract

Heat the almond milk and coffee together in the microwave for 2 minutes or until the desired temperature is reached.

Meanwhile, add all the other ingredients to a blender. Add the hot liquid and blend until smooth and creamy. (Be careful when blending hot liquids, and vent the blender as needed to release pressure.) Enjoy!

note

Most people will probably want to add more Super Sweet Blend.

And yet through it all she knew that this love of humanity,

this mad desire to serve and to help,

in no way detracted from his love for her. Nay, it intensified it, made it purer and better, adding to the joy of perfect intercourse the poetic and subtle fragrance of ever-recurring pain.

BARONESS EMMUSKA ORCZY - *THE ELUSIVE PIMPERNEL*

velvety drinkable custard

FOUNDATION FATS | SERVES I

¾ cup unsweetened almond milk

¾ cup water

1 egg

2 tablespoons whey protein powder

1 tablespoon refined coconut oil

2 teaspoons salted butter

½ teaspoon vanilla extract

2 doonks THM Pure Stevia Extract Powder

¹⁄₁₆ teaspoon salt

⅛ teaspoon glucomannan (scant)

Heat the almond milk and water until the desired temperature is reached. (I heat them for 2 minutes in the microwave.)

Meanwhile, add all the other ingredients to a blender. When the liquid is hot, add it to the blender as well and blend immediately. (Be careful when blending hot liquids, and vent the blender to relieve pressure as necessary.) Blend until smooth and creamy, then enjoy! I like to top mine with a little cinnamon.

note

• If the raw egg idea scares you, use a pasteurized egg. These can be purchased at many grocery stores or you can make your own (Google it).

• Feel free to add some maple extract and/or cinnamon!

"You are like a star upon my path which guides me on the upward way," said he. "Our souls are set together upon the finding of honor, and how shall we hold each other back when our purpose is the same?"

SIR ARTHUR CONAN DOYLE - *SIR NIGEL*

velvety maple latte

1 cup brewed coffee

1 cup unsweetened almond milk

2 tablespoons whey protein powder

2½ teaspoons THM Super Sweet Blend
(or more, to taste)

2 teaspoons refined coconut oil

1 teaspoon salted butter

1 teaspoon maple extract

½ teaspoon cinnamon

½ teaspoon vanilla extract

⅛ teaspoon salt (scant)

Heat the coffee and almond milk together to your desired temperature. (I microwave them together in a glass measuring cup for 2 minutes.)

Meanwhile, add the other ingredients to a blender. When the coffee and almond milk are hot, add them to the blender and blend until frothy and creamy. (Be careful when blending hot liquids, and vent the blender to relieve pressure as necessary.) Taste and add additional sweetener if desired.

note

• I'm not a coffee lover, so this ratio of coffee to almond milk was good for me. If you want a stronger coffee flavor, replace some of the almond milk with additional coffee. You could also try replacing the coffee with a strongly-brewed tea of your choice!

• I like strong flavors, so if you find the maple or cinnamon to be overpowering, feel free to decrease them. I'm just not a coffee drinker so I was looking for other flavors to balance it out.

velvety ginger cookie sip

1 cup water

1 cup unsweetened almond milk

1 chai spice tea bag

2 tablespoons whey protein powder

½ tablespoon refined coconut oil

½ tablespoon salted butter

2 teaspoons THM Super Sweet Blend
 (or more, to taste)

1½ teaspoons ginger

½ teaspoon each butter extract, maple extract

¼ teaspoon baking powder

3 doonks THM Pure Stevia Extract Powder

Dash each cinnamon, salt

Add the water, almond milk, and tea bag to a large mug or glass measuring cup and microwave for 3 minutes, then let it steep for 5 minutes while you add the rest of the ingredients to a blender. (Always be careful when blending hot liquids, and vent the blender as necessary to release pressure.)

Remove the tea bag and add the hot liquid to the blender as well. Blend until smooth. Taste and add more sweetener and/or spice as desired. Enjoy!

note

I'm referring to the dried, powdered ginger from the spice aisle. You may wish to start with less. I don't think mine was very strong.

If you're tired of pumpkin, this ginger cookie flavor is a nice change that still breathes a fall vibe. I always look forward to cooler weather because I love hot drinks – and hot drinks in the middle of a South Carolina (and now Louisiana) summer just don't jive. My first try at this ginger cookie sip was majorly BLAND, so the next time around I upped the flavor significantly. All the ingredients are here for a reason, folks. Lately I've been using collagen instead of whey protein in a lot of drinks because I prefer the non-flavor of collagen, but the whey protein really adds creaminess here, as does the butter. Even the baking powder is in here for a reason – it adds the cookie flavor!

velvety autumn sip

1 cup unsweetened almond milk

1 cup water

1-2 Rooibos tea bags

2 tablespoons whey protein powder

1 tablespoon refined coconut oil

½ tablespoon salted butter

2 teaspoons apple cider vinegar
   (or more, to taste)

¼ teaspoon each cinnamon, ginger

3-4 doonks THM Pure Stevia Extract Powder

Dash red pepper

Dash vanilla extract

Heat the almond milk and water and steep the tea bags to make a strong tea.

Add the second set of ingredients and the tea to a blender and blend until frothy. (Be careful when blending hot liquids, and vent the blender as needed to relieve pressure. Alternatively, use an immersion blender.) Taste and add more sweetener, spices, apple cider vinegar, and/or red pepper as desired.

I used Rooibos tea in this for a deep, rich fall flavor, but you can definitely substitute another earthy-flavored tea of your choice. I think Oolong would be good (and add even more metabolism rev)! As always, feel free to adjust the flavors to your own personal taste buds. I probably would've added a little more ACV if I wasn't trying to keep this recipe more moderate for the blog.

In all their affliction he was afflicted, and the angel of his presence saved them: in his love and in his pity he redeemed them; and he bare them, and carried them all the days of old. ISAIAH 63:9

velvety peppermint sip

1 cup unsweetened almond milk

1 cup water

1-2 peppermint tea bags

2 tablespoons whey protein powder

1 tablespoon refined coconut oil

½ tablespoon butter

3-4 doonks THM Pure Stevia Extract Powder

Dash each peppermint extract, vanilla extract

Dash salt

Add the peppermint tea bags to the almond milk and water and heat in the microwave for 3 minutes. Blend all the ingredients, including the hot liquid, until smooth. (Be careful when blending hot liquids, and vent the blender as needed to relieve pressure. Alternatively, use an immersion blender.) Taste and add more peppermint extract, sweetener, and/or salt if needed. Enjoy!

note

You could use coffee for part of the liquid in here in place of the water.

the velvety golden detox

1 cup unsweetened almond milk

1 cup water

1 chai spice tea bag

2 teaspoons thinly-sliced fresh ginger

1 med. lemon (peeled)

2 tablespoons whey protein powder

2½ teaspoons THM Super Sweet Blend

2 teaspoons refined coconut oil

1 teaspoon salted butter

½ teaspoon vanilla extract

¼ teaspoon turmeric

⅛ teaspoon glucomannan

⅛ teaspoon salt (scant)

Heat the almond milk, water, tea bag, and fresh ginger together in the microwave for 2½ minutes. (You could also bring the ingredients to a boil on the stovetop.) Let it steep for a few minutes. You want the flavors to strengthen, but don't let it cool off too much because you won't be reheating after blending the ingredients together.

Meanwhile, add all the other ingredients to a blender. After the tea has steeped, remove the tea bag and add the liquid (and ginger) to the blender and blend immediately so the glucomannan doesn't clump. Blend until smooth. (Be careful when blending hot liquids, and vent the blender as needed to relieve pressure.) If you like, you can strain any lemon and ginger pulp out of the drink before sipping. I don't bother. (Are you surprised?)

note

• I highly, highly recommend fresh ginger for the best taste, but you can try substituting the dried, powdered form from the spice aisle if you prefer. I would try ¼ teaspoon and increase from there if desired. If you have ginger juice, that would be a better alternative to dried ginger, but I'm not sure how much you would use. I also recommend using a real lemon, not bottled lemon juice. It just tastes so much better!

• Feel free to use a different kind of tea (like a ginger tea!) if you prefer. You can add more fresh ginger as well for a spicier drink.

cranberry wassail

LOW CARB/LOW FAT | YIELDS 1 QUART (3-4 SERVINGS)

5 cups water

1 cup whole cranberries

3 cinnamon spice tea bags

Zest from one orange

2 teaspoons apple cider vinegar

1 teaspoon THM Super Sweet Blend

½ teaspoon vanilla extract

¼ teaspoon allspice

⅛ teaspoon each cardamom, ground cloves

⅛ teaspoon THM Pure Stevia Extract Powder

¹⁄₁₆ teaspoon salt

Whisk all ingredients together in a saucepan, bring to a boil, use a potato masher to mash the cranberries, and simmer (uncovered) over medium heat for one hour. Strain and serve. If the wassail is too strong for your liking, dilute it with more water. Adjust the sweetness as desired.

Since this festive drink doesn't have any protein, enjoy it with a meal or snack that includes protein...or add some collagen to the wassail itself!

note

• Feel free to double, triple, or quadruple the batch!

• You could probably cook this in a slow cooker for a few hours (on High until it starts to bubble around the edges, then Low). Crack the lid open for the first hour, then cover it so too much liquid doesn't evaporate.

> They proved that a seal pup could swim or not swim at birth by stating the proposition very bellicosely and then following it up with an attack on the opposing man's judgment, common sense, nationality, or past history. JACK LONDON - *THE SEA WOLF*

cranberry nog

1 cup unsweetened almond milk
1 cup water
⅔ cup cranberries

2 tablespoons whey protein powder
⅛ teaspoon THM Pure Stevia Extract Powder
Hearty dash salt
Hearty dash orange extract, vanilla extract
½ teaspoon glucomannan

Heat the almond milk, water, and cranberries together until they are your desired temperature. (I do this in a huge mug in the microwave for 3 minutes.)

Add the rest of the ingredients and blend with an immersion blender until smooth. Taste, increase the sweetener and/or extracts if desired, and enjoy!

Yep, this Cranberry Nog is yet another recipe in my scheme to get more glucomannan down the hatch! Glucomannan balances the blood sugar, slows down the absorption of fat, and helps you feel full while eating less calories. Another cool use for this drink: chug it after a Healthy Carbs meal to help fill you up. It works.

A lot of stores have cranberries on sale (like, $1/bag!) around Thanksgiving and Christmas, so we always stock up and freeze them to use throughout the year.

note

• Different brands of glucomannan can vary in strength, so if the brand you're using makes this drink slimy, decrease the amount or just embrace the slime and enjoy it for all its health and weight loss benefits. This amount in the brand I use is not slimy but does make the drink fairly thick and foamy. It's so filling! This drink will thicken as it cools, so I don't recommend making it ahead and refrigerating it unless you want a glucomannan pudding.

• Want a Healthy Carbs drink? Add a few wedges of peeled orange in with the cranberries!

peanut butter cookie nog

1 cup unsweetened almond milk

1 cup water

3 tablespoons defatted peanut flour

2 tablespoons collagen

2 teaspoons THM Super Sweet Blend
  (or more, to taste)

½ teaspoon vanilla extract

⅛ teaspoon baking powder

⅛ teaspoon salt (scant)

2 doonks THM Pure Stevia Extract Powder

½ teaspoon glucomannan

Heat the almond milk and water together to reach your desired temperature. (I do this in the microwave in a huge mug.)

Add the rest of the ingredients and blend with an immersion blender until smooth. Taste and add more sweetener and/or salt if necessary to balance the flavors. Blend again. Enjoy!

note

• I don't recommend using whey protein powder in this recipe. The flavor just didn't pair well with the peanut flour when I tried it.

• Different brands of glucomannan can vary in strength, so if the brand you're using makes this drink slimy, decrease the amount or just embrace the slime and enjoy it for all its health and weight loss benefits. This amount in the brand I use is not slimy but does make the drink fairly thick and foamy. It's so filling! This drink will thicken as it cools, so I don't recommend making it ahead and refrigerating it unless you want a glucomannan pudding.

drinkable chocolate custard

HEALTHY FATS | YIELDS 5½ CUPS (6-7 SERVINGS)

2½ cups unsweetened almond milk

1½ cups half and half

3 eggs

¼ cup cocoa powder

½ teaspoon salt

½ teaspoon glucomannan

¼ cup THM Super Sweet Blend

1 tablespoon salted butter

1 teaspoon vanilla extract

Blend the first section of ingredients together until smooth. Pour the mixture into a non-stick saucepan and cook over medium-high heat just until it starts to bubble, whisking often. (When you can tell the custard is starting to thicken, turn the heat down to medium so it doesn't start cooking too hard and get lumpy.) As soon as the custard starts to bubble, pull it off the heat. Don't overcook!

Add the rest of the ingredients and whisk until smooth. Pour into cups and enjoy warm!

If you have leftovers to refrigerate, they will firm up to a pudding texture! Delicious!

The really cool thing about this hot chocolate recipe is that it's good hot or cold! When hot, it's a rich, thick, warming river of chocolate. After it's been refrigerated, it thickens to a pudding consistency that reminds me exactly of the chocolate pudding I used to love to get at our local pizza buffet as a kid. I've only had one or two chocolate Jello pudding cups in my lifetime, but I'd say it's similar to those as well. How cool is that?

note

• This is more salt and sweetener than I would typically use, but I just thought the recipe needed it this time! Heat and glucomannan tend to mask sweetness, so these amounts were perfect for me. You may wish to start with less of each, then increase to match your taste buds.

• I haven't tried this, but I bet you could leave out the cocoa powder and decrease the sweetener and salt for a vanilla version! You may want to add an extra teaspoon of vanilla extract.

• If you're having trouble with the custard separating or getting lumpy, use a lower heat and pull the custard off the burner before you think it's done. It will continue to thicken with residual heat.

LIGHT CHOCOLATE
ICE CREAM • PG 311

ice cream + frozen desserts

ice cream tips

Ice cream is one of the easiest healthy desserts to make (in my unbiased opinion)! Blend some stuff in a blender, pour it into an ice cream churn, eat. For this cookbook I experimented with many different ways of doing ice cream varying the ingredients, calorie load, and time commitment, so there should be a recipe for everyone!

» THE EQUIPMENT «

» **BLENDER:** I use a blender to blend all my ice cream ingredients together until smooth before pouring them into the ice cream maker.

» **IMMERSION BLENDER:** Sometimes I use an immersion blender instead of a full-size blender to reduce cleanup. An immersion blender is also handy for blending additional ingredients into a hot cooked custard ice cream base without the danger of a pressure buildup.

» **ICE CREAM CHURN:** I have used a Cuisinart ICE-21 1.5-quart automatic countertop ice cream churn for many years and love it. It's so easy to use! You simply keep the aluminum insert in your freezer, take it out when you want to make ice cream, place it on the churn base and insert the churn paddle thingy, turn the machine on, pour your ice cream mixture in, and enjoy your soft-serve ice cream in 20-30 minutes! No ice or rock salt needed. (When the ice cream is finished, remove it from the canister with a plastic spatula to avoid scratching the surface of the freezer canister. If you want a firmer product, put the ice cream in your freezer in a sealed container for an hour or so.) You can use a traditional ice-and-rock-salt churn for my recipes, but they usually come in much larger sizes so you may need to multiply my recipes to fit the recommended volume for your particular churn. All of my recipes are formulated for a 1.5-quart ice cream churn.

A countertop ice cream churn is well worth the money! They are so easy to use and clean, and they churn out my favorite healthy dessert of all time! If you don't have an ice cream maker and don't want to invest in one, you have a couple of options:

» Use your blender. Quite a few ice cream recipes can be made using a blender, but the texture won't be as nice. Simply freeze the ice cream mixture in ice cube trays, soften the cubes a bit, and blend them with a little unsweetened almond milk or cream in a high-powered blender until a soft-serve consistency is reached. Freeze the ice cream in your freezer for an hour or so to firm up or enjoy right away.

» Try the plastic bag/ice/rock salt method. (Google will show you how.)

» Freeze the ice cream mixture in popsicle molds! Not quite the same as ice cream, but you'll get a refreshing treat! You should probably only make a partial recipe if using this method unless you have a lot of popsicle molds.

» THE INGREDIENTS «

» **CREAM:** Put simply, the more cream you use, the creamier and softer and more scoopable your ice cream will be. The trick is to find a happy medium between "calorie overload" and "good ice cream." I use various amounts in my recipes depending on my mood and the occasion and try to keep my servings of my richer recipes on the more moderate side.

» HALF AND HALF: Half and half isn't as calorie dense as cream but stays creamier than almond milk when frozen, so I often use it as part of the volume in my ice cream recipes.

» CANNED COCONUT MILK: This makes a great dairy-free ice cream base! You can find a few recipes using canned coconut milk in this section. I purchase Thai Kitchen brand from Walmart and other local grocery stores. (You can find a Basic Dairy-Free Ice Cream recipe on page 239 of *Necessary Food*.)

» UNSWEETENED ALMOND, CASHEW, OR COCONUT MILK (the very light kind from the carton with about 40 calories per cup): I use this to make up the rest of the volume for the ice cream, just like you would use milk in regular ice cream recipes. Nut and coconut milks tend to get more icy than dairy milk does when frozen, so if a recipe isn't as creamy and smooth as you'd like, try substituting more cream or half and half in place of some almond milk. Keep in mind that this increases the calorie load!

» COTTAGE CHEESE: Cottage cheese is one of my favorite "secret ingredients" to make recipes creamy without a lot of extra calories. You can't taste it (provided that you don't use too much), and it adds a nice protein boost! I've also used Greek yogurt, regular yogurt, and kefir in some of the recipes in this book depending on the taste I was going for. I don't recommend substituting Greek yogurt for cottage cheese in ice cream recipes unless you're OK with the tangy flavor it will add.

» EGGS: Eggs (especially their yolks) can really improve the texture and taste of homemade ice creams! Cooking a custard base for an ice cream and chilling it before churning takes time, but the results are worth it. You can add raw eggs for extra richness if you're comfortable with that, but the ice cream's consistency will be better if the eggs are cooked into the ice cream base.

» SWEETENER: I used to use THM Pure Stevia Extract Powder to sweeten all my ice cream recipes...until I found that xylitol helps keep them from freezing so hard and improves the texture of the ice cream! Now I usually use mostly xylitol with a few doonks of stevia for extra sweetening power if needed. (I've tried making ice cream with all xylitol but found that the amount I needed to use left me with an aftertaste.) In my experience, xylitol dissolves just fine when blended into an ice cream base whether you cook it or not, but if you have a problem with crystals in your ice cream, try powdering the granulated sweetener in a coffee grinder before adding it. Xylitol is poisonous to dogs and gives some people an upset stomach if they're not used to it, so if you're not into using it you could try substituting erythritol or your favorite granulated sweetener that measures like sugar. I haven't tested anything other than xylitol so I'm not sure if other sugar alcohols will have the same anti-freezing effect in ice cream or not. I prefer the taste (or lack thereof) of xylitol over erythritol. You could also try substituting THM Gentle Sweet for both the stevia and the xylitol (to taste); try xylitol-free Gentle Sweet if you want to avoid xylitol. As always, feel free to add more sweetener to my ice cream recipes since my sweet tooth isn't as strong as some of yours!

» VEGETABLE GLYCERIN: This is a clear liquid that helps give ice cream a creamy texture and stay scoopable instead of icy when frozen, then thawed. It also helps keep the ice cream from creating a thick frozen layer on your ice cream canister. From what I've read, vegetable glycerin is safe for diabetics and doesn't spike blood sugar like regular sugar does. I cannot deny or confirm that, but I only use small amounts in my recipes. I made ice cream without vegetable glycerin for awhile, but once I started using it, I haven't made ice cream without it because it improves the texture so much! I always purchase Essential Depot brand from

Amazon, but you can often find vegetable glycerin in the skincare section of grocery or health food stores. A lot of vegetable glycerin is food grade, but if you find one with a poison warning on the label, I suggest finding another brand. I've heard that some vegetable glycerin made for use in cake frostings can have a funky taste in ice cream, so I'd stay away from those.

» **GLUCOMANNAN:** Glucomannan is a natural thickening agent made from the konjac root. Xanthan gum is similar, and they can generally be substituted for each other in the same amount. I've found that adding glucomannan to my ice cream recipes makes them nice and creamy, but I did leave it out of a few recipes when I wanted a more sherbet-like texture. Since glucomannan can clump when it comes into contact with liquid, I add it to the blender last, then immediately put the lid on and blend everything together. Different brands of glucomannan can vary in strength, so if you're using a stronger brand and find that it gives your ice cream a strange texture, try reducing the amount.

» **AIR:** The more air ice cream has in it, the fluffier and softer it will be! This is why I use an ice cream churn. I've also started blending the heavy cream into my cooked ice cream bases to incorporate extra air before churning.

≫ STORING ICE CREAM ≪

» So what if you have leftovers? No, really, sometimes you have leftover ice cream. (Or at least you should. Theoretically.) I recommend storing leftover ice cream in a shallow container with a really good seal. (The shallower the container, the faster the ice cream will thaw to a scoopable consistency at room temperature.) I usually use Tupperware containers.

» When you freeze ice cream leftovers, they will eventually freeze hard. How fast they get hard and exactly how hard they get will vary according to the ingredients you used. When you're ready to eat your ice cream leftovers, simply let them thaw at room temperature until they are your desired consistency. The meltier they are, the creamier they'll be, so don't skimp on thaw time, especially for lighter ice cream recipes!

» DO NOT pour the ice cream mixture into your countertop ice cream churn without turning it on first! If the canister is not rotating with the blades in place before you pour the ice cream mixture into it, the mixture will instantly freeze to the frozen canister and then the blades won't be able to move. You will have a gigantic ice-cream-ice-cube of a fail.

» Make sure your ice cream machine canister is completely frozen before trying to make ice cream, otherwise your ice cream will not freeze properly.

(Your ice cream maker's instruction manual will have information on how long your specific model takes to freeze.) When you first get your ice cream maker and freeze the canister, I recommend letting it freeze for 48 hours to make sure it's completely frozen. For subsequent batches, I like to give my ice cream canister 24 hours in the freezer just to be on the safe side. If you make ice cream extremely frequently, you might want to invest in an extra freezer canister for your ice cream machine.

custard tips

When making ice cream custard bases and puddings, I use a nonstick or stainless steel saucepan over medium heat. Whisk the custard often, and when it starts to get hot, whisk constantly to avoid burning. (Sometimes I turn the heat down a bit when I can tell the custard is almost ready to start cooking.) As soon as the custard starts to bubble slightly, pull it off the heat and keep whisking until thickened. (It will continue to thicken as it cools.) If the custard or pudding contains eggs, the thickening will be almost instantaneous, and you should not keep cooking after that point or you'll end up with scrambled eggs. If the custard doesn't noticeably thicken, place it back over low heat a little longer, still whisking. When in doubt, pull it off the heat and don't overcook! If you have trouble with lumpy puddings, try a lower heat. People with gas stoves will have to be extra vigilant when making custard because gas stoves tend to run hotter with a very direct heat. If your custard or pudding ends up lumpy, you can always strain it. Custard-making is definitely an art, but once you do it a few times you'll get a feel for when your custard is almost done and ready to be pulled off the burner. If you never have luck making custard this way, try the traditional tempering method.

basic vanilla scoopable ice cream

2 cups half and half

2 cups unsweetened almond milk

2 eggs

2 egg yolks

⅛ teaspoon salt

¾ teaspoon glucomannan

1 cup heavy whipping cream

¼ cup xylitol (or more, to taste)

1 tablespoon vegetable glycerin

2 teaspoons vanilla extract

3 doonks THM Pure Stevia Extract Powder

Add the first set of ingredients to a saucepan and blend with an immersion blender until smooth. Add the glucomannan slowly while blending to avoid clumping. Cook the ice cream mixture just until it starts to bubble, whisking occasionally, then pull it off the heat. Add the second set of ingredients and blend with an immersion blender for 1-2 minutes. Let the mixture cool on the counter, then cover and refrigerate for several hours or overnight to chill completely.

When the ice cream base has chilled completely, churn it in a 1½-quart automatic ice cream churn according to manufacturer's directions. Transfer the finished ice cream to an airtight, shallow container and freeze to firm up before eating. I prefer to freeze it overnight until all the way firm, then let it thaw on the counter for 10 minutes before scooping for best taste and texture. (Or longer, for an even creamier texture.)

For years I've tried to find a moderate-calorie homemade ice cream that's scoopable out of the freezer! Storebought sugar-free ice creams are convenient and yummy, but they're often expensive and full of questionable ingredients. Unfortunately homemade ice creams (even the sugary homemade ice cream my family used to make) freeze hard if you don't eat them right after churning. Lots of cream and other fats help ice cream stay softer and creamier after freezing, but they also make it really calorie dense – and I like to enjoy ice cream on a regular basis.

This recipe is the culmination of years of experimentation and research and is a delicate balance of ingredients with a dose of science. I don't recommend replacing ingredients or varying the procedure, unless you're willing to experiment and accept the results, because everything is in here for a reason. I've tried to figure out which elements help ice cream stay softer after being frozen and combined them in a way that gives me a scoopable end result while not overloading the calories.

I don't usually count calories, but I did for this recipe out of curiosity. There are only 159 calories in a half cup serving! (This is how ice cream is usually measured for nutrition, but when I say the recipe serves 8, I'm being more realistic and calculating ¾ cup servings.) A lot of my older recipes are even lighter than this one, but they take longer to thaw to an eatable consistency when leftovers are frozen for an extended period of time.

extreme chocolate ice cream

ICE CREAM

1½ cups heavy whipping cream

⅓ cup + 1 tablespoon xylitol
  (or more, to taste)

1 tablespoon vegetable glycerin

¼ teaspoon salt

⅛ teaspoon THM Pure Stevia
  Extract Powder

3 oz. unsweetened baker's chocolate
  (chopped)

2 cups half and half

1½ cups unsweetened almond milk

½ teaspoon glucomannan

2 tablespoons cocoa powder

1 teaspoon vanilla extract

TRUFFLE SWIRL

1 oz. unsweetened baker's chocolate

2 tablespoons xylitol

1½ tablespoons salted butter

3 tablespoons unsweetened almond milk

¼ teaspoon xanthan gum

Heat the first section of ice cream ingredients together in a saucepan on the stove (or a bowl in the microwave) just until the mixture starts to bubble around the edges. Remove from heat, add the chocolate, and let it stand for 5 minutes. Blend with an immersion blender until smooth. Add the half and half and almond milk a little at a time while blending to incorporate. Do the same with the glucomannan. Add the cocoa powder and vanilla and blend until smooth. Chill completely before churning the mixture in an automatic ice cream churn according to manufacturer's directions.

Meanwhile, make the truffle swirl. Melt the chocolate, xylitol, and butter together in the microwave (or a double boiler) just until they can be whisked together until smooth. Add the almond milk one tablespoon at a time, whisking between each addition. Sprinkle the xanthan gum in while whisking to avoid clumps. Whisk until the mixture thickens, then set aside.

When the ice cream has finished churning, transfer it to a shallow airtight container. Use a spoon to dollop the truffle mixture into the ice cream and swirl it to create ribbons. Freeze the ice cream awhile to let it firm up before serving. If leftovers freeze hard, let them thaw to a scoopable consistency, then enjoy.

Based off of one of my favorite Dairy Queen treats, this is definitely one of the best ice creams I've ever made, both in taste and texture. It tastes like high quality storebought chocolate ice cream! And that truffle swirl. Its fudgy chewiness is the bomb.

note

• The xylitol in the ice cream and the truffle swirl keep both from freezing so hard.

• Make a batch of the truffle swirl to freeze on its own and chop up for use in milkshakes!

butter pecan frozen custard

CANDIED PECANS

1 cup pecan halves

1 tablespoon salted butter

1 tablespoon xylitol

ICE CREAM

2 cups half and half

2 cups unsweetened almond milk

2 eggs

4 egg yolks

⅓ cup xylitol (or more, to taste)

2 tablespoons salted butter

2 tablespoons natural peanut butter

1 tablespoon vegetable glycerin

¼ teaspoon salt

¼ teaspoon maple extract

⅛ teaspoon + 1 doonk THM
    Pure Stevia Extract Powder

1 cup heavy whipping cream

2 teaspoons vanilla extract

Toast the pecans in a nonstick pan with the butter and xylitol over medium-low heat till golden brown and syrupy. Let the pecans cool in the pan, then fold them into the ice cream by hand when it's done churning.

To make the ice cream, blend the first section of ingredients with an immersion blender in a saucepan, then cook the mixture over medium heat until it just starts to bubble, whisking often. Pull the pan off the heat and add the cream and vanilla, blending again until smooth. Chill the mixture completely, then churn in an automatic ice cream churn according to manufacturer's directions. Transfer the ice cream to a shallow airtight container and fold in the toasted pecans. Freeze to firm up before serving. If leftovers freeze hard, let them thaw to a scoopable consistency, then enjoy the rich creaminess.

I've inherited a love of butter pecan ice cream from both of my grandpas, and while I love the simple butter pecan recipe in *Necessary Food*, I wanted to go all out with a frozen custard version one day. This recipe is one of the best, richest ice creams I've ever made and has an amazing texture!

note

• This recipe is a little sweeter than my other ice cream recipes, so you may not want to just double the sweetener willy nilly.

• The peanut butter adds a subtle richness that mimics *real* creamery-level butter pecan. The flavor using two tablespoons is very mild and fits well with the butter pecan vibe, but I'm admittedly a peanut butter lover so if you don't want a hint of peanut butter flavor, decrease the amount to one tablespoon or use almond butter (which is more neutral) in its place.

• Thaw your homemade ice cream leftovers at room temperature until they're getting melty around the edges for the most creamy texture.

brianafinger ice cream

HEALTHY FATS | SERVES 5-6

3 cups unsweetened almond milk

½ cup + 2 tablespoons heavy whipping cream

½ cup cottage cheese

¼ cup + 2 tablespoons natural peanut butter

1 tablespoon vegetable glycerin

1 teaspoon vanilla extract

⅛ teaspoon + 3-4 doonks THM
   Pure Stevia Extract Powder

⅛ teaspoon salt (scant)

¾ teaspoon glucomannan

½ tablespoon salted butter

½ cup unsweetened coconut flakes

50 grams 85% dark chocolate
   (2 wrapped candy bar sections from
   the Moser Roth bars found at Aldi)

Make the ice cream by blending the first section of ingredients together until smooth and churning in an automatic ice cream churn according to manufacturer's directions.

While the ice cream is churning, toast the coconut in the butter in a skillet on the stovetop. When the coconut is toasted, transfer it to a freezer-safe container and chop/shave the dark chocolate over it. Put this in the freezer to chill until the ice cream is finished churning.

When the ice cream is finished churning, transfer the ice cream to the freezer container and stir the coconut flakes and chocolate into

the ice cream. Serve immediately or freeze for an hour or so to firm it up some more.

Homemade ice cream, especially light ice cream like this, is best fresh, but if you have leftovers, freeze them in a shallow airtight container, then thaw for 30 minutes on the counter before eating.

This recipe was made in the era before I learned that xylitol really improves the texture and scoopability of homemade ice cream. Feel free to replace part of the stevia with a few tablespoons of xylitol (sweeten to taste).

no-bake cookie ice cream

1⅔ cups unsweetened almond milk

1 cup heavy whipping cream

1 cup half and half

1 cup pasteurized egg whites

¼ cup + 2 tablespoons xylitol
   (or more, to taste)

⅓ cup cottage cheese

1 tablespoon vegetable glycerin

2 teaspoons vanilla extract

⅛ teaspoon salt

2 doonks THM Pure Stevia Extract Powder

¾ teaspoon glucomannan

COOKIE CRUMBLE

½ cup unsweetened coconut flakes

¼ cup + 2 tablespoons old-fashioned oats

1½ tablespoons salted butter (melted)

1½ tablespoons natural peanut butter

2 teaspoons cocoa powder

1¼ teaspoons THM Super Sweet Blend
   (or more, to taste)

Blend the first section of ingredients together until smooth, adding the glucomannan right before blending to avoid clumping. Churn in an automatic ice cream churn according to manufacturer's directions.

Meanwhile, stir the cookie crumble ingredients together and freeze to harden. When the ice cream is done churning (it will be a soft serve consistency), transfer it to a shallow airtight container and stir in the cookie crumble pieces with a spatula. Freeze the ice cream for a few hours to firm up before serving.

If leftovers freeze hard, just let them thaw to a scoopable consistency before eating. (I like to thaw this ice cream till fairly soft for ultimate creaminess since the ice cream part is relatively low in fat.)

note

The oats in the cookie crumble contribute a little over 2 grams net carbs per serving. You're welcome to try substituting more coconut flakes for some or all of the oats.

candy cane ice cream

HEALTHY FATS | SERVES 8

2 cups half and half

2 cups unsweetened almond milk

4 egg yolks

⅛ teaspoon salt

1 teaspoon glucomannan

1 cup heavy whipping cream

¼ cup xylitol (or more, to taste)

1 tablespoon vegetable glycerin

1 teaspoon each peppermint extract,
   vanilla extract

3 doonks THM Pure Stevia Extract Powder

5-6 drops red food coloring

Blend the first set of ingredients until smooth (I use an immersion blender) and cook in a nonstick kettle just until the mixture starts to bubble, whisking often. As soon as it starts to bubble, pull it off the heat.

Add the second set of ingredients. Peppermint extracts can vary in strength, so start with less than 1 teaspoon and work your way up, tasting as you go. Blend these ingredients into the ice cream base; I use an immersion blender so I don't have to blend hot liquids in a covered blender. Let the ice cream base cool to room temperature, then refrigerate to chill completely before churning (overnight is great). Churn the ice cream in an automatic countertop ice cream churn according to manufacturer's directions. Transfer to a shallow sealable container and swirl 5-6 drops of red food coloring into the ice cream with a spatula for a candy cane effect. Freeze to firm up before serving. Ice cream frozen for long periods will freeze hard, but when stored in a shallow container, it thaws to scoopable consistency in about 10 minutes on the kitchen counter!

This Candy Cane Ice Cream is one of my favorite ice creams to date; even my DAD said it was good, and from the guy who dramatically shivers from the aftertaste every time he takes a bite of something sweetened with an alternative sweetener, that's saying a lot! (He often enjoys my savory recipes, but he would rather do without sweets than detect any aftertaste.) This ice cream is good right after churning, but it's actually meant to be eaten when it's harder, like a scooped ice cream. If you let it freeze hard in the freezer for a few hours or overnight, it will thaw to a scoopable texture at room temperature in about 10 minutes! The key is to use a shallow container so it thaws faster. The texture is amazing!

note

Feel free to add some crushed sugar-free peppermints or a chocolate ganache swirl to take it over the top! The Plain Hot Fudge Sauce (page 413) or Peanut Butter Hot Fudge Topping (page 414) from *Necessary Food* would be great toppings. Or serve with Bri's Best Fudgy Brownies on page 391 of this book!

pecan pie ice cream

HEALTHY FATS I SERVES 8

ICE CREAM

2 cups half and half

2 cups unsweetened almond milk

1 cup heavy whipping cream

5 egg yolks

1 teaspoon cinnamon

1 teaspoon molasses

⅛ teaspoon each ground cloves, salt

¾ teaspoon glucomannan

¼ cup xylitol (or more, to taste)

1 tablespoon vegetable glycerin

2 teaspoons vanilla extract

½ teaspoon butter extract

3 doonks THM Pure Stevia Extract Powder

CRUST PIECES

¼ cup + 2 tablespoons Briana's Baking Mix

2 tablespoons water

1 tablespoon salted butter (softened)

¼ teaspoon THM Super Sweet Blend

½ cup pecan halves and pieces

CARAMEL

¼ cup heavy whipping cream

2 tablespoons unsweetened almond milk

2 tablespoons salted butter

1½ teaspoons Truvia

First, make the ice cream base. Blend the first section of ice cream ingredients until smooth. Add the mixture to a nonstick kettle and cook over medium-high heat, stirring often. Remove the kettle from the heat as soon as the mixture starts to bubble. Whisk in the second section of ingredients, then cool the mixture to room temperature. Refrigerate to chill completely.

Before churning the ice cream, make the crust pieces and caramel. Mix the first 4 crust ingredients until crumbs form, then bake with the pecans on a baking sheet at 350° until they start to brown (about 15-20 minutes). Stir occasionally. Remove the crumbs and pecans from the oven, transfer them to another container (such as the container you want to put your ice cream in), and put them in the freezer to chill before you add the freshly-churned ice cream.

To make the caramel, whisk the ingredients together in a nonstick saucepan over medium-low heat. Simmer (uncovered) until the caramel reaches a golden-brown color, stirring occasionally. (This takes 20-30 minutes.) Remove the caramel from the heat and let it cool to room temperature before stirring it into the ice cream.

When the crust pieces and caramel have cooled, churn the chilled ice cream mixture in a countertop ice cream maker according to manufacturer's directions. Transfer the ice cream to a shallow sealable container and gently stir in the crust pieces, pecan halves, and caramel by hand. Don't overmix; you want to be able to distinguish all the different elements. Freeze for several hours to firm up before serving. Ice cream that is frozen for an extended period of time will freeze hard, but just let it thaw at room temperature for 40-50 minutes to return it to the ultimate scoopable texture.

angelic peanut butter cup ice cream

HEALTHY FATS | SERVES 8

1½ cups half and half

1½ cups unsweetened almond milk

1 cup pasteurized egg whites

⅔ cup low-fat cottage cheese

¼ cup vanilla whey protein powder

¼ cup + 1 tablespoon xylitol (or more, to taste)

3 tablespoons cocoa powder

2 tablespoons defatted peanut flour

1 tablespoon vegetable glycerin

1 teaspoon vanilla extract

⅛ teaspoon THM Pure Stevia
   Extract Powder

⅛ teaspoon salt

1 teaspoon glucomannan

PEANUT BUTTER CUP SWIRL

⅓ cup defatted peanut flour

⅓ cup water

1 tablespoon refined coconut oil (melted)

2½ teaspoons THM Super Sweet Blend

¼ teaspoon glucomannan

Hearty dash salt

Blend the ice cream ingredients until smooth. Churn in an automatic countertop ice cream churn according to manufacturer's directions. Don't under-churn! The mixture will stop moving in the churn while it's still pretty soft, but just let it keep churning for 10-15 more minutes to firm up a little more and incorporate more air into the ice cream. The end result will still be a soft serve consistency, but nice and creamy and not super melty.

While the ice cream is churning, make the peanut butter swirl by whisking the ingredients together to a peanut butter consistency.

When the ice cream is done churning, transfer it to a shallow airtight container. Use a spatula or spreader to swirl the peanut butter mixture through the ice cream, then freeze it to firm up before serving. If leftovers are frozen solid, let them warm up at room temperature for about 15 minutes to let them thaw to a scoopable texture. (The shallower the container, the quicker and more evenly it will thaw.) You can always nuke your serving for a few seconds to make it creamier.

angelic birthday cake ice cream

1½ cups unsweetened almond milk

1½ cups half and half

1 cup pasteurized egg whites

⅔ cup low-fat cottage cheese

¼ cup + 1 tablespoon xylitol (or more, to taste)

¼ cup vanilla whey protein powder

1 tablespoon vegetable glycerin

2 teaspoons vanilla extract

½ teaspoon each almond extract, butter extract

¼ teaspoon baking powder

2 doonks THM Pure Stevia Extract Powder

4 drops yellow food coloring

1 teaspoon glucomannan

Blend the ice cream ingredients for about 30 seconds. Churn in an automatic countertop ice cream churn according to manufacturer's directions. Don't under-churn! The mixture will stop moving in the churn while it's still pretty soft, but just let it keep churning for 10-15 more minutes to firm up a little more and incorporate more air into the ice cream. The end result will still be a soft serve consistency, but nice and creamy and not super melty.

When the ice cream is done churning, transfer it to a shallow airtight container, then freeze it to firm up before serving. If leftovers are frozen solid, let them warm up at room temperature for about 15 minutes to let them thaw to a scoopable texture. (The shallower the container, the quicker and more evenly it will thaw.) You can always nuke your serving for a few seconds to make it creamier.

I like to top my birthday cake ice cream with a little bit of peanut butter, but if you want to stay on the lower calorie side, keep that to a minimum or use peanut butter made with defatted peanut flour. A few (very few) sprinkles add to the birthday cake vibe but are obviously not sugar free. I doubt 20 sprinkles are going to make a huge dent in your progress, to be very honest, but that will be upon your own head.

These "angelic" ice cream recipes are on the lighter side so they may not be as creamy as some, but they remind me a lot of the specialty low calorie, low sugar, high protein ice cream pints on the market these days and are my new favorite evening snack!

foundational frozen custard

⅓ cup refined coconut oil

3 cups unsweetened almond milk

2 eggs

4 egg yolks

¼ cup + 2 tablespoons xylitol (or more, to taste)

1 tablespoon vanilla extract

¼ teaspoon salt

2 doonks THM Pure Stevia Extract Powder

½ teaspoon glucomannan

Melt the coconut oil in a saucepan on the stovetop. Add the rest of the ingredients except the glucomannan and blend with an immersion blender. Add the glucomannan slowly while blending to avoid clumps. Cook over medium heat just until the mixture starts to bubble, whisking often. Pull it off the heat immediately. Cool, then chill completely before churning.

Churn in an automatic ice cream churn according to manufacturer's directions. Transfer to a shallow airtight container and enjoy immediately, or freeze for a few hours to firm up. Let leftovers thaw to a scoopable consistency before eating.

This frozen custard makes a terrific creamy French vanilla ice cream! (Psst – it's dairy free!) Add some Superfood Brownies (page 393) and Foundational Peanut Butter Topping (page 490) for a Foundation Fats ice cream sundae!

note

• The chilled custard doubles as a nice spoonable pudding! (It's not thick enough for a pie filling.) If you want a chocolate pudding or a chocolate frozen custard, blend in some cocoa powder and extra sweetener after cooking the custard.

• I bet this custard would make great vanilla pudding pops! Blend in some cocoa powder and extra sweetener after cooking the custard for chocolate pops.

light chocolate ice cream

3 cups unsweetened almond milk

9 egg yolks

¼ cup + 1 tablespoon xylitol
(or more, to taste)

¼ cup cocoa powder

3 tablespoons refined coconut oil
(not melted)

1 teaspoon plain gelatin

⅛ teaspoon salt

2 doonks THM Pure Stevia Extract Powder

½ teaspoon glucomannan

Blend all the ingredients together in a high-powered blender until smooth and emulsified. Let the mixture rest a bit, then blend again until it gets a little lighter in color. Churn in an automatic ice cream churn according to manufacturer's directions. If you like, you can freeze the ice cream for a few hours for a firmer texture before serving.

Once frozen overnight, this ice cream will get firmer but won't freeze rock hard. Let it sit out on the counter for 10-15 minutes to let it soften up a bit before scooping.

note

• Scared of using raw egg yolks? Use yolks from pasteurized eggs. You can buy these or make your own (Google it).

• If you don't need this ice cream to be Foundation Fats compatible, I recommend adding a tablespoon or two of vegetable glycerin (with the rest of the ingredients in the blender) for a softer, creamier texture.

Who satisfieth thy mouth with good things;
so that thy youth is renewed like the eagle's.

PSALM 103:5

café au lait ice cream

HEALTHY FATS | SERVES 8

2 (13.66 oz.) cans full-fat coconut milk

1 (13.66 oz) can light coconut milk

⅓ cup xylitol (or more, to taste)

2 tablespoons espresso instant coffee powder

1 tablespoon vegetable glycerin

2 teaspoons vanilla extract

⅛ teaspoon salt

3 doonks THM Pure Stevia Extract Powder

Blend the ingredients together until smooth, then churn in an automatic ice cream churn according to manufacturer's directions. Transfer the ice cream to a shallow airtight container and freeze for a few hours to firm up before serving. If leftovers freeze hard, just let them thaw to a scoopable consistency before eating. Coconut milk ice creams tend to be icier than dairy ice creams, so they're best when eaten on the melty side.

The French term "café au lait" means "coffee with milk" and describes the strength of the coffee flavor in this ice cream well. I guess it's not technically ice cream because it contains no cream, but it's delicious!

note

• I used Medaglia D'Oro brand espresso instant coffee, which I found at my local grocery store. I believe it's available from Walmart as well. I don't recommend using plain ol' instant coffee; it doesn't taste as good. Feel free to make the coffee flavor stronger with more espresso powder if you like.

• Feel free to add a dash of hazelnut, caramel, or maple flavoring to replicate your favorite coffee shop flavor!

• Make a float with this ice cream and some cold (or hot) coffee!

creamy red raspberry sherbet

2 (13.66 oz.) cans full-fat coconut milk
2 cups red raspberries (fresh or frozen)
⅓ cup xylitol (or more, to taste)
1 tablespoon vegetable glycerin
2 teaspoons vanilla extract
⅛ teaspoon THM Pure Stevia
    Extract Powder

Blend the ingredients together until smooth, then churn in an automatic ice cream churn according to manufacturer's directions. Transfer the ice cream to a shallow airtight container and enjoy immediately or freeze for a few hours to firm up before serving. If leftovers freeze hard, just let them thaw to a scoopable consistency before eating. Coconut milk ice creams tend to be icier than dairy ice creams, so they're best when eaten on the melty side.

note

I bet the blended mixture would be good frozen as popsicles!

Technically sherbet in the USA must contain a small percentage of milkfat. This recipe obviously does not, but the texture reminds me of a creamy raspberry sherbet! The vibrant color and taste along with the silky-smooth texture make this one of my favorite ice cream recipes. You can taste the coconut milk in this recipe as well as my other coconut milk based ice cream recipes, but the key is finding flavors that pair well with the coconut. Red raspberry certainly does!

strawberry cardamom superfood ice cream

2 cups unsweetened almond milk

1 cup frozen diced okra (thawed)

1 cup strawberries

½ cup cottage cheese

½ cup heavy whipping cream

1 tablespoon vegetable glycerin

1 teaspoon vanilla extract

⅛ teaspoon + 3 doonks THM
  Pure Stevia Extract Powder

⅛ teaspoon ground cardamom
  (or more, to taste)

⅛ teaspoon salt

½ teaspoon glucomannan

Blend all the ingredients together until smooth. Strain if desired (I do not). Churn the mixture in an automatic countertop ice cream churn according to manufacturer's directions. Transfer the ice cream to a shallow sealable container and serve immediately or freeze for an hour or so until the desired firmness is reached.

Leftovers frozen for an extended period of time will freeze hard, but if you thaw them in the refrigerator for 3-4 hours or on the counter for 30-40 minutes, they'll taste great!

note

• I recommend using frozen okra, not fresh, because frozen okra has been blanched. The blanching process helps cut some of the sliminess for which okra is known and helps the okra blend better.

• This recipe was made in the era before I learned that xylitol really improves the texture and scoopability of homemade ice cream. Feel free to replace part of the stevia with a few tablespoons of xylitol (sweeten to taste).

Take my love; my Lord, I pour at Thy feet its treasure-store.
  Take myself, and I will be ever, only, all for Thee.
FRANCES RIDLEY HAVERGAL - "TAKE MY LIFE, AND LET IT BE"

strawberry frozen kefir

HEALTHY FATS, HEALTHY CARBS, OR LOW CARB/LOW FAT | SERVES 5-6

3 cups milk kefir

2 cups sliced strawberries

¼ cup xylitol (or more, to taste)

1 tablespoon vegetable glycerin

2 teaspoons vanilla extract

3 doonks THM Pure Stevia Extract Powder

Blend the ingredients until smooth. Churn in an automatic countertop ice cream churn according to manufacturer's directions. Transfer the frozen kefir to a shallow airtight container and enjoy immediately or freeze to firm up to your desired consistency. (I like the frozen kefir best when it's a little firmer.)

Leftover frozen kefir is actually nearly scoopable right out of the freezer, and it gets even softer as it sits at room temperature for a few minutes.

The tang of the kefir plays well with strawberry, giving this "ice cream" a bright, refreshing flavor. It's almost sherbet-like in texture. I didn't want to call it "ice cream" since it doesn't have any cream in it, so I called it what it is: Strawberry Frozen Kefir!

note

• The type of kefir you use will determine the fuel type of this frozen kefir. If you use single-fermented low-fat kefir (regular low-fat store-bought kefir), it's Healthy Carbs. If you use double-fermented low-fat kefir, it's Low Carb/Low Fat. If you use double-fermented full-fat kefir, it's Healthy Fats.

• Some kefir is actually lactose free, so keep that in mind if you have allergies. I used Green Valley Organics brand of low-fat kefir. It was super thick and creamy - and lactose free.

• Feel free to substitute your favorite fruit or berry for the strawberries! I think peaches or cherries would be great in this with double-fermented low-fat kefir for a Healthy Carbs option.

• Kefir is not pronounced "KEE-fur." It's "kuh-FEAR."

creamy black cherry soft serve

2½ cups plain low-fat yogurt

2 cups dark sweet cherries

1½ cups low-fat cottage cheese

¼ cup xylitol (or more, to taste)

1 tablespoon vegetable glycerin

2 teaspoons vanilla extract

⅛ teaspoon THM Pure Stevia Extract Powder

Blend the ingredients together until smooth, then churn in an automatic ice cream churn according to manufacturer's directions. Transfer the ice cream to a shallow airtight container and enjoy immediately or freeze for a few hours to firm up before serving. If leftovers freeze hard, just let them thaw to a scoopable consistency before eating. (I like to thaw this ice cream for about an hour for ultimate creaminess since it's low fat, but the time will vary according to the size of the storage container.)

Ryan loved the creaminess of this cherry soft serve! The cottage cheese is the key to the creaminess; it creates a better texture than using all yogurt.

note

• Feel free to add ½ cup chopped cherries by hand after churning for some texture.

• I used homemade regular yogurt, not Greek yogurt, because that's what I had on hand. You're welcome to try Greek yogurt in its place for extra protein, but it may have a tangier flavor and thicker texture. You could also try using low-fat kefir in place of the yogurt.

• If you notice any cottage cheese flavor right after churning, try freezing the ice cream firm before thawing and eating.

• I bet the blended mixture would be good frozen as popsicles!

• I ate this with a quick peanut butter sauce made with defatted peanut flour, THM Super Sweet Blend and salt to taste, and water to the right consistency.

peach ice cream

1 cup unsweetened almond milk

¾ teaspoon glucomannan

3 cups sliced peaches

¼ cup xylitol

1 cup low-fat cottage cheese

½ cup half and half

½ cup pasteurized egg whites

1 tablespoon vegetable glycerin

1 teaspoon vanilla extract

2 doonks THM Pure Stevia Extract Powder

Add the glucomannan to the almond milk in a nonstick saucepan while whisking so the glucomannan doesn't clump. Add the peaches and xylitol and bring to a boil. Simmer for 10 minutes, then remove from the heat and cool to room temperature.

Add the cooled peach mixture to a blender with the rest of the ingredients. Blend until smooth, then churn in an automatic ice cream churn according to manufacturer's directions. Enjoy immediately or freeze for a few hours to firm up before serving.

Leftovers frozen long-term will freeze hard, but if you let the container sit out on the counter for an hour before serving, the ice cream will soften up nicely. Since it doesn't have a high fat content to make it super creamy, I like to eat it on the soft side.

TIP ▼

In general, let your ice cream churn longer than you think is necessary to incorporate more air. I let mine churn until it's hard enough that it no longer moves through the ice cream churn paddles *or* until it's been churning for awhile with no noticeable change in texture. The final firmness of your ice cream will depend on the ingredients used and the amount of fat it contains. Make sure your ice cream freezer bowl is frozen solid and your ice cream base is cold before churning for best results.

single-serve peach frozen yogurt

1 med.-lg. peach (sliced, frozen)
⅔ cup low-fat Greek yogurt
⅓ cup unsweetened almond milk
1-2 doonks THM Pure Stevia Extract Powder
Dash vanilla extract

Blend the ingredients together until smooth. I used a Vitamix with a tamper to get the thick mixture to blend; if you don't have a tamper you may need to stop the blender a few times and scrape down the sides with a spatula to encourage the mixture to incorporate.

Freeze the mixture in a bowl in the freezer for an hour or until the desired consistency is reached, stirring often for best results. Enjoy!

I love to use this simple peach frozen yogurt as a post-running snack! I usually run in the evening, and since I don't like to eat super calorie-dense things right before I go to bed, this frozen yogurt fits the bill perfectly and still gives me the protein I need after working out. I blend it up before I go running, then put it in the freezer to firm up so I can enjoy it when I come back in. This isn't ideal for texture (it's best to be able to stir it frequently while it freezes for a smoother texture), but it still works and I have a refreshingly cold treat waiting for me when I'm finished running!

single-serve mocha chip frozen yogurt

HEALTHY FATS | SERVES 1

⅔ cup Greek yogurt

3 tablespoons half and half

1-2 tablespoons sugar-free chocolate chips

1 tablespoon THM Super Sweet Blend

1½ teaspoons espresso instant coffee powder

1 teaspoon cocoa powder

Dash vanilla extract

Dash salt

Whisk the ingredients together and enjoy as-is or freeze for 40 minutes to a frozen yogurt consistency, stirring often for best texture.

I definitely prefer ice cream to frozen yogurt, but when it comes to making a quick snack that's full of protein and light on calories, a single-serve frozen yogurt is the way to go! This mocha chip version is super refreshing. If you don't want to wait for it to freeze, just enjoy it as flavored yogurt.

note

• Use low-fat Greek yogurt, replace the half and half with unsweetened almond milk, and use only a sprinkling of chocolate chips for a Low Carb/Low Fat option.

• I used far more sweetener in this yogurt than I typically would because the chocolate and coffee flavors combined with the yogurt just seemed to need it! I used Super Sweet Blend instead of my typical stevia in this recipe because it pairs better with the slightly bitter/tangy notes of coffee, chocolate, and yogurt.

THE TASK IS
NOT YOURS
to complete,
but neither are you
free to desist from it.
MISHNAH (AVOT 2:21)

single-serve pb&j soft serve

HEALTHY FATS | SERVES 1-2

1 cup cottage cheese
1 cup frozen strawberries
2 tablespoons natural peanut butter
3 doonks THM Pure Stevia Extract Powder

Blend all the ingredients together in a high-powered blender until smooth. I used a Vitamix; the tamper works well to get thick things to blend smoothly. If you don't have a blender with a tamper you may need to stop the blender and scrape the sides periodically or add a little liquid. A food processor or immersion blender may also work.

 note

For a Low Carb/Low Fat version, use low-fat cottage cheese and 2-3 tablespoons defatted peanut flour in place of the peanut butter.

Thus saith the Lord, thy redeemer, and he that formed thee from the womb, I am the Lord that maketh all things; that stretcheth forth the heavens alone; that spreadeth abroad the earth by myself. ISAIAH 44:24

For by him were all things created, that are in heaven, and that are in earth, visible and invisible, whether they be thrones, or dominions, or principalities, or powers: all things were created by him, and for him: And he is before all things, and by him all things consist. COLOSSIANS 1:16-17

mango soft serve for one

1 cup frozen mango chunks
1 cup low-fat cottage cheese
2 doonks THM Pure Stevia Extract Powder

Blend the ingredients together until smooth, then enjoy! You can pop it in the freezer for a bit if you want it to be firmer, but I like it right after blending.

I actually used an immersion blender to make this, but a regular blender with a tamper or even a food processor would probably work. If you have trouble blending the mixture because it's too thick, try an immersion blender (really, it works!) or add some almond milk. If you do this it will be runnier so you'll probably need to pop it in the freezer after blending to firm it up a bit.

This is one of the easiest, yummiest ways to beat the heat in the summer!

Ye that love the Lord, hate evil.
PSALM 97:10A

note

• I know many of you are going to look at this recipe and say, "Nope - don't like cottage cheese." To me, the mango does a great job of hiding the cottage cheese flavor, but if the idea weirds you out or you can indeed taste the cottage cheese and don't like it, try substituting part or all of the cottage cheese with low-fat Greek yogurt for a frozen yogurt version. I prefer the creaminess of cottage cheese to the tanginess of Greek yogurt so the cottage cheese version will always be my personal pick.

• Strawberry and mango pair very well together, so feel free to use part frozen mango chunks, part frozen strawberries! I get my frozen mango from Walmart.

single-serve peanut butter ice cream

HEALTHY FATS I SERVES I

1 cup crushed ice

⅓ cup cottage cheese

¼ cup unsweetened almond milk

2 tablespoons whey protein powder or collagen

2 tablespoons half and half

1½ tablespoons natural peanut butter

2 doonks THM Pure Stevia Extract Powder

¼ teaspoon glucomannan

Blend all the ingredients together in a high-powered blender until smooth (the mixture will be thick). Transfer to a bowl and stick it in the freezer for 30-40 minutes to firm up, stirring every 10-15 minutes for optimum texture. Enjoy!

note

• Whey protein powder makes this recipe slightly creamier, but I prefer the taste when it is made with collagen. My taste buds just don't like protein powder very well.

• You could use 2 tablespoons defatted peanut flour instead of the peanut butter, but I prefer the texture and taste when using peanut butter. The oil in natural peanut butter tends to separate, so I like to take advantage of that and use the stiff, dry peanut butter that is left behind. This cuts back on fat but preserves the intense peanut flavor. If you decide to use defatted peanut flour and low-fat cottage cheese, this recipe would be Low Carb/Low Fat.

• If you prefer a little extra sweetness, add a little THM Super Sweet Blend to round things out.

single-serve mint chocolate chip ice cream

1 cup crushed ice

⅓ cup fresh spinach

⅓ cup cottage cheese

⅓ cup half and half

2 tablespoons collagen

1 teaspoon THM Super Sweet Blend
   (or more, to taste)

2 doonks THM Pure Stevia Extract Powder

Small dash each mint extract,
   peppermint extract (to taste)

¼ teaspoon glucomannan (rounded)

Chopped 85% dark chocolate or
   sugar-free chocolate chips

Blend the first section of ingredients in a blender until smooth. Be sure to use only a small amount of the mint and peppermint extracts at first, then increase to taste if desired. It's easy to get too much (but the strength will dissipate a bit when frozen)! Stir the chopped chocolate or chocolate chips into the ice cream by hand, then put the ice cream in the freezer for 30-60 minutes until the desired consistency is reached, stirring often. Enjoy! You can use this as a dessert or a snack on its own since it contains protein. Hey, you could even eat it for breakfast if you want!

It probably comes as no surprise to you that I like to top this ice cream with peanut butter.

note

• Don't have spinach? Leave it out, add a drop of green food coloring (or omit entirely and have a white mint chocolate chip ice cream), and miss out on the green benefits.

• I used a Vitamix with a tamper to blend this up. If your blender doesn't have a tamper or another way to coax the mixture into the blades, you may need to add a little more liquid to get it to blend; unsweetened almond milk, more half and half, or a little cream would work. If you do this, you may need to freeze it a little longer to bring it to the right consistency.

instant frozen chocolate pudding

LOW CARB/LOW FAT I SERVES 1

9 ice cubes

½ cup unsweetened almond milk

2 tablespoons collagen

1½ tablespoons cocoa powder

2 teaspoons THM Super Sweet Blend
(or more, to taste)

½ teaspoon vanilla extract

¼ teaspoon baking powder

Hearty dash salt

Slight dash almond extract

¾ teaspoon glucomannan

Blend all the ingredients together until smooth. Let the mixture sit for a bit, then blend again. The pudding will be very thick, so scrape down the sides of the blender with a spatula in between blending if necessary to help it mix (or use a tamper if your blender comes with one). My Vitamix does a good job. Don't be afraid to let it blend for a good while to let the pudding thicken and get creamy as the glucomannan and collagen react. I like to put the pudding in a glass and freeze it for a few minutes while I clean the blender so it gets even more firm.

This is a variation on the Instant Frozen Coffee Pudding on page 249 of *Necessary Food* – and this one is dairy free! The baking powder and almond extract are in there for a flavor that mimics one of my favorite fast food ice cream treats – the Wendy's Frosty.

note

• For a creamier version (not dairy free), replace part of the almond milk with a few tablespoons of half and half or whipping cream. This puts it into the Healthy Fats category. (3 tablespoons half and half can squeeze into the Low Carb/Low Fat category.)

• Mix-ins welcome! Sugar-free chocolate chips, brownie chunks, etc.

Do not have your concert first and tune
your instrument afterward. Begin the day with God.
HUDSON TAYLOR

instant frozen blueberry pudding

1 cup frozen blueberries

½ cup unsweetened almond milk

4 ice cubes

2 tablespoons collagen

2 teaspoons THM Super Sweet Blend

½ teaspoon vanilla extract

Hearty dash salt

½ teaspoon glucomannan

Blend all the ingredients together until smooth. Let the mixture sit for a bit, then blend again. The pudding will be very thick, so scrape down the sides of the blender with a spatula in between blending if necessary to help it mix (or use a tamper if your blender comes with one). My Vitamix does a good job. Don't be afraid to let it blend for a good while to let the pudding thicken and get creamy as the glucomannan and collagen react.

note

If you think this frozen pudding needs to be creamier, try adding 2 tablespoons cottage cheese. I really don't think it's necessary, though! The frozen berries give this frozen pudding a great texture.

This is definitely my favorite of the instant frozen puddings. I love blueberry stuff, and this recipe has a creamy soft serve texture that is so refreshing! Since blueberries are higher in natural sugars than many other berries, this frozen pudding belongs in a Healthy Carbs category. If you want to stay Low Carb/Low Fat, try using frozen raspberries (or another strong-flavored berry) instead of blueberries!

instant frozen lemon pudding

12 ice cubes

½ cup unsweetened almond milk

1 lg. lemon (peeled)

2 tablespoons collagen

½ teaspoon vanilla extract

⅛ teaspoon THM Pure Stevia Extract Powder

Hearty dash salt

¾ teaspoon glucomannan

Blend all the ingredients together until smooth. Let the mixture sit for a bit, then blend again. This pudding isn't quite as thick as some of the other frozen pudding recipes, but if necessary, scrape down the sides of the blender with a spatula in between blending to help it mix (or use a tamper if your blender comes with one). Don't be afraid to let it blend for a good while to let the pudding thicken and get creamy as the glucomannan and collagen react.

Oh, the frothy, lemony goodness! I love the texture of this one – it's just a little softer than the other frozen pudding recipes and it reminds me of the Frosted Lemonade from Chick-fil-A! The real lemon adds a lot here, and I'm not responsible for what happens if you use bottled lemon juice instead.

note

• For a creamier version (not dairy free), replace part of the almond milk with a few tablespoons of half and half or whipping cream. This puts it into the Healthy Fats category. (3 tablespoons half and half can squeeze into the Low Carb/Low Fat category.) You could even add 2 tablespoons cottage cheese (Low Carb/Low Fat).

• I like it tart, but if you want it to be sweeter, add some THM Super Sweet Blend.

• Don't like lemon? Try it with limes instead! 1 large lemon made about ½ cup chopped lemon wedges.

ice cream fried taco for one

1 low-carb tortilla
½ cup sugar-free vanilla ice cream of choice
Refined coconut oil (for frying)
THM Super Sweet Blend and cinnamon

Heat a dollop of coconut oil in a skillet. (You want it to be good and hot before adding the ice cream taco so it browns instantly.)

Place a half cup dollop of ice cream in the center of a low-carb tortilla and fold each side over to make a square package shape. Secure with toothpicks.

Fry the taco on both sides until lightly golden brown on each side; don't fry too long or all the ice cream will melt. Fry it seam side down first, then flip so the seam side is up once the ice cream starts melting. Sprinkle each side of the tortilla generously with Super Sweet Blend and cinnamon while it's still wet with oil. Remove toothpicks and enjoy (quickly)!

This gal loves her fried tacos and her ice cream, so this combination was a no-brainer. It's kind of a mess, but it works and it's so good!

note

• I used Breyers Carb Smart Vanilla Ice Cream for convenience in this recipe. It's sweetened with Splenda, which isn't ideal but is OK as a personal choice item once in awhile. Carb Smart melts quickly, so a harder homemade ice cream might actually hold up better in this recipe.

• You could add a drizzle of melted sugar-free chocolate chips and some toasted coconut for extra crunch after frying if you want to get fancy.

peppermint brownie ice cream cake

HEALTHY FATS | SERVES 12

BROWNIES

⅔ cup Briana's Baking Mix

⅔ cup oat fiber

⅔ cup cocoa powder

¼ cup THM Gentle Sweet (or more, to taste)

2 tablespoons THM Super Sweet Blend

2 teaspoons baking powder

¾ teaspoon xanthan gum

½ teaspoon salt

16 tablespoons salted butter (softened)

1 cup unsweetened almond milk

1 cup water

2 eggs

¼ cup egg whites

PEPPERMINT ICE CREAM

2 cups heavy whipping cream

2 cups unsweetened almond milk

½ cup cottage cheese

1 tablespoon vegetable glycerin

1 teaspoon vanilla extract

½ teaspoon peppermint extract

¼ teaspoon THM Pure Stevia Extract Powder

⅛ teaspoon salt

4 drops red food coloring

1 teaspoon glucomannan

10 sugar-free peppermints
  (coarsely chopped)

FUDGE

3 tablespoons salted butter

2 tablespoons refined coconut oil

2 tablespoons cocoa powder

2 teaspoons THM Super Sweet Blend

¼ cup + 2 tablespoons heavy whipping cream

Chopped sugar-free peppermints
  (for garnish)

BROWNIES: Whisk the dry ingredients. Add the wet ingredients and beat until smooth. Pour the brownie batter into a greased 9"x13" pan and smooth the top. (For foolproof removal from the pan, line the pan with parchment paper.) Bake at 350° for 25 minutes. Let the brownies cool, then refrigerate until completely chilled.

ICE CREAM: (make after brownie is chilled) Blend all the ice cream ingredients except the peppermints in a blender until smooth. Churn the mixture in an automatic countertop ice cream churn. When the ice cream is done churning, transfer it to a shallow container, stir the chopped peppermints in by hand, and freeze for 40 minutes (or until the ice cream is firm enough to support a layer of brownie as you assemble the cake).

ASSEMBLY: Cut the brownie layer in half lengthwise so you have two pieces of brownie that are 13" long. Carefully remove them intact from the baking pan and place one on a serving platter. Top the brownie with half the ice cream and smooth it with a spatula, then top that with the other piece of brownie. Spread the remaining ice cream on top. Freeze the ice cream cake in a level spot in your freezer (this is important) until it is structurally solid.

FUDGE: Melt the butter and coconut oil together. Whisk in the cocoa powder and Super Sweet Blend. Whisk in the cream, but only whisk until the mixture has thickened. If you whisk it too long, the fudge will clump.

ASSEMBLY: Pour and/or spread the fudge mixture on top of the ice cream cake, then top with chopped peppermints. The fudge layer will harden quickly on the cold cake. Wrap the cake in tinfoil and freeze solid. The cake can be stored in the freezer for a few days if necessary.

SERVING: Slowly thaw the ice cream cake in the refrigerator for 3 hours before serving. Let the cake sit out at room temperature for half an hour, then slice into 12 slices with a sharp knife. Serve. Freeze leftover cake slices between wax paper or tinfoil so you can thaw them individually as the need arises (10-15 seconds in the microwave on "defrost" works great).

Be still my beating heart. Layers of chocolate brownie glued together with creamy peppermint ice cream - topped with chocolate fudge and peppermint bits. It's the stuff dreams are made of. It also happened to be my 21st birthday cake!

peppermint ice cream sandwiches

CHOCOLATE COOKIE PIECES

¾ cup Briana's Baking Mix

¼ cup + 2 tablespoons cocoa powder

1 tablespoon THM Super Sweet Blend

¾ teaspoon xanthan gum

¼ teaspoon salt

10 tablespoons salted butter (melted)

¼ cup Greek yogurt

PEPPERMINT ICE CREAM

2 cups heavy whipping cream

2 cups unsweetened almond milk

½ cup cottage cheese

1 tablespoon vegetable glycerin

1 teaspoon vanilla extract

½ teaspoon peppermint extract

¼ teaspoon THM Pure Stevia Extract Powder

⅛ teaspoon salt

4 drops red food coloring

1 teaspoon glucomannan

10 sugar-free peppermints (chopped) (optional)

First, make the chocolate cookie pieces. Whisk the dry ingredients, then add the wet ingredients and mix with a hand mixer until a stiff dough is formed. Divide the dough in half. Line two baking sheets with silicone mats and use your hands to press each half of the dough onto one of the baking sheets in a rectangle approx. 9" wide and 7½" tall. The dough will be fairly thin, like a cracker.

Score each rectangle of dough into 8 equal pieces with a sharp knife. Bake the cookie pieces at 350° for 5 minutes, then remove them from the oven, gently transfer the silicone baking mats from the hot baking sheets to wire racks, and put the racks and silicone baking mats (with the cookie pieces on top, of course) into the freezer to chill.

Make the ice cream. Blend all the ice cream ingredients (except the peppermints) together until smooth. Churn in an automatic countertop ice cream churn according to manufacturer's directions. Transfer the ice cream to a wide, shallow container and stir the chopped peppermints in by hand. Put the ice cream in the freezer for 30 minutes to firm up before assembling the ice cream sandwiches.

To assemble the ice cream sandwiches, gently remove the chilled cookie pieces from the baking mats. Place a large spoonful of ice cream on top of a cookie piece, then top with another cookie piece and use an offset spatula to add more ice cream and clean up around the sides as needed. Assemble all eight sandwiches this way, then put them in a sealable container and freeze them until completely firm. (You'll probably have some ice cream left over, so just eat it or freeze it for dessert later.)

Let the ice cream sandwiches thaw on the counter for 10-15 minutes before eating.

frozen key lime pie

HEALTHY FATS I SERVES 8

CRUST

1 cup almond flour

¼ cup oat fiber

1½ teaspoons THM Super Sweet Blend

⅛ teaspoon xanthan gum

6 tablespoons salted butter (melted)

FILLING

½ cup + 2 tablespoons key lime juice

1 egg

3 egg yolks

1½ tablespoons THM Super Sweet Blend
  (or more, to taste)

1 tablespoon vegetable glycerin

1 teaspoon vanilla extract

¼ teaspoon glucomannan

¾ cup sour cream

1 cup heavy whipping cream

Make the crust first. Whisk the dry ingredients, then add the butter and mix with a fork to form a dough. Press into the bottom and up the sides of a greased 9" pie plate, then bake at 350° for 10 minutes. Cool completely before filling.

To make the filling, whisk the first set of ingredients together in a saucepan on the stovetop, adding the glucomannan slowing while whisking to avoid clumping. Cook over medium heat, whisking often, just until the pudding thickens. Once it reaches a certain temperature, it thickens instantly. Don't wait for bubbles to appear; just pull the pan off the heat immediately and whisk in the sour cream. Let the pudding cool to room temperature but don't refrigerate.

When the pudding is cool, beat the cream until stiff, then fold it into the pudding with a spatula. Spread the filling into the cooled crust, cover, and freeze until firm. Serve frozen. Thaw 40 minutes before slicing, then let it thaw a few more minutes before serving for the best texture. Top with homemade whipped cream and lime slices if desired. Freeze leftovers as individual slices for easy grabbing.

This frozen key lime pie has a refreshing lime tartness and a creamy texture! The crust really takes it up a notch, but I've made it crustless before too for an even easier dessert. I bet the filling mixture would be great frozen as popsicles as well!

note

I like my key lime pie tart and limey. Reduce the lime juice to ½ cup and add more sweetener if you prefer.

frozen pumpkin pie

PECANS

24 pecan halves

1 tablespoon butter

THM Super Sweet Blend, salt,
   black pepper (to taste)

FILLING

1 (15 oz.) can pumpkin

⅔ cup cottage cheese

⅓ cup unsweetened almond milk

4-6 tablespoons xylitol

1 tablespoon vegetable glycerin

1 teaspoon each butter extract,
   maple extract, vanilla extract

¾ teaspoon pumpkin pie spice

⅛ teaspoon salt

2 doonks THM Pure Stevia Extract Powder

2 tablespoons unsweetened almond milk

1 teaspoon plain gelatin

1 cup heavy whipping cream

First, toast the pecans so they can cool down. Melt the butter in a skillet on the stovetop, then add the pecans and toast over medium-high heat until darker in color and fragrant. Sprinkle with Super Sweet Blend, salt, and pepper to taste. (I'm not joking about the pepper - it's good!) Set aside to cool.

To make the filling, blend the first section of ingredients in a blender until smooth. Whisk the gelatin into the almond milk, then heat the mixture until it starts to bubble. (I do this in the microwave.) Add the gelatin mixture to the heavy whipping cream while beating with a hand mixer. Beat until stiff peaks form. Fold the pumpkin mixture into the whipped cream by hand with a spatula until uniform in color. Pour into an ungreased 9" pie plate and smooth the top. Top the pie with the cooled pecans, 3 halves to each piece. Cover and freeze the pie until firm, then serve.

The pie will freeze solid if frozen for an extended period of time; in this case, let it thaw on the counter for 30 minutes before cutting. Let the pieces thaw a little longer for optimum texture (or nuke for a few seconds). I recommend cutting the whole pie and freezing leftovers in individual slices for quick desserts.

fruit slush

2 cups chopped watermelon

2 cups chopped pineapple

1½ cups chopped strawberries

1½ cups blueberries

2 med. oranges (peeled,
   seeds removed, chopped)

1 lg. grapefruit (peeled,
   seeds removed, chopped)

1 cup sugar-free soda of choice
   (I used Honest Fizz Ginger Ale)

3 tablespoons xylitol (or more, to taste)

1-2 tablespoons lemon or lime juice

Combine the fruit in a mixing bowl and mash with a potato masher to get some juices flowing and break up the big chunks. Add the soda, xylitol, and lemon or lime juice and stir to combine. Taste and add more sweetener and/or more lemon or lime juice for additional "zing" if desired. Spread the fruit slush into a shallow airtight container and freeze solid. (You could also freeze it in individual cups for quicker thawing.) Thaw to a slushy consistency before serving. (Thaw time will depend on the container you used, but expect 30-45 minutes.) You can break it apart with a meat fork a bit, then serve with a spoon.

note

• I used fresh pineapple, but pineapple canned in its own juice should work as well. Drain before using.

• Make sure your sugar-free soda is sweetened with a good sweetener, like stevia or erythritol. Alternatively, you could use an unsweetened flavored sparkling water in place of the sugar-free soda and just add more sweetener to the slush recipe.

chocolate-covered peanut butter ice cream bars

HEALTHY FATS | YIELDS 15 BARS

1½ cups heavy whipping cream

1½ cups half and half

1 cup unsweetened almond milk

⅔ cup natural peanut butter

¼ cup xylitol (or more, to taste)

1 tablespoon vegetable glycerin

1 teaspoon vanilla extract

⅛ teaspoon THM Pure Stevia Extract Powder

¾ teaspoon glucomannan

DIPPING CHOCOLATE

¾ cup refined coconut oil

5 tablespoons salted butter

1½ oz. unsweetened baker's chocolate

1 tablespoon THM Super Sweet Blend
   (powdered after measuring)

Add the first section of ingredients to a blender and blend until smooth. (Add the glucomannan right before blending so it doesn't clump.) Churn in an automatic ice cream churn according to manufacturer's directions. Spread the finished ice cream into a foil-lined 9"x13" pan and freeze until semi-firm. Slice into 15 bars and freeze until completely firm before dipping.

Melt the dipping chocolate ingredients together in the microwave or in a double boiler just until they can be whisked together, stirring often. Let the chocolate cool until it's close to room temperature before dipping so the ice cream bars don't melt immediately on contact. Stir the chocolate well before dipping. When the bars are frozen hard, dip them in the chocolate. I like to place them in the chocolate and flip twice to coat. (Letting the bars sit in the chocolate a bit instead of flipping them instantly allows more chocolate to stick.) Place the dipped ice cream bars on a foil-lined pan to let the chocolate coating harden, then store them in a sealed container in the freezer.

These ice cream bars are so convenient to just keep in the freezer for when you need a quick ice cream treat...and they're amazing! These bars are bitable straight out of the freezer, but let them thaw for 10-15 minutes before eating for ultimate creaminess.

note

• You could probably use melted sugar-free chocolate chips in place of the dipping chocolate mixture for a thicker coating.

• Stir frozen berries or nuts into the leftover dipping chocolate for instant candy clusters!

peanut butter cookie doughsicles

HEALTHY FATS I YIELDS 12 POPSICLES

1 cup unsweetened almond milk

½ cup defatted peanut flour

½ cup cottage cheese

½ cup half and half

3 tablespoons xylitol (or more, to taste)

2 tablespoons refined coconut oil (softened)

½ teaspoon vanilla extract

¼ teaspoon baking powder

¼ teaspoon salt

2 doonks THM Pure Stevia Extract Powder

½ teaspoon glucomannan

Blend the ingredients together until smooth. Pour into popsicle molds and freeze until firm (several hours or overnight). Since these are pretty light, feel free to enjoy two or three!

note

The number of popsicles you get depends on the size of your molds.

mochasicles

1½ cups brewed coffee

1 cup unsweetened almond milk

4 eggs

¼ cup xylitol (or more, to taste)

3 tablespoons cocoa powder

2 tablespoons refined coconut oil (softened)

¼ teaspoon salt (scant)

2 doonks THM Pure Stevia Extract Powder

1 teaspoon glucomannan

1 teaspoon vanilla extract

Blend the first section of ingredients until smooth, adding the glucomannan right before blending to avoid clumping. Pour the blended mixture into a nonstick kettle and cook just until it starts to bubble and get thick, stirring often. Remove the kettle from the heat immediately and whisk in the vanilla. Pour the pudding mixture into popsicle molds and freeze for several hours or overnight until firm.

strawberry delight popsicles

CREAM CHEESE FILLING
4 oz. reduced-fat cream cheese
¼ cup sour cream
½ teaspoon THM Super Sweet Blend
¼ teaspoon vanilla extract
2 doonks THM Pure Stevia Extract Powder

¾ teaspoon Knox gelatin
1 tablespoon hot tap water

½ cup heavy whipping cream

CRUST PIECES
½ cup Briana's Baking Mix
2 tablespoons salted butter (melted)
2 tablespoons water
1 teaspoon THM Super Sweet Blend

1½ cups coarsely-chopped fresh strawberries

Make the cream cheese filling ahead of time so it can set up. Beat the first five ingredients until smooth. Whisk the gelatin into the hot water, then add it to the cream cheese mixture while beating with a hand mixer and beat until smooth. Add the cream and beat for several minutes until the cream thickens and ridges start to appear while beating. Refrigerate the cream cheese mixture for several hours before assembling the popsicles.

Make the crust pieces by beating all the crust ingredients together and mashing the dough flat onto a baking pan with a fork. Broil for a few minutes until browning on top, then remove from the oven and crumble into small pieces. Transfer the crumbs to another container and freeze to quickly chill before assembling the popsicles.

Stir the chilled crumbs and chopped strawberries into the chilled cream cheese mixture, then use a spoon to push the mixture into popsicle molds. Insert sticks and freeze for several hours until firm. The pops are best after they have been at room temperature for a few minutes to soften.

note

Use a scant teaspoon of gelatin if using beef gelatin instead of Knox gelatin.

strawberry kiwi popsicles

LOW CARB/LOW FAT | YIELDS 12 POPSICLES

2 cups strawberry puree

¼ cup xylitol

2 doonks THM Pure Stevia Extract Powder
(or more, to taste)

Peeled and sliced kiwifruit

Blend the strawberry puree, xylitol and stevia.

Place kiwi slices in popsicle molds. (The kiwi is mostly just for looks. I use 2-3 slices per popsicle, so it's not enough to knock you into Healthy Carbs territory.) Pour the strawberry mixture over the kiwi slices and tap the molds to eliminate air bubbles. Freeze until firm.

These popsicles are SO easy to make, and their vibrant flavor is perfect for summer!

note

Xylitol gives these popsicles a nice texture, but you can substitute with another sweetener. The pops will just be harder and icier.

VANILLA
PUDDING
CAKE • PG 350

briana's baking mix

LOW CARB / LOW FAT | YIELDS 7 ½ CUPS

3 cups coconut flour
2 cups oat fiber
1½ cups golden flaxmeal
1 cup whey protein powder
1½ teaspoons xanthan gum

Combine all ingredients in a plastic container with a tight lid (I use a Tupperware container) and shake thoroughly. Store in a cool, dry place.

A quarter cup serving of this baking mix contains 4.4 grams of fat and 3.34 grams of net carbs, as well as 6.27 grams of protein.

Using a blend of alternative flours provides the best result in recipes, and it's so much easier to pull out one container of homemade baking mix instead of 5 different containers every time I want to make something! Like many low-carb flours, my baking mix needs plenty of liquids and "conditioners" (water, eggs, sour cream, Greek yogurt, etc.) in order to turn out something fluffy and moist, and my recipes take that into account.

My mix is a little sturdier and soaks up more liquid than THM Baking Blend. You should be able to use THM Baking Blend in most of the recipes in this book in place of my baking mix, but it's always safest to use the ingredients with which recipes are formulated. I really recommend mixing up a batch of my baking mix to use in my recipes for best results. If you do want to try substituting, you'll need a little more THM Baking Blend than my mix called for in recipes. General rule of thumb is to start with 1 cup of THM Baking Blend for every ¾ cup of my baking mix called for in a recipe, then add more flour or liquid if needed. (In small amounts of only a few tablespoons, you can probably substitute THM Baking Blend in the same amount.)

note

• Oat fiber brands vary drastically and can have a very negative impact on any recipes you make with this baking mix. You need to use a brand that has a very light color and flavor. I've always purchased LifeSource brand from Netrition.com and had very good success with it. I can't personally vouch for any other brands.
• Almond flour could probably be substituted for the golden flaxmeal.
• Need to be dairy free? Try substituting collagen for the whey protein powder.
• Glucomannan could probably be substituted for the xanthan gum.
• I do not suggest substituting for the oat fiber or coconut flour unless you are planning to create your own unique flour blend.

cream cheese chocolate chip brownie cake

½ cup Briana's Baking Mix

½ cup cocoa powder

2½ tablespoons THM Super Sweet Blend
(or more, to taste)

1½ teaspoons baking powder

1 teaspoon glucomannan

¼ teaspoon salt

1 cup water

4 eggs

CREAM CHEESE FILLING

1 (8 oz.) pkg. reduced-fat cream cheese

2 teaspoons THM Super Sweet Blend

½ teaspoon vanilla extract

Sugar-free chocolate chips

Whisk the dry ingredients. Add the water and eggs and mix. Spread the batter into a greased 8"x8" pan.

Beat the cream cheese, Super Sweet Blend, and vanilla together until smooth. Dollop the mixture onto the cake in 9 blobs, in the center of what will become each piece. Top with a sprinkling of sugar-free chocolate chips (or chopped 85% dark chocolate for a more economical version).

Bake at 350° for 40 minutes or until a toothpick comes out cleanly and the cake appears to be done all the way through. You can let it cool a little to solidify before eating it warm, but I prefer the texture cold after refrigeration.

Why do I call it "brownie cake"? Because the texture reminds me of a cross between a brownie and a cake! It's more moist and fudgy than a cake but more cakey than a brownie. Whatever it is, it's awesome. (Of course adding cheesecake and chocolate chips makes anything awesome, right?) The best part about this recipe is that it really doesn't take very many ingredients and it's so simple to make!

note

Different brands of glucomannan can vary in strength, so if you notice an odd texture in the cake, try decreasing the amount a bit. If you don't have glucomannan, you should be able to use xanthan gum in the same amount.

lemon cream cheese cake

HEALTHY FATS I SERVES 9

½ cup Briana's Baking Mix

½ cup oat fiber

2½ tablespoons THM Super Sweet Blend
(or more, to taste)

1½ teaspoons baking powder

1 teaspoon glucomannan

¼ teaspoon salt

¹⁄₁₆ teaspoon turmeric (for color)

¾ cup water

½ cup lemon juice

4 eggs

1 teaspoon vanilla extract

CREAM CHEESE FILLING

1 (8 oz.) pkg. reduced-fat cream cheese

2 teaspoons THM Super Sweet Blend

½ teaspoon vanilla extract

Whisk the dry ingredients. Add the wet ingredients and mix. Spread the batter into a greased 8"x8" pan.

Beat the cream cheese, Super Sweet Blend, and vanilla together until smooth. Dollop the mixture onto the cake in 9 blobs, in the center of what will become each piece. Push the cream cheese blobs down into the batter a bit.

Bake at 350° for 40-45 minutes or until a toothpick comes out cleanly and the cake appears to be done all the way through. The cake is good (kind of a custardy texture) when warm, but it's meant to be eaten cold after overnight refrigeration. The lemon flavor and sweetness level out overnight and the cake sets up to an amazing texture!

Commit thy works unto the Lord,
and thy thoughts shall be established.
PSALM 16:3

cream cheese chocolate chip muffin

¼ cup water

1 egg

2 tablespoons Briana's Baking Mix

1½ tablespoons cocoa powder

1 tablespoon THM Super Sweet Blend
    (or more, to taste)

½ teaspoon glucomannan

¼ teaspoon baking powder

Dash salt

2 tablespoons reduced-fat cream cheese

Sugar-free chocolate chips

Whisk the water and egg together in a large mug or a small ceramic bowl. Add the dry ingredients and whisk until smooth. Drop the cream cheese into the center and top with a sprinkle of sugar-free chocolate chips.

Microwave for 1 minute, 20 seconds, then check on it. I microwave mine for about 1 minute and 40 seconds, but the time may vary by microwave. I like it to be a little wet in the center yet so it's not overdone.

Enjoy warm because it will solidify as it cools (thanks to the glucomannan). I like to take a bite of the cream cheese center with each bite! I recommend adding a little protein on the side if eating this as a meal or snack on its own.

This is officially my favorite mug muffin!

note

• Different brands of glucomannan can vary in strength, so if you notice an odd texture in the cake, try decreasing the amount a bit.

• The sweetness was good for me since the cream cheese and chocolate chips balance things out, but feel free to add more sweetener. You could also mix some sweetener into the cream cheese before adding it to the cake, but I didn't feel like creating an extra step.

vanilla cream cheese chocolate chip muffin

HEALTHY FATS I SERVES I

2 tablespoons Briana's Baking Mix

1½ tablespoons oat fiber

1 tablespoon THM Super Sweet Blend
(or more, to taste)

½ teaspoon glucomannan

¼ teaspoon baking powder

Dash salt

¼ cup water

1 egg

1 teaspoon vanilla extract

2 tablespoons reduced-fat cream cheese

Sugar-free chocolate chips

Whisk the dry ingredients in a small ceramic bowl, then add the water, egg, and vanilla and whisk until smooth. Place the cream cheese in the center of the batter and top with sugar-free chocolate chips. Microwave for 1 minute and 20 seconds, then check, microwaving longer if needed. (I like to keep my microwave muffins on the slightly underdone side for best texture.)

Your heavenly Father
knoweth that ye have
need of all these things.
MATTHEW 6:32B

note

• Feel free to add sweetener to the cream cheese; I don't because with the sweetened chocolate chips I don't need it, and I like to keep things simple.

• The chocolate chips really make this, but some chopped fresh strawberries on top of this muffin after microwaving would probably be good as well.

• Using good oat fiber and glucomannan is imperative in recipes like this!

vanilla pudding cake

FOUNDATION FATS | SERVES 8

¾ cup oat fiber

½ cup collagen

2 tablespoons THM Super Sweet Blend
   (or more, to taste)

1½ teaspoons baking powder

¾ teaspoon glucomannan

¼ teaspoon salt

5 eggs

¾ cup water

4 tablespoons salted butter (softened)

2 teaspoons vanilla extract

Whisk the dry ingredients. Add the wet ingredients and mix well.

Spread batter into a greased 9" cake pan with a square of parchment paper on the bottom and bake at 350° for 40 minutes or until the top is dry and a toothpick comes out cleanly. Let the cake cool a bit to solidify before slicing and serving.

This cake is good warm or cold, but I like it best cold with sliced strawberries.

TOPPING SUGGESTIONS ▼

foundation fats butter, cinnamon, and
Waffle & Pancake Syrup (page 491),
most low-carb lemon curds,
Hot Chocolate Custard (page 434)
healthy fats sliced berries or
Blueberry Topping (page 493)

This cake has an amazing taste and texture; it's so soft and moist! When warm it's a bit custardy, like the Vanilla Pudding Cake for One, but I formulated this recipe with less glucomannan so it has a great texture when cold as well. (The single-serve pudding cakes gum up when refrigerated due to the high concentration of glucomannan.)

note

• The flours listed are imperative for the great texture of this cake. Do not substitute whey protein powder for the collagen.

• I tried making this cake dairy free, but it needed the butter for flavor. Perhaps a butter-flavored coconut oil would work?

vanilla pudding cake for one

FOUNDATION FATS I SERVES I

2 teaspoons refined coconut oil

1 egg
2 tablespoons water
½ teaspoon vanilla extract

2 tablespoons collagen
1½ tablespoons oat fiber
2 teaspoons THM Super Sweet Blend
½ teaspoon glucomannan
¼ teaspoon baking powder
Dash salt

Melt the coconut oil in a ceramic bowl. (A small cereal bowl size works well.) I do this in the microwave. Add the egg, water, and vanilla and whisk. Add the dry ingredients and whisk until smooth. The batter will be very liquidy.

Microwave for a minute, then check and see if you want to nuke it any longer. At one minute mine is fairly soft, which I like. 1½ minutes cooks it all the way through so it's a regular cake and not a pudding cake any longer. Times may vary with each microwave, so find what you like. Enjoy warm.

To stay in Foundation Fats territory, eat it plain, top with a little unsweetened almond milk, or make a glaze with some butter, sweetener, and cinnamon! For a regular Healthy Fats meal, top with some strawberries.

I love my "pudding cakes" because they're easy to make, full of protein and healthy fats, and have a texture close to that of a boxed cake mix! This vanilla version tastes like a vanilla custard in cake form and makes a great dessert, but since it contains protein you can also use it as breakfast or a snack on its own!

note

• Try adding a dash of lemon juice or your favorite extract – or add a healthy dose of cinnamon for a spice version!
• I do not recommend substituting whey protein powder for the collagen.
• Using good oat fiber and glucomannan is imperative in recipes like this!

chocolate pudding cake for one

2 teaspoons refined coconut oil

1 egg
2 tablespoons water

2 tablespoons collagen
1½ tablespoons cocoa powder
2½ teaspoons THM Super Sweet Blend
   (or more, to taste)
½ teaspoon glucomannan
¼ teaspoon baking powder
Dash salt

Melt the coconut oil in a ceramic bowl. (A small cereal bowl size works well.) I do this in the microwave. Add the egg and water and whisk. Add the dry ingredients and whisk until smooth. (Feel free to add more sweetener!) The batter will be very liquidy.

Microwave for a minute, then check and see if you want to nuke it any longer. At one minute, mine is a little underdone in the center, which I like. 1½ minutes cooks it all the way through so it's a regular chocolate cake and not a pudding cake any longer. Times may vary with each microwave, so find what you like. Enjoy warm.

To stay in Foundation Fats territory, top with a little unsweetened almond milk. For a regular Healthy Fats meal, top with a dab of Reddi-wip or some sugar-free ice cream. Enjoy as breakfast, snack, or dessert!

note

• Many people will probably want more sweetener, so taste and adjust to your own preferences.
• I do not recommend substituting whey protein powder for the collagen.

mocha pudding cake for one

2 teaspoons refined coconut oil

1 egg
2 tablespoons water

2 tablespoons collagen
1 tablespoon oat fiber
2 teaspoons THM Super Sweet Blend
   (or more, to taste)
1½ teaspoons cocoa powder
1½ teaspoons espresso instant coffee powder
½ teaspoon glucomannan
¼ teaspoon baking powder
Dash salt

Melt the coconut oil in a ceramic bowl. (A small cereal bowl size works well.) I do this in the microwave. Add the egg and water and whisk. Add the dry ingredients and whisk until smooth. (Feel free to add more sweetener, cocoa powder, or instant coffee!) The batter will be very liquidy.

Microwave for a minute, then check and see if you want to nuke it any longer. Times may vary with each microwave, so find what you like. I like mine on the soft side! Enjoy warm.

To stay in Foundation Fats territory, top with a little unsweetened almond milk. For a regular Healthy Fats meal, top with a dab of Reddi-wip, some sugar-free chocolate syrup, and/or sugar-free chocolate chips! An extra layer of chocolate really takes this cake up a notch. Since this cake contains protein, it can be used as breakfast or a snack on its own, but it also makes a great dessert after a meal.

note

I do not recommend substituting whey protein powder for the collagen.

peanut butter pudding cake for one

LOW CARB / LOW FAT | SERVES 1

3 tablespoons defatted peanut flour

1 tablespoon oat fiber

1½ tablespoons collagen

2 teaspoons THM Super Sweet Blend
(or more, to taste)

¼ teaspoon glucomannan

¼ teaspoon baking powder

⅛ teaspoon salt

¼ cup water

3 tablespoons egg whites

Whisk the dry ingredients. Add the water and egg whites and whisk again. Microwave in a small ceramic bowl, checking at 1 minute, 15 seconds. You can microwave it longer if you like, but I recommend keeping it slightly underdone in the center so it's soft and melt-in-your-mouth. Top with chopped strawberries and enjoy!

note

• Do not substitute whey protein powder for the collagen.

• I've made a Healthy Fats version of this using 1 egg in place of the egg whites and omitting the glucomannan. This version is a little more muffin-like and doesn't have the pudding cake feel if glucomannan isn't your thing.

pound cake with strawberries

¾ cup coconut flour

⅔ cup oat fiber

2 teaspoons baking powder

¼ teaspoon xanthan gum

¼ teaspoon THM Pure Stevia Extract Powder

8 tablespoons salted butter (softened)

6 eggs

¾ cup water

½ cup sour cream

2 teaspoons vanilla extract

Whisk the dry ingredients.

Beat the butter until smooth, then add the eggs two at a time, beating between each addition. Add the water, sour cream, and vanilla and mix till smooth.

Add wet ingredients to dry and mix well.

Spread batter into greased loaf pan. Bake at 350° for approximately 75 minutes or until a toothpick comes out cleanly and the center of the cake is not mushy. Let the cake cool in the pan 15 minutes, then take it out and let it cool at least another 25-30 minutes before slicing.

Serve the pound cake with sliced strawberries and almond milk or whipped cream. It's good warm or cold, but the texture is a teensy bit better after overnight refrigeration.

In my testing, I found that this combination of flours instead of using my baking mix gave me the best pound cakey texture.

note

• I bet leftovers would make good French toast!

• If you want the pound cake to be sweeter, add some granulated sweetener to the stevia listed. The stevia alone sweetens this perfectly for me. In certain recipes it just *works*, and I use it where I can to save money.

cinnamon roll cupcakes

CUPCAKES

1 cup Briana's Baking Mix

1 cup oat fiber

2 tablespoons THM Super Sweet Blend
   (or more, to taste)

2½ teaspoons baking powder

1½ teaspoons cinnamon

½ teaspoon salt

8 tablespoons salted butter (softened)

4 eggs

1 cup + 2 tablespoons water

¾ cup egg whites

1 tablespoon vanilla extract

FROSTING

1 (8 oz.) pkg. reduced-fat cream cheese

1 tablespoon THM Super Sweet Blend
   (powdered after measuring)
   (or more, to taste)

½ teaspoon vanilla extract

¼ teaspoon cinnamon

¼ teaspoon maple extract

1 cup heavy whipping cream

To make the cupcakes, whisk the dry ingredients. In a separate bowl, beat the butter and eggs very well, then add the dry ingredients and the rest of the wet ingredients and mix well. Divide the batter among 18 greased muffin tin holes (about ¼ cup batter in each) and bake at 350° for 18-20 minutes or until a toothpick comes out cleanly and the tops are dry, not squishy. Let the cupcakes cool in the pans for 10 minutes, then remove and chill before frosting (overnight is great).

To make the frosting, beat the first section of ingredients until smooth. Add the cream and beat until thick and stiff. Frost the cupcakes and top with a dusting of additional cinnamon if desired.

note

• Feel free to add extra cinnamon to the batter if you're a spice lover. I didn't want to overtake the cupcakes with overwhelming cinnamon.

• This frosting makes a yummy dip for strawberries!

chocolate peppermint cupcakes

HEALTHY FATS I YIELDS 18 CUPCAKES

CUPCAKES

1⅓ cups Briana's Baking Mix

⅔ cup cocoa powder

2½ tablespoons THM Super Sweet Blend

2½ teaspoons baking powder

½ teaspoon xanthan gum

½ teaspoon salt

1 cup + 2 tablespoons water

¾ cup egg whites

½ cup olive oil

4 eggs

1 teaspoon vanilla extract

FROSTING

1 (8 oz.) pkg. reduced-fat cream cheese

2 teaspoons THM Super Sweet Blend

½ teaspoon peppermint extract

¼ teaspoon vanilla extract

8 sugar-free peppermints (crushed)

¾ cup heavy whipping cream

For the cupcakes, whisk the dry ingredients. Add the wet ingredients and mix well. Divide the batter among 18 cupcake tin holes. (I like to use paper liners for less mess and no chance of sticking, but if you don't have any, grease the cupcake tins.) Bake at 350° for 20-22 minutes or until a toothpick comes out cleanly. Leave the cupcakes in the pans for 10 minutes, then remove them and let them cool completely before frosting. For the frosting, beat the first set of ingredients together until smooth. Add the cream and beat until thick. Frost the cooled cupcakes, then refrigerate the cupcakes to chill completely before serving.

> **THE PEOPLE**
> are more important
> than the process.
> TIM THOMAS

peppermint pudding cake

HEALTHY FATS | SERVES 12

CAKE

1⅓ cups Briana's Baking Mix

⅔ cup cocoa powder

2½ tablespoons THM Super Sweet Blend

2½ teaspoons baking powder

½ teaspoon xanthan gum

½ teaspoon salt

1 cup + 2 tablespoons water

¾ cup egg whites

½ cup olive oil

4 eggs

1 teaspoon vanilla extract

PUDDING

2 ½ cups unsweetened almond milk

1 cup heavy whipping cream

1 cup half and half

4 eggs

1 tablespoon Knox gelatin

¼ teaspoon salt

½ teaspoon glucomannan

3 tablespoons Truvia

1 tablespoon salted butter

2 teaspoons vanilla extract

1 teaspoon peppermint extract

2 doonks THM Pure Stevia Extract Powder

2-3 drops red food coloring

Sugar-free chocolate chips or chopped
  85% dark chocolate (for garnish)

Whisk the dry ingredients. Add the wet ingredients and beat until smooth. Divide the batter among three 9" greased cake pans and bake at 350° for 14 minutes or until a toothpick comes out cleanly. Remove the cakes from the oven and let them cool in the pans. Remove the cakes from the pans gently after 5-10 minutes and let them continue cooling on wire racks. Cover and refrigerate the cake layers to chill completely before frosting (overnight is great).

Blend the first section of pudding ingredients together until smooth, adding the glucomannan right before blending so it doesn't clump. Pour the mixture into a nonstick kettle and cook over medium-high heat just until it starts to bubble, stirring occasionally. As soon as the mixture starts to bubble, pull it off the heat and whisk in the second section of ingredients. (Start with ½ teaspoon of peppermint extract, then add more a dash at a time until it tastes right to you. Peppermint extracts can vary in strength and you don't want to use too much!) Let the pudding cool, then refrigerate it for several hours or overnight to firm up.

When the cake layers and pudding have been chilled, you're ready to assemble the layer cake. Place one cake layer on a cake stand and top it with one-third of the pudding mixture. The pudding will be firm; this is good for the strength of the cake. Just plop the pudding onto the cake layer and use an offset frosting spreader to spread it out close to the edges of the cake. Top with another cake layer and press it down to cement it firmly. Top this cake layer with more pudding, then the last cake layer. For the top pudding layer I recommend whisking the remaining peppermint pudding to a smoother consistency before spreading it onto the top of the cake (an offset spreader really helps get the nicest finish). I don't recommend doing this to the other layers because it's nice to leave the gelatin undisturbed for support, but on the top it doesn't matter. Top the cake with some sugar-free chocolate chips or chopped 85% dark chocolate for garnish. Refrigerate for a few hours to firm up, then serve.

note

Add ¾ teaspoon gelatin to the pudding if using beef gelatin.

carrot cake

HEALTHY CARBS | SERVES 10-12

2 cups oat flour

¾ cup oat fiber

1 tablespoon baking powder

1½ teaspoons cinnamon

¾ teaspoon ginger

⅜ teaspoon THM Pure Stevia Extract Powder

⅜ teaspoon salt

2 cups finely-grated carrot

¾ cup low-fat Greek yogurt

½ cup water

1½ cups egg whites

1 teaspoon cream of tartar

FROSTING

4 oz. reduced-fat cream cheese (softened)

¾ cup low-fat cottage cheese

½ teaspoon vanilla extract

1½ teaspoons THM Super Sweet Blend

Cinnamon (for garnish)

Whisk the dry ingredients in a large mixing bowl. (Yes, I mean a *large* mixing bowl. You'll see why in a bit.) Add the carrots, Greek yogurt, and water and mix with a hand mixer. (The mixture will be very thick.)

In a separate bowl, beat the egg whites and cream of tartar until stiff peaks form. The egg whites will expand a LOT. Pour the egg whites into the mixing bowl with the other ingredients and fold them in on low speed with a hand mixer. Finish the job by hand with a spatula until the batter is just mixed. It's OK if there are a few streaks left. Pour the batter into two greased 9" cake pans and bake at 350° for 21 minutes or until a toothpick comes out cleanly. Let the cakes cool in the pans for 10 minutes before removing them and letting them cool completely on the counter.

For the frosting, beat the cream cheese until smooth. Add the cottage cheese, vanilla, and sweetener and beat until relatively smooth.

To assemble the cake, place one cake layer on a cake stand and spread the frosting on top. Top with the second cake layer. Dust the top of the cake with cinnamon. Refrigerate to chill completely before serving. Store in the refrigerator. A small squirt of fat-free Reddi-wip and a drizzle of sugar-free syrup on top for serving wouldn't be a bad idea!

This cake may not be a traditional carrot cake, but I love it! It contains a good amount of protein, so enjoy it as a breakfast, snack, or dessert.

note

• The fat from the cream cheese comes to 2.4 grams per serving if the cake is cut into 10 slices.

• When beaten with a hand mixer, the cottage cheese loses much of its texture. If you put the frosting between the cake layers instead of on top of the cake, you don't even notice the cottage cheese!

carrot cake for one

HEALTHY CARBS | SERVES 1

⅓ cup oat flour

⅓ cup finely-grated carrot

¼ cup egg whites

2 tablespoons oat fiber

2 tablespoons Greek yogurt

1 tablespoon water

½ teaspoon baking powder

¼ teaspoon cinnamon

⅛ teaspoon ginger

2 doonks THM Pure Stevia Extract Powder

1/16 teaspoon salt

FROSTING

1½ tablespoons reduced-fat
   cream cheese (softened)

2 tablespoons low-fat cottage cheese

Dash vanilla extract

Sprinkle of THM Super Sweet Blend (to taste)

Mix the cake ingredients together well. Pour the batter into a well-greased 2-cup glass oven-safe dish and bake at 350° for 30 minutes or until a toothpick comes out cleanly. Take the cake out of the oven and let it cool. Remove from baking dish, freeze until well chilled, then slice it in half horizontally.

To make the frosting, mash the ingredients together with a fork to reduce the cottage cheese to a fairly smooth texture. Spread the frosting onto the bottom half of the cake, top with the top half, and add a dab of Reddi-wip and a little cinnamon on top. Enjoy as breakfast, snack, or dessert! (This is probably enough for 2 dessert servings, but if you're having it for breakfast, eat the whole thing! It contains protein on its own.)

note

• The cottage cheese works. If you mash it up and put the frosting between the cake layers instead of on top of the cake, you don't notice the texture.

• I do not recommend microwaving the cake because the carrots probably won't get soft.

peach & blueberry oat cake

HEALTHY CARBS | SERVES 6-8

1½ cups oat flour

¾ cup oat fiber

1½ teaspoons baking powder

1½ teaspoons cinnamon

½ teaspoon salt

⅜ teaspoon glucomannan

¼ teaspoon THM Pure Stevia Extract Powder

1¼ cups egg whites

½ cup water

1 teaspoon molasses

1 teaspoon vanilla extract

¾ cup sliced peaches (thawed if frozen)

¾ cup blueberries (thawed if frozen)

Whisk the dry ingredients. Add the wet ingredients and mix well. Fold in the peaches and blueberries.

Spread the batter into a greased 9" cake pan with a square of parchment on the bottom. Bake at 350° for 45-50 minutes until a toothpick comes out cleanly and the cake is still a little soft in the center but not mushy. Let it cool down before cutting and eating. It's good warm, but I prefer it cold. Crumble it into almond milk, drizzle with sugar-free syrup, or top with low-fat cottage cheese or yogurt and berries!

I love to eat this cake cold with almond milk for breakfast! It has a great texture and balanced sweetness with pops of flavor from the fruit.

note

• Soft fruits work best in this cake. I didn't have good luck with apples.

• This cake is not overly sweet; it's more of a breakfast cake. If you want it sweeter, I recommend adding some granulated sweetener like THM Super Sweet Blend or Gentle Sweet.

blender banana muffins

3 cups oat flour

1½ cups mashed banana

1½ cups egg whites

1 tablespoon baking powder

1 tablespoon refined coconut oil (melted)

1 tablespoon apple cider vinegar

2 teaspoons cinnamon

1 teaspoon vanilla extract

¼ teaspoon THM Pure Stevia Extract Powder

¼ teaspoon salt

Blend the ingredients together until smooth. Pour into greased muffin tins, filling the holes three-quarters of the way full. (I made 12 standard-sized muffins and 6 mini muffins.)

Bake at 375° for 18-20 minutes (about 12 minutes for mini muffins) or until a toothpick inserted into the center of a muffin comes out cleanly. Let cool for a few minutes before digging in. The muffins are also good cold (or cut in half, toasted, and topped with a smidgen of butter).

note

• The coconut oil adds a trace amount of fat per muffin and improves the texture.

• I recommend sticking to 2 standard-sized muffins as the majority of your carb source in a Healthy Carbs fuel setting.

morning glory muffins

2 cups oat flour

1 cup oat fiber

2½ teaspoons baking powder

1 teaspoon each cinnamon, ginger

⅜ teaspoon THM Pure Stevia Extract Powder

⅜ teaspoon salt

1½ cups egg whites

1 cup grated carrot

¾ cup grated apple

¾ cup pineapple chunks
canned in juice (drained)

½ cup water

1 teaspoon molasses

Unsweetened shredded coconut (for garnish)

Whisk the dry ingredients. Add the wet ingredients and beat well with a hand mixer. (I like to beat it long enough that the pineapple chunks break down a little.) Fill greased muffin tin holes with ¼ cup of batter each, garnish with a small amount of shredded coconut, and bake at 375° for 18 minutes or until a toothpick comes out cleanly.

I like these muffins warm, but the flavor is actually best after they have been refrigerated overnight. The pineapple flavor is more prominent.

note

The shredded coconut is a fat source, so go easy on it. There are 5 grams of fat in one tablespoon of shredded coconut, so as long as you don't use more than a tablespoon over 2-3 muffins (what I consider a serving size), you're fine. If you want to eat these muffins with a smidgen of butter, just leave the coconut off because the butter would be your added fat source.

oat bran muffins

HEALTHY CARBS | YIELDS 12 MUFFINS

2½ cups oat bran

1 cup egg whites

1 cup water

1 tablespoon THM Super Sweet Blend

2 teaspoons baking powder

2 teaspoons plain gelatin

1½ teaspoons cinnamon

1 teaspoon salt

1 teaspoon vanilla extract

1 teaspoon maple extract

Mix the ingredients together. Divide batter among 12 greased muffin tin holes (approx. ¼ cup of batter in each hole). Bake at 350° for 20 minutes or until done. Store in the refrigerator but reheat before eating. (The gelatin gives them a bit of a "chew" when warm, which I love, but makes them stiff when cold.)

I would make these muffins over and over again because they're so easy and I love the texture! They're very good warm: dense, and a bit chewy. While they're pretty basic, they make a great blank canvas for toppings and don't have the gooiness of muffins made with oat flour. The texture is similar to that of bran muffins, or maybe an English muffin; they don't rise a lot and are very hearty. Top them with some berry jam!

zucchini spice muffins

2 cups oat flour

2 cups grated zucchini

1½ cups egg whites

1 cup oat fiber

¾ cup water

2½ teaspoons baking powder

2½ teaspoons cinnamon

1 teaspoon molasses

1 teaspoon vanilla extract

½ teaspoon salt

⅜ teaspoon THM Pure Stevia Extract Powder

¼ teaspoon ground cloves

Mix the ingredients together well with a hand mixer. Taste and add some extra sweetener (preferably a granulated sweetener like THM Super Sweet Blend or Gentle Sweet) if the batter isn't sweet enough for you.

Fill greased muffin tin holes with ¼ cup of batter each. Bake at 375° for 20 minutes or until a toothpick comes out cleanly. I prefer these muffins cold out of the refrigerator (the sweetness and flavor really develops after refrigeration), but they're also good toasted and topped with a smidgen of butter and a few sugar-free chocolate chips. (Keep your added fat to 5 grams per serving or less to stay within Healthy Carbs boundaries.)

note

• We grate and freeze zucchini in 2-cup bags during the summer, so I used one of those bags that I thawed - liquid and all. Freshly-grated zucchini should work as well, but it may not break down as much in the muffins.

• No, I do not recommend baking this as a loaf of zucchini bread. I'm guessing it would be kind of mushy in the center.

pumpkin chip muffins

HEALTHY CARBS | YIELDS 12 STANDARD AND 12 MINI MUFFINS

3 cups oat flour

1½ cups canned pumpkin

1½ cups egg whites

¾ cup water

1 tablespoon refined coconut oil

1 tablespoon apple cider vinegar

2½ teaspoons baking powder

2 teaspoons cinnamon

1 teaspoon molasses

1 teaspoon vanilla extract

⅜ teaspoon THM Pure Stevia Extract Powder

⅜ teaspoon each ground cloves, salt

¼ cup sugar-free chocolate chips or
chopped 85% dark chocolate +
a few more for sprinkling on top

Blend everything but the chocolate chips together until smooth. (I do this in our Vitamix blender, but I'm sure you could also use a hand mixer.) Taste and add more sweetener if desired. Fold in the chocolate chips by hand and pour the batter into 12 (greased) standard-sized muffin tin holes and 12 mini muffin tin holes. Fill each hole ¾ of the way full. Top the batter with a sprinkling of additional chocolate chips and bake at 375° for 18 minutes (about 12 minutes for the mini muffins) or until a toothpick inserted into the center of a muffin comes out cleanly. Let the muffins cool for 10-15 minutes for best texture before eating. Store leftovers in the refrigerator. These muffins are good cold but do reheat well in the microwave.

Since I used only oat flour in these muffins for budget reasons, they're going to be denser than your typical pumpkin chip muffins made with white flour, but I love them. They have the best taste and texture if they're warm, and they reheat well in the microwave!

note

• The coconut oil adds a trace amount of fat per serving but improves the texture of the muffins. Between the coconut oil and chocolate chips there are about 2.5 grams of fat per standard-sized muffin. Stick to 2 muffins to stay within Healthy Carbs guidelines. If you want to have more muffins or have a smidgen of butter or cream cheese on your muffins, go lighter on the chocolate chips and/or omit the coconut oil.

• Feel free to use more sweetener, especially if you use 85% dark chocolate instead of sugar-free chocolate chips. I recommend adding some granulated sweetener (such as THM Super Sweet Blend) if you want to increase the sweetness. Start with a few teaspoons and taste as you go. Don't omit the chocolate! It really balances the flavors and adds some oomph to a muffin made completely with oat flour. I'm not saying that the muffins aren't good without the chocolate; I'm just saying that the chocolate is in there for a reason.

pumpkin chip mug muffin

2 teaspoons chia seeds

3 tablespoons Briana's Baking Mix
¾ teaspoon pumpkin pie spice
½ teaspoon baking powder
⅛ teaspoon + 1 doonk THM Pure
　Stevia Extract Powder
Dash salt

¼ cup + 1 tablespoon water
3 tablespoons canned pumpkin
½ teaspoon maple extract

Sugar-free chocolate chips or
　chopped 85% dark chocolate

Grind the chia seeds to powder in a coffee grinder. Whisk the ground chia and the rest of the dry ingredients together. Add the water, pumpkin, maple extract, and a few chocolate chips and stir with a spatula to mix well. The batter will be very thick, so just smash it against the side of the bowl with the spatula to combine the ingredients evenly.

Spread the batter into a small ceramic or glass ramekin (I didn't need to grease mine), top with some additional chocolate chips, and microwave for 3 minutes or until the top center looks mostly done.

This soft, cakey bowl of chocolate-studded yumminess happens to be egg free! I used ground chia seeds as the binder in this recipe, producing a soft, moist muffin. It's a unique texture that took me by surprise at first, but now I'm hooked. I've only tried black chia seeds so far, which can give baked goods an odd color, not gonna lie. My mom took one look at this muffin and said, "NO ONE is going to make that." The chia seeds tend to mask flavor, so you may need to oversweeten and overspice just a bit (hence the ¾ teaspoon of pumpkin pie spice in one muffin).

note

As always, feel free to add more sweetener than I did! I found that stevia worked well in this, but you could always use a few teaspoons of THM Super Sweet Blend in its place.

pumpkin cheesecake muffins

HEALTHY FATS | YIELDS 12 MUFFINS

1 cup Briana's Baking Mix

1 tablespoon THM Super Sweet Blend

1½ teaspoons baking powder

½ teaspoon ginger

¼ teaspoon xanthan gum

¼ teaspoon each cloves, salt

⅛ teaspoon THM Pure Stevia Extract Powder

¾ cup canned pumpkin

½ cup egg whites

½ cup water

2 eggs

3 tablespoons refined coconut oil (melted)

1 tablespoon apple cider vinegar

CHEESECAKE TOPPING

4 oz. cream cheese (softened)

¼ cup Greek yogurt

1 egg

¼ teaspoon vanilla extract

2 doonks THM Pure Stevia Extract Powder

Whisk the dry ingredients. Add the wet ingredients and beat until smooth. Divide the muffin batter among 12 greased muffin tin holes.

Beat the cream cheese until smooth. Add the rest of the cheesecake topping ingredients and beat again. Top off the muffin batter with the cheesecake batter. (You can swirl the cheesecake batter into the muffin batter if you like, or just leave it on top like I did.) Smooth the tops.

Bake at 350° for 30 minutes or until a toothpick comes out cleanly and the cheesecake part is set. Let the muffins cool for 5 minutes, then remove them from the muffin tin and let them cool on wire racks. Refrigerate overnight before eating for best results. I prefer these muffins cold.

As written, the cheesecake layer is fairly thin – like a "baked frosting" of sorts. If you want a higher cheesecake to muffin ratio you could double or triple the batch of cheesecake batter and make 18 muffins instead! I personally didn't want too much calorie-dense cheesecake – just enough to top off the pumpkin.

the best blueberry muffins

HEALTHY FATS | YIELDS 12 MUFFINS

½ cup Briana's Baking Mix

½ cup oat fiber

½ cup collagen

2 tablespoons THM Super Sweet Blend
   (or more, to taste)

1½ teaspoons baking powder

½ teaspoon glucomannan

¼ teaspoon salt

6 eggs

5 tablespoons salted butter (melted)

⅓ cup water

2 teaspoons vanilla extract

1 cup frozen blueberries

Get the blueberries out before mixing up the muffins so they're not straight out of the freezer, but don't thaw them before mixing them into the batter. (If using fresh blueberries, you might not need to bake the muffins as long.)

Whisk the dry ingredients. Add the wet ingredients and mix. Fold in the blueberries by hand. Stir as little as possible.

Divide the batter among 12 greased muffin tin holes. Bake at 350° for 25 minutes or until the tops are dry. Let cool in the pan, then remove. Let the muffins cool down before eating to solidify. The taste and texture is best after refrigeration.

When I was a little girl, my mom made the best blueberry muffins. This recipe is my recreation of that boxed muffin mix, and it's the most normal muffin texture I've had using alternative flours! I like these blueberry muffins best cold, but they're good warm too, especially with a little butter on top.

note

• The flours listed are imperative for the great texture of these muffins. Do not substitute whey protein powder for the collagen.

• I tried making these muffins dairy free, but they needed the butter for flavor. Perhaps a butter-flavored coconut oil would work?

blueberry muffin for one

¼ cup oat flour

2 tablespoons oat fiber

1½ teaspoons THM Super Sweet Blend
   (or more, to taste)

¼ teaspoon baking powder

⅛ teaspoon glucomannan

⅛ teaspoon each cinnamon, salt

3 tablespoons egg whites

3 tablespoons water

Dash vanilla extract

⅓ cup frozen blueberries

Whisk the dry ingredients. Add the wet ingredients and mix well. Stir in the blueberries.

Pour the batter into a greased oven-safe ceramic bowl. Bake at 350° for 26-28 minutes or until it's not wet on top but is still a little gooey in the center when you press on it. Let it cool for a few minutes to solidify before digging in and enjoying it warm. I recommend topping it with a teaspoon of salted butter; this really makes it!

note

I've only tried baking this muffin because I wasn't having success with oat flour muffins in the microwave. You're welcome to try microwaving it, but I think the oven will work best.

> GOD'S IN HIS HEAVEN—
> All's right with the world!
> ROBERT BROWNING - "PIPPA PASSES"

PEANUT BUTTER
COOKIES • PG 388

candies, cookies + bars

peanut butter cups

HEALTHY FATS | YIELDS 24 CANDIES

PEANUT BUTTER LAYER

1 cup natural peanut butter
  (well-stirred and creamy)
¼ cup refined coconut oil (softened)
1 tablespoon THM Super Sweet Blend
½ teaspoon vanilla extract
¹⁄₁₆ teaspoon salt
3 tablespoons oat fiber

CHOCOLATE

1 (3.5 oz.) bar 85% dark chocolate
¾ cup refined coconut oil
3½ teaspoons THM Gentle Sweet
  (or more, to taste)

Mix the peanut butter, coconut oil, sweetener, vanilla, and salt together with a hand mixer. Add the oat fiber one tablespoon at a time until the mixture returns to a typical natural peanut butter thickness. I used 3 tablespoons of oat fiber, but my natural peanut butter was from a new jar that had just been stirred so it wasn't super thick like some natural peanut butters can get if they're not stirred correctly. The end result should be easily spooned into candy liners; if anything, err on the thin side so the peanut butter mixture won't be too dry once refrigerated. Taste and add more sweetener if desired.

Make the chocolate by melting the chocolate bar, coconut oil, and sweetener together in a microwave. Stir at 20-second intervals so the chocolate doesn't burn. (Alternatively, you could melt the chocolate in a double boiler.) Taste and add more sweetener if necessary; I like dark chocolate.

Divide half the chocolate mixture among 24 mini cupcake tin liners, then freeze to harden. When the chocolate is firm, divide the peanut butter mixture among the liners. Top with the remaining chocolate, then put the candies in the freezer to firm up. (If you have chocolate left over, freeze it on its own and enjoy.) You can store the candies in the freezer or refrigerator; I prefer the fridge for a more traditional peanut butter cup texture.

note

I use Smucker's brand natural peanut butter (from Walmart) that contains just peanuts and salt and has a very intense peanut flavor.

SERVING SIZES ▼

It's so hard to note serving sizes on candy recipes because they're so subjective! Serving sizes vary according to your metabolism and what else you're eating along with the candy. In general, I'd stick with 2-4 pieces per serving depending on how heavy the rest of your meal or snack is. Most candy recipes don't have a lot of protein, so include some protein along with them to round out your meal or snack.

raspberry crémes

RASPBERRY FILLING

1 (8 oz.) pkg. reduced-fat cream cheese

2 tablespoons refined coconut oil (melted)

1 teaspoon raspberry extract

½ teaspoon vanilla extract

3 doonks THM Pure Stevia Extract Powder

1 drop red food coloring

CHOCOLATE

1 (3.5 oz.) bar 85% dark chocolate

¾ cup refined coconut oil

3½ teaspoons THM Gentle Sweet
   (or more, to taste)

Beat the filling ingredients together until smooth. Put the filling into a sealable plastic bag, seal, and snip a hole in one bottom corner for piping. Set aside.

To make the chocolate coating, melt the chocolate bar, coconut oil, and sweetener together in the microwave, stirring every 20 seconds or so to prevent the chocolate from burning. (You could also use a double boiler for this.) Taste and add more sweetener if desired. (I happen to like dark chocolate.)

Fill 24 mini muffin tin holes with liners. Divide half of the chocolate mixture among the liners and freeze to firm up. When the chocolate is firm, pipe some raspberry filling into each liner until all the filling is gone. Spoon the rest of the chocolate mixture over the raspberry filling in each liner and freeze. (If you have chocolate left over, just freeze it to eat on its own.) When the crèmes are firm, transfer them to a sealable container and store in the fridge.

note

Want to switch things up? Try using orange, maple, or mint/peppermint extract instead of raspberry! (Adjust the color.)

mounds of coconut treats

1 (13.66 oz.) can light coconut milk

½ cup + 2 tablespoons coconut oil (softened)

1 tablespoon THM Super Sweet Blend
   (or more, to taste)

2 teaspoons vanilla extract

¼ teaspoon salt

½ teaspoon xanthan gum

4 cups unsweetened coconut flakes

75 grams 85% dark chocolate (3 pieces
   of Moser Roth chocolate from Aldi)

2 teaspoons coconut oil

Blend the first section of ingredients together in a blender or food processor, adding the xanthan gum right before blending so it doesn't clump. Add the coconut and pulse to break up the flakes just a bit (but don't blend until smooth). Pour the coconut mixture into a foil-lined 8"x8" pan, spread out, and refrigerate until firm. Cut into 36 squares, then put the pan in the freezer to super chill. When the squares are nice and cold, remove them from the pan and spread them out on foil on a cookie sheet. Melt the chocolate and coconut oil together in a microwave or double boiler, stirring often. Drizzle the melted chocolate over the coconut squares, then refrigerate or freeze to firm up the chocolate. Store the finished squares in a sealed container in the fridge.

These little squares are on the soft side and remind me of the inside of the classic chocolate-covered coconut candy bar!

note

Feel free to use your favorite sugar-free chocolate chips in place of the 85% dark chocolate.

joyous almond bites

2 cups unsweetened coconut flakes

1 cup oat fiber

1 tablespoon + 1 teaspoon
   THM Super Sweet Blend

½ teaspoon xanthan gum

¼ teaspoon salt

⅛ teaspoon THM Pure Stevia Extract Powder

75 grams 85% dark chocolate (3 pieces of
   Moser Roth chocolate from Aldi) (chopped)

¾ cup refined coconut oil (melted)

½ cup water

1 teaspoon vanilla extract

28 whole almonds

Whisk the first section of ingredients. Add the coconut oil, water, and vanilla and mix well with a hand mixer.

Use your hand to press the dough together into a big blob, then scoop it with a 1-tablespoon cookie scoop. Use your fingers to squish the blobs together into little mounds, then press an almond into the center of each. Store in an airtight container.

These little candy bites are made up of coconut flakes, chocolate chunks, and almonds! If you're not a nut fan (or have a nut allergy), just leave off the almonds. No problem, mate. Want to make them a little more fancy? Drizzle with some melted 85% dark chocolate or sugar-free chocolate chips.

But seek ye first the kingdom of God, and his righteousness;
and all these things shall be added unto you. MATTHEW 6:33

snickerdoodle truffles

HEALTHY FATS I YIELDS 25 TRUFFLES

¾ cup oat fiber

½ cup Briana's Baking Mix

1 tablespoon THM Super Sweet Blend
(or more, to taste)

½ teaspoon xanthan gum

½ teaspoon baking powder

½ teaspoon cinnamon

⅛ teaspoon THM Pure Stevia Extract Powder

⅛ teaspoon salt

¼ cup refined coconut oil

4 tablespoons salted butter

4 oz. reduced-fat cream cheese

½ cup water

1 teaspoon vanilla extract

1 teaspoon molasses

Cinnamon for rolling

Whisk the first section of ingredients. Soften the coconut oil, butter, and cream cheese together in the microwave. Add the softened ingredients, water, vanilla, and molasses to the dry ingredients and mix well with a hand mixer until a dough forms.

Scoop into balls with a 1- tablespoon cookie scoop. Chill the balls in the fridge or freezer for a bit, then roll them smooth between your hands. Roll in cinnamon to coat lightly, then store in an airtight container in the fridge.

These easy truffles taste like unbaked snickerdoodle or cinnamon roll dough! I LOVE the bold flavor of pure cinnamon on the exterior. Traditionally snickerdoodles are rolled in cinnamon sugar, so I tried that with these truffles but used xylitol instead of sugar. Unfortunately, the xylitol absorbed water when I put these truffles in the fridge, so I was left with "sweating" truffles. In round 2, I rolled them in straight cinnamon and actually MUCH preferred the bold flavor of cinnamon on its own!

note

I don't recommend substituting coconut oil for the butter in this recipe because the butter is needed for both taste and texture.

easy chocolate cake truffles

HEALTHY FATS | YIELDS 18 TRUFFLES

⅔ cup Briana's Baking Mix

⅓ cup cocoa powder

2 teaspoons THM Super Sweet Blend

1 teaspoon espresso instant coffee powder

½ teaspoon xanthan gum

¼ teaspoon baking powder

¼ teaspoon salt

⅛ teaspoon THM Pure Stevia Extract Powder

½ cup refined coconut oil (melted)

½ cup water

2 oz. cream cheese (softened)

½ teaspoon vanilla extract

Whisk the dry ingredients. Add the wet ingredients and beat with a hand mixer until a dough forms. Refrigerate or freeze the dough until you can scoop it into balls with a cookie scoop. Freeze the balls for a few minutes, then roll them smooth with your hands and dip them into your choice of coating. Store in the refrigerator.

These silky-smooth chocolate truffles remind me of a cross between Lindt truffles and the homemade truffle recipes that include squished-up chocolate cake and cream cheese. My healthy version doesn't require any cake baking and comes together in a jiffy! If you want to dip them in a melted chocolate coating, I suggest freezing the truffles first so the chocolate sticks better.

COATING SUGGESTIONS ▼

melted sugar-free chocolate, cocoa powder, unsweetened coconut flakes, chopped nuts, sugar-free chocolate chips, crushed sugar-free peppermints

note

• You can increase, decrease, or omit the coffee powder as you see fit. In this amount, it doesn't add a strong flavor.

• If you're sensitive to the taste of stevia, I recommend adding some extra THM Super Sweet Blend or THM Gentle Sweet in its place (to taste).

peanut butter cookie dough fudge

HEALTHY FATS | YIELDS 36 SQUARES

1 cup Briana's Baking Mix

1 tablespoon + 2 teaspoons
   THM Super Sweet Blend

⅜ teaspoon xanthan gum

⅛ teaspoon salt

1 cup natural peanut butter
   (well-stirred and creamy)

¼ cup refined coconut oil

¼ cup water

½ teaspoon vanilla extract

Whisk the dry ingredients. Soften the peanut butter and coconut oil together. Add them, the water, and the vanilla to the dry ingredients and mix with a hand mixer until a dough forms. Press the dough into a foil-lined 8"x8" pan. Cover and freeze until semi-firm, then score into 36 squares with a knife. Freeze until totally firm, then break the squares apart and store in a sealable container in the freezer. I prefer this fudge right out of the freezer. It's soft enough to bite, and it has a better consistency when frozen than it does when kept in the refrigerator.

brianafinger truffle fudge

HEALTHY FATS | YIELDS 36 SQUARES

FUDGE
¾ cup unsweetened almond milk
1 tablespoon Knox gelatin

1 cup refined coconut oil
8 tablespoons salted butter
½ cup + 2 tablespoons oat fiber
½ cup cocoa powder
½ cup unsweetened almond milk (cold)
1 tablespoon Truvia (or more, to taste)
1 tablespoon THM Super Sweet Blend
1 teaspoon xanthan gum
1 teaspoon vanilla extract
³⁄₃₂ teaspoon salt

TOPPINGS
¼ cup natural peanut butter

½ tablespoon butter
½ cup unsweetened coconut flakes
½ teaspoon THM Super Sweet Blend

Whisk the gelatin into ¾ cup almond milk. Microwave for 1½ minutes to dissolve.

Meanwhile, add the rest of the fudge ingredients to a high-powered blender. (I used a Vitamix; you could try using a food processor if you don't have a good blender.) There is no need to soften the coconut oil or butter. Add the hot almond milk/gelatin mixture to the blender and blend until everything is smooth and emulsified, like a chocolate mayonnaise consistency. Taste and add more Truvia if desired. Blend again if you chose to add more sweetener. Spread the fudge mixture into a foil-lined 8"x8" pan.

Dollop the peanut butter over the top of the fudge and use a knife or fork to swirl it into the top.

Toast the coconut flakes in the butter with the Super Sweet Blend in a small saucepan on the stovetop. Sprinkle the toasted coconut on top of the fudge (it's OK if the coconut is still warm).

Cover the fudge and refrigerate overnight to firm up completely, then slice the fudge into 36 squares. Store in the refrigerator.

note
• If using beef gelatin, add an extra ¾ teaspoon.
• Most people will probably want to add more sweetener to the fudge layer. I suggest upping the Truvia, not the Super Sweet Blend (less concentrated sweeteners pair better with chocolate recipes). If you don't have Truvia, try THM Gentle Sweet in its place. I've found that Gentle Sweet doesn't seem quite as strong as Truvia, so you may need a little more.
• The fudge part alone without the toppings is a Foundation Fats treat.
• Find Chocolate Truffle Fudge and Peanut Butter Truffle Fudge recipes on pages 298-299 of *Necessary Food!*

BRIANAFINGER
TRUFFLE FUDGE

PEPPERMINT
TRUFFLE FUDGE

peppermint truffle fudge

HEALTHY FATS | YIELDS 36 SQUARES

¾ cup unsweetened almond milk

1 tablespoon Knox gelatin

1 cup refined coconut oil

8 tablespoons salted butter

¾ cup oat fiber

½ cup unsweetened almond milk (cold)

¼ cup collagen

2 tablespoons THM Super Sweet Blend
   (or more, to taste)

2 teaspoons vanilla extract

1 teaspoon xanthan gum

3/32 teaspoon salt

9-12 drops peppermint essential oil (to taste)

4 drops red food coloring

Melted 85% dark chocolate or sugar-free
   chocolate chips for drizzling on top

Whisk the almond milk and gelatin together and heat until just starting to bubble. (I use a microwave.)

Meanwhile, add the rest of the ingredients to a high-powered blender. Do not soften the coconut oil or butter first. Start with the lower amount of sweetener and peppermint oil because you can always add more later but you can't take any out! Add the hot almond milk/gelatin mixture and blend until emulsified and smooth, like mayonnaise.

Taste and add more sweetener or peppermint oil if desired. I've found that the flavors tend to intensify with time, so I would err on the lighter side. Blend again if you added anything, then pour the mixture into a foil-lined 8"x8" pan. Refrigerate until firm (overnight for the best taste), then cut into 36 squares.

The fudge as-is is Foundation Fats, but a drizzle of chocolate is nice and makes it a regular Healthy Fats dessert. Just melt some sugar-free chocolate and drizzle over the top, then refrigerate to harden.

note

• The butter is necessary for richness and I don't recommend replacing it with more coconut oil.

• If using beef gelatin, add an extra ¾ teaspoon.

• If you're not comfortable with ingesting essential oils, use your favorite peppermint extract to taste. I find that peppermint essential oil provides a much more authentic peppermint taste and since it is emulsified into this recipe with other oils, I am comfortable with using it. Please do your own research and make your own decision. I am not a doctor, nutritionist, or anything of the sort.

trail mix bark

CHOCOLATE

¾ cup refined coconut oil

4 tablespoons salted butter

¼ cup cocoa powder

2½ teaspoons THM Super Sweet Blend
   (or more, to taste)

Dash salt

1 cup salted cashew halves and pieces

1 cup unsweetened coconut flakes

1 cup roasted pumpkin seeds

1 cup fresh or frozen cranberries (chopped)

1 teaspoon THM Super Sweet Blend

Make the chocolate mixture first. Soften the coconut oil and butter just until they can be whisked together. Powder the Super Sweet Blend in a coffee grinder, then whisk it, the cocoa powder, and salt into the butter and coconut oil. Set aside.

Mix the second set of ingredients together and distribute evenly in a foil-lined 9"x13" pan. Pour the chocolate mixture over the top. The chocolate is what holds everything together, so make sure it's coating everything, distributing it with a spatula as needed. Freeze to firm up, then break into pieces. Store in the fridge for a softer result, or the freezer for more crunch and less mess (my preference).

note

• You could use 1¼ cups of your favorite melted sugar-free chocolate chips in place of the homemade chocolate – measure after melting.

• Feel free to add more of a less concentrated sweetener to the chocolate mixture if you have a big sweet tooth or are sensitive to the taste of stevia.

peanut butter cookies

8 tablespoons salted butter (softened)

½ cup natural peanut butter

3 oz. reduced-fat cream cheese

¼ cup + 2 tablespoons xylitol
(or more, to taste)

1 teaspoon molasses

2 eggs

3 tablespoons water

1 teaspoon vanilla extract

¾ cup oat fiber

½ teaspoon baking powder

¼ teaspoon baking soda

¼ teaspoon salt

Beat the first section of ingredients well. Add the eggs, water, and vanilla and beat again. Add the dry ingredients and mix.

Scoop cookies with a 1½- tablespoon cookie scoop onto ungreased cookie sheets. Spread the cookies out a bit with your fingers or a spoon. (The dough is too soft to make the traditional crosshatch pattern on the tops of the cookies with a fork, but you can try!) Bake at 350° for about 14 minutes (check at 10 so you don't overbake), then cool on the pans for 3 minutes before transferring the cookies to wire racks to finish cooling. When warm, they're a bit cakey and fragile. I prefer them cold; they're firmer with more chew.

Ryan really liked these cookies and told me that they were a success! They're not the same as traditional peanut butter cookies because they don't have the crisp chewiness that comes with gluten and caramelized sugar, but if the husband is happy, that's good enough for me.

note

• I used xylitol for a more sugar-like texture in these cookies, but you're welcome to experiment with other sweeteners.

• These cookies would make amazing ice cream sandwiches!

chocolate chip cookie pie

HEALTHY FATS | SERVES 8

¾ cup oat fiber

⅔ cup natural almond butter

⅔ cup water

6 tablespoons salted butter (melted)

1½ tablespoons chia seeds (ground to powder after measuring)

1 tablespoon + 1 teaspoon THM Super Sweet Blend (or more, to taste)

1 teaspoon molasses

1 teaspoon vanilla extract

½ teaspoon baking soda

⅜ teaspoon salt (my almond butter was not salted)

⅓ cup sugar-free chocolate chips

Mix the ingredients together well, then fold in the chocolate chips. Spread into a greased 9" cake pan with parchment paper on the bottom. (Batter will be thick.) Bake at 350° for 18-20 minutes. It will be underdone and soft in the center, but it won't have a glossy, wet look on top.

This cookie pie is best cold. Because there are no eggs to act as a binder, it doesn't hold together well when warm. It still tastes great warm, and would be terrific topped with some vanilla ice cream, but if you want to pick it up like a slice of cookie pie, eat it cold.

This is one of my favorite recipes from this book. It's egg free so it holds its shape best when cold, but it's delightfully moist and cookie-dough-y.

note

• Use natural peanut butter in place of the almond butter for a peanut butter chocolate chip cookie pie.

• If your nut butter is salted, you'll probably need to decrease the salt in the recipe. I used Cadia natural almond butter, which is made entirely of almonds and nothing else.

• If using chopped dark chocolate instead of sugar-free chocolate chips, consider adding more sweetener to the dough.

• If the oil has separated from your natural nut butter, be sure to stir it well before measuring for accurate results in recipes.

bri's best fudgy brownies

HEALTHY FATS | SERVES 9

½ cup natural almond butter

4 tablespoons salted butter

1½ oz. unsweetened baker's chocolate

½ cup + 2 tablespoons oat fiber

¼ cup + 3 tablespoons xylitol (or more, to taste)

2 tablespoons chia seeds (ground to
   powder after measuring)

⅜ teaspoon salt (my almond butter
   was not salted)

¾ cup water

1 teaspoon vanilla extract

Melt the almond butter, butter, and chocolate together in a microwave or double boiler just until they can be whisked together, stirring periodically.

Whisk the dry ingredients. Add the chocolate mixture, water, and vanilla to the dry ingredients and combine with a spatula. Stir just enough to combine evenly.

Spread into a greased 8"x8" pan and bake at 350° for about 35 minutes. The brownies will be set in the center but still look slightly underdone. Let the brownies cool awhile to continue to firm up before cutting and enjoying. Store in the fridge.

Here's another recipe for my egg-free friends! These brownies are good warm or cold (although they do need some time to solidify after coming out of the oven), and they're SO fudgy! If you want to reheat a cold brownie, a few seconds in the microwave will do the trick, but I love them cold with ice cream on top.

note

• You won't taste the almond butter, but it provides the right texture and structure for these brownies. I used Cadia natural almond butter, which is made entirely of almonds and nothing else. Look for almond butter with no added sugar in the ingredients, and use a crunchy almond butter if you like nuts in your brownies! If you're OK with a peanut butter flavor, you could try replacing the almond butter with natural peanut butter. If your nut butter is salted, you'll probably need to decrease the salt in the recipe.

• I used xylitol for a more sugar-like texture in these brownies, but you're welcome to experiment with other sweeteners. If your taste buds are really sensitive to sugar alcohols, like mine are, you'll like the taste of these brownies best after overnight refrigeration. The sweetness settles out.

• These brownies are delicious with the Extreme Chocolate Ice Cream on page 298! They're also perfect for cutting up and stirring into milkshakes.

gooey brownies

HEALTHY CARBS | SERVES 9

1⅓ cups oat flour

¼ cup + 2 tablespoons cocoa powder

1½ tablespoons THM Super Sweet Blend

1 teaspoon baking powder

¼ teaspoon salt

1 cup frozen diced okra (thawed)

¾ cup egg whites

¾ cup water

Whisk the dry ingredients. Blend the wet ingredients until smooth. Pour the wet ingredients into the dry ingredients and stir by hand with a spatula just until mixed. Pour into a greased 8"x8" pan and bake at 350° for about 17 minutes or until the top looks done and the center isn't too squishy when you press on it. Remove the brownies from the oven, let them cool, then refrigerate overnight before cutting and eating. Store in the refrigerator.

If you want a warm brownie, wait until the day after baking and heat one in the microwave for a few seconds.

note

I recommend using frozen diced okra because it has been blanched before freezing. Blanching helps cut some of the slime and makes the okra disintegrate into your brownies better.

superfood brownies

FOUNDATION FATS | SERVES 9

1½ cups frozen diced okra (thawed)
½ cup + 2 tablespoons warm water
¼ cup + 1 tablespoon refined coconut oil
3 eggs

½ cup oat fiber
¼ cup + 2 tablespoons cocoa powder
1½ - 2 tablespoons THM Super Sweet Blend
1 teaspoon baking powder
¼ teaspoon salt

Blend the okra, water, coconut oil, and eggs together in a blender just until smooth.

Whisk the dry ingredients. Add the blended mixture to the dry ingredients and beat with a hand mixer just until mixed.

Spread the batter into a greased 8"x8" glass baking dish and bake at 350° for 24 minutes. The center may still feel underdone, but that's OK. Let the brownies cool, then refrigerate them overnight before cutting and serving. Store in the refrigerator.

note

I recommend using frozen diced okra because it has been blanched before freezing. Blanching helps cut some of the slime and makes the okra disintegrate into your brownies better.

I used a significant amount of okra in this recipe because I've really been trying to eat more of this special vegetable. When I created the recipe I was still using a Ninja blender that was losing some of its power after years of hard use, and it didn't blend the okra as finely as I would've liked, hence the okra specks that you see in the picture. The okra adds a bit of an "earthy" flavor to these brownies; I'm not going to lie and say that you can't taste it a little. I put enough in this recipe that I expected to taste it, and I don't mind a bit! I definitely recommend refrigerating these brownies overnight before eating them – and once they're fully chilled…mmm, are they ever good! Every single bite contains lots of good okra and coconut oil to nourish your body.

superfood single brownie

⅓ cup frozen diced okra
1 tablespoon refined coconut oil

1 egg
2 tablespoons water

1½ tablespoons oat fiber
1 tablespoon cocoa powder
2 teaspoons THM Super Sweet Blend
  (or more, to taste)
¼ teaspoon baking powder
1/16 teaspoon salt

Thaw the diced okra with the coconut oil in the microwave.

Blend the okra, coconut oil, egg, and water until smooth.

Whisk the blended mixture with the rest of the ingredients until smooth.

Pour the mixture into a greased 2-cup glass dish and microwave for 1 minute and 30 seconds, or until the brownie is just dry on top. Enjoy warm or cold.

The okra gives this brownie a nice traditional brownie texture that I love! I recommend using frozen okra in this recipe because it has been blanched, which helps cut some of the okra slime and breaks the okra down better before use in recipes. I can personally taste the earthiness of the okra a little in this brownie and in every other recipe in which I've used okra, but it's not a flavor that I mind as long as there's another strong flavor, like chocolate, to mask it. I just love knowing that I'm getting a dose of healthy veggies in my dessert!

pecan pie cheesecake bars

HEALTHY FATS I SERVES 9

CRUST
¾ cup Briana's Baking Mix

½ cup finely-chopped pecans

4 tablespoons salted butter (melted)

1 egg

1½ teaspoons THM Super Sweet Blend

½ teaspoon cinnamon

¼ teaspoon baking powder

CHEESECAKE
1½ (8 oz.) pkgs. cream cheese
   (room temperature)

1 cup sour cream (room temperature)

2 eggs (room temperature)

2-3 teaspoons THM Super Sweet Blend

1 teaspoon vanilla extract

½ teaspoon maple extract

¼ teaspoon cinnamon

Chopped pecans

Sugar-free chocolate chips

Mix the crust ingredients together and press into a greased 8"x8" glass baking dish. Do not prebake the crust.

Beat the cheesecake ingredients together until smooth. Taste and add more sweetener if desired. Pour onto the crust. Sprinkle with chopped pecans and sugar-free chocolate chips and bake at 350° for 35 minutes or until set. Refrigerate to chill completely before serving (overnight is great).

Why are they called "Pecan Pie Cheesecake Bars" instead of just "Pecan Pie Cheesecake"? Because I made them in a non-fancy 8"x8" pan, not a spring-form pan. I just didn't feel right calling this recipe "cheesecake" since it wasn't made in a cheesecake pan. It's basically cheesecake though. Cheesecake with an amazing pecan crust, a creamy filling with a hint of maple, and nuts and chocolate chips on top.

note

Some caramel sauce would be the perfect topping for this cheesecake! There's an easy caramel sauce recipe in *Necessary Food*.

raspberry crumble bars

HEALTHY FATS | SERVES 9

JAM

1½ cups red raspberries

1 cup water

¼ cup chia seeds

2 teaspoons THM Super Sweet Blend
(or more, to taste)

CRUST

12 tablespoons salted butter (softened)

1 cup oat fiber

¾ cup Briana's Baking Mix

¼ cup + 2 tablespoons water

1 tablespoon + 1 teaspoon THM Super
Sweet Blend (or more, to taste)

1 teaspoon vanilla extract

⅛ teaspoon salt

TOPPING

½ cup unsweetened coconut flakes

¼ cup old-fashioned oats

½ teaspoon THM Super Sweet Blend

Make the jam first so it can cool down a bit. Bring the jam ingredients to a boil in a saucepan, stirring occasionally, then take the pan off the heat.

Mix the crust ingredients together with a hand mixer to form a crumbly dough. Set aside ¾ cup of the crust mixture and press the remainder into a greased 8"x8" pan. Bake at 350° for 10 minutes.

To the reserved ¾ cup of crust mixture, add the coconut flakes, oats, and Super Sweet Blend and mix.

When the crust is done prebaking, pour the jam on top and spread it out evenly. Press the topping mixture with your hand so it clumps together a bit and distribute it evenly over the jam. Bake at 350° for 25 minutes. You can eat the bars warm, but they're pretty soft and more of a scoopable dessert than bars. I recommend refrigerating the bars to chill completely before cutting and serving.

Of course these bars are great on their own, but I also like to eat them crumbled up into some almond milk. For some reason they remind me of a breakfast pastry when I do that! There's an abundance of crumb topping on these bars, so they can be a little messy. They're more of a plate-and-fork bar than a pick-up-with-your-hands bar.

note

• I used frozen raspberries, but fresh would probably work too.

• Oats are a Healthy Carbs ingredient, but this amount only adds 1.28 grams net carbs per serving.

• Measure flours correctly by spooning the flour into a measuring cup with another measuring cup, then leveling it off with a knife to avoid packing the flour and getting a dry result!

coconut cream pie bars

CRUST

½ cup oat fiber

⅓ cup Briana's Baking Mix

1½ teaspoons THM Super Sweet Blend

¼ teaspoon xanthan gum

¼ teaspoon salt

¼ cup + 1 tablespoon coconut oil (softened)

2 tablespoons water

FILLING

1 (13.66 oz.) can full-fat coconut milk

1 cup unsweetened coconut flakes

2 eggs

2 egg yolks

1 tablespoon + 1 teaspoon
    THM Super Sweet Blend

2 teaspoons vanilla extract

¼ teaspoon salt

Whisk the dry crust ingredients. Add the coconut oil and water and mix to form coarse crumbs. Press into a greased 8"x8" pan and bake at 350° for 5 minutes.

Mix the filling ingredients together and pour on top of hot crust. Spread the coconut out evenly. Bake at 350° for about 40 minutes or until almost set in the center (but still a little jiggly). Cool, then refrigerate the bars to chill completely before cutting and serving.

If you use collagen to make my baking mix, these bars are dairy free! Whether or not you follow a dairy-free diet, you'll enjoy these creamy bars reminiscent of a coconut cream pie.

The ETERNAL GOD is thy REFUGE, and underneath are the everlasting arms.
DEUTERONOMY 33:27A

trail mix snack bars

1½ cups unsweetened coconut flakes

1½ cups roasted pumpkin seeds

1 cup pecans or nuts of choice (chopped)

1 cup fresh or frozen cranberries (chopped)

⅔ cup Briana's Baking Mix

½ cup sugar-free chocolate chips

¼ cup chia seeds

2 tablespoons THM Super Sweet Blend
   (or more, to taste)

¾ teaspoon xanthan gum

¾ teaspoon salt

½ teaspoon cinnamon

1 cup water

½ cup refined coconut oil (melted)

Mix the first section of ingredients together. Add the water and coconut oil and mix again. Press the dough into a 9"x13" pan, then refrigerate to firm up. Once the bars are firm, slice into 24 pieces. Store in fridge.

I would stick to 2-3 squares in a serving. If using them on their own as a snack, add some protein, such as collagen in your coffee or tea.

These bars have a really neat combination of tastes and textures. The pop of cranberry really adds something. I always stock up on cranberries around the holidays when they're really cheap and freeze them for the rest of the year.

note

• I think the xanthan gum adds a cool texture (and it helps hold the bars together), but if you find them to be slimy, you could probably decrease it to ½ teaspoon.

• None of my ingredients were salted. Use less salt if some of yours were.

chocolate peanut butter snack bars

HEALTHY FATS I YIELDS 9 (OR 16)

2 cups unsweetened coconut flakes

6 tablespoons salted butter (melted)

¼ cup Briana's Baking Mix

¼ cup defatted peanut flour

¼ cup natural peanut butter

1½ tablespoons THM Super Sweet Blend

1 teaspoon vanilla extract

½ teaspoon salt

TOPPING:

½ cup natural peanut butter

¼ cup + 2 tablespoons refined
   coconut oil (melted)

2 tablespoons cocoa powder

1 tablespoon THM Super Sweet Blend
   (or more, to taste) (ground to powder)

Mix the first section of ingredients together and press into a greased 8"x8" pan. Bake at 350° for 12 minutes, then chill completely before adding the chocolate topping.

To make the topping, melt the coconut oil, then whisk in the peanut butter, cocoa powder, and powdered sweetener. Pour the chocolate mixture over the chilled crust and refrigerate to firm up. Cut into 9 squares (or 16, since they're rather rich) and store in the fridge.

These bars are based off of my Brianafinger Bars (*Necessary Food*, page 328), but they don't have any oats, make a smaller batch, and are more peanut buttery. I wasn't going for this, but when I tasted these I thought, "Oh, I bet that's close to what a scotcheroo tastes like!" I've never actually had a scotcheroo, so I can't say for sure...haha. A dash of butterscotch extract in the top layer would probably make the resemblance even stronger.

note

• If you're sensitive to the taste of stevia you may want to use 2½ - 3 tablespoons THM Gentle Sweet (or more, to taste) in place of the Super Sweet Blend. Less concentrated sweeteners tend to pair better with chocolate if you have sensitive taste buds. As always, feel free to add more sweetener.

• If the oil separates out of your natural peanut butter, stir it well before measuring to ensure accurate results.

brianafinger bar for one

HEALTHY FATS | SERVES 1

CRUST

3 tablespoons finely-shredded unsweetened
   coconut flakes

1 tablespoon Briana's Baking Mix

2 teaspoons salted butter (melted)

½ teaspoon THM Super Sweet Blend

TOPPING

1 tablespoon refined coconut oil

1 tablespoon natural peanut butter

1-2 teaspoons THM Gentle Sweet

1 teaspoon cocoa powder

Combine the crust ingredients with a fork until evenly mixed and press into the bottom of a foil-lined mini loaf pan. Broil for a few minutes until the edges are toasty brown. Put the pan in the freezer to cool.

Meanwhile, melt the topping ingredients together (I use a microwave) and whisk until smooth. When the crust is completely chilled, pour the topping on top and return it to the freezer until firm. Enjoy!

This Brianafinger Bar is based off of the full-size recipe on page 328 of *Necessary Food*. It's pretty rich and calorie-dense so I keep it for a once-in-awhile treat if I intend to eat the whole thing. It does make a rather large cookie bar, so cutting it in half is a good option, especially if you're eating it with a meal that already contains quite a bit of fat. This is the kind of thing I like to save for when I'm on my own for supper and don't feel like cooking much. I might eat something light, like a salad with some chicken or salmon on top, then have this (the whole thing!!) for dessert to fill in the cracks. You can have plenty of fats, but it's best to be smart with them and not have them all at the same time!

note

• If you use regular unsweetened coconut flakes, the crust may be more crumbly.

• For a non-coconut option, you can replace the coconut flakes with almond flour and add 2 teaspoons water. This makes a softer crust than the coconut does.

• It's important to let the crust chill completely before pouring the topping mixture on top or else the topping will soak down into the crust.

MOCHA CHEESECAKE
PG 425

desserts

peach cobbler with biscuit topping

HEALTHY CARBS I SERVES 9

4 cups chopped peaches (peeled)

1-2 tablespoons THM Super Sweet Blend
   (amount will vary based on
   sweetness of peaches)

1 teaspoon cinnamon

½ teaspoon vanilla extract

BISCUIT TOPPING

1 cup oat flour

½ cup low-fat Greek yogurt

½ cup egg whites

2 teaspoons refined coconut oil (melted)

1 teaspoon baking powder

⅛ teaspoon THM Pure Stevia Extract Powder

⅛ teaspoon salt

I like to use a hamburger chopper to roughly chop my peaches and get the juices flowing. If using frozen peaches, thaw them, chop them, then drain them well. If they're pretty mushy (either from being frozen or from being overripe), I suggest adding ½ teaspoon xanthan gum to the peach mixture to thicken it while baking. Sprinkle it over the peaches in a fine layer and stir quickly to prevent clumping.

Add the Super Sweet Blend, cinnamon, and vanilla to the chopped peaches and stir to coat. Pour the mixture into a greased 8"x8" baking pan.

Whisk the biscuit topping ingredients together to mix well. Blob it on top of the peaches with a spoon, then spread it out evenly. You can sprinkle the top of the cobbler with additional Super Sweet Blend and cinnamon if you like.

Bake the cobbler at 350° for 40 minutes or until a toothpick inserted into the biscuit topping comes out cleanly and the center feels done. Let the cobbler cool for 15 minutes before serving for best results. Refrigerate leftovers and enjoy them for breakfast with a lean protein source such as low-fat cottage cheese or Greek yogurt or some collagen in your morning tea.

I've eaten this cobbler warm from the oven as well as cold from the fridge. It makes a special Sunday morning breakfast! Just add a side of low-fat cottage cheese or Greek yogurt for protein. I enjoy my cobbler with a splash of unsweetened almond milk, a squirt of fat-free Reddi-wip, or some low-fat ice cream (such as the Basic Soft Serve recipe on page 241 of *Necessary Food*).

note

• Feel free to add more sweetener to this cobbler recipe if you like your desserts really sweet. I prefer to use less – just call me European. (My grandpa, who has spent quite a bit of time in Germany, tells me often that European desserts are generally a lot less sweet than American desserts are.)

• The coconut oil adds a very small amount of fat per serving, and I like the texture it adds.

single-serve peach cobbler

HEALTHY CARBS | SERVES 1

1 med.-lg. peach (thawed and drained
   if frozen, chopped)
1 teaspoon THM Super Sweet Blend
   (or more, to taste)
Dash vanilla extract
Dash cinnamon

BISCUIT TOPPING
¼ cup oat flour
2 tablespoons full-fat sour cream
2 tablespoons egg whites
¼ teaspoon baking powder
1 doonk THM Pure Stevia Extract Powder
Dash salt

Stir the first section of ingredients together
and pour into a ceramic or glass ramekin.

Whisk the biscuit topping ingredients together
and pour over the top of the peaches.

Microwave for 2 minutes. The topping will
look done after about a minute, but you need
to nuke it a little longer than you think. Let
the cobbler cool for a few minutes before
digging in for best texture. You can use this
as a dessert after a Healthy Carbs or Low
Carb/Low Fat meal, or add some protein (like
low-fat cottage cheese) on the side and call
it breakfast. (Between the peach and the oat
flour, this recipe contains roughly 30 grams
net carbs, so keep additional carbs minimal.)

note

• I used full-fat sour cream as my allotted fat in
this recipe because I like the texture it gives the
topping. If you don't have sour cream or want to
use your 5 grams of fat elsewhere, use fat-free
Greek yogurt in its place. For a dairy-free option,
I would try substituting the sour cream with
unsweetened applesauce, but the result will be
gooier.

• Feel free to top with some unsweetened almond
milk, fat-free Reddi-wip, and/or low-fat ice cream
(such as the Basic Soft Serve recipe on page 241
of *Necessary Food*).

• I haven't tried baking this recipe, but that would
probably work. Bake at 350° until a toothpick
inserted through the topping comes out cleanly.

cherry cobbler

1 (26 oz.) can tart cherries canned in water (undrained)

1-2 tablespoons THM Super Sweet Blend (or more, to taste)

1 tablespoon oat flour

¾ teaspoon xanthan gum

½ teaspoon cinnamon

½ teaspoon vanilla extract

⅛ teaspoon salt

BISCUIT TOPPING

1 cup oat flour

½ cup low-fat Greek yogurt

½ cup egg whites

2 teaspoons refined coconut oil (melted)

1 teaspoon baking powder

⅛ teaspoon THM Pure Stevia Extract Powder

⅛ teaspoon salt

Stir the filling ingredients together gently with a spatula to combine. (Sprinkle the xanthan gum into the mixture in a fine layer before stirring to avoid major clumping.) Pour into a greased 8"x8" pan.

Whisk the topping ingredients until smooth. Spread over the filling. Top with a sprinkle of cinnamon if you like. Bake at 350° for 30 minutes or until a toothpick inserted into the topping comes out cleanly and the top feels done in the middle. Let the cobbler cool for a few minutes before digging in. Feel free to top with a squirt of Reddi-wip, some unsweetened almond milk, or some low-fat, sugar-free ice cream.

note

• A 26-oz. can of cherries holds about 3 cups of cherries and a little over ½ cup of juice. If you can't find canned cherries, you could try cooking down fresh or frozen tart cherries (pitted, of course!) in some water, then using the cooked cherries and resulting juice in this recipe.

• The coconut oil adds only a trace amount of fat per serving and improves the texture of the topping.

pumpkin torte

HEALTHY FATS I SERVES 15

PUMPKIN LAYER

1 (15 oz.) can pumpkin

1 cup unsweetened almond milk

¾ cup heavy whipping cream

3 eggs

3 tablespoons THM Super Sweet Blend

¾ teaspoon pumpkin pie spice

¼ teaspoon salt

CRUMBS

12 tablespoons salted butter (softened)

1 cup chopped pecans

¾ cup Briana's Baking Mix

¾ cup oat fiber

2½ tablespoons THM Super Sweet Blend

1½ teaspoons baking powder

1 teaspoon vanilla extract

Beat the pumpkin layer ingredients together, then pour into a greased 9"x13" pan.

Mix the crumb ingredients together (I use a hand mixer) to form crumbs, then distribute these evenly into the pumpkin mixture using a spatula. Some will be submerged; some will stick above the surface and get nice and golden brown.

Bake at 350° for 30 minutes. Let the torte cool down a few minutes to solidify before serving. Serve warm with homemade sweetened whipped cream or healthy vanilla ice cream. Refrigerate leftovers. (It's good cold, too.)

This is my version of the infamous Pinterested pumpkin dump cake – the kind with the pumpkin filling, yellow cake mix, and 2 sticks of melted butter. I've actually never tried the real thing so maybe I shouldn't tout this as the healthy version of it, but that's kind of the spin I was going for when creating this recipe. That and a pecan streusel-topped pumpkin cobbler of sorts. Meant to be eaten warm with whipped cream or vanilla ice cream. When it came out of the oven, this dessert also reminded me of a pumpkin torte I ate once upon a time (when I ate such things… kidding…I still do once in awhile…), so Pumpkin Torte it became. And then I looked at all kinds of pumpkin torte recipes in a huge church cookbook we have and realized that "pumpkin torte" means many different things. Why is life so complicated??

pumpkin donuts

HEALTHY FATS | YIELDS 12 MINI DONUTS

½ cup Briana's Baking Mix
2½ teaspoons THM Super Sweet Blend
2 teaspoons baking powder
1 teaspoon pumpkin pie spice

½ cup canned pumpkin
3 eggs
3 tablespoons refined coconut oil (melted)

GLAZE
1 oz. cream cheese (softened)
2 tablespoons refined coconut oil (softened)
1 doonk THM Pure Stevia Extract Powder
Dash maple extract
2 tablespoons unsweetened
   almond milk (cold)

Whisk the dry ingredients. Add the wet ingredients and mix well. Bake in a greased mini donut maker by 2-tablespoonfuls for 3-4 minutes or until the donuts don't feel too squishy when you press down lightly on the tops. Chill the donuts before glazing.

To make the glaze, whisk the first four ingredients together until mostly smooth (they might not emulsify completely until you add the cold almond milk). Add the almond milk and whisk until smooth and emulsified.

Dip the chilled donuts in the glaze, then return them to the fridge or freezer to harden the glaze. If you have enough glaze left, double dip the donuts after chilling. Store in the refrigerator.

note

No donut maker? Try baking these in greased mini muffin tins at 350° until a toothpick comes out cleanly and the tops aren't too squishy when you press on them lightly.

fresh strawberry pie

CRUST

½ cup Briana's Baking Mix

¼ cup oat fiber

½ teaspoon plain gelatin

1/16 teaspoon xanthan gum

1/16 teaspoon salt

1 doonk THM Pure Stevia Extract Powder

3 tablespoons salted butter (cold, cubed)

¼ c + 2 tablespoons cold water

1 tablespoon heavy whipping cream

CREAM CHEESE LAYER

1 (8 oz.) pkg. reduced-fat cream cheese

½ cup sour cream

1 teaspoon THM Super Sweet Blend
   (or more, to taste)

½ teaspoon vanilla extract

⅛ teaspoon THM Pure Stevia Extract Powder

1½ teaspoons Knox gelatin

2 tablespoons very hot tap water

1 cup heavy whipping cream

STRAWBERRY LAYER

1 cup strawberries

½ cup water

1½ teaspoons THM Super Sweet Blend
   (or more, to taste)

¾ teaspoon Knox gelatin

¼ teaspoon glucomannan

3 cups sliced fresh strawberries

CRUST: Pulse the dry ingredients in a food processor. Add the butter and pulse until crumbs form. Add the water and heavy whipping cream and pulse until a dough forms. Remove the dough, press it together with your hands, and chill in the freezer for 10 minutes. After chilling, roll the dough out between two silicone baking mats or sheets of plastic wrap. Invert the dough into a greased 9" pie plate and gently arrange it in the plate, patching tears and cutting off extra dough as necessary. Flute the edges of the pie crust if desired and bake at 350° for 15 minutes or until the edges start to lightly brown and the dough is no longer wet. Let the crust cool completely before filling.

CREAM CHEESE LAYER: Beat the first section of ingredients together with a hand mixer until smooth. Whisk the gelatin into the hot water and add it to the cream cheese mixture immediately while beating. Add the cream and beat for a few minutes until the mixture thickens and slight ridges start to appear. Pour the cream cheese mixture into the cooled pie crust and refrigerate until it starts to set up before adding the strawberry layer.

STRAWBERRY LAYER: Bring 1 cup strawberries, the water, and Super Sweet Blend to a boil, then simmer (uncovered) for 5 minutes. Remove from the heat and blend with an immersion blender. Add the gelatin and glucomannan and blend again. Stir in the fresh sliced strawberries by hand and refrigerate for 15-20 minutes to cool before spreading the strawberry mixture on top of pie. Refrigerate the completed pie for several hours or overnight to firm up. It's best to eat the pie within 24 hours of assembly for the freshest result.

note

• If using beef gelatin, add ⅜ teaspoon to the cream cheese layer. Add a rounded ⅛ teaspoon to the strawberry layer.

• If you prefer, just top the pie with sliced fresh strawberries (tossed with some sweetener if you like) and don't bother with the strawberry glaze. This will give you a more vibrantly-colored, crisper result.

blueberry cheesecake delight

HEALTHY FATS **I SERVES 9**

CRUST

1 cup Briana's Baking Mix

2 teaspoons THM Super Sweet Blend

¼ teaspoon xanthan gum

5 tablespoons salted butter (softened)

CHEESECAKE FILLING

1 (8 oz.) pkg. reduced-fat cream cheese

½ teaspoon vanilla extract

⅛ teaspoon THM Pure Stevia Extract Powder

½ cup heavy whipping cream

BLUEBERRY TOPPING

1½ cups blueberries

¾ cup water

1½ teaspoons THM Super Sweet Blend

1 teaspoon lemon juice

⅛ teaspoon THM Pure Stevia Extract Powder

1 teaspoon Knox gelatin

½ teaspoon glucomannan

2 cups fresh blueberries

CRUST: Whisk the dry ingredients. Beat in the butter with a hand mixer until crumbs form. Press into a greased 8"x8" pan and bake at 350° for 7 minutes. Cool completely.

CHEESECAKE FILLING: Beat the cream cheese, vanilla, and stevia until smooth. Add the cream and beat until thick and fluffy. Spread over the cooled crust.

BLUEBERRY TOPPING: Bring the first five ingredients to a boil in a saucepan and simmer (uncovered) for five minutes. Take off the heat and blend with an immersion blender until smooth. Blend in the gelatin and glucomannan, adding the glucomannan while blending so it doesn't clump. Stir in the fresh blueberries gently and cool the blueberry topping to room temperature before spreading it onto the top of the delight.

Refrigerate the delight overnight to set up completely. Serve.

I always grew up calling layered cream cheese desserts "delights," but apparently that isn't the universal norm. While we were dating, my Canadian now-husband asked me if I ever make "blueberry cheesecake," and then proceeded to describe what I had always called "blueberry delight." In case you're not familiar with a delight, I've included both terms in this recipe's name so we're all in agreement.

note

• If using beef gelatin, add an extra ¼ teaspoon.

• Want a 9"x13" version? Just double the recipe.

lemon cheesecake delight

CRUST

1 cup Briana's Baking Mix

2 teaspoons THM Super Sweet Blend

¼ teaspoon xanthan gum

5 tablespoons salted butter (softened)

CHEESECAKE LAYER

1 (8 oz.) pkg. reduced-fat cream cheese

½ teaspoon vanilla extract

⅛ teaspoon THM Pure Stevia Extract Powder

½ cup heavy whipping cream

LEMON LAYER

1½ cups water

½ cup lemon juice

2 eggs

2 teaspoons THM Super Sweet Blend
(or more, to taste)

1 teaspoon Knox gelatin

1 teaspoon vanilla extract

¼ teaspoon salt

⅛ teaspoon THM Pure Stevia Extract Powder

1⁄16 teaspoon turmeric (for color)

CRUST: Whisk the dry ingredients. Beat in the butter with a hand mixer until crumbs form. Press into a greased 8"x8" pan and bake at 350° for 7 minutes. Cool completely.

CHEESECAKE LAYER: Beat the cream cheese, vanilla, and stevia until smooth. Add the cream and beat until thick and fluffy. Spread over the cooled crust.

LEMON LAYER: Whisk or use an immersion blender to blend the ingredients until smooth in a saucepan on the stovetop. Cook over medium heat until the mixture just starts to bubble, whisking often, then pull it off the heat. Transfer the lemon pudding to a bowl and cover with plastic wrap, putting the wrap in contact with the surface of the pudding to prevent a skin from forming. Chill for several hours or overnight to firm up.

When the lemon pudding is firm, invert it onto the cheesecake layer of the delight so what was the top of the pudding is now the bottom. Use a spatula to spread the pudding and smooth the top, but spread as little as possible so it doesn't look lumpy and the gelatin doesn't lose its strength. You can top the delight with whipped cream for serving if it doesn't look pretty, but if you're careful when spreading the lemon layer you can omit the extra step (and extra calories).

I like to refrigerate the delight for a few hours before serving to ensure that everything is cold and will keep its shape. It holds up fine, so you can even make the delight a day in advance of serving.

note

If using beef gelatin instead of Knox gelatin, add ¼ teaspoon.

peppermint delight

CRUST
1 cup almond flour
3 tablespoons cocoa powder
2 teaspoons THM Super Sweet Blend
3 tablespoons salted butter (melted)

PEPPERMINT FILLING
2 (8 oz.) pkgs. reduced-fat cream
    cheese (softened)
2 tablespoons THM Gentle Sweet
    (or more, to taste)
½ teaspoon vanilla extract
½ - ¾ teaspoon peppermint extract
⅛ teaspoon + 2 doonks THM
    Pure Stevia Extract Powder
4 drops red food coloring (optional)

¾ cup heavy whipping cream
½ cup unsweetened almond milk

2 tablespoons very hot tap water
1 tablespoon Knox gelatin

For the crust, whisk the dry ingredients. Add the melted butter and mix with a hand mixer. Press the crust mixture into a greased 8"x8" pan and set aside.

For the peppermint filling, beat the cream cheese until smooth. Add the sweeteners, vanilla, food coloring, and ½ teaspoon peppermint extract. Beat until smooth. Taste and add more Gentle Sweet and/or an additional ¼ teaspoon of peppermint extract if desired. Add the cream and almond milk while beating and beat until smooth and thick. Whisk the gelatin into the hot water to dissolve and immediately add it to the peppermint filling while beating so the gelatin doesn't clump. Beat until smooth. Pour the filling over the crust, then cover and refrigerate overnight to firm up.

You can either eat this as a no-bake peppermint cheesecake, or you can top it with whipped cream and garnish with chopped sugar-free peppermints and dark chocolate for a decadent peppermint delight.

note

If using beef gelatin, add an extra ¾ teaspoon.

no-bake pumpkin cheesecake

CRUST

1 cup Briana's Baking Mix

4 tablespoons salted butter (melted)

¼ cup water

1½ teaspoons THM Super Sweet Blend

¼ teaspoon xanthan gum

CHEESECAKE

1½ (8 oz.) pkgs. cream cheese (softened)

1 cup canned pumpkin

½ cup sour cream

1 tablespoon THM Super Sweet Blend
   (or more, to taste)

½ teaspoon cinnamon

½ teaspoon vanilla extract

¼ teaspoon each ginger, ground cloves

⅛ teaspoon THM Pure Stevia Extract Powder

2 teaspoons Knox gelatin

2 tablespoons very hot tap water

½ cup heavy whipping cream

Mix the crust ingredients together with a hand mixer until crumbs form. Press into a greased 8"x8" pan.

Beat the first set of cheesecake ingredients together until smooth. Whisk the gelatin into the hot water, then add it to the cheesecake mixture while beating. Beat until smooth. Add the cream and beat until thick. Pour the cheesecake mixture over the crust and smooth it out. Refrigerate for several hours until firm (or overnight).

note

If using beef gelatin, add an extra ½ teaspoon.

Nevertheless I am continually with thee: THOU HAST HOLDEN ME BY MY RIGHT HAND. Thou shalt guide me with thy counsel, and afterward receive me to glory. Whom have I in heaven but thee? and there is none upon earth that I desire beside thee. My flesh and my heart faileth: BUT GOD IS THE STRENGTH OF MY HEART, and my portion for ever.

PSALM 73:23-26

classic cheesecake

CRUST

2 cups almond flour

6 tablespoons salted butter (melted)

¼ cup Briana's Baking Mix

1½ teaspoons THM Super Sweet Blend

CHEESECAKE

4 (8 oz.) pkgs. reduced-fat cream
    cheese (room temperature)

4 eggs (room temperature)

16 oz. full-fat sour cream (room temperature)

⅔ cup heavy whipping cream
    (room temperature)

3½ tablespoons THM Super Sweet Blend
    (or more, to taste)

2 teaspoons vanilla extract

1 teaspoon cream of tartar

Mix the crust ingredients together and press into a greased 10" spring-form pan. Bake at 350° for 8 minutes. Set crust aside and turn oven down to 325°.

To make the cheesecake, beat the cream cheese until smooth. Add the eggs and beat well. Add the other ingredients and beat for 2 minutes. Pour the cheesecake batter over the crust, wrap a piece of wide tinfoil around the cheesecake pan, and place the pan in a larger pan filled with half an inch of water. Place the whole contraption in the oven and bake at 325° for 1 hour and 20 minutes or until set in the center. Turn the oven off, open the oven door, and let the cheesecake cool in the oven for 10 minutes. Remove the cheesecake from the oven, cool, then refrigerate overnight before slicing and serving.

Like all cheesecakes, this one gets better as it sits. 2-day-old cheesecake is the best, in both sweetness, and texture! This recipe has a softer set than my other cheesecakes; it's not as dense due to the addition of some heavy whipping cream.

note

• Check out one of my other cheesecake recipes for a nut-free crust if you like. I wanted to go a more graham cracker-esque route with this one.

• Because this cheesecake has a softer set and isn't as dense as my other recipes, it's also less structurally sound and more prone to cracking. You could use full-fat cream cheese for a richer, firmer result if desired.

• I like THM Super Sweet Blend, and I like things not so sweet. This amount of sweetener was great for me, but Ryan wanted it to be sweeter. If you have picky taste buds, use THM Gentle Sweet in place of the Super Sweet Blend – as much as needed to make the cheesecake as sweet as you like it. Or use 2 tablespoons THM Super Sweet Blend and 3 tablespoons THM Gentle Sweet for a more budget-friendly option, and add more Gentle Sweet if needed. Tasting and adjusting the sweetener is the best method to ensure happiness with the end result. That's what I do! Sweet toppings can help balance things if you didn't make the cheesecake sweet enough. Try the Blueberry Topping from page 493, the Caramel Sauce from page 413 of *Necessary Food*, or a sugar-free chocolate sauce. Or just decorate with sliced strawberries.

MAKING CHEESECAKE ▼

Cheesecake has a reputation for being difficult, but it's actually really easy to make! If you want a pretty cheesecake without cracks on top, use full-fat ingredients and bring all ingredients to room temperature before mixing them up. Baking the cheesecake in a water bath and letting it slowly cool in the oven after baking helps as well. Cheesecake has become one of my favorite desserts to make because a) it is so easy, b) it is usually enjoyed by most people, even if it's healthy, and c) leftovers.

black raspberry cheesecake

HEALTHY FATS I SERVES 14-16

CRUST

¼ cup + 2 tablespoons Briana's Baking Mix

3 tablespoons oat fiber

1 teaspoon THM Super Sweet Blend

¼ teaspoon xanthan gum

¼ teaspoon salt

5 tablespoons salted butter (softened)

2 tablespoons Greek yogurt

BLACK RASPBERRY SWIRL

1 (10 oz.) pkg. black raspberries (1½ cups)

⅓ cup water

⅛ teaspoon xanthan gum

Dash salt

2-3 teaspoons THM Super Sweet Blend
  (or more, to taste)

CHEESECAKE

4 (8 oz.) pkgs. reduced-fat cream
  cheese (room temperature)

16 oz. full-fat sour cream
  (room temperature)

4 eggs (room temperature)

3 tablespoons THM Gentle Sweet
  (or more, to taste)

2 tablespoons THM Super Sweet Blend

1 teaspoon cream of tartar

1 teaspoon vanilla extract

CRUST: Whisk the dry ingredients. Add the butter and Greek yogurt and mix with a hand mixer until crumbs form. Press into a greased 10" spring-form pan and bake at 350° for 6 minutes. Remove from the oven.

Turn the oven down to 325°.

SWIRL: Make the black raspberry swirl next so it can cool a bit. Blend the raspberries, water, xanthan gum, and salt together until smooth. (If using frozen, thawed raspberries, use the juice and all.) Transfer to a saucepan on the stovetop and bring to a boil, then simmer for 5 minutes. While it is heating, add THM Super Sweet Blend to taste. After the raspberry mixture has simmered for 5 minutes, press it through a sieve with the back of a spoon to remove the seeds. You should have about a cup of thick raspberry syrup left.

CHEESECAKE: Beat the cream cheese until smooth. (I do this in a stand mixer.) Add the rest of the ingredients and beat for 2 minutes. Pour the cheesecake mixture onto the pre-baked crust. Dollop the raspberry sauce onto the top of the cheesecake in separate blobs, then run a knife through the blobs to make a nice swirled pattern.

Place the cheesecake pan into a piece of wide aluminum foil and wrap the foil around the sides of the pan, then place the contraption into a larger pan filled with half an inch of water. Bake at 325° for one hour or until set. (At one hour, mine still jiggles a little in the middle. I like this because it makes for a creamier cheesecake, but feel free to leave it in until it's set all the way through.) Turn the oven off, leave the door open a crack, and leave the cheesecake in the hot oven for 10 minutes to cool slowly.

Remove the cheesecake from the oven, let it cool, then refrigerate to chill completely before cutting and serving (overnight is perfect).

Introducing my 22nd birthday cake: a beautiful Black Raspberry Cheesecake featuring a creamy basically-vanilla base with a festive fuchsia swirl. I sure hope you try it, because this is my favorite cheesecake recipe to date!

note

• Please taste and add more sweetener if you like! I prefer my cheesecakes not very sweet, so most people will probably want to add more sweetener. I recommend adding more of the less concentrated sweetener for the best taste. (I combine sweeteners to get the best taste for the best price.) Feel free to substitute with the sweeteners you have; just taste and adjust.

• I like to use reduced-fat cream cheese because a) the cheesecake is calorie-dense enough as it is, and b) the reduced-fat cream cheese makes a creamier, not-so-stiff cheesecake. I do use full-fat sour cream, though. This is the combination of ingredients that I've found gives the best texture.

• Cheesecake improves with age! I actually waited 2 days to cut into this one because of the way my schedule worked out.

peanut butter chocolate cheesecake

CRUST

1 cup Briana's Baking Mix

1 tablespoon THM Super Sweet Blend

¼ teaspoon xanthan gum

¼ teaspoon salt

4 tablespoons salted butter

1½ oz. unsweetened baker's chocolate

CHEESECAKE

3 (8 oz.) pkgs. reduced-fat cream
  cheese (room temperature)

16 oz. full-fat sour cream
  (room temperature)

1½ cups natural peanut butter
  (well-stirred and creamy)

5 egg yolks (room temperature)

2 tablespoons THM Gentle Sweet
  (or more, to taste)

2 tablespoons THM Super Sweet Blend

1 teaspoon vanilla extract

5 egg whites (room temperature)

1 teaspoon cream of tartar

GANACHE

75 grams 85% dark chocolate (3 sections
  from the Moser Roth brand
  chocolate found at Aldi)

2-3 teaspoons THM Gentle Sweet
  (or more, to taste)

¼ cup heavy whipping cream

¼ cup unsweetened almond milk

CRUST: Whisk the dry ingredients. Melt the butter and chocolate together, stirring every 20-30 seconds so the chocolate doesn't burn. (I do this in the microwave, but a double boiler works too.) Add the chocolate mixture to the dry ingredients and mix well. Press into a greased 10" spring-form pan and bake at 350° for 5 minutes. Turn the oven down to 325°.

CHEESECAKE: Beat the first section of ingredients together until smooth. Beat the egg whites and cream of tartar together until stiff peaks form. Gently fold the egg whites into the cheesecake mixture until the two are just mixed together. Pour the cheesecake mixture onto the crust and smooth the top. Place the spring-form pan in a large piece of wide foil to protect the bottom from leaking, then put this contraption into a larger pan filled with half an inch of water. Bake at 325° for one hour or until set, then turn the oven off, open the oven door, and leave the cheesecake in the oven for another ten minutes. Remove the cheesecake from the oven, let it cool completely, then refrigerate overnight.

GANACHE: The next day, make the ganache. Melt the chocolate in the microwave or double boiler, stirring often. Add the Gentle Sweet, then whisk in the cream and almond milk 2 tablespoons at a time. Whisk until emulsified and smooth. Spread or pipe the ganache onto the cheesecake, then refrigerate to firm up the ganache. Serve.

Since I don't like to have entire cheesecakes sitting in my fridge due to the temptation to overindulge in some pretty high-calorie dessert, I tested this one twice at church functions. My dear church friends get experimented upon quite often. In this particular case, I labeled the first cheesecake as "Sugar-Free Peanut Butter Chocolate Cheesecake." The second one bore a sign reading, "New and (Hopefully) Improved Peanut Butter Chocolate Cheesecake." The general consensus was one of enjoyment, although one or two people remarked that they would've liked more sweetener in the chocolate ganache topping. So if you like stuff pretty sweet, add some more sweetener to your liking. You know me…dark chocolate fan right here.

I took the second version of this cheesecake to the evening fellowship meal at church that fateful day in April 2017 when Ryan first showed up. He struck up a conversation with me before we went through the food line, so we ended up sitting together and I remember being very nervous when I saw that he had taken some of my experimental cheesecake. (This was before I even knew why he was there.) I guess he liked it.

note

I usually use Smucker's brand natural peanut butter from Walmart. Make sure it's stirred well and isn't really thick or the cheesecake will be dry.

mocha cheesecake

HEALTHY FATS | SERVES 14-16

CRUST

1 cup Briana's Baking Mix

1 tablespoon THM Super Sweet Blend

¼ teaspoon xanthan gum

¼ teaspoon salt

4 tablespoons salted butter

1½ oz. unsweetened baker's chocolate

CHEESECAKE

3 (8 oz.) pkgs. reduced-fat cream
cheese (room temperature)

16 oz. full-fat sour cream
(room temperature)

6 egg yolks (room temperature)

2 tablespoons THM Super Sweet Blend

1 tablespoon THM Gentle Sweet
(or more, to taste)

1 teaspoon vanilla extract

¼ teaspoon salt

2 tablespoons cocoa powder

2 tablespoons espresso instant coffee powder

6 egg whites (room temperature)

1 teaspoon cream of tartar

CRUST: Whisk the dry ingredients. Melt the butter and baker's chocolate together in the microwave or in a double boiler, stirring often to prevent burning. Add the melted mixture to the dry ingredients and mix with a hand mixer. Press into a greased 10" spring-form pan and bake at 350° for 5 minutes. Remove the crust from the oven and turn the oven down to 325°.

CHEESECAKE: Beat the first section of ingredients together until smooth. Divide the batter into two bowls. To one bowl, add the cocoa powder and mix. Mix the espresso powder into the other bowl. Beat the egg whites with the cream of tartar until stiff peaks form. Add half the egg whites to each bowl and gently fold them in by hand with a spatula. (It's OK if there are still a few white streaks.) Pour the chocolate batter over the cheesecake crust. Gently spoon the coffee batter over the chocolate batter and use an offset spreader to smooth it out. Put the cheesecake pan in a piece of wide foil and wrap the foil up around the sides of the pan. Place the pan inside another larger pan that can hold water and add half an inch of water. Put the whole contraption in the oven and bake for 1 hour at 325°. The cheesecake should be just set in the middle. Open the oven door, turn the oven off, and let the cheesecake cool in the oven for 10 minutes. Remove the cheesecake from the oven, let it cool to room temperature, then cover and refrigerate overnight before cutting and serving.

note

I recommend a good quality espresso instant coffee powder for this recipe. (See page 9 for my recommendation.) I'm not a huge coffee lover, so if you want to increase the amount of coffee or add some coffee extract, be my guest! As always, feel free to increase the sweetener as well; THM Gentle Sweet would be a good one to increase in this recipe.

amazing turtle cheesecake

CRUST

¼ cup + 2 tablespoons Briana's Baking Mix

3 tablespoons oat fiber

1 teaspoon THM Super Sweet Blend

¼ teaspoon xanthan gum

¼ teaspoon salt

5 tablespoons salted butter (softened)

2 tablespoons Greek yogurt

CHEESECAKE

2½ (8 oz.) pkgs. reduced-fat cream
    cheese (room temperature)

3 tablespoons oat fiber

2 tablespoons THM Super Sweet Blend

1 tablespoon THM Gentle Sweet

1 teaspoon vanilla extract

¼ teaspoon salt

16 oz. full-fat sour cream
    (room temperature)

6 eggs (room temperature)

½ cup sugar-free chocolate chips

CARAMEL TOPPING

1 cup heavy whipping cream

8 tablespoons salted butter

2½ teaspoons THM Super Sweet Blend

2 teaspoons molasses

½ teaspoon vanilla extract

⅜ teaspoon xanthan gum

ADDITIONAL TOPPINGS

Chopped pecans

Sugar-free chocolate chips

CRUST: Whisk the dry ingredients, then add the wet ingredients and mix well. Press into a greased 10" spring-form pan and bake at 350° for 6 minutes. Turn the oven down to 325° to prepare for baking the cheesecake.

CHEESECAKE: Beat the first six ingredients (cream cheese through salt) together until smooth. Add the sour cream and beat again. Add the eggs and beat well until everything is thoroughly incorporated. Fold in the chocolate chips. Pour the cheesecake batter over the hot crust. Place a large piece of foil around the bottom of the spring-form pan and set the pan in a larger pan with a lip. (I use a pizza pan with sides.) Fill the larger pan with half an inch of water. Put the whole contraption in the oven and bake at 325° for 1 hour and 5 minutes or until the cheesecake is set. Turn the oven off, crack the door open, and let the cheesecake cool in the oven for 10 minutes. Remove the cheesecake from the oven.

CARAMEL: Make the caramel while the cheesecake is cooling in the oven so both will still be warm when you're ready to use the caramel. Heat the cream and butter in a nonstick pan; whisk in the rest of the ingredients while the butter melts. (Add the xanthan gum while whisking so it doesn't clump.) Bring the mixture to a slow boil, then cover and cook for 7 minutes or until thickened, adjusting the heat downwards as far as possible while still retaining a slow boil. Doing it this way produces a lot of caramel sauce without as much intense caramel flavor. If you'd like more flavor and less sauce, leave the caramel uncovered and cook longer if necessary until the caramel reaches your desired caramelization. Whisk occasionally to keep the caramel from burning, especially if you decide to cook it longer.

When the cheesecake and caramel are both done, top the cheesecake with your desired amount of chopped pecans and sugar-free chocolate chips. Pour the caramel sauce over the cheesecake. (The warm caramel will melt the chocolate chips a little, which I like.)

Garnish with additional chopped pecans and chocolate chips. Refrigerate the cheesecake overnight to chill and set completely before removing from the pan, cutting, and serving.

quick pumpkin cheesecakes

2 tablespoons almond flour (optional)

4 oz. cream cheese (softened)

5 tablespoons canned pumpkin

2 tablespoons Greek yogurt or sour cream

1 egg

2 teaspoons THM Super Sweet Blend
(or more, to taste)

¼ teaspoon pumpkin pie spice (rounded)

SUGGESTED TOPPINGS ▼

a squirt of Reddi-wip, chopped pecans

Spread a tablespoon of almond flour in the bottom of each of two small ramekins. (Omit this if you don't care about having a crust.)

Beat the cheesecake ingredients together until smooth and pour half into each ramekin.

Bake the cheesecakes at 350° for 35 minutes or until set.

The cheesecakes will be a custardy texture if you eat them warm (as is any cheesecake). I prefer to refrigerate them and enjoy them cold.

vanilla custard chia "tapioca"

2 cups unsweetened almond milk
1 cup half and half
3 eggs
½ teaspoon molasses
¼ teaspoon salt (rounded)

¼ cup + 2 tablespoons chia seeds

2 tablespoons THM Super Sweet Blend
1 tablespoon salted butter
1 teaspoon vanilla extract

Whisk the first section of ingredients very well in a nonstick saucepan. Whisk in the chia seeds and turn the heat to medium. Cook until the mixture just starts to bubble, whisking often, especially towards the end. Pull the pan off the heat and whisk in the Super Sweet Blend, butter, and vanilla. Taste and add more sweetener if desired. Refrigerate overnight to thicken, then enjoy!

This "tapioca" is good warm or cold. If I heat it up for breakfast, stirring a little bit of peanut butter into it to melt is super yummy. (Add some extra protein, such as collagen in your coffee or tea, to make it a meal.)

Did any of y'all grow up eating a rich and creamy vanilla tapioca pudding? I remember it from church potlucks...how we children would fill up red plastic drinking cups with the stuff and enjoy it to the very last bite. The base of it was almost custardy, which is why I included eggs in this recipe, like I was making a vanilla pudding. Of course if you're following a low-glycemic eating plan, tapioca is out because of its high glycemic index (and therefore its impact on blood sugar). By happy accident, chia seeds do a great job of mimicking the texture of tapioca! The chia seeds do add a slight flavor of their own, but nothing too distracting. The pudding is good warm, but I think it's more traditional when refrigerated and served cold. It will thicken up in the refrigerator.

single-serve vanilla chia "tapioca"

1 cup unsweetened almond milk

½ cup light canned coconut milk

½ cup water

¼ cup chia seeds

½ teaspoon vanilla extract

⅛ teaspoon THM Pure Stevia Extract Powder

1/16 teaspoon salt

Whisk the ingredients together in a small saucepan and bring to a boil. Refrigerate overnight to thicken, then enjoy! You can top the "tapioca" with some berries or use it as a blank canvas for your favorite extracts and/or spices.

The chia seeds in this "tapioca" pudding have 12 grams of protein, so this can be a meal or snack on its own. It makes a great dessert too!

note

Any coconut flavor disappears when the pudding is refrigerated overnight - to my taste buds, at least, and I'm not really a coconut fan! If you want a non-coconut option, you could try substituting half and half in its place.

single-serve strawberry chia "tapioca"

HEALTHY FATS | SERVES I

1 cup unsweetened almond milk

½ cup strawberries

½ cup water

2 tablespoons collagen

½ teaspoon vanilla extract

3 doonks THM Pure Stevia Extract Powder

³⁄₃₂ teaspoon salt

3 tablespoons chia seeds

Blend everything but the chia seeds until smooth. (I do this in a saucepan with an immersion blender, but a regular blender would work fine.) Pour the mixture into a saucepan, whisk in the chia seeds, and bring to a boil. Once the mixture comes to a boil, pull it off the heat. Refrigerate overnight to thicken. Enjoy!

note

• This yields a tapioca-like pudding of a medium consistency. For a thicker pudding, use 4 tablespoons chia seeds.

• I don't recommend substituting whey protein powder for the collagen.

• If you don't have a dairy intolerance and want to increase the creaminess in this, add 2 tablespoons cottage cheese and/or 2 tablespoons half and half. Add before blending.

chai spice rice pudding

2 cups unsweetened almond milk

2 cups water

1 cup uncooked brown rice (not instant)

½ cup light canned coconut milk

½ teaspoon each cinnamon,
   ground cardamom, salt

½ teaspoon molasses

4 drops orange essential oil

1½ tablespoons THM Super Sweet Blend
   (or more, to taste)

1 teaspoon vanilla extract

½ teaspoon almond extract

Stir the almond milk, water, brown rice, and coconut milk together and refrigerate (covered) overnight.

The next day, add the spices, salt, and orange oil to the rice mixture and bring to a boil in a nonstick saucepan. Cook (covered) for 50 minutes or until the rice is soft, stirring occasionally. Whisk in the Super Sweet Blend and extracts, then cover and simmer for 5 minutes before serving. Add a little extra almond milk if the rice pudding is too thick.

Feel free to add some cranberries or a small amount of fruit! I like to enjoy the rice pudding warm as a Healthy Carbs dessert with a smidgen of butter, but it's good cold, too. If you add some protein on the side, it makes a great breakfast. The rice pudding reheats well.

Rice pudding made with brown rice instead of white rice doesn't get as soft, but it's still completely enjoyable. I do like to eat leftovers cold out of the fridge, but the rice is softer if you reheat it a bit in the microwave. Do NOT use instant brown rice in this recipe! I have not had good luck with instant brown rice; it stays crunchy no matter how I cook it!

note

• The light coconut milk adds less than 2 grams of fat per serving.

• If you're not comfortable ingesting essential oils or don't have orange oil, add a dash of orange extract at the end with the vanilla extract.

• I've found that soaking the rice overnight helps the rice get softer, but it's not required. If you don't want to soak it, just omit that step and expect the rice to take a little longer to cook.

chocolate rice pudding

3 cups cooked brown rice (unseasoned)
¾ cup unsweetened almond milk
⅔ cup light canned coconut milk
2 tablespoons THM Super Sweet Blend
   (or more, to taste)
¾ teaspoon salt

2 tablespoons cocoa powder
1 teaspoon vanilla extract

Cook the brown rice, almond milk, coconut milk, Super Sweet Blend, and salt together in a 10" saucepan on the stovetop. (The large surface area helps it thicken faster.) Bring the rice pudding to a boil, reduce the heat, and simmer uncovered for 15 minutes, stirring occasionally. Remove the pan from the heat and whisk in the cocoa powder and vanilla. Serve.

Sometimes I like to serve the rice pudding with a drizzle of almond milk and a small amount of sliced banana. The texture and flavor of the rice pudding is best fresh. (The rice gets harder after leftovers are refrigerated.) However, I definitely don't mind having leftovers cold for breakfast with some protein on the side.

Ryan and I both enjoyed this comforting, creamy rice pudding. Brown rice will never get as soft as white rice, but it's still very enjoyable!

note

• If the rice pudding is too thick, add a splash of almond milk. If it's too thin, cook longer to reduce.
• I don't recommend cooking the pudding after adding the cocoa powder; this brings out bitter notes in the cocoa and the texture of the pudding isn't as nice and creamy.
• The light coconut milk adds 2.25 grams of fat per serving.
• I recommend using freshly cooked rice that is still warm to make this recipe. I don't think cold leftover rice would release as much starch into the liquid to thicken the rice pudding, and the rice itself would not be as soft (but you're welcome to try).
• Don't use instant brown rice; it doesn't soften as well as regular brown rice.

hot chocolate custard

2 eggs

1 cup unsweetened almond milk

1 tablespoon THM Super Sweet Blend
(or more, to taste)

1 tablespoon cocoa powder

2 teaspoons refined coconut oil

½ teaspoon vanilla extract

⅛ teaspoon salt

¼ teaspoon glucomannan

TOPPINGS

1 teaspoon salted butter

THM Super Sweet Blend

Whisk the eggs in a small saucepan. Add the rest of the ingredients and whisk again. (Don't worry - the coconut oil will melt eventually.) Add the glucomannan while whisking so it doesn't clump. Heat the custard on medium-high heat until it's just starting to bubble, whisking often. When the custard starts to bubble, turn the burner off, pull the custard off the stove, and whisk it continuously. Once the burner has cooled off a bit, put the pan back on the burner and keep whisking until the custard thickens. Pull the custard off the burner a little bit before you think it's done so the custard doesn't get too hot and curdle. This is my lazy woman's way of avoiding tempering eggs to make a nice smooth custard and it usually works. Just keep whisking and when in doubt, use less heat. Top the custard with a teaspoon of butter and additional Super Sweet Blend. Enjoy!

This custard is a melt-in-your mouth milk chocolate version of the Hot Custard on page 375 of *Necessary Food*, but this version has twice the volume with close to the same amount of calories!

note

• I used an electric burner stove when creating this recipe. On a gas stove, use a lower heat all the way around, and once the custard starts to bubble, turn the burner down as far as it will go (but don't turn it off).

• For a vanilla version, use the following ingredients: 2 eggs, 1 cup unsweetened almond milk, 1 tablespoon salted butter, 2 teaspoons THM Super Sweet Blend (or more, to taste), ½ teaspoon vanilla extract, ⅛ teaspoon salt, and ⅛ teaspoon glucomannan. Follow the same directions.

hot pumpkin custard

2 eggs

⅔ cup unsweetened almond milk

⅓ cup canned pumpkin

2 teaspoons refined coconut oil

¼ teaspoon pumpkin pie spice (rounded)

⅛ teaspoon THM Pure Stevia Extract Powder

⅛ teaspoon salt

Hearty dash vanilla extract

¼ teaspoon glucomannan

TOPPINGS

1 teaspoon salted butter

THM Super Sweet Blend

Cinnamon

Whisk the eggs in a small saucepan. Add the rest of the ingredients and whisk again. (Don't worry - the coconut oil will melt eventually.) Add the glucomannan while whisking so it doesn't clump. Heat the custard on medium-high heat until it's just starting to bubble, whisking often. When the custard starts to bubble, turn the burner off, pull the custard off the stove, and whisk it continuously. Once the burner has cooled off a bit, put the pan back on the burner and keep whisking until the custard thickens. Pull the custard off the burner a little bit before you think it's done so the custard doesn't get too hot and curdle. This is my lazy woman's way of avoiding tempering eggs to make a nice smooth custard and it usually works. Just keep whisking and when in doubt, use less heat.

Top the custard with a teaspoon of butter and a sprinkling of cinnamon and Super Sweet Blend. Enjoy! It's great warm, but if you want to think ahead and chill the custard in the refrigerator before eating, it tastes like the inside of a pumpkin pie!

note

I used an electric burner stove when creating this recipe. On a gas stove, use a lower heat all the way around, and once the custard starts to bubble, turn the burner down as far as it will go (but don't turn it off).

fried apple pie

HEALTHY CARBS & HEALTHY FATS | SERVES 1

1 cup chopped apple of choice
¾ teaspoon THM Super Sweet Blend
   (or more, to taste)
½ teaspoon cinnamon
Dash each ground cloves, salt

½ Joseph's Reduced Carb/Flax,
   Oat Bran & Whole Wheat
   Lavash Bread
Reduced-fat cream cheese
Refined coconut oil (for frying)
Additional cinnamon and
   THM Super Sweet Blend

Stir the first section of ingredients together and microwave for 2 minutes to soften the apples.

Spread the apple mixture on one side of the lavash piece. Spread some reduced-fat cream cheese on the other side and fold the lavash over onto itself. Fry in coconut oil until crispy and golden brown on each side, then sprinkle with some additional cinnamon and Super Sweet Blend and enjoy!

A word to the wise: don't omit the cloves! The cloves are what really trigger the "McDonald's apple pie" taste button in my brain. If anyone's wondering, I used Granny Smith apples in this recipe. Mmm…I love their tartness, and they hold up great for baking.

note

For a Healthy Carbs version, you could omit the cream cheese and use just 1 teaspoon coconut oil for frying. Obviously this version isn't as decadent, but it might still fill your apple pie craving.

Ye are my witnesses, saith the Lord, and my servant whom I have chosen: that ye may know and believe me, and understand that I am he: before me there was no God formed, neither shall there be after me. I, even I, am the Lord; and beside me there is no saviour. I have declared, and have saved, and I have shewed, when there was no strange god among you: therefore ye are my witnesses, saith the Lord, that I am God. ISAIAH 43:10-12

pb&j fried taco

HEALTHY FATS | SERVES I

1 low-carb tortilla

1-2 tablespoons natural peanut butter

½ cup sliced strawberries
   (fresh are best, but frozen work too)

THM Super Sweet Blend

Refined coconut oil (for frying)

Spread the peanut butter onto the low-carb tortilla. You can spread it in the center like I did, place the strawberries on top, and fold up the edges nice and purty...or you can just spread it on one half of the tortilla, put the strawberries on top, and fold it over like a typical quesadilla. Tastes the same. Sprinkle a little Super Sweet Blend onto the strawberries before folding the tortilla. Fry in coconut oil on both sides until golden brown, then enjoy!

note

• You could use a peanut butter made from defatted peanut flour to cut back on calories if you like. Just mix up some peanut flour, water, salt, and sweetener to your desired taste and texture.

• If you want a little more "goop" inside your fried taco, you could add a little cream cheese.

WHAT'S A FRIED TACO? ▼

Fried tacos are my "comfort food" go-to! Frying a low-carb tortilla in coconut oil turns it into something crispy and delicious! While I really do enjoy my fried tacos, I try not to eat them too often because processed foods like low-carb tortillas should only be used in moderation and can cause weight loss stalls if used too often. Look for reduced-carb wraps with 6 grams net carbs or less. I've used many different brands, most of them found at my local discount grocery store. Enjoy these fried tacos as dessert after a meal, or add protein and eat them for breakfast or a snack! There are some lunch options in the Main Dishes section as well.

creamy pumpkin chocolate fried taco

HEALTHY FATS I SERVES I

1 low-carb tortilla

2 tablespoons reduced-fat cream cheese

2 tablespoons canned pumpkin

1 tablespoon sugar-free chocolate chips
  (or chopped 85% dark chocolate)

½ - 1 teaspoon THM Super Sweet Blend

⅛ teaspoon pumpkin pie spice

Dash salt

Refined coconut oil (for frying)

Spread the cream cheese and pumpkin in the center of the low-carb tortilla. Top with the chocolate chips, Super Sweet Blend, pumpkin pie spice, and a dash of salt. Mash the ingredients together a bit with a spoon to combine the flavors so you don't get one giant bite of only cream cheese or only pumpkin. Fold the sides of the tortilla over like you're wrapping a present and secure the flaps with 2 toothpicks. Fry the package in coconut oil on both sides until brown and crispy, then remove the toothpicks and enjoy!

note

I used ½ teaspoon THM Super Sweet Blend because I don't like my stuff to be killer sweet, but feel free to use more to your own personal tastes, especially if you use dark chocolate instead of sugar-free chocolate chips.

"How can a man have too much religion?" cried Alleyne earnestly. "It is the one thing that availeth. A man is but a beast as he lives from day to day, eating and drinking, breathing and sleeping. It is only when he raises himself, and concerns himself with the immortal spirit within him, that he becomes in very truth a man. Bethink ye how sad a thing it would be that the blood of the Redeemer should be spilled to no purpose."

SIR ARTHUR CONAN COYLE - *THE WHITE COMPANY*

peanut butter banana fried taco

PEANUT BUTTER

¼ cup defatted peanut flour

3 tablespoons water

½ teaspoon THM Super Sweet Blend
   (or more, to taste)

¼ teaspoon cinnamon

⅛ teaspoon salt (scant)

1 low-carb tortilla

½ lg. banana (sliced)

THM Super Sweet Blend and
   cinnamon (for dusting)

Whisk the peanut butter ingredients together. Arrange the banana slices on one half of the tortilla and spread the peanut butter on the other half, then fold the tortilla over onto itself. For a true Healthy Carbs recipe, spray a nonstick pan lightly with cooking spray and fry the taco on both sides until golden brown, then dust with Super Sweet Blend and cinnamon and enjoy.

The peanut flour contains 4 grams of fat, so a teaspoon of coconut oil for frying technically takes this into Healthy Carbs & Healthy Fats, combining fats and carbs. (Although it could be argued that the defatted peanut flour is your lean protein source and thus you don't need to count the fat in it.) Occasionally I treat myself and use a teaspoon of coconut oil to fry the taco for a crispier, less chewy result.

The peanut flour contains 16 grams of protein, so you don't need to add any more protein to complete your meal. I personally need more food than this to hold me over for a few hours if I'm eating this taco for breakfast, so I like to eat it with a side of homemade yogurt for even more protein and a few more carbs to give me a true Healthy Carbs meal. As an afternoon snack, this taco on its own would be fine for me.

note

You can use the peanut butter recipe as a Low Carb/Low Fat condiment! Feel free to omit the cinnamon and add some vanilla extract.

snacks + appetizers

greek yogurt variations

HEALTHY FATS OR LOW CARB/LOW FAT | SERVES 4

VANILLA (LC/LF)

1 (500 gram) container low-fat Greek yogurt
(about 2 cups)

⅓ cup half and half or unsweetened
almond milk

½ teaspoon vanilla extract

⅛ teaspoon THM Pure Stevia Extract Powder
(or more, to taste)

PEANUT BUTTER (HF)

1 (500 gram) container Greek yogurt
(about 2 cups)

⅓ cup half and half or unsweetened
almond milk

3 tablespoons natural peanut butter

⅛ teaspoon THM Pure Stevia Extract Powder
(or more, to taste)

NOTE: If a stronger peanut butter flavor is desired, add a tablespoon or two of defatted peanut flour. If you use low-fat yogurt and defatted peanut flour in place of the peanut butter, this would be LC/LF. You may need to add more peanut flour than the peanut butter called for, plus some extra salt and sweetener to round out the flavors.

KEY LIME PIE (LC/LF)

1 (500 gram) container low-fat Greek yogurt
(about 2 cups)

⅓ cup half and half or unsweetened
almond milk

1 tablespoon lime juice

½ teaspoon vanilla extract

5-6 doonks THM Pure Stevia Extract Powder
(or more, to taste)

1 drop each green and yellow food coloring

ORANGE (LC/LF)

1 (500 gram) container low-fat Greek yogurt
(about 2 cups)

⅓ cup half and half or unsweetened
almond milk

½ teaspoon vanilla extract

½ teaspoon orange extract

⅛ teaspoon THM Pure Stevia Extract Powder
(or more, to taste)

1 drop each red and yellow food coloring

Whisk the ingredients together for the flavor you want to make. Adjust the half and half/almond milk according to your desired thickness, and adjust the sweetness to your liking as well. Some THM Gentle Sweet would be a good option for adding a kick of extra sweetness if needed. The flavor of the yogurt is best after overnight refrigeration.

Because of the additions to the yogurt, it probably won't keep quite as long as plain Greek yogurt. It will keep for at least a week in the fridge; if the added liquid separates out a bit, just give the yogurt a stir.

note

Using half and half to thin down the yogurt adds 2.3 grams of fat per serving.

single-serve greek yogurt variations

HEALTHY FATS, HEALTHY CARBS, OR LOW CARB/LOW FAT | SERVES 1

FOUNDATION (LC/LF)

½ cup low-fat Greek yogurt (or a single-serve container of low-fat Greek yogurt)

1-2 tablespoons half and half or unsweetened almond milk (to desired consistency)

1 doonk THM Pure Stevia Extract Powder (or more, if desired)

VANILLA (LC/LF)

Dash vanilla extract

PEANUT BUTTER (HF)

1 tablespoon natural peanut butter

Squirt of Reddi-wip and sugar-free chocolate chips for topping (optional)

NOTE: Use defatted peanut flour instead of peanut butter and keep the chocolate chips to a garnish amount to make this LC/LF.

TOASTED COCONUT (LC/LF)

Dash each coconut extract, vanilla extract

Dash liquid smoke (optional)

Toasted coconut flakes for topping (optional, HF)

KEY LIME PIE (HF)

1 additional doonk THM Pure Stevia Extract Powder

Hearty dash lime juice

Dash vanilla extract

1 drop green food coloring

Squirt of Reddi-wip and a sprinkling of low-carb granola or toasted coconut flakes (to mimic pie crust) for topping (optional)

NOTE: Omit the granola or coconut flakes for LC/LF.

CHUNKY MONKEY (HF)

1 tablespoon natural peanut butter

Dash banana extract

Sprinkling of sugar-free chocolate chips

NOTE: Use defatted peanut flour instead of peanut butter and keep the chocolate chips to a garnish amount to make this LC/LF.

BANANA CREAM (HC)

Dash each banana extract, vanilla extract

½ lg. banana (sliced)

NOTE: Omit the sliced banana for LC/LF.

ORANGE CREAM (HC)

Dash orange extract

Chunks of orange/tangerine/clementine

NOTE: Omit the orange chunks for LC/LF.

Start with the foundation ingredients, then add the mix-ins from your desired variation. Feel free to add more sweetener to taste. Whisk until smooth, then top with any additional toppings. Enjoy!

L-R:
TOASTED COCONUT
PEANUT BUTTER

L-R:
KEY LIME PIE
CHUNKY MONKEY

Here are seven easy ways to turn your thick and tangy Greek yogurt into deliciously smooth, flavored yogurt using very few ingredients! Greek yogurt has a lot less carbs than regular yogurt does – and a whole lot of protein for the volume! However, it's really thick, and sometimes it's downright sour! My favorite way to make Greek yogurt more palatable (i.e. more like regular yogurt) is to add a little liquid – half and half or almond milk – and a little sweetener.

I usually use a doonk or two of THM Pure Stevia Extract Powder, but the liquid squirt stevia bottles like you can find at Walmart are an even easier option!

note

If you're making a Healthy Fats variation, the Greek yogurt can be full fat.

ORANGE CREAM

BANANA CREAM

VANILLA

regular yogurt variations

HEALTHY CARBS I YIELDS 2 QUARTS

VANILLA YOGURT

8 cups plain low-fat yogurt

¼ cup + 2 tablespoons water (nearly boiling)
2 tablespoons THM Super Sweet Blend
   (or more, to taste)
1 tablespoon THM Just Gelatin or
   2½ teaspoons Knox gelatin

2 teaspoons vanilla extract
⅛ teaspoon salt
⅛ teaspoon THM Pure Stevia Extract Powder

Whisk the Super Sweet Blend and gelatin into the very hot water, adding the gelatin while whisking. If it doesn't dissolve immediately, let it sit for a few minutes and whisk again. Whisk the gelatin mixture into the yogurt, adding it while whisking. Whisk in the vanilla, salt, and stevia. If making another flavor, add the cinnamon or lemon juice now as well. Taste and add more sweetener if desired. Refrigerate overnight to set up. Do not whisk or stir the yogurt after the gelatin has set; it will get clumpy. The "gelatinized" yogurt gets a little watery and separates a little after a few days, but it tastes fine.

note

Don't forget to save enough plain yogurt to make your next batch!

CINNAMON YOGURT   Reduce to 1 teaspoon vanilla extract. Add ¾ teaspoon cinnamon.

LEMON YOGURT Reduce to 1 teaspoon vanilla extract. Add 2½ tablespoons lemon juice.

Homemade yogurt is a really easy thing to put in my husband's lunch, and I often leave the yogurt as regular yogurt instead of straining it into Greek yogurt so it lasts longer. We go through it quickly! Homemade yogurt tends to be runnier than storebought yogurt, so I devised this method of thickening it and giving it more body. It takes on a gello salad or panna cotta texture which is really neat! I eat it on its own or pair with fruit, granola, baked oatmeal, or regular oatmeal.

yogurt parfaits

....

HEALTHY FATS, HEALTHY CARBS, OR LOW CARB/LOW FAT

....

Need something special to serve to company? Want a quick and easy snack or dessert? Yogurt parfaits fit the bill perfectly! They're customizable so you can feed them to anyone or use them in any fuel type with a few tweaks. Here are the tools you need to make an awesome parfait:

LOW CARB/LOW FAT

(can be used with any fuel type)

Vanilla, Key Lime Pie, or Orange
   Greek Yogurt (page 443)

Blueberry Topping (page 493)

Fresh berries – strawberries, blueberries,
   raspberries, blackberries

HEALTHY FATS

Peanut Butter Greek Yogurt (page 443)

Peanut Butter Granola (page 47)

HEALTHY CARBS

Vanilla, Cinnamon, or Lemon Yogurt (page 446)

Easy Granola (*Necessary Food*, page 34)

Chopped fresh fruit – bananas, kiwifruit,
   mangoes, oranges, pineapple

note

You could add a few ounces of softened cream cheese to the Vanilla Greek Yogurt from page 443 for use in a decadent Healthy Fats yogurt parfait!

VANILLA GREEK YOGURT PG 443
PEANUT BUTTER GRANOLA PG 47
BLUEBERRY TOPPING PG 493

pb&j power bowl

1 cup plain low-fat yogurt

2 tablespoons collagen

1-2 teaspoons baobab powder (to taste)

3 doonks THM Pure Stevia Extract Powder

½ cup frozen red raspberries

2 tablespoons defatted peanut flour

Whisk the collagen, baobab powder, and stevia into the yogurt. Add the raspberries and peanut flour and stir just enough to swirl. Enjoy!

The frozen raspberries super chill the yogurt and give this bowl a neat pop! The baobab powder offers a nutritional boost. (You can omit it if you don't have it, but you may need to decrease the sweetener.)

note

• I used homemade yogurt – regular, not Greek – because it's what I had on hand and I like that it's thinner than Greek yogurt. For a Low Carb/Low Fat version of this snack, use ¾ cup low-fat Greek yogurt + a splash of almond milk in place of the regular yogurt.

• I don't recommend using whey protein powder in place of the collagen in this recipe.

carrot cake greek yogurt snack

¾ cup low-fat Greek yogurt

¼ cup finely-grated carrot

2 tablespoons half and half

¼ teaspoon cinnamon

2 doonks THM Pure Stevia Extract Powder

Dash vanilla extract

Whisk the ingredients together and garnish with the toppings of your choice.

TOPPINGS ▼

a sprinkling of chopped pecans, a few chopped unsweetened dried cranberries, ¼ teaspoon molasses, THM Super Sweet Blend

chewy peanut butter protein bites

HEALTHY FATS | YIELDS 36 SQUARES

2 cups defatted peanut flour
¾ cup Briana's Baking Mix
¼ cup whey protein powder
1 teaspoon Knox gelatin
1 teaspoon THM Super Sweet Blend
¾ teaspoon xanthan gum
½ teaspoon salt
¼ teaspoon THM Pure Stevia Extract Powder

1½ cups warm water
⅔ cup refined coconut oil (melted)
1 tablespoon vegetable glycerin
1 teaspoon vanilla extract
Dash maple extract

Whisk the dry ingredients. Whisk the wet ingredients separately, then add them to the dry ingredients and mix with a hand mixer. A thick dough will form. Press this into a foil-lined 8"x8" pan with a spatula and refrigerate to firm up. When the fudge has firmed up a bit, use a sharp knife to slice it into 36 squares, then cover and refrigerate overnight to finish setting up. Enjoy! Store in refrigerator.

Each of these squares has over 5 grams of protein! Eat 3-4 for a great snack. The main fat source is good ol' coconut oil, which is great for your metabolism. I like to store these protein bites in the fridge because they get too firm to eat if kept in the freezer. However, if you want to be able to pack up a few of these bites in a baggie for when you're out and about running errands, freezing them first would be a good idea so they take longer to thaw.

note

• If using beef gelatin, add ¼ teaspoon.
• I added the vegetable glycerin for a softer, slightly sticky texture. (This is an ingredient I use in ice cream to achieve a smooth, creamy texture, and it has very little impact on blood sugar.) If you don't have it on hand, just omit it.
• For a dairy-free option, use collagen to make my baking mix and replace the whey protein powder in this recipe with collagen or another non-dairy protein powder.

chocolate chip cookie dough protein butter

¾ cup vanilla whey protein powder

½ cup oat fiber

1 tablespoon THM Super Sweet Blend
(or more, to taste)

½ teaspoon baking powder

¼ teaspoon salt

Handful of sugar-free chocolate chips or
chopped 85% dark chocolate

½ cup natural peanut butter
(well-stirred and creamy)

2 tablespoons refined coconut oil

1 teaspoon plain gelatin

1 teaspoon vanilla extract

½ cup hot tap water

Whisk the first section of ingredients. Melt the peanut butter and coconut oil together, then whisk in the gelatin and vanilla. Add the water and whisk again. Add the wet ingredients to the dry ingredients and stir with a spatula until well-mixed. (If the dough is crumbly and not a smooth cookie dough texture, add a little extra water.) Chill the cookie dough in a jar in the fridge for several hours before digging in. This can be kept in the fridge for a few days. Eat it with a spoon or spread it on a Light Rye Wasa cracker to balance the sweetness.

There are about 12 grams of protein per serving in this protein butter!

note

Not a fan of peanuts? Try cashew butter or almond butter for a milder-flavored cookie dough!

cinnamon "sugar" cottage cheese toast

HEALTHY CARBS | SERVES 1

2 slices sprouted bread
½ cup low-fat cottage cheese
THM Super Sweet Blend
Cinnamon

Toast the bread. Top each slice with half of the cottage cheese and sprinkle Super Sweet Blend and cinnamon on top. Enjoy!

This easy toast makes a great snack or breakfast – protein already included!

note

I like the Aldi SimplyNature Knock Your Sprouts Off Sprouted 7 Grain Bread, but any sprouted or fermented bread made with whole grains will work.

goldmine salsa

HEALTHY CARBS | YIELDS 2 QUARTS

6 lg. Roma tomatoes (chopped)

1 lg. green bell pepper (chopped)

1 lg. onion (chopped)

½ cup fresh cilantro (chopped)

1 jalapeño pepper (seeds removed, chopped)

4 med. garlic cloves (minced)

1 cup whole kernel corn

1 cup crushed pineapple canned
   in juice (drained)

Juice of 2-3 med. limes

1 teaspoon salt (or more, to taste)

Chop the tomatoes, bell pepper, onion, cilantro, and jalapeño by hand or use a food processor to pulse them to your desired consistency. Stir the chopped vegetables and remaining ingredients together in a bowl, then taste and adjust as desired. Feel free to add more salt, more garlic, some THM Super Sweet Blend, or more jalapeños to round out the flavors. (As written, this salsa isn't that spicy, so feel free to leave the seeds in the jalapeño and/or add more jalapeños if you like heat.) You could even add some rinsed and drained canned black beans. Refrigerate overnight to let the flavors develop before serving.

This salsa is so fresh and has plenty of non-tomato ingredients, which I like. As written, the flavors are fairly conservative, so make it your own!

guacamole

HEALTHY FATS | YIELDS 3 CUPS (⅓ CUP PER SERVING)

3 cups mashed avocado (6 sm. avocados)

1 med. Roma tomato (chopped)

Juice of 1 med. lime

½ teaspoon salt

¼ teaspoon each cumin, garlic powder,
   onion powder, black pepper

Cayenne pepper (to taste)

Mix the ingredients together; I like to leave mine a little chunky, but make it as smooth as you like. Taste and adjust salt, spices, and acidity if needed. Serve as a dip with non-starchy veggies or on salads or fajitas.

Cover leftovers with plastic wrap in contact with the surface of the guacamole to keep air out. This will help keep it from turning brown, but it's always prettiest fresh.

baba ghanoush

1 (1 lb.) eggplant
Oil of choice

2 tablespoons tahini
1 tablespoon lemon juice
⅜ teaspoon salt (or more, to taste)
¼ teaspoon garlic powder

Olive oil and smoked paprika (for garnish)

Slice the eggplant in half lengthwise. Brush the cut sides of the eggplant with your oil of choice, or just spray it with cooking spray like I did. Place the eggplant cut side down on a cookie sheet and roast in the oven (uncovered) at 400° for 30 minutes or until completely tender. Let the eggplant cool on the pan for 15 minutes. Scrape the flesh out of the skins into a colander. Squeeze the eggplant to drain excess liquid, then let it sit in the colander for a few minutes to keep draining.

Transfer the eggplant to a food processor or bowl and add the tahini, lemon juice, salt, and garlic powder. Process until mostly smooth, or just stir it by hand with a meat fork like I did to avoid washing appliances. (It will have more texture when mixed by hand.) Taste and add more salt if desired. Garnish with olive oil and plenty of smoked paprika and serve with cucumbers or other non-starchy veggies. You could also bake some low-carb pitas for "pita chips."

Some people would say this dip serves 4 as an appetizer, but let's be realistic: in all honesty, it serves 2 if you're lucky. Baba ghanoush is my new favorite thing.

note

Feel free to multiply this recipe. Just make sure your eggplant(s) are completely tender before removing from the oven, increasing the bake time if needed.

roasted red pepper hummus

HEALTHY CARBS & HEALTHY FATS | YIELDS 3 ½ CUPS

2 (15.5 oz.) cans chickpeas (rinsed, drained)
1 (12 oz.) jar roasted red peppers (drained)
¼ cup tahini
3 tablespoons lemon juice
2 tablespoons olive oil
1½ teaspoons each garlic powder,
    smoked paprika, salt
¼ teaspoon THM Super Sweet Blend (optional)

Olive oil and smoked paprika (for garnish)

Blend the ingredients together until smooth and creamy. I used a Vitamix blender with a tamper and scraped down the sides occasionally; a food processor may also work. Taste and add sweetener if desired to round out the flavors. You could also add some cayenne pepper to make it spicy. Blend again after any additions. Garnish with olive oil and smoked paprika and serve immediately, or chill in the refrigerator first. Serve with your veggies of choice. Since you're already combining carbs and fats, carrots are fair game!

This is one of those times where you should just skip trying to calculate carbs and fats and enjoy a combination of fuels as a treat. It's easier that way. I tried to make hummus with less olive oil and tahini to stay in Healthy Carbs mode, but it was a no-go so I went all out with this recipe. I'm glad I did, because this is one of the most amazing things I've ever put in my mouth! It's SO creamy!

What a blow it must be when a man with imagination marries
the beautiful bundle of clothes that he's been building ideals around,
and finds that she's just a weak, whining, cowardly mass of affectations!

F. SCOTT FITZGERALD - "BERNICE BOBS HER HAIR"

basic cauliflower "hummus"

1 med. head fresh cauliflower

3 tablespoons olive oil
3 tablespoons tahini
1 tablespoon lemon juice
1 teaspoon salt (or more, to taste)
¾ teaspoon each garlic powder, onion powder
½ teaspoon black pepper

Olive oil and smoked paprika (for garnish)

Trim the stems off the cauliflower head, chop it into florets, and steam it in a small amount of water in a covered saucepan until crisp-tender (not mushy). Drain the cauliflower in a colander for 15 minutes.

Transfer the steamed cauliflower to a mixing bowl, add the rest of the ingredients, and use an immersion blender to blend it to your desired consistency. (The immersion blender will give you greater control over the texture; a regular blender will make it too smooth. A food processor may work, if you have one.)

Taste and add more salt and/or seasonings if desired. Chill, or garnish with olive oil and smoked paprika and serve immediately.

This cauliflower-based dip has many hummus elements, but since it contains no chickpeas, it's obviously not a traditional hummus. It is an addictingly creamy snack item that fits perfectly in a Healthy Fats setting because there are no carb sources involved (unlike traditional hummus)! Serve it with non-starchy veggies of your choice, such as red and yellow bell pepper strips, cucumbers, and celery.

note

I recommend using fresh cauliflower over frozen in hummus and mashed cauliflower recipes for best texture.

french onion veggie dip

HEALTHY FATS I YIELDS I PINT

16 oz. reduced-fat sour cream

1 tablespoon + 1 teaspoon dried minced onion

1½ teaspoons onion powder

1 teaspoon parsley flakes

1 teaspoon Worcestershire sauce

½ teaspoon each salt, black pepper

Mix the ingredients together and enjoy!

note

• I don't recommend replacing the sour cream with Greek yogurt.

• Feel free to add a few tablespoons of mayonnaise for a richer dip, if desired.

This is one of my favorite recipes in the book. I've always loved storebought French onion dip, and this one doesn't have any funky ingredients! As written, the dip is quite light, but it's full of flavor. You can serve it with any non-starchy veggies such as cucumbers, celery, broccoli, radishes, and the like, but I've always been a carrots 'n dip gal so sometimes I go to town with this dip and a bag of carrots for a completely healthy combination of carbs and fats.

marshmallowy fruit dip

LOW CARB/LOW FAT | YIELDS 1½ CUPS

¼ cup very hot tap water
½ teaspoon Knox gelatin

1 cup low-fat cottage cheese
¼ cup half and half
2 teaspoons THM Super Sweet Blend
1 teaspoon vanilla extract
¼ teaspoon orange extract
½ teaspoon glucomannan

Whisk the gelatin into the hot water to dissolve. Let it sit for a few minutes, then add the rest of the ingredients (except the glucomannan). Blend with an immersion blender until smooth, adding the glucomannan slowly while blending so it doesn't clump. Refrigerate for several hours or overnight to firm up before serving. You could eat half the batch and still be under 5 grams of fat (if using 1% cottage cheese).

This fruit dip has such a creamy texture – almost like marshmallow cream! The fat is low, so you can enjoy it with fruit in a Healthy Carbs meal or snack. The dip is delicious on apples and strawberries, but it's dangerously addictive on small banana sections…. Don't overdo it on the bananas, though; they're pretty high in natural sugars.

note

If using beef gelatin, add ⅛ teaspoon.

"Great excellences, my dear Prue," I sometimes allow myself to say, "lie concealed in the depths of character, like pearls at the bottom of the sea. Under the laughing, glancing surface, how little they are suspected! Perhaps love is nothing else than the sight of them by one person."
GEORGE WILLIAM CURTIS - "TITBOTTOM'S SPECTACLES"

fiesta dip

HEALTHY FATS I SERVES 15

1 lb. ground beef (cooked, chopped, drained)

1½ (8 oz.) pkgs. cream cheese (softened)
1 cup Greek yogurt
1-2 tablespoons sriracha (to taste)
2 teaspoons each chili powder, cumin
1 teaspoon each cilantro, dill, onion powder, salt

1 (10 oz.) can diced tomatoes with
   green chilies (drained)
2 cups shredded cheddar cheese
Sliced black olives and jalapeños (optional)

Prepare the ground beef. Beat the cream cheese, Greek yogurt, sriracha, and seasonings until smooth. Fold in the cooked ground beef. Spread into a greased 9"x13" pan.

Top with the drained tomatoes, cheese, and optional olives and jalapeños. Bake (uncovered) at 350° for 25 minutes or until the cheese is melted and bubbly. To stay in Healthy Fats mode, enjoy with a spoon or veggies.

When I take a baked chip dip to a party, I usually just take a bag of regular ol' tortilla chips to go along with it, then use a spoon or some veggies to eat mine (celery and cucumbers are some of my favorites). Works like a charm, and everyone's satisfied.

buffalo chicken dip

4 cups shredded cooked chicken breast

2 (8 oz.) pkgs. reduced-fat cream cheese

1½ cups shredded cheddar cheese

1 cup reduced-fat sour cream

5 tablespoons Louisiana-style hot sauce

1½ teaspoons each chili powder, onion powder

¾ teaspoon salt

Beat the ingredients together with a hand mixer or stand mixer until smooth. Spread into a 10" circular baking dish. Bake (uncovered) at 350° for 30 minutes.

If you have company coming you can assemble this dip ahead of time, refrigerate it until party time, then bake it fresh. Serve with non-starchy veggies such as cucumbers and celery...or crackers for the general public.

note

If you don't care for the flavor of hot sauce, feel free to decrease the amount.

greek dip

2 (8 oz.) pkgs. reduced-fat cream cheese

1 cup shredded mozzarella cheese

1 cup reduced-fat sour cream

1 tablespoon lemon juice

1 teaspoon each basil, dill weed,
    garlic powder, oregano

¾ teaspoon salt

½ teaspoon black pepper

2 cups fresh spinach

1 (13.75 oz.) can quartered artichoke hearts
    (drained, chopped fine)

1 cup chopped tomato

1 cup sliced black olves

Sliced black olives and oregano (for garnish)

Beat the first section of ingredients together with a hand mixer until smooth. Add the vegetables and beat well to break them down a bit. Spread the dip into a 9"x13" baking dish, garnish with additional sliced olives and oregano, and bake (uncovered) at 350° for 30 minutes. Serve with non-starchy veggies of your choice (like cucumbers), or crackers for the general public.

"To have that many skilled physicians swarm a room means you must be doing something right." Those were the words of my husband, Dr. Ryan, when I brought a pan of this dip into the hospital for him and his resident co-workers.

note

This would also be good as a cold dip, without baking!

"Then must you strive to be worthy of her love. BE BRAVE AND PURE, fearless to the strong and humble to the weak; and so, whether this love prosper or no, you will have fitted yourself to be honored by a maiden's love, which is, in sooth, the highest guerdon which a true knight can hope for."
SIR ARTHUR CONAN COYLE - *THE WHITE COMPANY*

refried bean dip

3 (16 oz.) cans fat-free refried beans
(the already-seasoned kind)

2 cups fat-free Greek yogurt
2 teaspoons lime juice
1 teaspoon dill weed

½ med. head iceburg lettuce (shredded)
2-3 med. Roma tomatoes (chopped, drained)
1 cup shredded cheddar cheese
⅓ cup sliced black olives

Stir the refried beans to get them nice and creamy, then spread into the bottom of a 9"x13" pan.

Stir the Greek yogurt, lime juice, and dill together and spread over the refried beans.

Top with the lettuce, tomatoes, cheese, and olives, in that order. Serve with tortilla chips for the average Joe, and eat it with a spoon or veggies yourself. Or bake up some low-carb or sprouted tortillas as chips if you feel like going to the effort.

You can make this dip a few hours ahead. I don't recommend refrigerating it overnight before serving; the lettuce won't be as crisp.

note

There are about 2.75 grams of fat per serving from the cheese and olives.

veggie pizza

DOUGH

3 cups shredded part-skim mozzarella cheese
3 oz. reduced-fat cream cheese

1½ cups Briana's Baking Mix
2 teaspoons baking powder
½ teaspoon each garlic powder, salt

3 eggs
¼ cup water

TOPPING

2 (8 oz.) pkgs. reduced-fat cream cheese
⅔ cup mayonnaise
1 teaspoon each dill weed, onion powder,
    oregano, parsley flakes

2 cups chopped broccoli florets
1 cup chopped tomato
1 med. bell pepper (chopped)
1 med. carrot (peeled, grated)
½ cup shredded cheddar cheese

To make the dough, melt the cheese and cream cheese in a saucepan on the stovetop over medium-low heat, stirring occasionally. Cook until the cheeses have softened and can be combined with a spatula.

Meanwhile, whisk the dry ingredients. Add the eggs and water and combine roughly with a fork.

When the cheese has melted, pull the pan off the heat and add the flour and egg mixture and use your hand to knead the dough until the ingredients are mixed.

Line a cookie sheet with parchment paper. Press the dough out onto the parchment with greased hands to cover the pan the width of the parchment paper. Bake at 350° for 15 minutes or until baked through in the center. (Do not overbake. The crust will solidify even more once chilled.) Cool completely before adding the toppings.

Beat the cream cheese, mayo, and seasonings together until smooth. Spread evenly over the cooled crust. Top with the chopped broccoli, tomato, pepper, and carrot, then sprinkle the cheese on top. Cover and refrigerate for 1-2 hours before slicing and serving. (A pizza cutter works well for slicing.) It keeps well, so you could even make it the night before.

This is definitely one of my favorite recipes in this book. It's so fresh and flavorful! Where I come from, cold veggie pizza is a very popular potluck food and party appetizer.

note

• Carrots are not non-starchy veggies, but one medium carrot spread over 16 servings is only a garnish amount.
• The seasoned cream cheese topping would make an excellent Ranch-style veggie dip! I would add some low-fat sour cream to lighten it up a bit and make it not so thick.

pigs in a blanket

1½ cups shredded part-skim
    mozzarella cheese
2 oz. reduced-fat cream cheese

¾ cup Briana's Baking Mix
1 teaspoon baking powder
¼ teaspoon garlic powder

1 egg
¼ cup water

6 beef hot dogs (cut in half)

Melt the cheese and cream cheese in a saucepan on the stovetop over medium-low heat, stirring occasionally. Cook until the cheeses have softened and can be combined with a spatula.

Meanwhile, whisk the dry ingredients. Add the egg and water and combine roughly with a fork.

When the cheese has melted, pull the pan off the heat and add the flour and egg mixture and use your hand to knead the dough until the ingredients are mixed.

Line a cookie sheet with parchment paper. Press the dough out onto the parchment with greased hands to form a rectangle 12" wide by 8" high. Cut it once horizontally and five times vertically to form 12 rectangles of dough. Wrap a section of dough around each hot dog half and seal the edges of the dough.

Bake the "pigs" on the parchment-lined cookie sheet at 350° for 40-45 minutes or until the tops are golden brown and firm to the touch and the dough is baked through. Let them cool a few minutes before serving to firm up (and cool down!). Serve with ketchup and/or the Cow Sauce on page 478.

note

The dough firms up if leftovers are refrigerated (because of the cheese), but reheat in the microwave and they're good to go again!

easy jalapeño poppers

HEALTHY FATS | SERVES 14

14 med.-lg. jalapeños

1 (8 oz.) pkg. reduced-fat cream cheese
½ cup shredded mozzarella cheese
½ cup real bacon bits
¼ teaspoon garlic powder

Smoked paprika (for garnish)

Slice the jalapeños in half and remove the stems, seeds, and membranes. (Wear gloves if you don't want your hands to sting later.) Beat the cream cheese, mozzarella cheese, bacon bits, and garlic powder together until smooth. Use a spoon to spread the mixture into the jalapeño halves, place the jalapeño poppers on a cookie sheet, sprinkle with smoked paprika, and bake at 350° for 30 minutes.

I took these jalapeño poppers into the hospital for Ryan and his co-workers and they got scarfed up quickly! If you want to get fancy, you could top them with the cracker topping from the Jalapeño Popper Dip on page 399 of *Necessary Food*, but I wanted to keep these super easy.

deviled eggs

HEALTHY FATS | YIELDS 24 DEVILED EGGS

12 hardboiled eggs

¼ cup + 1 tablespoon mayonnaise
¼ cup sour cream
1 tablespoon yellow mustard
2 teaspoons apple cider vinegar
¼ teaspoon each salt, black pepper
⅛ teaspoon THM Super Sweet Blend

Smoked paprika (for garnish)

Slice the eggs in half lengthwise. Use a spoon to gently scrape the yolks out of the eggs into a bowl.

Add the rest of the ingredients to the yolks and mix with a hand mixer until smooth. Pipe the yolk mixture back into the eggs using a piping bag or a sandwich bag with one corner snipped off. Garnish the deviled eggs with smoked paprika.

note

If you're dairy free, try using more mayonnaise in place of the sour cream. You may need to decrease the vinegar and salt. I used reduced-fat sour cream to lighten these eggs up a bit.

raspberry jalapeño baked brie

HEALTHY FATS | SERVES 8

JAM
¾ cup red raspberries
½ lg. jalapeño (seeds removed, diced)
¼ cup water
1 teaspoon THM Super Sweet Blend
⅛ teaspoon salt (scant)

1 (8 oz.) fresh Brie round

Make the jam ahead of time. Bring the jam ingredients to a boil in a small saucepan, mashing the berries with a spoon after they've softened. Simmer (uncovered) for 5 minutes. Let the jam cool, then refrigerate to thicken. (The jam is not that spicy, so feel free to use the whole jalapeño and/or leave the seeds in for more kick.)

When the jam is cold and your company has arrived, bake the Brie. Leave the rind on for baking; it can be eaten, or each person can peel it off his own serving. Bake the Brie uncovered at 350° for 12-14 minutes or until soft. Top with the cold jam and serve. Enjoy with non-starchy veggies like cucumbers and celery, low-carb tortillas turned into chips, Ryvita or Wasa crackers (watch the carbs), or a spoon.

fresh nacho pizzas

HEALTHY FATS | SERVES 2

2 low-carb tortillas
⅔ cup shredded cheese of choice

⅔ cup chopped Roma tomato
⅔ cup chopped fresh cilantro
1 med. jalapeño (chopped)

1 med. avocado (sliced)
Sour cream and salsa
Salt and pepper

Spread half the cheese onto each tortilla and bake on a cookie sheet at 425° for 8 minutes.

Spread half the tomato, cilantro, and jalapeño onto each tortilla and return to the oven for 5 more minutes.

Top the pizzas with the sliced avocado, as much sour cream and salsa as desired, and a hearty shake of salt and pepper to season, then enjoy them while they're still crunchy! (I like to cut each pizza into 4 wedges with a pizza cutter so they're easy to pick up.)

I call them fresh because they're full of fresh ingredients, including fresh avocado that really takes them over the top. I call them nachos because the crunchy tortilla and melted cheese is definitely reminiscent of a nacho! While these are in the snack category, they can also be supper.

note

• Remove some of the jalapeño seeds to remove some of the heat if you're not a spice lover.
• I like to use Roma tomatoes in most of my recipes because they're firmer and less juicy than a beefsteak tomato.

He maketh the storm a calm, so that the waves thereof are still.
Then are they glad because they be quiet;
so he bringeth them unto their desired haven.
Oh that men would praise the Lord for his goodness,
and for his wonderful works to the children of men!
PSALM 107:29-31

BLUEBERRY JAM
PG 487

sauces, spices, spreads + syrups

perfect barbecue sauce (and pulled pork)

LOW CARB/LOW FAT | YIELDS 6 CUPS SAUCE

½ cup salted butter

4 cups no-sugar-added ketchup

½ - 1 cup water

2 tablespoons THM Super Sweet Blend

2 tablespoons apple cider vinegar

1 tablespoon yellow mustard

1 tablespoon Worcestershire sauce

2 teaspoons each chili powder, salt

1 teaspoon each onion powder, black pepper

1 teaspoon molasses

Melt the butter in a saucepan, then add the rest of the ingredients and whisk to combine. Taste and add more sweetener if desired. Simmer (uncovered) for 20 minutes. Store in the refrigerator.

Based off of my mom's favorite barbecue sauce recipe, this is definitely my favorite healthy barbecue sauce to date! It's a sweet barbecue, so adjust that according to your family's preferences. I love it on everything from grilled chicken to haystacks to green beans to brown rice! I kind of love barbecue sauce....

This barbecue sauce contains butter, which would normally be a Healthy Fats ingredient, but if you use ¼ cup of sauce or less in a serving, the fat stays within Low Carb/Low Fat boundaries and can be used in any fuel setting. Pair the sauce with a lean meat such as chicken or turkey breast or pork tenderloin to stay in LC/LF territory, or use it with a fattier meat for an HF meal.

note

Start with ½ cup water in the sauce, then add an additional ½ cup if you prefer a thinner sauce.

PULLED PORK ▼

To make barbecue pulled pork for 12-14 people, cook a 4 pound pork loin in a slow cooker on High for 4 hours, flipping it over halfway through. Drain the juice (reserving it for another use if desired), break the pork loin into chunks, and add 3 cups of barbecue sauce. Simmer on Low for 4 hours, stirring occasionally (do this with a meat fork to shred the pork finer). Serve with additional sauce as desired. This pulled pork would be Healthy Fats since pork loin is not a lean meat.

bri's kickin' barbecue sauce

LOW CARB/LOW FAT I YIELDS 1¾ CUPS

1½ cups no-sugar-added ketchup

2 tablespoons salted butter

2 tablespoons sriracha (feel free to decrease this for less heat)

2 teaspoons apple cider vinegar

1-2 teaspoons THM Super Sweet Blend (or more, to taste)

1 teaspoon liquid smoke

¾ teaspoon each chili powder, dry mustard, paprika

½ teaspoon maple extract

Dash orange extract

Whisk the ingredients together in a small saucepan and simmer for ten minutes. Taste and add more sweetener and/or spice as desired. Store in the refrigerator. This sauce is Low Carb/Low Fat as long as you stick with ¼ cup per serving or less.

Leave to thy God to
ORDER & PROVIDE;
in ev'ry change
He faithful will remain.

KATHRINA VON SCHLEGEL
"BE STILL, MY SOUL"

As a South Carolina girl – born and raised – barbecue is an integral part of my life. While a mound of sweet, tangy, and juicy pulled pork with a side of coleslaw will always be my favorite way to eat barbecue, I enjoy a variety of sauces and styles. This sauce is thick with a kick, full of deep flavor with some fruity notes, and perfect for basting onto a rack of baby back ribs. Adjust the sweetness level to your own personal taste (as written it has a definite sweet note but isn't overly sweet) and feel free to add more or less sriracha depending on how much you like heat. I'm not a big spice fan, but I put a little more in this sauce than usual. I'd say it's on the upper end of medium on the spice scale, but some of you spice-handling firemouths will probably take one lick and laugh me out of the state.

bri's adobo sauce

4 ancho chiles (stems and seeds removed)

1 lg. onion (chopped)

5 lg. garlic cloves (peeled)

2 cups water

1 (28 oz.) can diced tomatoes
(no salt added, undrained)

1 (6 oz.) can tomato paste

3 tablespoons apple cider vinegar

Juice from 3 med. limes

1 tablespoon + 1 teaspoon
THM Super Sweet Blend

2 teaspoons each cumin, oregano,
smoked paprika, salt

1 teaspoon black pepper

Smash the garlic cloves with the flat of a knife. Roast the chiles, onion, and garlic in a Dutch oven on the stovetop over medium-high heat until the onion starts to brown, stirring occasionally. Add the rest of the ingredients and bring to a boil, then turn the heat down and simmer (uncovered) for 30 minutes. Blend with an immersion blender until smooth, then use in a recipe or refrigerate for later and use on all the things.

note

This sauce makes a great Low Carb/Low Fat salad dressing!

Disclaimer: this is my play on adobo sauce. It may or may not be authentic, but it is now one of my favorite sauces to keep in the fridge. This sauce has a nice body to it and leaves a lingering heat in the back of the throat (but it's not overwhelmingly spicy). I use it like a barbecue sauce on pretty much everything.

SUGGESTIONS FOR USE ▼

dipping sauce // stir into brown rice // salad dressing // pizza or quesadilla topping // enchilada sauce // toss with veggies before roasting // broasted chicken drumsticks (page 98) // chicken salad // Adobo Pork Tacos (page 86) // Adobo Baked Beans (page 212)

cow sauce

1 cup mayonnaise

½ cup reduced-fat sour cream

3 tablespoons no-sugar-added ketchup

3 tablespoons Dijon mustard

2 tablespoons yellow mustard

2 teaspoons THM Super Sweet Blend
   (or more, to taste)

2 teaspoons lemon juice

1½ teaspoons onion powder

½ teaspoon smoked paprika

15 drops liquid smoke

Whisk the ingredients together until smooth. Taste and add more sweetener if desired. Store in fridge.

Ryan tasted this and immediately guessed what fast food condiment it was replicating. (Hint: It's typically served with chicken…and never on Sundays.) He said I nailed it! Try using this as a dipping sauce for the Pan-Fried Chicken Strips on page 105.

note

You could try thinning this down with water to use as a salad dressing!

pineapple sweet & sour sauce

1 (20 oz.) can pineapple chunks
    canned in juice (drained)
1 cup water
¼ cup no-sugar-added ketchup
¼ cup rice vinegar
1 teaspoon molasses
1 med. garlic clove
½ teaspoon salt
¼ teaspoon black pepper
⅛ teaspoon THM Pure Stevia Extract Powder

Blend the ingredients together until smooth, then cook (uncovered) in a large skillet on the stovetop. It's good to use a large skillet with plenty of surface area because the sauce will take less time to reduce. Bring to a boil and simmer for 15 minutes or until the volume is reduced by about half, stirring occasionally. Store in the refrigerator. I've kept this in the fridge for 2-3 weeks, but if it smells funny, toss it.

Use this condiment as a dipping sauce for grilled chicken, eat it over salad as a low-fat dressing, or pair it with some Wasa Light Rye crackers and low-fat cottage cheese for a light snack. Use it like salsa and think outside the box! You could even use it to marinate chicken or make the Sweet & Sour Rice on page 207.

note

If you want a smoother, thicker sauce, feel free to add a bit of xanthan gum before blending. I would start with ¼ teaspoon. I decided not to add xanthan gum this time because I wanted the sauce to have as bold and bright a flavor as possible, plus I know that some people either don't have xanthan gum or don't like it and to me, the sauce really doesn't need it.

creamy sweet onion dressing

HEALTHY FATS I YIELDS 1¾ CUPS

½ cup mayonnaise

½ cup olive oil

½ cup water

¼ cup Dijon mustard

2 teaspoons dried minced onion

2 teaspoons onion powder

1½ teaspoons poppy seeds

1 teaspoon THM Super Sweet Blend

¼ teaspoon each salt, black pepper

Combine all the ingredients in a dressing bottle and shake to combine. Store in the fridge. Shake again before serving.

EASY TOSSED SALAD ▼

Make a big bowl of mixed greens and top it with your choice of non-starchy veggie toppings and shredded cheese. I did this for a fellowship meal using what I had on hand and topped my lettuce with chopped cucumber, shredded carrot (more than I would usually use in a Healthy Fats setting because it was going to a public event and most people like shredded carrots on their salad), and shredded cheddar cheese. Right before serving, toss the salad and toppings with enough dressing to wet the greens adequately. (I used 4-5 quarts of greens for this whole batch of dressing.) Only dress as much salad as you'll use immediately because leftovers will wilt. If you want to get fancy, you could use sliced strawberries, candied pecans, and feta cheese as toppings.

The creamy honey mustard notes and subtle onion flavor of this dressing have made it my new favorite! I used it on a simple tossed salad that I took to a fellowship meal, where it got gobbled up in a hurry.

He that covereth a transgression
SEEKETH LOVE;
but he that repeateth a matter
separateth very friends.
PROVERBS 17:9

balsamic & lime vinaigrette

HEALTHY FATS | YIELDS 1½ CUPS

1 cup olive oil

¼ cup balsamic vinegar

¼ cup water

2 tablespoons lime juice

1½ teaspoons each onion powder, parsley flakes

1 teaspoon THM Super Sweet Blend

1 teaspoon each basil, oregano

½ teaspoon each salt, black pepper

Blend the ingredients together until smooth and emulsified. Store in the refrigerator. Shake before serving.

I love to use this dressing on a simple salad of spinach and mozzarella cheese. It's the easiest side dish you could think of, but it feels special.

asian vinaigrette

HEALTHY FATS | YIELDS 1¾ CUPS

¾ cup olive oil

⅓ cup reduced-sodium soy sauce

⅓ cup rice vinegar

2 tablespoons natural peanut butter

2 tablespoons lime juice

1 tablespoon sriracha

2½ teaspoons THM Super Sweet Blend

½ teaspoon each garlic powder, ginger

¼ teaspoon salt

Combine all the ingredients in a dressing bottle and shake to combine. Store in the fridge. Shake again before serving.

USES ▼

Asian Chicken Salad (page 173) // toss with shredded cabbage to make an Asian coleslaw // on lunch wraps // tossed with sautéed cabbage

mushroom soup/gravy

HEALTHY FATS I YIELDS 2 ¼ CUPS

1 tablespoon salted butter

1 (8 oz.) can mushrooms (drained)

2 med. garlic cloves (minced)

2 teaspoons chives

1 cup unsweetened almond milk

½ cup shredded mozzarella cheese

½ cup sour cream

¼ teaspoon black pepper

Dash salt (to taste)

Sauté the mushrooms, garlic, and chives in the butter until fragrant and softened. Turn down the heat and add the rest of the ingredients. Simmer (don't boil), stirring occasionally, until everything is melted. Blend with an immersion blender until smooth, then reheat if needed. You can use this as gravy over pork chops or mashed caulitoes, or enjoy it on its own as a soup! I haven't tried this, but I bet it would work in casseroles in place of cream of mushroom soup.

bri's sweet & spicy rub

LOW CARB/LOW FAT | YIELDS ½ CUP

¼ cup dehydrated tomato powder

1 tablespoon + 2 teaspoons salt

1 tablespoon THM Super Sweet Blend

1 tablespoon each chili powder, smoked paprika

2 teaspoons onion powder

½ teaspoon black pepper

Mix the ingredients together and store in a sealed container at room temperature.

I've used this spice rub on quite a few different things – roasted carrots, salad, meats of all sorts. I bet it would be a great seasoning for roasted chickpeas as well!

note

To make dehydrated tomato powder, I just dehydrate tomato slices from our garden, then powder them in a coffee grinder, but you can purchase tomato powder from Amazon if you'd rather do that.

CHICKEN INSTRUCTIONS ▼

This spice rub is great on bone-in chicken thighs for a Healthy Fats meal! Sprinkle the thighs generously with the spice rub, then bake at 350° for one hour or until done.

pumpkin butter

LOW CARB / LOW FAT | YIELDS 9 CUPS

12 cups baked pumpkin flesh

4 teaspoons cinnamon

2 teaspoons each ginger, salt

2 teaspoons molasses

2 teaspoons vanilla extract

½ teaspoon each chili powder,
   ground cloves, nutmeg

¼ teaspoon THM Pure Stevia Extract Powder

¼ cup apple cider vinegar

2 tablespoons THM Super Sweet Blend
   (or more, to taste)

Cook the first set of ingredients together in a slow cooker on High for two hours, stirring occasionally. (I used a 6-quart slow cooker.)

Blend the mixture together in a high-powdered blender until smooth (be very careful when blending hot stuff like this and vent your blender as needed; alternatively you could try using an immersion blender). Return it to the slow cooker. Whisk in the apple cider vinegar and Super Sweet Blend, then taste and add more cinnamon and/or sweetener if desired. Cook on High (with the slow cooker lid left open a crack to let water evaporate) for 3 hours or until the desired consistency is reached, stirring occasionally.

Store the pumpkin butter in the fridge (freezing it would probably work too, but canning pumpkin butter is not recommended because it is often too dense to be heated properly).

Update 5 months later - I just discovered that I still have a jar of this pumpkin butter in my fridge and it's still good, so I guess that tells you how well it keeps. Toss it if it grows mold or smells funny.

note

I don't know if this would work with canned pumpkin or not. I'm pretty sure it would be a lot stronger and thicker - maybe too thick. I think a safer idea would be to buy a pumpkin (preferably a pie pumpkin), bake it in the oven in a big roaster pan (covered) until tender, then scoop the flesh out and use it in this recipe.

blueberry jam

LOW CARB/LOW FAT I YIELDS 6 CUPS

1 quart blueberries

3 cups water

2 tablespoons lemon juice

3 tablespoons THM Super Sweet Blend
 (or more, to taste)

1 tablespoon + 1 teaspoon Knox gelatin

¼ teaspoon THM Pure Stevia Extract Powder

⅛ teaspoon salt

2½ teaspoons glucomannan

Bring the first three ingredients to a boil in a saucepan, then simmer (uncovered) for ten minutes, stirring occasionally.

Blend the mixture carefully with an immersion blender until smooth. (If you don't have an immersion blender, you can try to do this in a regular blender, but always be very careful when blending hot liquids and vent the blender as necessary to avoid a pressure build-up.)

Add the second set of ingredients and blend again. Add the glucomannan last while blending to avoid clumping. Taste and add more Super Sweet Blend if desired.

Bring the mixture to a boil again and simmer for an additional 5 minutes, stirring often. Transfer to storage containers, let cool to room temperature, then freeze for long-term storage. For short-term storage, the refrigerator is fine.

I love this blueberry jam on toast, Greek yogurt, cottage cheese, and waffles for an extra burst of flavor and color. The trick to the great texture is to use a combination of gelatin and glucomannan for a jam that isn't slimy but still holds together when spread on warm toast. Oh, it's delightful! This recipe is a jam, not a jelly, so it's a looser consistency than jelly and includes all the good fiber from the blueberry skins.

note

• If you're using beef gelatin, add an extra teaspoon.

• I haven't tried canning this jam, and to be honest, I don't know if it would work or not. I know there are various things that need to be considered when canning to make sure that you don't end up growing bad bacteria, but I don't know what those things are – yet. Maybe someday I'll get a chance to experiment with it.

This sickness is not unto death, but for the glory of God. JOHN 11:4B

chunky cinnamon applesauce

HEALTHY CARBS | YIELDS 1½ CUPS

3 cups peeled, cored, chopped apples
½ cup water

½ teaspoon THM Super Sweet Blend
¼ teaspoon cinnamon
Dash salt

Combine the apples and water in a saucepan on the stovetop. Cover and bring to a boil, reduce heat, and simmer for 20 minutes, stirring occasionally. Mash to desired consistency with a potato masher. Add the rest of the ingredients and continue to simmer uncovered for 5-10 minutes to evaporate excess liquid. Mash again for a finer consistency if you like. Taste and add more sweetener, salt, and/or cinnamon as desired. Serve warm or cold.

I grew up on my grandma's homemade cinnamon applesauce. I love to eat this version on its own or as a topping on pancakes, waffles, or low-fat cottage cheese or Greek yogurt.

note

• I used Gala apples. Adjust the sweetness according to your personal preference and the sweetness of the apples you use.
• This is a small batch of applesauce meant for use as a topping. Feel free to multiply if you would like a larger batch. You may need to cook a larger batch longer.

chocolate peanut butter hardshell ice cream topping

HEALTHY FATS | YIELDS I CUP (8-12 SERVINGS)

½ cup refined coconut oil

½ cup natural peanut butter

2 teaspoons THM Super Sweet Blend
(or more, to taste)

3 tablespoons cocoa powder

If you want to ensure a smooth texture, powder the Super Sweet Blend in a coffee grinder before using it in this recipe.

Soften the coconut oil, peanut butter, and Super Sweet Blend together just until you can whisk them together. Whisk in the cocoa powder. Let the topping cool on the counter before serving so it's not hot. Drizzle slowly over ice cream to give it time to harden and watch the magic happen! Keep leftovers in the fridge and reheat to melt before using.

So this topping probably doesn't pair the best with coffee ice cream, but that's what I had on hand for pictures. Chocolate, vanilla, or peanut butter ice cream would all be delicious covered in this crunchy goodness!

note

• For a mini version of this recipe that makes 1-2 servings, follow the instructions above with 1 tablespoon refined coconut oil, 1 tablespoon natural peanut butter, ¼ teaspoon THM Super Sweet Blend, and 1 ⅛ teaspoons cocoa powder.

• Stir frozen berries and/or nuts into leftover liquid hardshell topping to make instant candy clusters!

foundational peanut butter topping

¼ cup defatted peanut flour

1 teaspoon THM Super Sweet Blend

⅛ teaspoon salt

⅛ teaspoon glucomannan

Dash vanilla extract

6 tablespoons unsweetened almond milk

2 tablespoons refined coconut oil

Whisk the dry ingredients. Whisk in the almond milk. Add the coconut oil and microwave in thirty-second intervals, whisking at each interval, until the coconut oil melts and everything can be whisked together smoothly. You can thin the sauce down with extra almond milk if you like. Serve.

Make a Foundation Fats sundae with Superfood Brownies (page 393), Foundational Frozen Custard (page 310), and this peanut butter topping!

> Take this rule: whatever weakens your reason, impairs the tenderness of your conscience, obscures your sense of God, or takes off your RELISH OF SPIRITUAL THINGS; IN SHORT, WHATEVER INCREASES the strength and authority of your body over your mind, that thing is sin to you, however innocent it may be in itself.
> SUSANNA WESLEY (LETTER, JUNE 8, 1725)

waffle & pancake syrup

LOW CARB / LOW FAT | YIELDS 1¼ CUPS

1½ cups water

¼ cup xylitol (or more, to taste)

1 tablespoon + 1 teaspoon oat fiber

1 teaspoon refined coconut oil

1 teaspoon molasses

1 teaspoon each maple extract, vanilla extract

¼ teaspoon salt

2 doonks THM Pure Stevia Extract Powder

½ teaspoon glucomannan

Add all the ingredients to a saucepan, adding the glucomannan slowly while whisking so it doesn't clump. Bring to a boil and boil lightly (uncovered) for 10 minutes, whisking occasionally. It should become a nice caramel color. Serve. Store leftovers in the fridge and reheat before using.

I used xylitol in this syrup recipe for a more caramelly, sugary result. You can find a similar recipe using THM Super Sweet Blend in *Necessary Food* on page 416. That recipe isn't quite as thick as this one.

note

The syrup will thicken even more as it cools. I like a thick syrup so it coats my pancakes and isn't watery like sugar-free syrups tend to be, but if it's too thick for you, add a little more water.

cranberry syrup

LOW CARB / LOW FAT | YIELDS 1½ CUPS

1 cup cranberries (chopped)

1 cup water

2-3 teaspoons THM Super Sweet Blend
 (or more, to taste)

½ teaspoon vanilla extract

¼ teaspoon glucomannan

2 doonks THM Pure Stevia Extract Powder

Dash salt

Combine all the ingredients in a small saucepan (adding the glucomannan while whisking so it doesn't clump). Bring to a boil, then simmer until thickened to a syrup consistency. Store in the refrigerator.

This simple cranberry syrup (which thickens to more of a sauce consistency once refrigerated) is great on waffles, pancakes, toast, Greek yogurt, cottage cheese, and cheesecake! I bet it would be good on pork loin or grilled chicken as well!

blueberry topping

2 cups blueberries

2 cups water

2 teaspoons lemon juice

1 teaspoon Knox gelatin

¼ teaspoon glucomannan

5 doonks THM Pure Stevia Extract Powder

³⁄₃₂ teaspoon salt

Whisk the ingredients together in a saucepan and bring to a boil. (Add the glucomannan while whisking so it doesn't clump.) Take the blueberry topping off the stove, let it cool, then refrigerate it overnight to thicken. Stir before serving to make it more of a sauce consistency.

This topping is great on waffles – and the yogurt parfaits on page 447!

note

• If using beef gelatin, add an extra ¼ teaspoon of gelatin.

• I decided to use mostly gelatin instead of a larger amount of glucomannan to thicken this sauce because I know some people don't like the texture of glucomannan. I personally prefer the taste and texture of toppings like this thickened mostly with gelatin, but if you prefer glucomannan, feel free to use it exclusively and omit the gelatin. I'd start with ½ teaspoon of glucomannan (adding it while whisking so it doesn't clump), then add additional glucomannan in ⅛ teaspoon increments if necessary until the desired thickness is reached. Remember that the sauce will continue to thicken up as it cools.

• Because this sauce is thickened mostly with gelatin, it is meant for use with cold items. If it gets warm, it will lose its gelled properties.

resources

Visit **BRIANA-THOMAS.COM/CONVENIENTFOODRESOURCES**
for future book corrections (let's hope there aren't any), links to the products
I use, and helpful resources!

Go to BRIANA-THOMAS.COM/NECESSARYFOOD to purchase my
first cookbook! *Necessary Food* is full of classic Mennonite church cookbook
recipes made healthy – along with many classic Briana-style originals.

494

yogurt
tutorial

Why make your own yogurt? Well, I personally think it tastes a lot better than storebought yogurt! Homemade Greek yogurt in particular is less tangy than the storebought kind. Depending on where you live, homemade yogurt may be cheaper to make than to buy, and if you go through a lot of yogurt, the savings may be worth your time. Once you get the drill down, making yogurt is so easy. There's also the added benefit of knowing exactly what's in your yogurt and being able to make it whatever flavor you want!

Using skim milk gives you more fuel type options. Regular skim yogurt is Healthy Carbs, while skim Greek yogurt is Low Carb/Low Fat. Full-fat Greek yogurt is Healthy Fats, but full-fat regular yogurt combines carbs and fats (not ideal for weight loss).

....

1» Bring a gallon of skim milk to a boil over medium heat in a large covered kettle. (This takes about 45-55 minutes.) Bringing the milk to a boil slowly keeps the yogurt from being slimy.

2» Take the milk off the heat after it has achieved a slow boil. Let the milk cool to bathwater temperature (about one hour).

3» If a film has formed over the top of the milk, remove it, then stir a half cup of room temperature plain yogurt or Greek yogurt into the warm milk. The milk needs to be warm enough to allow the cultures to do their thing but not so hot that it kills them.

4» Cover the milk and put it in the oven with the oven light on overnight or for at least six hours (until the milk comes together into one big curd).

5» At this point you can drain off any whey pooled around the yogurt curd, then whisk the yogurt smooth before storing it in the fridge. If you want to make Greek yogurt, you'll need to strain a lot of the whey off. To do so, place a large piece of straining cloth over a strainer in the sink. Pour the yogurt into the cloth and tie the corners of the cloth up over a wooden spoon to form a bag. Hang the wooden spoon suspending the yogurt over a tall container to catch the whey. (Alternatively you can just omit the wooden spoon trick and suspend the cloth-lined colander by its handles inside a larger bowl to catch the whey. I've included pictures of both methods.)

6» Let the yogurt strain for an hour or two in the fridge, dumping the accumulated whey as needed to keep the yogurt from hanging in the whey. Drain as long as needed to reach your desired thickness; the thickness of your cloth will affect the straining time. The more whey you drain off, the fewer carbs your yogurt will have. I aim for 7-8 cups of remaining yogurt for a Greek-style yogurt. Store the strained yogurt in the fridge in a sealed container.

≫ Don't forget to save some homemade yogurt (regular or Greek) to start your next batch!

≫ On a gas stove I've had some trouble with milk burning and sticking to the bottom of my kettle, so I usually keep the heat lower than I would on an electric stove (between 2 and 3 on a gas stove) and pull it off the heat before it's actually boiling. (I pull it off when it's really hot and I can tell it's right on the edge of boiling.)

≫ The straining cloth I used at home was just a loosely-woven fabric that we bought at Walmart. Cheesecloth holes are too big and the yogurt will run through it, but a double layer might work. I'm currently using a piece of an old curtain that I found at a thrift store; it works great! I'm sure you can buy yogurt straining bags online as well. You should be able to see through the cloth you use,

but the holes shouldn't be so open that the yogurt solids can run through.

≫ Regular unstrained yogurt can be runny, so I try to pour off any easily-discarded whey that has collected around the yogurt curd before whisking the yogurt smooth and storing it in the fridge. Yogurt tends to thicken up a bit in the fridge as it ages, so that can help too.

≫ If your yogurt won't set up into a curd in the oven, try using a new starter, add the room temperature starter to your warm milk when the milk is between 110° and 115° (measure with a thermometer instead of just using your finger), let it culture longer in the oven (I always leave it in the oven overnight), and make sure your oven light is working correctly.

"Once you get
the drill down,
making yogurt
is so easy."

MEET THE
designers

Abigail Nicole and Grace Elizabeth were born in Walnut Creek, Ohio, three years apart. Growing up on a hundred acre farm meant hard work with a side of exploring creeks, woods, and collapsing outbuildings. Many summer days were spent with family, friends and pets, rich in adventure and color. As teenagers we were co-workers at a local print shop as graphic designers. Today our paths are quite diverse. Abigail, founder of the Abiart greeting card line, and husband Ryan live on a five acre wilderness near the small town of Wilmot. The Abiart mission is speaking life through unique paper goods to women of all ages while raising funds for children in Haiti. Grace spent a greater part of the past 2 years living in the city of Panagiouda, Greece, working with refugees. Grace has dedicated this season to being a voice of freedom to vulnerable women from around the world. Designing *Convenient Food* as a sister team has been a pleasure and felt like "the good ole days." Grace will be returning to Greece shortly, far from color palettes, computer screens, and tranquility. Abigail is eagerly awaiting the arrival of a firstborn, ready to embrace this new chapter of life-possibly far from tranquil as well. Our prayer is that you enjoy the design details on these pages that only accent the wisdom and talent of Mrs. Briana Thomas Burkholder.

vist abiartcreative.com
or call 330.440.3418 for
more information

....

follow Grace in Greece
on Instagram @graceafull

alphabetical index

ICE CREAM + FROZEN DESSERTS

SNACKS + APPETIZERS

SAUCES, SPICES, SPREADS + SYRUPS

FIND A *fuel type index*

AT BRIANA-THOMAS.COM/CONVENIENTFOODRESOURCES